# THE AGRARIAN PROBLEM
# IN THE SIXTEENTH CENTURY

# THE AGRARIAN PROBLEM IN THE SIXTEENTH CENTURY

RICHARD HENRY TAWNEY

ISBN: 978-93-89679-43-4

Published: 1912

LECTOR HOUSE LLP
E-MAIL: lectorpublishing@gmail.com

# THE AGRARIAN PROBLEM
# IN THE SIXTEENTH CENTURY

### BY

## R.H. TAWNEY

*"And if the whole people be landlords, or hold the Lands so divided among them, that no one Man, or number of Men, within the Compass of the Few or Aristocracy, overbalance them, the Empire (without the interposition of force) is a Commonwealth."* —HARRINGTON, *Oceana.*

### WITH 6 MAPS

## TO
## WILLIAM TEMPLE AND ALBERT MANSBRIDGE

### PRESIDENT AND SECRETARY
### OF THE
### WORKERS' EDUCATIONAL ASSOCIATION

# PREFACE

This book is an attempt to trace one strand in the economic life of England from the close of the Middle Ages to the beginning of the Civil War. As originally planned, it included an account of the relations of the State to trade and manufacturing industry, the growth of which is the most pregnant economic phenomenon of the period. But I soon found that the material was too abundant to be treated satisfactorily in a single work, and I have therefore confined myself in the following pages to a study of agrarian conditions, whose transformation created so much distress, and aroused such searchings of heart among contemporaries. The subject is one upon which much light has been thrown by the researches of eminent scholars, notably Mr. Leadam, Professor Gay, Dr. Savine, and Professor Ashley, and its mediæval background has been firmly drawn in the great works of Maitland, Seebohm, and Professor Vinogradoff. The reader will see that I have availed myself freely of the results of their investigations. But I have tried, as far as the time at my disposal allowed, to base my picture on original authorities, both printed and manuscript.

The supreme interest of economic history lies, it seems to me, in the clue which it offers to the development of those dimly conceived presuppositions as to social expediency which influence the actions not only of statesmen, but of humble individuals and classes, and influence, perhaps, most decisively those who are least conscious of any theoretical bias. On the economic ideas of the sixteenth century in their relation to agrarian conditions I have touched shortly in Part III. of the book, and I hope to treat the whole subject more fully on some future occasion. If in the present work I have given, as I am conscious that I have, undue space to the detailed illustration of particular changes, I must plead that one cannot have the dessert without the dinner, and that a firm foundation of fact, even though as tedious to read as to arrange, is a necessary preliminary to the higher and more philosophical task of analysing economic conceptions. The reader who desires to start with a bird's-eye view of the subject is advised to turn first to the concluding chapter of Part III.

One word may be allowed in extenuation of the statistical tables, which will be found scattered at intervals through the following pages. In dealing with modern economic conditions it is increasingly recognised that analysis, to be effective, must be quantitative, and one of the disadvantages under which the student of all periods before the eighteenth century labours is that for large departments of life, such as population, foreign trade, and the occupations of the people, anything approaching satisfactory quantitative description is out of the question. The difficulty in the treatment of agrarian history is different. Certain classes of manorial documents offer material which can easily be reduced to a statistical shape. Indeed one difficulty is its very abundance. The first feeling of a person who sees a manuscript collection such as that at Holkham must be "If fifty maids with fifty mops—," and a sad consciousness that the mop which he wields is a very feeble one. But historical statistics should be regarded with more than ordinary scepticism, inasmuch as they cannot easily be checked by comparison with other sources of information, and it may reasonably be asked whether it is possible to obtain figures that are sufficiently reliable to be used with any confidence. Often, no doubt, it is not possible. The strong point of surveyors was not always arithmetic. The forms in which their information has been cast are sometimes too various to permit of it being used for the purpose of a summary or a comparison. Even when figures are both accurate and comparable the student who works over considerable masses of material will be fortunate if he does not introduce some errors of his own. The tables printed below are marred by all these defects, and I have included them only after considerable hesitation. I have tried to prevent the reader from being misled by pointing out in an appendix what I consider to be their principal faults and ambiguities. But no doubt there are others which have escaped my notice.

It remains for me to express my gratitude to those whose kind assistance has made this work somewhat less imperfect than it would otherwise have been. I have to thank the Warden and Fellows of All Souls College, the Senior Bursar of Merton College, the Clerk of the Peace for the County of Warwick, and the Earl of Leicester for permission to examine the manuscripts in their possession. The maps illustrating enclosure are taken from the beautiful maps of the All Souls estates; my thanks are due to the College for allowing me to use them, and to Mr. W. Tomlinson, of the Oxford Tutorial Class at Longton, for helping me to prepare them for reproduction. Circumstances preventing me from working in the Record Office, I was so fortunate as to secure the co-operation of Miss Niemeyer and Miss L. Drucker, who have transcribed for me a large number of surveys and rentals. How much I owe to their help will be apparent to any one who consults my footnotes and references. Among those who have aided me with advice and information I must mention Professor Vinogradoff, Professor Unwin, and Professor Powicke, the late Miss Toulmin Smith, Mr. Kenneth Leys, Mr. F.W. Kolthammer, Lieut.-Colonel Fishwick, Dr. G.H. Fowler, and the Hon. Gerard Collier. Especially great are my obligations to Mr. R.V. Lennard and Mr. H. Clay, who have read through the whole of the following pages in manuscript or in proof, and who have helped me with numberless criticisms and improvements.

In conclusion I owe two debts which are beyond acknowledgment. The first is to my wife, who has collaborated with me throughout, and without whose constant assistance this book could not have been completed. The second is to the members of the Tutorial Classes conducted by Oxford University, with whom for the last four years it has been my privilege to be a fellow-worker. The friendly smitings of weavers, potters, miners, and engineers, have taught me much about problems of political and economic science which cannot easily be learned from books.

R.H.T.

MANCHESTER, *April 1912.*

# CONTENTS



## PART II
## THE TRANSITION TO CAPITALIST AGRICULTURE

## PART III
## THE OUTCOME OF THE AGRARIAN REVOLUTION

# LIST OF MAPS

# THE AGRARIAN PROBLEM
# IN THE SIXTEENTH CENTURY

## INTRODUCTION

Any one who turns over the Statutes and State Papers of the sixteenth century will be aware that statesmen were much exercised with an agrarian problem, which they thought to be comparatively new, and any one who follows the matter further will find the problem to have an importance at once economic, legal, and political. The economist can watch the reaction of growing markets on the methods of subsistence farming, the development of competitive rents, the building up of the great estate, and the appearance, or at any rate the extension, of the tripartite division into landlord, capitalist farmer, and landless agricultural labourer, the peculiar feature of English rural society which has been given so much eulogy in the eighteenth century and so much criticism in our own. From a legal point of view the great feature of the period is the struggle between copyhold and leasehold, and the ground gained by the latter. Before the century begins, leases for years, though common enough on the demesne lands and on land taken from the waste, are the exception so far as concerns the land of the customary tenants. When the century closes, leasehold has won many obstinately resisted triumphs; much land that was formerly held by copy of court roll is held by lease; and copyhold tenure itself, through the weakening of manorial custom, has partially changed its character. The copyholders, though still a very numerous and important class, are already one against which the course of events has visibly begun to turn, and economic rent, long intercepted and shared, through the fixity of customary tenure, between tenant and landlord under the more elastic adjustments of leasehold and competitive fines, begins to drain itself into the pockets of the latter. Politically, one can see different views of the basis of wealth in conflict, that which measures it by the number of tenants "able to do service" contending with that which tests it by the maximum pecuniary returns to be got from an estate, and which treats the number of tenants as quite a subordinate consideration. The former is the ideal of philosophical conservatives, is supported, for military and social reasons, by the Government, and survives long in the North; the latter is that of the new landed proprietors, and wins in the South.

And its victory results in much more than a mere displacement of tenants. It means ultimately a change in the whole attitude towards landholding, in the doctrine of the place which it should occupy in the State, and in the standards by which the prosperity of agriculture is measured, drawing a line between modern English conceptions and those of the sixteenth century as distinct as that which exists between those of the Irish peasantry and Irish landlords, or between the standpoint of a French peasant and that of the agent of a great English estate. The decline of important classes alters the balance of rural society, though the Crown for a long time tries to maintain it, and the way is prepared both for the economic and political omnipotence which the great landed aristocracy will exercise over England as soon as the power of the Crown is broken, and for the triumph of the modern English conception of landownership, a conception so repugnant both to our ancestors and to the younger English communities,[1] as in the main a luxury of the richer classes. If it had not been for the undermining of the small farmer's position in the sixteenth century, would the proposal[2] to enfranchise copyholders have been thrown out in 1654, and would the enclosures[3] of the eighteenth century have been carried out with such obstinate indifference to the vested interests of the weaker rural classes? Would England have been unique among European countries in the concentration of its landed property, and in the divorce of its peasantry from the soil?

From a wider point of view the agrarian changes of the sixteenth century may be regarded as a long step in the commercialising of English life. The growth of the textile industries is closely connected with the development of pasture farming, and it was the export of woollen cloth, that "prodigy of trade,” which first brought England conspicuously into world-commerce, and was the motive for more than one of those early expeditions to discover new markets, out of which grew plantations, colonies, and empire. Dr. Cunningham[4] has shown that the system of fostering the corn trade, which was embodied in the Corn Bounty Act of 1689, and which was a principle of English policy long after the reason for it had disappeared, was adopted in a milder form in the reign of Elizabeth with the object of checking the decline in the rural population. Again, new agricultural methods were a powerful factor in the struggle between custom and competition, which colours so much of the economic life of the period, and, owing to this fact, they

---

[1] See the land legislation of the Australasian Colonies.

[2] The Instrument of Government (December 1653) established a franchise qualification of rent or personal estate to the value of £200. This certainly would have enfranchised a large number of copyholders and leaseholders, some of whom were much better off than the small freeholders. For an estate of £299, 15s. 4d. left at death by a tenant "Husbandman"" see *Nottingham Borough Records* under the year 1599 (vol. iv. pp. 249–252). It was made up as follows: "Money in purse and his clothes, £15; value of beasts, £74; corn sowne in fields, £35; value of furniture in hall, £2, 13s.; in parlour, £5, 14s., and other miscellaneous possessions." For wills of husbandmen and yeomen see *Surtees Society*, vol. lxxix., pp. 181–182, 263–264, 294, 310. For the restoration of the franchise to the freeholders, see Gardiner, *The Commonwealth*, iii. 78.

[3] Hammond, *The Village Labourer*, 1760–1832. One may add—if English statesmen had studied the history of customary tenures in England, would they have deferred until 1870 legislation protecting tenant right in Ireland? See Lord Morley's description of the Irish cultivator "as a kind of copyholder or customary freeholder" (*Life of Gladstone*, vol. ii. p. 281).

[4] Cunningham, *Growth of English Industry and Commerce, Modern Times*, Part i. pp. 85–88, 101–107, 540–543.

produced reactions which spread far beyond their immediate effect on the classes most closely concerned with them. The displacement of a considerable number of families from the soil accelerated, if it did not initiate, the transition from the mediæval wage problem, which consisted in the scarcity of labour, to the modern wage problem, which consists in its abundance. Throughout the sixteenth and seventeenth centuries municipal[5] authorities were engaged in a prolonged struggle to enforce their exclusive economic privileges against the rural immigrant who had lost his customary means of livelihood and who overcrowded town dwellings and violated professional byelaws; while the Government prevented him from moving without a licence, and when he moved, straitened[6] his path between the Statute of Inmates on the one hand and the House of Correction on the other. Observers were agreed that the increase in pauperism[7] had one capital cause in the vagrancy produced by the new agrarian régime; and the English Poor Law system, or the peculiar part of it providing for relief of the able-bodied, which England was the first of European countries to adopt, came into existence partly as a form of social insurance against the effect of the rack rents and evictions, which England was the first of European countries to experience. Whatever uncertainty attaches to the causes and effects of the agrarian problem, there can be no doubt that those who were in the best position to judge thought it highly important. If it is not a watershed separating periods, it is at least a high range from which both events and ideas descend with added velocity and definiteness. To the economic historian the ideas are as important as the events. For though conceptions of social expediency are largely the product of economic conditions, they acquire a momentum which persists long after the circumstances which gave them birth have disappeared, and act as over-ruling forces to which, in the interval between one great change and another, events themselves tend to conform.

A consideration of these great movements naturally begins with those contemporary writers who described them. Though the books and pamphlets of the age contain much that is of interest in the development of economic theory, their writers rarely attempted to separate economic from other issues, and economic speculation usually took the form of discussions upon particular points of public policy, or of a casuistry prescribing rules for personal conduct in difficult cases. Such a difficult case, such a problem of public policy, was offered by the growth of competitive methods of agriculture. The moral objections felt to the new conditions caused them to be a favourite subject with writers of sermons and pamphlets, and made the sins of the encloser, like those of the usurer, one of the stand-bys of the sixteenth century preacher. There is, therefore, a considerable volume of writings dealing with the question from the point of view of the teacher of morality. At the same time the political significance of the movement, and the fact

[5] See *e.g. Records of the Borough of Reading*, vol ii. pp. 36, 94, 156; vol. iii., 131, and those of Leicester, Norwich, Nottingham, and Southampton, *passim*; also below, pp. 275–277.

[6] "Mr. Secretary Cecil said, ... If we debar tillage, we give scope to the Depopulator, and then, if the poor being thrust out of their houses go to dwell with others, straight we catch them with the Statute of Inmates; if they wander abroad, they are within the danger of the Statute of the Poor to be whipt" (D'Ewes' *Journal of the House of Commons*, 1601, pp. 674–675).

[7] See below, pp. 273–275.

that the classes concerned were important enough to elicit attempts at protection on the part of the Government, called forth a crop of suggestions and comments like those of More, Starkey,[8] Forest,[9] the author of the Commonwealth[10] of England, and, at a later date, Powell[11] and Moore.[12] Further, the new agricultural methods were explained by persons interested in the economics of agriculture, such as Fitzherbert,[13] Tusser,[14] Clarkson,[15] who surveyed the manors of the Earl of Northumberland in 1567, Humberstone[16] who did the same for those of the Earl of Devonshire, and Norden.[17] The accounts of surveyors, a dull but indispensable tribe, are reliable, as they are usually statements of facts which have occurred within their own experience, or at any rate, generalised descriptions of such facts. The same may be said of the evidence of John Hales, who was employed by the Government in investigating the question, and who had to explain it in such a way as to convince opponents, and to get legislation on this subject through a bitterly hostile Parliament. The description given by writers like Latimer,[18] Crowley,[19] and Becon[20] are valuable as showing the way in which the movement was regarded by contemporaries; but they are mainly somewhat vague denunciations launched in an age when the pulpit was the best political platform, and their very positiveness warns one that they are one-sided and must be received with caution. Still, they mark out a field for inquiry, and one may begin by setting out the main characteristics of the agrarian changes as pictured in their writings.

The movement originates, they agree, through the covetousness[21] of lords of

[8] E. E. T. S., *England in the Reign of King Henry the Eighth*, Part II.: "A Dialogue between Cardinal Pole and Thomas Lupset, Lecturer in Rhetoric at Oxford, by Thomas Starkey, Chaplain to the King," edited by J.M. Cowper (date of composition about 1538).

[9] E. E. T. S., as above, Part I. (Appendix). *The Pleasant Poesye of Princelie Practise*, by Sir William Forest (date of composition 1548).

[10] *The Commonweal of this Realm of England*, edited by Elizabeth Lamond (date of composition 1549; the author was almost certainly John Hales).

[11] Powell, *Depopulation Arraigned*, 1636.

[12] *The Crying Sin of England in not Caring for the Poor, wherein Enclosure such as doth unpeople Towns and Common Fields is Arraigned, Convicted, and Condemned by the Word of God*, by John Moore, Minister of Knaptoft, in Leicestershire, 1653.

[13] Fitzherbert, *Boke of Husbandry*, 1534. *Surveyinge*, 1539.

[14] Tusser, *Five Hundred Points of Husbandry*.

[15] *Northumberland County History*, vol. i. p. 350 and passim.

[16] Surveys *temp.* Philip and Mary of various estates belonging to the Earl Devon (*Topographer and Genealogist*, i. p. 43).

[17] Norden, *The Surveyor's Dialogue* (1607).

[18] Sermons by Hugh Latimer, sometime Bishop of Worcester (Everyman's Library, J.M. Dent & Co.).

[19] Crowley, Select Works (E.E.T.S., 1872).

[20] Becon, *Jewel of Joy*. Extract quoted in England in the reign of King Henry the Eighth (Part I., p. lxxvi.).

[21] "For looke in what partes of the realm doth growe the fynest and therefore dearest woll, there noblemen and gentlemen, yea, and certeyn abbotes, holy men no doubt, not contenting them selfes with the yearely revenues and profytes, that were wont to grow to their forefathers and predecessours of their landes, nor being content that they live in rest and pleasure nothinge profitting, yea much noyinge, the weal publique, leave no grounde for tillage, thei inclose al into pasture; thei throw doune houses; they plucke downe townes,

manors and large farmers, who have acquired capital in the shape of flocks of sheep, and who, by insisting on putting the land to the use most profitable to themselves, break through the customary methods of cultivation. The outward sign of this is enclosing, the cutting adrift of a piece of land from the common course of cultivation in use, by placing a hedge or paling round it, and utilising it according to the discretion of the individual encloser, usually with the object of pasturing sheep. This is accompanied by land speculation and rack-renting, which is intensified by the land-hunger which causes successful capitalists,[22] who have made money in trade, to buy up land as a profitable investment for their savings, and by the sale of corporate property which took place on the dissolution[23] of the monasteries and the confiscation of part of the gild estates. The consequence is, first, that there is a scarcity of agricultural produce and a rise[24] in prices, which is partly (it is supposed) attributable to the operations of the great graziers who control the supplies of wool, grain, and dairy produce, and secondly and more important that the small cultivator suffers in three ways. Agricultural employment is lessened. Small holdings are thrown[25] together and are managed by large capi-

---

and leave nothing standynge, but only the churche to be made a shepehouse" (More's *Utopia*, Book I., p. 32, Pitt Press Series).

[22] "The Grazier, the Farmer, the Merchants become landed men, and call themselves gentlemen, though they be churls; yea, the farmer will have ten farms, some twenty, and will be a Pedlar-merchant" (*King Edward's Remains: A Discourse about the Reformation of many Abuses*). "Look at the merchants of London, and ye shall see, when by their honest vocation God hath endowed them with great riches, then can they not be content, but their riches must be abrode in the country, to bie fermes out the handes of worshipful gentlemen, honest yeomen, and poor laborynge husbands" (*Lever's Sermons*, Arber's Reprints, p. 29).

[23] "Do not these ryche worldlynges defraude the pore man of his bread, ... and suffer townes so to decay that the pore hath not what to eat, nor yet where to dwell? What other are they, then, but very manslears? They abhorre the names of Monkes, Friars, Chanons, Nounes, etc., but their goods they gredely gripe. And yet where the cloysters kept hospitality, let out their fermes at a reasonable pryce, noryshed scholes, brought up youths in good letters, they doe none of all these thinges" (Becon, *Works*, 1564, vol. ii. fols. xvi., xvii.).

[24] "A proclamation set fourthe by the King's Majestie with the assent and consent of his dear uncle Edward, Duke of Somerset ... and the said cattell also by all lyklyhode of truth should be more cheape beynge in many men's handes as they be nowe in fewe, who may holde them deare and tarye the avantage of the market" (Brit. Mus. *Lansdown*, 238, p. 205). See also E. E. T. S.: "Certayne causes gathered together, wherein is showed the decaye of England only by the great multitude of shepe" (date 1550–1553), and *The Commonweal of this Realm of England, passim*, especially pp. xlv.-lxvii. It is worth noting that Hales, who was quite conversant with the effect on general prices of an increase in the supply of money, thought that the rise which took place in his day was in some measure due to monopolists. He describes his third Bill as ensuring that "ther wolde have byn within fyve yeares after the execution therof suche plentie of vitteyll and so good cheape as never was in England" (*Commonweal*, p. lxiii.).

[25] Proclamation as before: "Of late by thynclosinge of landes and erable grounds, many have byn drevyn to extreme povertie, insomuche that wheareas in tyme past, tenne, twentie, yea in some places C. or CC. Chrysten people hathe byn inhabytynge ... nowe ther is nothynge kept but sheepe and bullocks. All that lande, whiche heretofore was tilled and occupied by so many men, is nowe gotten by insaciable gredyness of mynde into one or two men's handes, and scarcely dwelled upon with one poore shepherd."

talists, with the result that he is driven off the land, either by direct eviction, or by a rise in rents and fines, or by mere intimidation. At the same time the commonable[26] area, consisting of the common waste, meadow, and pasture of the manor is diminished, with the result that the tenants who are not evicted suffer through loss of the facilities which they had previously had for grazing beasts without payment. There is, in consequence, a drift into the towns and a general lowering in the standard of rural life, due to the decay of the class which formerly sent recruits to the learned professions, which was an important counterpoise to the power of the great landed proprietors, and which was the backbone of the military forces of the country.[27]

The picture drawn by the literary authorities suggests questions, some of which have been satisfactorily cleared up and some of which are still obscure. Dissertations as to method are usually more controversial than profitable, and we do not propose at this point to give any detailed account of the order in which these problems have been taken up by previous scholars, to pass any judgment upon the different kinds of evidence which they have used, or to offer any estimate of the value of their conclusions. If we are at all successful in our presentation of the subject, the reader will discover for himself the nature of the evidence upon which we have relied, and where we differ from and agree with the treatment of other writers. All we can attempt here is to give a short statement of some of the principal issues which demand attention, a statement which does not pretend to be exhaustive, but which may serve to indicate the more salient features of the ground over which we shall travel.

As to the counties mainly affected by the agrarian changes there is now substantial agreement. The work of Mr. Leadam[28] and Professor Gay[29] seems to have put the geographical distribution of the movement towards enclosure, or at least of those enclosures which produced hardships, upon a fairly firm basis. We can say with some confidence that it mainly affected the Midlands and eastern counties, from Berkshire and Oxfordshire in the south to Lincoln and Norfolk in the north-east, and that it was least important in the south-western counties of Cornwall and Devon, and in the south-eastern counties of Kent and Essex, much of which had been enclosed before the sixteenth century began, and in the northern counties of Lancashire, Westmoreland, Cumberland, Northumberland, and Durham, though, by the end of the sixteenth century, parts of the two latter counties, at any rate, were considerably affected by it. Again, the same authors have offered a statistical estimate of the extent of the movement which, while it is manifestly defective, and while it can only be used with great caution to support arguments as to the practical effect of enclosures, does offer some guide to the imagination,

---

[26] "There be a manie a M cottagers in England, which, havinge no land to live of theire owne but their handie labours, and some refreshinge upon the said commons, yf they were sodenly thrust out from that commoditie might make a great tumult and discorde in the commonwealth" (*Commonweal of England*, pp. 49–50).

[27] See below, pp. 341–344.

[28] Leadam, *Domesday of Enclosures*.

[29] *Trans. Royal Hist. Soc.*, vol. xiv. and vol. xvii.; *Quarterly Journal of Economics*, vol. xvii. See also Gonner, *Common Land and Inclosure*, pp. 132–152.

and is, at least, a valuable check on the conjectures made by contemporaries without any statistics at all and on a basis merely of their personal impressions. Finally, the difficult question of the security of copyhold tenants as against the landlords who desired to evict them seems to have been put in the right perspective by the evidence which Dr. Savine[30] has adduced to prove that, in the case of copyholds of inheritance, a plaintiff who could show a clear title could get legal redress.

On the other hand, certain points must still be pronounced highly obscure. The first is a simple one. The agrarian changes are usually summed up under the name of "Enclosure." But what exactly did enclosing mean? Contemporary writers represent it as almost always being carried out by lords and large farmers against the interests of the smaller tenantry. But there is abundant proof that the tenants themselves enclosed; and as they can hardly be supposed to have been forward in initiating changes which damaged their own prospects, ought we not to begin by drawing a distinction between the piecemeal enclosures made by the peasantry, often after agreement between neighbours, from which they hoped to gain, and the great enclosures made by lords of manors from which the peasants obviously lost? Further, different authorities assign different degrees of importance to different aspects of the movement. Mr. Johnson[31] holds, for example, that the enclosure of the common waste, as distinct from the enclosure of the arable fields, was relatively unimportant. Such a view, however, is not easily reconciled with the constant complaints which relate clearly to the enclosing of common wastes and pastures and with the state of things depicted in the surveys.[32] Again, the writings of the period speak as though the movement were mainly one from arable to pasture farming. But this was questioned as long ago as the first thorough study of the question—that of Nasse[33]—and the doubts which he threw on their view of the problem are supported by Mr. Leadam by means of the statistics which he has drawn from the returns of the Commission of 1517, though his conclusions are in their turn disputed by Professor Gay. In fact no one who examines the picture given by the Commissions and by surveys and field maps can help feeling that the word "enclosing," used by contemporaries as though it bore its explanation on its face, covered many different kinds of action and has a somewhat delusive appearance of simplicity.

Moreover, who gained and who suffered by the enclosures, and to what extent? If the movement deserves to be called an agrarian revolution, it was certainly one which left a great many holders of small landed property intact, and perhaps

---

[30] *Quarterly Journal of Economics*, vol. xix. See below, pp. 287–297.

[31] Johnson, *The Disappearance of the Small Landowner*, p. 40.

[32] See below, pp. 218–221 and 237–253.

[33] Nasse, *The Land Community of the Middle Ages* (translated for the Cobden Club by Colonel Ouvry, 1871), pp. 81–91: "With regard to the proper agricultural character of these movements they are represented commonly as having been caused by an exclusively pure pasture husbandry, which expelled the tillage husbandman. Different circumstances, however, and witnesses show us closely that this, for the most part, was not the case." The discussion between Mr. Leadam and Professor Gay is contained in the *Trans. Royal Hist. Soc.*, New Series, vol. xiv. See also Miss Davenport, *Quarterly Journal of Economics*, vol. xi., and below, pp. 223–228.

even improved their position. Otherwise we can hardly account for the optimistic description of them, or of some of them, which is given in the late sixteenth and early seventeenth centuries by writers like Harrison,[34] Norden,[35] and Fuller,[36] or for the part which this class played in the Civil War. Nor can we say with confidence how the statistical evidence derived by Mr. Leadam and Professor Gay from the reports of Royal Commissions should be interpreted. The comparative smallness of the percentage of land which the Commissioners returned as enclosed has led to the view[37] that the importance of the whole movement was grossly exaggerated by the writers of the period, who created a storm in a tea-cup over changes which really affected only an inconsiderable proportion of the whole country. If this is so, it is not easy to explain either the continuous attention which was paid to the question by the Government, or the revolts of the peasantry, or the strong views of reasonable and fair-minded men with first-hand knowledge, such as John Hales.

There is obscurity not only as to the details, but as to the outlines of the movement. Different views have been expressed as to its origin, duration, and points of maximum intensity. Professor Ashley[38] puts the period of most rapid change from about 1470 to 1530. But these dates cannot be taken as in any way fixed. The greatest popular outcry[39] against enclosing occurred about the middle of the sixteenth century, in the years 1548 to 1550. As Miss Leonard[40] has shown, there was much enclosing in the seventeenth century, and about 1650[41] there was a crop of pamphlets against it similar in tone to the protests which occurred almost exactly a century before. It is especially difficult to determine how far back the movement should be carried. The first statute[42] against it, that of 1489, is an obvious landmark. But has it not been too readily accepted as an earlier limit? Hales[43] said that

[34] *Elizabethan England*, edited by Lothrop Withington, with introduction by F.J. Furnivall, p. 119.

[35] J. Norden, *The Surveyor's Dialogue*.

[36] Thomas Fuller, *Holy and Profane State*.

[37] Gay, *Quarterly Journal of Economics*, vol. xvii., p. 587: "Hysterical and rhetorical complaint ... condemned by its very exaggeration."

[38] Ashley, *Economic History*, vol. i. Part II., p. 286: "There were two periods of rapid change ... namely from c. 1470 to c. 1530, and again from about 1760 to 1830. After about 1530 the movement somewhat slackened."

[39] See below, Part III., chap. i.

[40] *Trans. Royal Hist. Soc.*, vol. xix. See also Gonner, *Common Land and Inclosure*, pp. 153–186. Professor Gonner is no doubt right in saying that "the view which regards inclosure ... as taking place mainly at two epochs, in the sixteenth and eighteenth centuries respectively ... gives an almost entirely false presentation of what occurred."

[41] Moore. *The Crying Sin of England in not Caring for the Poor*, 1653, and *A Scripture Word against Enclosure*, 1656. Moore's pamphlets provoked rejoinders, viz., *A Vindication of a Regulated Enclosure*, by Joseph Lee, 1656, *Considerations concerning Common Fields and Enclosures* (1654, Pseudonismus), and *A Vindication, of the Considerations concerning Common Fields and Enclosures, or a Rejoynder unto that Reply which Mr. Moore hath pretended to make unto those Considerations* (1656, Pseudonismus).

[42] 4 Henry VII. c. 19.

[43] "For the chief destruccion of Townes and decaye of houses was before the begynnynge of the reign of King Henry the Seventh" (The defence of John Hales, quoted p. lxiii. of

most of the "destruction of towns" had taken place before the beginning of the reign of Henry VII. The allusion to enclosing in the Chancellor's[44] speech to Parliament in 1483 shows that the movement must have already obtained considerable dimensions. Rous[45] had petitioned Parliament on the subject of depopulation in 1459, and in his History, which was published sometime between that date and 1486, he returned to the charge with a detailed account of the destruction of villages in his own county of Warwickshire. More convincing than either, the records of Manorial Courts[46] prove that the consolidation of holdings and collisions between the interests of commoners and sheep-farmers were quite common early in the fifteenth century. One may perhaps pause to remark that the question of the antecedent conditions, out of which the rapid agricultural changes of the sixteenth century arose, is a very important one, and the more important the more far-reaching those changes are thought to have been. It is surely incredible that the conversion of land to pasture, the growth of large pasture estates, and the eviction of customary tenants, should have occurred to the extent described, unless considerable minor changes preceded them, and without some premonitory rumblings to suggest the coming storm. In economic affairs new lines of organisation usually start on a small scale before they attain dimensions sufficiently striking to attract attention; and one would expect to be able to trace the leading motives of the agrarian changes of the Tudor period far back in the fifteenth century and even earlier, and that they would throw light on the nature of the subsequent movements. There is, further, some difference of opinion as to the causes which forced the agrarian problem to the front. Some contemporary authorities attribute it mainly to the growth of the woollen industry,[47] and in this they have been followed by most subsequent writers. On the other hand, the direct evidence supplied by price statistics seems to be not altogether reliable,[48] and in any case the woollen industry had been steadily growing for a hundred years before the complaints as to enclosure become general. This has led Dr. Hasbach[49] to argue that the change in agricultural methods was due less to the high price of wool than to the low price of grain, which was artificially reduced by the restrictions imposed on export under the Tudors, and which he holds to have produced such a fall in rent as to result in the adoption of pasture-farming. Other writers have emphasised the revolutionary effect of the general depreciation in the value of money[50] and the consequent

Miss Lamond's edition of *The Commonweal of this Realm of England*).

[44] Camden Society, 1854, lii.

[45] J. Rossus, *Historia Regum Angliæ* (T. Hearne).

[46] See below, pp. 161–162.

[47] See *e.g.* More's *Utopia* quoted above, and Pauli, *Drei volkswirthschaftliche Denkscriften aus der Zeit Heinrichs VIII. von England*. It is suggested that if the council will only fix the price which stappellers and clothmakers are to pay for raw wool, "it shall cause the pasturers of sheep to open their enclosures and suffer the more earth to be wrought by works of husbandry."

[48] See the discussion between Mr. Leadam and Professor Gay on the wool prices of Thorold Roger in *Trans. Royal Hist. Soc.*, New Series, vol. xiv. The best account of the price movements of the sixteenth century is contained in *Studien zur Geschichte der Englischen Lohnarbeiter*, Band I., by Gustaf F. Steffen.

[49] Hasbach, *A History of the English Agricultural Labourer*, pp. 31–33.

[50] See below, pp. 197–200 and 304–310.

growth of commercialism in the relations between landlord and tenant.

Finally, one may ask what was the effect of legislation against pasture-farming and evictions, and of the frequent administrative interference by which the Governments of the sixteenth and seventeenth centuries tried to check them. On a first view, at any rate, the whole history of the policy pursued in this matter, with one short interval from the autumn of 1549 to 1553, constitutes surely one of the most remarkable attempts to control changing economic conditions by Government action which has ever been made. Whether successful or unsuccessful, it throws much light on the ideas of the period with regard to the place in the State which should be occupied by the landholding classes, on the relative advantages from a political standpoint of large and small farming, and on the administrative machinery of Government. The opinion generally[51] adopted seems to be that the Acts forbidding conversion were entirely ineffective, and that the Government, if sincere, was outmanœuvred by the Local Authorities, whose duty it was to administer the laws, and whose interest lay in preventing their administration. Much evidence may be cited in support of this view. On the other hand, we have clear proof of the Council interfering on some occasions with apparent success; and further, it seems necessary to discriminate between the policies of different periods. One cannot argue, for example, that because the statutes protecting the poorer classes were not carried out by the rapacious oligarchy of adventurers which governed England from the fall of Somerset to 1553, therefore they were never used effectively in the reigns of Henry VIII., of Elizabeth, or of the first two Stuarts. Nor would one be right in assuming the existence in the sixteenth century of the identity of interest and policy between the great landlords and the Government which characterised the period from 1688 to 1832. One's conclusion on the whole question must depend less on direct evidence as to the success of the particular measures, which, in the nature of things, is not easily obtainable, than on the opinion which one forms of the degree of importance which the statesmen of the period assigned to the class of small cultivators, and of the ability of the Central Government to get its policy executed.

Such are some of the questions which are suggested by even a cursory survey of the agrarian problem. There are others which are less susceptible of summary statement, but which involve issues that are of some importance for the interpretation of economic history. Granted that it was inevitable that the subsistence husbandry of the mediæval village should give way to capitalist agriculture, in what light are we to regard the changes by which that great transformation was brought about? Ought we to think of the open field system as altogether incompatible with any improvement in agricultural technique, as the miracle of squalid perversity which it has appeared to some writers both of our own and of earlier ages, and as requiring the bitter discipline of pasture farming and evictions to shake it out of its deep rut of custom, and to make room for more progressive methods? Or are we to view it as permitting a good deal of mobility, and as already slowly developing a less rigid and cumbrous organisation when it was partially over-

[51] *e.g.* by Hasbach, *op. cit.* p. 37. Gay, *Trans. Royal Hist. Soc.*, vol. xviii. Contrast Miss Leonard, Trans. *Royal Hist. Soc.*, vol. xix. On the subject of the policy of the State towards the agrarian problem, see below, Part III., chap. i.

whelmed by rapid, and for the mass of the peasantry disastrous, changes? What place ought the agrarian revolution of the sixteenth century to be given in that transition from mediæval to modern conditions of agriculture which, starting in England, has spread eastwards through almost every European country, and which is beginning to-day even in India. How far does it compare and contrast with the enclosures of the period succeeding the fall of the Stuarts, and with the analogous developments which have taken place on the continent, and how far does it present special features peculiar to itself? What were the relations between it and other aspects of national life? Have the economic changes which took place in the world of agriculture any reflex in the social and political changes occurring in the century which divides the Reformation from the Civil War? How far did the redistribution of property which they effected contribute to the decline in the condition of the poorer classes which, according to most writers, took place in the sixteenth century, and to the creation of the commercial aristocracy whose influence becomes so pronounced after the Restoration? What was the result of these material developments in the realm of legal and economic ideas? Ought we to minimise the communalism of the mediæval village? Or should we think of the agrarian revolution of the sixteenth century as really a new and decided movement in the direction of economic individualism, a long step towards the growth of modern ideas of land ownership and of the right of the individual to follow unfettered his own discretion in matters of economic enterprise, which gather weight at the end of the seventeenth, and come to their own at the end of the eighteenth, century?

We cannot pretend to answer these questions. We leave them as riddles for the reader, with the words which a sixteenth century economist prettily prefaces to his analysis of the chief economic problems of his age:—"And albeit ye might well saye that there be men of greater witte then I; yet fools (as the proverb is) speake some times to the purpose, and as many headdes, so many wittes ... and though eche of theise by them selves doe not make perfitte the thing, yet when every man bringeth in his guifte, a meane witted man maye of the whole (the best of everie mans devise beinge gathered together) make as it were a pleasant garland and perfitte."[52]

In the following pages we shall deal with our subject in the following order: Chapter I. of Part I. will describe the chief classes of tenants as they are set out in rentals and surveys, and in particular the freeholders and customary tenants who formed the bulk of the landholders. Chapters II., III. and IV. will discuss in some detail the economic positions of the customary tenants both before and during the sixteenth century, the reasons for supposing that there had been a considerable growth in the prosperity of many of them before our period begins, and the gradual modification in the customary conditions of rural life, as illustrated both by the growth of competitive payments on those parts of the manor which were least controlled by custom, and by the attempts made by the peasantry themselves to overcome by enclosure the difficulties attaching to the methods of open field cultivation. Chapter I. of Part II. will examine the reason which led to more rapid changes in agricultural methods in the sixteenth century, and the growth of the

---

[52] Preface to *The Commonweal of this Realm of England* (ed. Lamond).

large leasehold farms upon which these changes can be most easily traced. Chapters II. and III. will discuss the reaction of these changes upon the peasantry and the question of the nature and security of their tenure. Chapter I. of Part III. will explain their political and social importance and the policy of the State towards them. In Chapter II. we shall endeavour to offer a summary of our main conclusions.

# PART I
# THE SMALL LANDHOLDER

"What comyn folke in all this world may compare with the comyns of England in riches, freedom, liberty, welfare, and all prosperity? What comyn folke is so mighty, so strong in the felde as the comyns of England?" — *State Papers, Henry VIII., vol. ii. p. 10.*

"My thynketh that as the wise husbandman makethe and maynteyneth his nursery of yonge trees to plante in the steede of the olde, when he seeth them begynne to fail, because he will be sure at all tymes of fruyte: so shulde politique governours (as the kynges maiestie and his councell mynde) provide for thencrease and mayntenance of people, so that at no tyme they maye lacke to serve his highnes and the commenwelthe." — *The defence of John Hales agenst certeyn sclaundres and false reaportes made of hym.*

# CHAPTER I

## THE RURAL POPULATION

### (a) The Classes of Landholders

If an Englishman of ordinary intelligence had been asked in the reign of Henry VIII. to explain the foundations of national prosperity, he would probably have answered that the whole wealth[53] of the country arises out of the labours of the common people, and that, of all who labour, it is by the work of those engaged in tillage that the State most certainly stands. True, it cannot dispense with handicraftsmen and merchants, for ours is an age of new buildings, new manufactures, new markets. The traders of Europe are already beginning to look west and east after the explorers; there are signs of an oceanic commerce arising out of the coastwise traffic of the Middle Ages; and Governments are increasingly exercised with keeping foreign ports open and English ports closed. But whether any particular artisan or trader is a profitable member of the commonwealth is an open question. Too many of the manufactures which men buy are luxurious[54] trifles brought from abroad and paid for with good English cloth or wool or corn or tin, if not with gold itself—articles whose use sumptuary legislation would do well to repress. As for merchants,[55] if like honest men they give their minds to navigation, well and good. But theirs is an occupation in which there is much room for "unlawful subtlety and sleight," for eking out the legitimate profits earned by the labour of transport, with underhand gains filched from the necessitous by buying cheap and selling dear, for speculations perilously near the sin of the usurers who traffic in time itself. Outside the circle of a few statesmen and financiers, the men of the sixteenth century have not mastered the secret by which modern societies feed and clothe (with partial success) dense millions who have never seen wheat

[53] Pauli, *Drei volkswirthschaftliche Denkschriften aus der Zeit Heinrichs VIII. von England*: How to reform the Realme in setting them to work, and to restore tillage. "The whole welth of the body of the realm riseth out of labours and workes of the common people."

[54] *The Commonweal of this Realm of England* (Lamond), p. 63: "And I marvell no man taketh heade unto it, what nombre first of trifles cometh hether from beyonde the seas, that we might either clene spare, or els make them within oure owne Realme, for the which we paie inestimable treasure every yeare, or els exchange substanciall wares and necessaries for them." E. E. T. S., *England in the Reign of King Henry VIII.*, Part II., p. 84: "Craftys men and makers of tryfullys are too many." Harrison in *Elizebethan England* (Withington), p. 15: "O how many trades and handicrafts are now in England whereof the Commonwealth hath no need!" &c.

[55] *e.g.* the prayer for merchants in Edward VI.'s *Book of Private Prayer*: "So occupy their merchandise without fraud, guile, or deceit."

or wool, though London and Bristol and Southampton are beginning to grope towards it. Looking at the cornfields which are visible from the centre of even the largest cities, they see that a small harvest means poverty and a good harvest prosperity, and that a decrease of a few hundred acres in the area sown may make all the difference between scarcity and abundance. A shortage in grain, which would cause a modern State to throw open its ports and to revise its railway tariff, sets a sixteenth century town[56] breaking up its pastures and extending the area under tillage. No man is so clearly a "productive labourer" as the husbandman, because no man so unmistakably adds to the most obvious and indispensable forms of wealth; and though, in the system of classes which makes up the State, there are some whose function is more honourable, there is none whose function is more necessary. In most ages there is some body of men to whom their countrymen look with pride as representing in a special degree the strength and virtues of the nation. In the sixteenth century that class consisted of the substantial yeoman. Men speak of them with the same swaggering affection as is given by later generations to the sea-dogs. The genius of England is a rural divinity and does not yet rule the waves; but the English yeomen have "in time past made all France afraid."[57] They absorb most of the attention of writers, both on the technique and on the social relations of agriculture. They are the feet[58] upon which the body politic stands—the hands which, by ministering to its wants, leave the brain free to act and plan. Let us begin by trying to see how the landholding classes were composed.

The manorial documents supply us with much information about the landholders, and though we cannot say what proportion[59] they formed of the popula-

---

[56] *Coventry Leet Book*, Part III., pp. 679–680.

[57] See Smith, *De Republica Anglorum*, Lib. I. c. 23: "These are they which in the old world got that honour to Englande ... because they be so manie in number, so obedient at the Lorde's call, so strong of bodie, so hard to endure paine, so courageous to adventure ... these were the good archers in times past, and the stable troops of footmen that affaide all France that would rather die all, than once abandon the knight or gentleman their captaine," and Harrison in *Elizabethan England* (Withington), pp. 11–13.

[58] E. E. T. S., *England in the Reign of King Henry VIII.*, Starkey's Dialogue, Part II., p. 49: "To the handes are resemblyd both craftysmen and warryarys.... To the fete the plowmen and tyllarys of the ground, beycause they, by theyr labour, susteyne and support the rest of the body."

[59] In this essay we are concerned only with the landholders, not with the wage workers. The relative number of persons holding land and of agricultural labourers without land is an important question on which it is not easy to get light. The surveys and rentals, a species of private census invaluable in giving information about the holders of property, tell us only the number of householders, and as the labourers employed in agriculture (like many of those employed in manufacturing industry) usually lived on the premises of their masters, they do not enable us to calculate the number of those living entirely by their labour. Still, since they include all tenants, whether holders of a cottage only or holders of land in addition, they enable us to say what proportion of heads of families held land, and what proportion had none, or none except a garden. This is of some importance. A tenant holding even as much as fifty acres can hardly have employed more than two or three agricultural labourers, and most tenants held less than this; so that in those places where the cottagers form a small proportion of the whole population we may conclude that a large proportion of the villagers were landholders (for the figures on this point see the tables given below).

tion, we ought to be able to say with some certainty the relative numbers of differ-

Unfortunately, we do not possess for the sixteenth century even such a loose estimate as was made by Gregory King at the end of the seventeenth. In 1688 he calculated that there were 16,560 families of nobles and gentlemen, 60,000 families of yeomen, 150,000 of farmers—presumably on lease—400,000 cottagers and poor, 364,000 labouring people and out-servants, obviously a very rough calculation, the most remarkable feature of which is the large number of yeomen. Poll Tax returns might give us the kind of information we require, since they included, or were meant to include, the whole population above a certain age, irrespective of whether they held land or not, and sometimes divided them roughly into classes. Thus on sixteen manors in the Norfolk Hundred of Thingoe the return to the Poll Tax of 1381 showed a population of 870 male and female inhabitants over fifteen years of age, of whom 9 were set down as knights, 53 as farmers, 102 as artificers, 344 as "labourers" (laboratores), 362 as "servants" (servientes). If, as is not improbable, the first four classes held land (the labourers being serfs working on the demesne), and the last consisted of farm and household employees who did not, this would put the landholding classes on these manors at a little more than half the total population over the age of fifteen. But this return was probably falsified to escape the tax; see Powell, *The East Anglian Rising*, App. I., and Oman, *The Great Revolt of 1381*. The figures published by Dr. Savine (*Oxford Studies in Social and Legal History*, vol. i., pp. 223–226) of the monastic population show that on the eve of the dissolution there were residing in 22 houses in Leicester, Warwick, and Sussex, 255 "hinds" and 76 "women servants," presumably employed on the demesne farm, which gives an average to each farm of about 11 hinds and about 3 women servants. In the Kentish Nunnery of St. Sexburge, Sheppey, the demesne farm employed a carter, a carpenter, two cowherds, a thatcher, a horse keeper, a malter, three shepherds. Best, describing his farming arrangements in Yorkshire in 1641 (*Surtees Society*, vol. xxxiii.), states: "Wee kept constantly five plowes goinge, and milked fowerteene kine, wherefore wee had always fower men, two boyes to go with the oxeploughe, and two good lusty mayde-servants." These were in each case only the permanent staff, and their comparatively small numbers suggest that much work must have been done by men who worked on their own land and only occasionally helped on the demesne, *i.e.* that the proportion of landholders to non-landholders was high. This conclusion agrees with the evidence of the surveys, which show that, especially in the East of England, many of both the free and the customary tenants' holdings were so small that they could hardly have made a living out of them without working as wage-labourers as well, and also with other indications as to the classes in rural society; *e.g.* out of 3780 persons mentioned in Worcestershire recognizances, 1591–1643, as either "labourers," "husbandmen," or "yeomen," 667 are entered as labourers, 1303 as husbandmen, 1810 as yeomen, the latter designation always, and the second usually, implying a holder of land (J.W. Willis Bund, *Kalendar of the Sessions Rolls*, 1591–1643, Part II.) On the other hand, conditions varied enormously from place to place. Where there was a considerable body of small landowners the number of hired labourers tended to be small, the work of cultivation being done by the holder and his family; *e.g.* we read of a manor in the seventeenth century where thirteen freeholders farmed 580 acres with the aid of only ten men-servants and shepherds before enclosure, and six or seven afterwards (Joseph Lee, *A Vindication of a Regulated Enclosure*).

Some of the surveys supply us with extreme cases of the opposite kind, where the whole manor consists of two or three holdings or of even one great estate, and where almost the whole of the population must have been working for wages; these illustrate Harrison's complaint that in many places "The land of the parish is gotten up into a few men's hands; yea, sometimes, into the tenure of one or two or three, whereby the rest are compelled betimes to be hired servants unto the others, or else to beg their bread in misery from door to door" (Withington's edition of *Elizabethan England*, p. 21). A protest made to the Coun-

ent classes among them. In the surveys and rentals of the period persons holding land may usually be divided roughly according to the nature of their tenure into three groups—freeholders, customary tenants, and leaseholders. This classification[60] of course is an elastic and tentative one, which raises almost as many questions as it settles. The customary tenure of one part of the country differs very much from the customary tenure of another part. Customary tenants include copyholders and the vast majority of tenants at will, who are holding customary land, and who are often entered under the latter heading merely because the surveyor did not trouble to set out their full description. But tenancy at will is sometimes used to describe the condition, not only of the holder of customary land, but also of men who are mere squatters on the waste or on the demesne, and who are not protected in their holdings by any manorial custom. Again, it is not always easy to draw a line between copyhold and leasehold. On a manor where the custom is least favourable to the tenants' interests the former shades into the latter. There is not much difference, for example, between a lease for thirty-three years and a copyhold for life. Again, the classification is one of tenures not of tenants. In parts of England, it is true, it does divide individual tenants with almost complete exhaustiveness and precision. In most districts, for example, the free tenant usually holds freehold land and nothing else, the customary tenant customary land and no other. But in East Anglia there is no such simplicity of arrangement, no such permanence of tenurial compartments. Many free tenants hold land which is said to be bond or villein or customary land; many customary tenants hold free land;

---

cil from Norfolk in 1631 against its policy of trying to keep down prices by insisting that all corn should be sold in the open market points out that in "the woodland and pasture part" of the country there are "a great many handicraftsmen which live by dressinge and combinge of wool, carding, spinning and weaving, etc., and the Townes there commonly very great consisting of such like people and other artificers with many poor, and none of them all ordinarilye having any corn but from the market." As to the "champion part" of the county, the document divides the rural population into three classes: "1. Tilth masters that have corn of their own growing and sell it to others. 2. Labourers that buy it at an under-price of them unto whom they worke. 3. Poore people that are relieved by good orders in every towne" (*Original Papers of the Norfolk and Norwich Archæological Society*, 1907). But the case of Norfolk was exceptional, owing to its position as the chief seat of the textile industries.

On the whole I am inclined to think that though the process of commutation which went on from 1350 onwards can hardly be explained except on the supposition that there was a considerable population of persons who held little land and were ready to eke out a living by working for wages, yet in the sixteenth century even the wage-working heads of families usually held a certain amount of land (even if only a garden) as well. This agrees with what we are told by contemporaries of the scarcity of wage-earners (see below, pp. 99–102). One may add, that in view of this, the fixing of maximum wages bears a somewhat different colour from that often given it. It was only practicable, one is inclined to say, because so few persons depended entirely on wages for a living. The social problem in the sixteenth century was not a problem of wages, but of rents and fines, prices and usury, matters which concern the small-holder or the small master craftsman as much as the wage-earner. The "working classes" were largely small property holders and small traders.

[60] The summary statement given above is liable to be misleading. The reader will find a fuller discussion of the questions arising in connection with it below in Part II., chap. iii.

many of both have added to their holdings by leasing parts of the demesne or of the waste, and though in this respect the Eastern counties are exceptional, it is in them often impossible to say in what class any individual should be placed.

Nevertheless, in spite of many marginal cases, we may perhaps find in the surveyors' classification a map of the broader features of the country through which we are to travel. Property holders, profit makers, and wage-earners are to-day inextricably confused, but to the economist who writes on our social problems 200 years hence it will not be altogether useless to know that his predecessors did in practice draw rough distinctions between these classes, and formed estimates of the numbers of each. Much of the agrarian problem of the sixteenth century turns on the question of the legal interest in their holdings enjoyed by different classes of tenants, and though we cannot hope to escape the pitfalls which await compilers of even the humblest census, a preliminary survey of their distribution in a few counties may not be altogether without value. The following figures are taken from the surveys and rentals of 118 manors.[61] The majority were made in the reign of Henry VIII., Edward VI., and Elizabeth. There are included, however, three from the latter half of the fifteenth century and three from the years between 1630 and 1650. Under the heading of customary tenants are grouped copyholders and tenants at will, as well as those who are called customary tenants in the rentals and surveys.

Scanty as they are, these figures show that there is the very greatest variety in the distribution of different classes of tenants in different parts of the country, and remind us that we must be careful how we generalise from the conditions of one district to those of another. When all localities are handled together, customary tenants form nearly two-thirds of the whole landholding population, freeholders about one-fifth, leaseholders between one-eighth and one-ninth. But in parts of the Midlands and in parts of the West the leaseholders are much more numerous than they are elsewhere; in Leicestershire they form over one-fifth, and are almost as numerous as the freeholders, while if we isolate the five Somersetshire and Devonshire manors which above are combined with those of Wiltshire, we find that in them the leaseholders exceed the freeholders by nearly two to one. Again, in Northumberland the preponderance of customary tenants (where they form 91 per cent. of the landholding population) over the two other classes is much more marked than it is in Wiltshire, and in Wiltshire it is greater than it is in the three Midland counties and in East Anglia. That customary tenants should overwhelmingly preponderate in Northumberland is intelligible enough. If the single great manor of Rochdale be removed, they preponderate almost as much in Lancashire. In those two wild counties mediæval conditions survive long after they have begun elsewhere to disappear. There has been no growth of trade to bring mobile leasehold tenures in its train, or to accumulate the wealth which the peasants need to enfranchise their servile tenancies. But why should they be so much more numerous in the southern counties than they are in the twenty-two Midland villages, where one would suppose the conditions to be much the same? Here, as often

[61] They include also tenants on the lands belonging to Cockersand Abbey, lying in many different parts of Lancashire, in 1503. For the sources from which this table is constructed and its defects, see Appendix II..

hereafter, we raise a question only to leave it unanswered.

TABLE I

| | Total | Freeholders | Customary Tenants | Lease-holders | Uncer-tain |
|---|---|---|---|---|---|
| Northumberland, six manors | 474 | 26 | 436 | 12 | |
| Lancashire, seven manors, and lands belonging to Cockers and Abbey | 1280 | 217 | 451 | 334[62] | 278 |
| Total | 1754 | 243 | 887 | 334 | 346 |
| | | (13.8%) | (50.5%) | (19.04%) | (15%) |
| Staffordshire, six manors | 356 | 44 | 272 | 23 | 17 |
| Leicestershire, nine manors | 618 | 134 | 311 | 124 | 49 |
| Northampton-shire, seven manors | 531 | 100 | 355 | 66 | 10 |
| Total | 1505 | 278 | 938 | 213 | 76 |
| | | (18.1%) | (62.3%) | (14.2%) | (5%) |
| Norfolk, twen-ty-five manors | 1011[63] | 316 | 596 | 53 | 50 |
| Suffolk, fourteen manors | 353 | 176 | 146 | 25 | 6 |
| Total | 1364[64] | 492 | 742 | 78 | 56 |
| | | (36%) | (54.3%) | (5.7%) | (4.1%) |
| Wiltshire, Somer-set, and Devon-shire, thirty-two manors | 1102 | 149 | 817 | 136 | |
| Hampshire, two manors | 259 | 8 | 251 | | |

[62] The Lancashire figures are unduly weighted by those of the single large manor of Rochdale, where, in 1626, there were 612 tenants. If this manor be omitted, there remain only 19 leaseholders on the other Lancashire manors. Like Northumberland, Lancashire seems to be (as one would expect) a county of customary tenants.

[63] There is an error of 4 in the Norfolk figures which I have been unable to trace and correct.

[64] There is an error of 4 in the Norfolk figures which I have been unable to trace and correct.

| Ten other manors in the south of England | 219 | 43 | 158 | 12 | 6 |
|---|---|---|---|---|---|
| Total | 1580 | 200 | 1226 | 148 | 6 |
|  |  | (12.6%) | (77.2%) | (9.3%) | (0.3%) |
| Grand Total | 6203[65] | 1213 | 3793 | 785 | 416 |
|  |  | (19.5%) | (61.1%) | (12.6%) | (6.7%) |

Yet there is one point emerging from these figures of which the explanation can hardly be in doubt. It will be noticed that in Norfolk and Suffolk combined the proportion of freeholders is about double what it is in the country as a whole. In the former county they form more than one-third of all the landholders, and in the latter they are almost equal to the other two classes together. The number of peasant proprietors in Suffolk is indeed quite exceptional, and is one of the most remarkable facts revealed by the surveys, drawing an unmistakable line between the land tenure of the east and that of the south-west and the northern border. In Wiltshire and Northumberland it is not uncommon to find villages where no freeholders at all are recorded. In Norfolk and Lancashire it is the exception for them to be in a majority. But on half the Suffolk manors summarised above they are the largest class represented, and on some they stand to the other landholders in a proportion of two, three, and even four to one. Is it fanciful, one may ask, to turn from the sixteenth century to the dim beginnings of things, to that first and greatest survey in which the land of England was described so that not an ox or an acre escaped valuation, and in which, before freehold tenure had been hammered into any precise legal shape, Suffolk and Norfolk abounded more than all other counties in *liberi homines* and *sochemanni*? Though a longer time separates these documents from Domesday[66] than separates them from us, perhaps it is not altogether fanciful. Rural life, except for one great catastrophe, has been very permanent. Unlike rural life to-day, it has been most permanent in its lower ranges. How ever often manors may have changed hands, there has been little to break the connection with the soil of peasants whose title is good, no change at all com-

---

[65] There is an error of 4 in the Norfolk figures which I have been unable to trace and correct.

[66] In Domesday Book 35 per cent. of all the tenants in Suffolk are *liberi homines*, 32 per cent. of all those in Norfolk are either *liberi homines* or *sochemanni*. See Vinogradoff, *The Growth of the Manor*, note 24 to chap. iii. Book III. (p. 376); Maitland, *Domesday Book and Beyond*, p. 23; Seebohm, *The English Village Community*, map opposite p. 85. Domesday also gives a large number of *liberi homines* and *sochemanni* in Leicestershire. In the table given above the Leicestershire manors come after Suffolk and Norfolk as having the third largest proportion of freeholders, viz., 21.6 per cent. The return of freeholders supplied to the Government in 1561 (Lansdowne MSS. V., 8, 9, 11, 12, 13, 14, 15) appear to be considerably understated, probably because only the more substantial men were thought worth mentioning. They are as follows: Beds 282, Berks 166, Essex 880, Notts 189, Oxon. 198, Herts 363, York 787, Lincoln 444. The large number in Essex is noteworthy.

parable to the buying out of small freeholders which took place in the eighteenth and nineteenth centuries. It may well be that the main outlines of the social system which the Domesday commissioners found already laid in the east of England crop out again after the lapse of between four and five hundred years. It may well be that Suffolk is a county of small freeholders in the days of Henry VIII. and Elizabeth, because it was a county of free men and socmen in the days of William I.

### (b) The Freeholders

In spite of the constant complaints of the sixteenth century writers that one effect of the agrarian changes was the decay of the yeomanry, we shall not in the following pages be much concerned with the freeholders. In our period the word "yeomen" was ceasing to be given the narrow semi-technical sense which it possessed in Acts of Parliament and legal documents, and was beginning to acquire the wide significance which it possesses at the present day. To the lawyer the yeoman meant a freeholder,[67] "a man who may dispend of his own free lande in yerely revenue to the summe of 40s. sterling," and if the word yeoman was used in its strict legal sense, the decay of the yeomanry ought to have meant a decline in the numbers of freeholders, such as occurred on a very large scale two and a half centuries later. But in this matter it seems that popular usage was more elastic than legal definition, and, except when the significance to be given it is defined by the context, the word itself is not an accurate guide to the legal position of those to whom it is applied. Writers on constitutional questions were careful to observe the stricter usage, because the 40s. freeholder occupied a position in the State, both as a voter and in serving on juries, from which persons who, though much wealthier, were not freeholders, were excluded. But the word yeoman was used, in speaking of agricultural conditions, to describe any well-to-do farmer beneath the rank of gentleman, even though he was not a freeholder. Thus Bacon[68] writes quite vaguely of "the yeomanry or middle people, of a condition between gentlemen and cottagers or peasants." Those who insisted that the military power of England depended on the yeomanry can hardly have meant to exclude well-to-do copyholders;[69] not only copyholders but even villeins[70] by blood were sometimes described as yeomen; and, in fact, even writers who, like Sir Thomas Smith,[71] use the word most clearly in its strict legal sense on one page, allow themselves to slip into using it in its wider and more popular sense on the next, when the social importance of the class and not its legal status is uppermost in their minds.

Nor is there much evidence that the freeholders suffered generally from the agrarian changes of the sixteenth century. It is true that there are some complaints from freeholders as to the loss of rights of pasture through the encroachments of large farmers upon the commonable area, some cases of litigation between them

[67] Smith, *De Republica Anglorum*, Lib I., c. 23.

[68] *History of King Henry VII.* (Lumley), pp. 70–72. He makes his meaning quite clear by saying "tenancies for years, lives, and at will, whereupon much of the yeomanry lived, were turned into demesnes."

[69] *Trans. Royal Hist. Soc.*, vol. xvii. (Savine, "Bondmen under the Tudors").

[70] *Ibid.*

[71] Smith, *De Republica Anglorum, loc. cit.*

and enclosing landlords. But, since their payments were fixed, there was no way of getting rid of them except by buying them out, and though this method, which was so important a cause of the decline of the small freeholder in the eighteenth and early nineteenth centuries, was occasionally employed to round off a great estate, it seems to have played a comparatively unimportant part in our period. There is no sign of any large diminution in their numbers, such as would have been expected if the movement had affected them in the same way as it did the customary tenants.

Indeed, if the accounts of contemporary writers may be trusted, it would appear that their position was actually improved in the course of the century. Though even among quite small men one occasionally finds a tenant by knight[72] service, the vast majority of freeholders held in free socage, owing fealty and suit of court, and paying a money rent, sometimes combined with the old recognitions[73] of dependent tenure, such as a gillyflower, a red rose, a pound of pepper, or a pound of cummin. But while on some manors some outward form of feudalism, such as homage and fealty, were still maintained, the decay of feudal relations in the middle order of society had combined with economic causes to better their condition, and the time was already not far distant when those who held by the more honourable tenure of knight service would insist on its being assimilated to the humbler and less onerous tenure of the socager. The agricultural services of the socage tenants had long disappeared. There are many instances of work on the demesne being done in the sixteenth century by copyholders; but there is in our records only one manor where it was exacted from the freeholders, and other obligations were tending to go the way of the vanished predial labour. Suits of court might be owing, and set down as owing in the surveys, but one may doubt very much whether they were often enforced. Owing to the fall in the value of money the fixed rent of the socager often yielded only a small income to the lord of the manor, and in a good many cases these payments had disappeared altogether before the end of the century, or were so unimportant as to be hardly worth the trouble of collecting. Surveyors for this reason were often little interested in them, and, while recording the acreage held by the customary tenants and leaseholders with scrupulous accuracy, did not always trouble to set out in detail the holdings of a class which was financially so insignificant, with the result that sometimes the freeholders shook themselves loose from all payments and services altogether. Nor, had the surveyors been as careful as the heads of the profession would have had them be, would they always have been successful in dealing with this very independent class. They may protest that "next[74] under the king" the freeholders

---

[72] MSS. of Earl of Leicester at Holkham. Billingford and Bintry MSS. No. 9 (Manor of Foxley, 1568).

[73] *e.g. ibid.*, Sparham MSS. No. 5, a freeholder pays "a pounde of cumming seede and a gillyflower" (*c.* 1590). R.O. Rentals and Surveys, Duchy of Lancaster, Portf. 6, No. 15: "nyne golden threads of vi.d." (1568). R.O. Land Rev. Misc. Bks., 182, fol. 1: a tenant "holds freely a cottage paying a red rose."

[74] Norden, *The Surveyor's Dialogue*, Book I., pp. 4–5, to which the farmer answers: "Fie upon you. Will you bring us to be slaves? Neither lawe, nor reason, nor least of all religion, can allowe what you affirme."

"may be said to be the lord's," but freehold lands have a way of getting mislaid[75] to the despair of manorial officials, as copyhold lands do to-day. When escheats occur, the holding cannot be found; when rents are overdue, distraint is impossible, because the bailiff does not know on whom to distrain. The suggestion that, as long as rents are paid and services discharged, the lord has any interest in the property of his freehold tenants, rouses instant resentment, and it would seem that by our period, at any rate in the south of England, the connection of the freeholders with the manor was a matter rather of form and sentiment than of substance. In fact freehold has almost assumed its modern shape.

In assuming its modern shape it has made this particular strand in rural life harder to unravel. By escaping from the supervision of the manorial authorities the freeholders escape at the same time from the economic historian, and since the facts of their position go so often unrecorded, we can speak of it with much less confidence than we can about that of the leaseholders and customary tenants. Out of over one hundred manors which we have examined, there are only twenty-two where it is possible to ascertain with any accuracy the acreage held by the freeholders, and, even on these, one too often meets cases in which the extent of the holding is either unknown to the surveyor, or in which he does not think it worth while to record it. Our results, such as they are, are set out in the table on pages 32 and 33.[76]

Combining the information supplied by these figures with that obtained from other sources, we can form a rough idea of the agrarian conditions under which the freeholders live. They are, in the first place, a most heterogeneous class, including on the one hand men of considerable wealth and position, and on the other mere cottagers. If we could trust the statistics given above we should have to say that the latter enormously outnumbered the former. But our impression is that, though, no doubt, a large number of freeholders were extremely small men, the preponderance of the latter was not nearly so marked as is suggested by the table. For one thing, it is difficult to reconcile it with the accounts given us of the substantial yeomen by the writers of the sixteenth and seventeenth centuries. For another thing, it is in dealing with the larger freeholders that the inclination of surveyors

[75] *Op. cit.*, Book III. Here is a bitter cry from the bailiff of a manor (Merton Documents, No. 4381). "Good sir let me entreat you yf the Colledge determyne to make survey this spring of the lands at Kibworth and Barkly to send Mr. Kay or me word a month or 3 weeks before your coming that we may have Beare and other necessaries, and I desire you to gather up all evidences that may be needful for the Lordshipp, for all testimony will be little enough, the Colledge land is so mingled with Mr. Pochin's freehold and others in our towne. There ys an awarde for keepinge in of the old wol (?) close in our fields for (from ?) Mr. Pochin's occupation, very needfulle for the ynhabitannts yf that awarde can be founde at the colledge where yt was loste." (For the remainder of this letter see Appendix I.) The Crown suffered especially, see Norden, *Speculum Britanniae*, Part I., pp. xl.-xliii. of introduction (Camden Society): "In many of his Majesty's manors, free holders, their rents, services, tenures and landes ... become strange and unknown ... and when escheates happen the lande that should redound to his Majesty cannot be found." In the common entry in manorial surveys under the heading of freeholders of "certain lands" we should probably take the word "certain" to mean "uncertain."

[76] For the sources and defects of this table see Appendix II..

to omit any estimate of the extent of the land is strongest, because it is naturally in their case that an estimate is most difficult to form. Probably, therefore, if we could obtain for the freehold tenancies figures even as full as we can for those of the customary tenants, we should find that the proportion holding between twenty and forty acres was considerably larger than these partial statistics would suggest.

In the second place, though we very rarely have direct information as to the proportion of their holdings used as arable, meadow, and pasture, such as is often supplied for other classes of tenants, we may say with some confidence that it is extremely improbable that their agricultural economy differed from that of the neighbouring copyholders,[77] and that the backbone of their living, except when the plots were so small as merely to supply them with garden produce, was therefore in almost every case tillage. If in any way they departed from the practice of their neighbours who were not freeholders, they did so probably only in being somewhat more alert and enterprising, somewhat more ready to use their security to break with custom and to introduce innovations. It is clear that many of them were very far from being tied down to the stagnant routine which some writers would have us believe is inseparable from all small scale farming. Often, indeed, they had enough initiative to realise the advantages of improved methods of cultivation, and on several manors of the sixteenth and seventeenth centuries the freeholders agreed with each other to survey their lands and separate them, so that they could be cultivated in severalty.[78] In many cases, again, they extended their holdings, which were sometimes large and sometimes mere patches of a few acres, by acting as farmers for the lord of the manor and leasing[79] the demesne or part of it. Above all they had nothing to fear from the agrarian changes which disturbed the copyholder and the small tenant farmer, and a good deal to gain; for the rise in prices increased their incomes; while, unlike many copyholders and the tenant farmers, they could not be forced to pay more for their lands.

**Table II**

Column Key

| A | Total Number of Tenants | K | 35 and under 40 Acres. | U | 85 and under 90 Acres. |
|---|---|---|---|---|---|
| B | Houses or Cottages only | L | 40 and under 45 Acres. | V | 90 and under 95 Acres. |
| C | Under 2½ Acres. | M | 45 and under 50Acres. | W | 95 and under 100 Acres. |
| D | 2½ and under 5 Acres. | N | 50 and under 55 Acres. | X | 100 and under 105 Acres. |

---

[77] See below, pp. 105–115.

[78] See *e.g. Northumberland County History*, vol. ix. p. 327, below, pp. 157–158, and *Calendar of Proceedings in Chancery, temp. Eliz.* B, b. 1, 58, Ll. 10, 62.

[79] Smith, *De Republica Anglorum*, Lib. I., c. 23: "These be for the most part fermors unto gentlemen." *Elizabethan England* (Withington), p. 120. "Yeomen" frequently occur in the sixteenth and seventeenth centuries as lessees of the Merton Manors.

| | | | | | |
|---|---|---|---|---|---|
| E | 5 and under 10 Acres. | O | 55 and under 60 Acres. | Y | 105 and under 110 Acres. |
| F | 10 and under 15 Acres. | P | 60 and under 65 Acres. | Z | 110 and under 115 Acres. |
| G | 15 and under 20 Acres. | Q | 65 and under 70 Acres. | A' | 115 and under 120 Acres. |
| H | 20 and under 25 Acres. | R | 70 and under 75 Acres. | B' | 120 and over. |
| I | 25 and under 30 Acres. | S | 75 and under 80 Acres. | C' | Uncertain. |
| J | 30 and under 35 Acres. | T | 80 and under 85 Acres. | | |

| | A | B | C | D | E | F | G | H | I | J | K | L | M | N | O | P | Q | R | S | T | U | V | W | X | Y | Z | A' | B' | C' |
|---|---|---|---|---|---|---|---|---|---|---|---|---|---|---|---|---|---|---|---|---|---|---|---|---|---|---|---|---|---|
| Norfolk, six manors | 139 | 25 | 33 | 12 | 17 | 9 | 10 | 2 | ... | 2 | 1 | 2 | ... | ... | ... | ... | ... | ... | ... | ... | ... | ... | 1 | 2 | ... | ... | ... | ... | 23 |
| Suffolk, four manors | 85 | 27 | 18 | 10 | 11 | 2 | ... | 1 | 1 | 3 | ... | ... | ... | 2 | 1 | ... | ... | ... | ... | 1 | ... | ... | ... | ... | ... | ... | ... | ... | 8 |
| Staffordshire, three manors | 24 | 7 | 4 | 2 | 3 | 1 | ... | 1 | 2 | ... | 1 | 1 | ... | ... | ... | ... | ... | ... | ... | ... | ... | ... | ... | 2 | ... | ... | ... | ... | ... |
| Lancashire, three manors | 9 | ... | 1 | 3 | 1 | 1 | 1 | ... | ... | ... | ... | ... | ... | 1 | ... | ... | ... | ... | ... | ... | ... | ... | ... | ... | ... | ... | ... | ... | 1 |
| Northants, four manors | 116 | 10 | 11 | 4 | 13 | 9 | 5 | 1 | 1 | 4 | 2 | 3 | 2 | ... | ... | 3 | ... | ... | ... | ... | ... | ... | ... | ... | ... | ... | ... | 3 | 45 |
| Wiltshire, one manor | 6 | ... | ... | ... | 2 | ... | ... | ... | ... | ... | ... | 1 | ... | 1 | ... | 1 | ... | ... | ... | ... | ... | ... | ... | ... | ... | ... | ... | 1 | ... |
| Leicestershire, one manor | 11 | 1 | 2 | 2 | 1 | ... | 1 | 1 | ... | ... | ... | ... | 1 | ... | ... | ... | ... | ... | ... | ... | ... | ... | ... | ... | ... | ... | ... | ... | 2 |
| Total, twenty-two manors | 390 | 70 | 69 | 33 | 48 | 22 | 17 | 6 | 4 | 9 | 4 | 7 | 3 | 4 | 1 | 4 | ... | ... | ... | 1 | ... | ... | 1 | 4 | ... | ... | ... | 4 | 79 |

The apparent immunity of the freeholders in the face of movements which overwhelmed other groups of tenants suggests indeed that economic causes alone, which all classes, whatever the legal nature of their tenure, would have experienced equally, are not sufficient to explain the sufferings of the latter. The situation in our period is not like that which arose in the eighteenth and early nineteenth centuries, when widening markets throw all the advantages of increasing returns on the side of the large wheat farmer, and the yeomanry sell their holdings to try their fortunes in the rapidly growing towns. The struggle is not so much between the large scale and small scale production of corn as between corn growing and grazing. The small corn grower, provided he has security of tenure, can still make a very good living.[80] From the point of view of the economist all the smaller men, whether freeholders, leaseholders, or customary tenants, are in much the same position. The decisive factor, which causes the fortunes of the former class to wax, and those of the two latter to wane, is to be found in the realm not of economics but of law. Leaseholders and many copyholders suffer, because they can be rack-rented and evicted. The freeholders stand firm, because their legal position is unassailable. Here, as so often elsewhere, not only in the investigation of the past but in the analysis of the present, the trail followed by the economist leads across a country whose boundaries and contours and lines of least resistance have been fashioned by the labour of lawyers. It is his wisdom to recognise that economic forces operate in a framework created by legal institutions, that to neglect those institutions in examining the causes of economic development or the distribution of wealth is as though a geographer should discuss the river system of a country without reference to its mountain ranges, and that, if lawyers have wrought in ignorance of economics, he must nevertheless consult their own art in order to unravel the effect of their operations.

From the larger standpoint of social and political organisation the freeholders constituted an element in society the very nature of which we can hardly understand, because our modern life offers no analogy to it. We tend to draw our social lines not between small properties and great, but between those who have property and those who have not, and to think of the men who stand between the very rich and the very poor, the men of whom our ancestors boasted as the "Commons of England," as men who do not own but are employed by owners. Independence and the virtues which go with independence, energy, a sober, self-respecting forethought, public spirit, are apt to become identified in our minds with the possession of wealth, because so few except the comparatively wealthy have the means of climbing beyond the reach of the stream of impersonal economic pressure which whirls the mass of mankind this way and that with the violence of an irresponsible Titan.

The sixteenth century was poor with a poverty which no industrial community can understand, the poverty of the colonist and the peasant. It lived in terror of floods and bad harvests and disease, of plague, pestilence, and famine. If one may judge by its churchyards, it had an infantile mortality which might make even Lancashire blush under its soot. Yet (and we do not forget the black page of the early Poor Law) it was possible for men who by our standards would be called poor to exercise that control over the conditions of their lives which is of the essence of freedom, and which in most modern communities is too expensive a privilege to be enjoyed by more than comparatively few. Such men were the freeholders. They formed a class which had security and independence without having affluence, which spanned the gulf between the wealthy and the humble with a chain of estates ranging from the few acres of the peasant proprietor to the many manors of the noble, which was not too poor to be below public duties nor too rich to be above them, which could feel that "it is a quietness to a man's mind to dwell upon his owne and to know his heire certaine."[81] Look for a moment at

[80] See below, pp. 105–115.
[81] Norden, *The Surveyor's Dialogue.*

the jolly picture drawn by Fuller,[82] who wrote at the very end of the period with which we are dealing: —

"The good yeoman is a gentleman in ore whom the next age may see refined, and is the most capable of genteel impressions when the Prince shall stamp.... France and Italy are like a die which has no points between cinque and ace, nobility and peasantry.... Indeed, Germany hath her boors like our yeomen; but by a tyrannical appropriation of nobility to some few ancient families their yeomen are excluded from ever rising higher to clarify their blood. In England the temple of honour is closed to none who have passed through the temple of virtue.

"He wears russet clothes, but makes golden payment, having tin in his buttons and silver in his pocket. He is the surest landmark whence foreigners may take aim of the ancient English customs, the gentry more floating after foreign fashions.

"In his house he is bountiful both to strangers and poor people. Some hold, when hospitality died, she gave her last groan among the yeomen of Kent. And still at our yeoman's table you shall have as many joints as dishes; no meat disguised with strange sauce; no straggling joint of a sheep in the midst of a pasture of grass, but solid, substantial food.

"He hath a great stroke in the making of a knight of the Shire. Good reason, for he makes a whole line in the subsidy book, where, whatsoever he is rated, he payeth without regret, not caring how much his purse be let blood, so it be done by the advice of the physicians of the state.

"In his own country he is a main man on juries; where, if the Judge open his eyes on a matter of law, he needs not to be led by the nose in matters of fact.... Otherwise (though not mutinous in a jury) he cares not whom he displeaseth, so he pleaseth his own conscience.

"In a time of famine he is the Joseph of the country and keeps the poor from starving ... and to his poor neighbour abateth somewhat of the high price of the market. The neighbour gentry court him for his acquaintance, which either he modestly waveth, or thankfully accepteth, but in no way greedily desireth.

"In war, though he serveth on foot, he is ever mounted on a high spirit, as being a slave to none, and subject only to his own Prince. Innocence and independence make a brave spirit, whereas otherwise one must ask his leave to be valiant on whom one depends. Therefore if a state run up all to noblemen and gentlemen, so that the husbandmen be only mere labourers or cottagers (which one calls but 'housed beggars'), it may have good cavalry, but never good bands of foot.... Wherefore to make good infantry it requireth men bred not in a servile or indigent fashion, but in some free and plentiful manner."

The ancestors of the yeomanry had suffered much in the anarchy of the fifteenth century, when the violent ejection of freeholders seems to have become <u>almost as common</u>[83] as it had been in the evil days before the reforms of Henry II.

[82] Fuller, *Holy and Profane State*. The concluding paragraph is obviously copied from Bacon's *History of King Henry VII.*

[83] Paston Letters, I. 12, II. 248. Plummer's edition of Fortescue, *On the Governance of England*, Intro., p. 21.

But the Tudor monarchy had put an end to that nightmare of lawlessness, and in any society governed by law this body of small property-owners was bound to be a powerful element, even though they had no occasion for making any concerted use of their power, as during the greater part of our period they had not. One must not, of course, exaggerate their importance, or forget that, though a special dignity was attached by opinion to all freeholders, they included in reality men of various economic positions. Many of them must have been quite poor. In the eastern counties, where they are most numerous, they frequently own not more than three or four acres apiece, and can hardly, one would suppose, have supported themselves without working for wages in addition to tilling their holdings. Nevertheless the part which they played in the routine of rural life was an indispensable one, and the very diversity of the elements which they included made them a link between different ends of the social scale. It was from the more substantial among them that the government was most anxious to recruit the military forces. The obligation of serving the State as voters and upon juries fell upon the 40s. freeholders. The security of their tenure caused them to be the natural leaders of the peasantry in resisting pressure from above. No efforts of Elizabeth's Government could induce the yeomanry of the North[84] Riding to abandon the old religion; and when tenants and lords fall out over common rights and enclosures, it is often the freeholders—though on occasion they enclose themselves—who speak[85] for the less independent classes and take the initiative in instituting legal proceedings. The upward movement which went on among this class in many parts of England meant a change in the distribution of material wealth which necessarily involved a corresponding change in the balance of social forces and in the control of political power. To Harrington,[86] who sought in the seventeenth century to find in economic causes an explanation of the revolution through which the country had passed, it seemed that the seeds of the civil war had been sown by the Tudor kings themselves in the care which they showed for the small proprietor. In destroying feudalism to establish the monarchy, they had raised a power which was more dangerous to the monarchy than feudalism itself. They had snapped the bond between landlord and tenant by the Statute of Retainers. They had given the tenant security by forbidding depopulation. Most important of all, by encouraging alienation they had caused an enormous transference of property from the upper to the middle and lower middle classes. "The lands in possession of the Nobility and Clergy of England till Henry VII. cannot be estimated to have over-balanced those held by the People less than four to one. Whereas, in our days, the Clergy being destroyed, the Lands in possession of the People over-balance those held by the Nobility at least nine in ten." But property is political power individualised and made visible. The destruction of the monarchy was only the political expression of an economic change which had begun in the reign of Henry VII. "He suffered the balance to fall into the power of the people.... But the balance being in the People,

[84] Atkinson's *Quarter Sessions of the North Riding of Yorkshire*, lists of recusants.

[85] *e.g. Topographer and Genealogist*, vol. iii. (quoted below, pp. 251–253), and Selden Society, *Select Cases in the Court of Star Chamber*, vol. ii., *Inhabitants of Thingden* v. *Mulsho*; also Holkham MSS., Burnham Documents, Bdle. 5, No. 94 (quoted below, p. 245 *n.*).

[86] Harrington's works, 1700 edition, p. 69 (*Oceana*), pp. 388–389 (*The Art of Law-giving*). See also Firth, *The House of Lords during the Civil War*, pp. 28–32.

the Commonwealth (though they do not see it) is already in the nature of them." We need not accept Harrington's view in its entirety in order to appreciate the significance of the change which he describes. Certainly the yeomanry were growing in political power, and were strong in that spirit of self-respect and pride in their order, which, when, as too often, it is confined to a single class, means social oppression, but which, when widely diffused throughout society, is the mother of public spirit and political virtue. The long discipline of tiresome public duties which they had borne throughout the Middle Ages had formed them into a body which was alive to political issues and conscious of political influence, and which, when participation in public affairs became not only a duty but a right, would use their power to press urgent petitions from one county after another upon the King and upon the Parliament, or by riding up from Buckinghamshire to protect Hampden at Westminster in 1642, or by fighting behind Cromwell in Cambridgeshire, or by fighting for the King in the West. Compared with the bulk of the population, they were a privileged class and stood by their own; it was they who restored the franchise to the 40s. freeholders in 1654 and refused to extend it to the copyholders. But the tenure of much of the land of England by men with whom, however poor, no landlord or employer could interfere, set a limit to the power of wealth, and made rural society at once more alert and more stubborn, a field where great ideas could grow and great causes find adherents. Political and religious idealism flourish bravely in a stony soil. What makes them droop is not poverty, but the withering shadow cast by complete economic dependence.

From such degrading subservience the freeholders, "slaves to none," were secure. As it was, they often left substantial fortunes to their children, and by the middle of the sixteenth century were already following the examples of their social superiors in entailing[87] their lands. One can quite understand therefore that there is nothing inconsistent between the glowing accounts of their prosperity at the end of the century given by Harrison and his lamentation over the decline of the rural population, or between the well-attested sufferings of the small cultivator in the sixteenth century and his equally well-attested importance in the seventeenth and early eighteenth. The explanation is that the freeholders, though most important politically, did not form the larger proportion of those substantial yeomen whose decay was lamented. The day of their ruin was to come. But for the next two centuries they were safe enough, and, if anything, gained on the class immediately above them, whose lands they bought or leased, into whose families they married, and with whose children their own competed in the learned professions, laying,

---

[87] It is stated by good authorities that between 12 Ed. IV., when the collusive action known as a common recovery used to evade the Statute *de donis conditionalibus* was confirmed by a judicial decision (Taltarum's case), and the introduction into settlements of "Trustees to preserve contingent remainders" by Sir Orlando Bridgeman and Sir Geoffrey Palmer under the Commonwealth, the tieing up of lands in one family was impossible (*e.g.* Johnson, *The Disappearance of the Small Landowner,* pp. 11–13). But in 1538 Starkey's Dialogue speaks strongly of the practice of entailing lands. "This faute sprange of a certayn arrogancy, whereby, wyth the entaylyng of landys, every Jake would be a gentylman, and every gentylman a knight or a lord" (E. E. T. S., *England in the Reign of Henry VIII.,* Part II. pp. 112–113, and pp. 195–196.)

as the historian of Suffolk[88] said, "such strong, sure and deep foundations that from thence in time are derived many noble and worthy families." Nothing in the life of the period caused more pride than the prosperity of this solid body of small property-owners, and the contrast which it offered to the downtrodden peasantry of the Continent. No loss has been sustained by the modern world greater than their disappearance.

### *(c) The Customary Tenants*

Important, however, as the freeholders were from a social and political standpoint, they were in most parts of England far inferior in point of numbers to those described as "customary tenants." It is with the latter class that we are mainly concerned, and leaving the leaseholders on one side for examination later,[89] we may summarise shortly certain features in their position. The number of customary tenants varied from one manor to another, according to the extent to which in different districts farmers holding by lease had been substituted for them, and on some by the middle of the sixteenth century there were none at all. But there are many indications that, down to the end of that century at any rate, and probably much longer, they formed over the great part of England the bulk of the landholding population. Of the revenues of 74 manors held by monastic[90] houses in 1535, £116 came from free, and £1310 from customary, tenants. On 81 of the 118 manors analysed above they are the most numerous class. When all the different districts are grouped together, they amount to about 61 per cent. of all landholders, and even this figure does not give an adequate idea of their numerical importance. As we have seen, Norfolk and Suffolk are quite peculiar in the multitude of freeholders they embrace, while the large number of leaseholders on one extensive Lancashire manor unduly weights the figures for that county. On the Midland manors 62 per cent., in Wiltshire, Devonshire, and Somerset 77 per cent., in Northumberland 91 per cent. of all those holding land are customary tenants. No doubt the area of land held under lease was growing in the course of the sixteenth, and still more in the course of the seventeenth, century, and its growth is an extremely important movement, of which something will be said later. But it seems true to say that, down to the end of the sixteenth century, both in numbers and payments, though not in prestige and influence, the customary tenants, as distinct from the freeholders and leaseholders, were by far the most important class in the agricultural life of the country.

Among the customary tenants, however, there are certain important subdivisions. There are in the first place, differences of legal status. Though villeinage by blood had been disappearing rapidly for several generations, partly through manumission on payment of a fine to the lord, partly through the absorption of migrating villeins into the growing industries of the towns, a certain number of villeins by blood lingered on into the sixteenth century. Dr. Savine[91] has estimated that

[88] Reyce, *Breviary of Suffolk*, p. 58, quoted *Victoria County History, Suffolk*.

[89] See below, pp. 200–213 and 283–287.

[90] *Oxford Studies in Social and Legal History*, vol. i. Savine, *English Monasteries on the Eve of the Dissolution*, pp. 156–159.

[91] *Trans. Royal Hist. Soc.*, vol. xvii.

there were at least as many as 500 villein families in 1485, and as many as 250 in the reign of Elizabeth; and the fact that they occur occasionally on our Norfolk[92] manors, and rather more often on those in Wiltshire[93] and Somersetshire, suggests that his list could be considerably extended on further investigation. Even in 1561 a borough surrenders an apprentice on the ground that he is a runaway villein.[94] Even in 1568 it is worth while in leasing[95] a manor to a farmer for the lord to reserve to himself the villeins upon it, together with other forms of property like quarries and advowsons.

One cannot, therefore, take the almost sanctimonious abhorrence of bondage expressed by the writers of the period quite at its face value. On the other hand, though villeinage by blood was still worth recording, since it offered an impecunious lord an opportunity for arbitrary taxation, and still sufficiently irksome for the rebels under Ket[96] (influenced perhaps by some dim memory of the German peasants' programme) to set its abolition among their demands, its practical importance was slight, and it was quite compatible with a good deal of prosperity on the part of those who were legally bondmen. How completely out of date it was by the middle of the sixteenth century is best shown by some of the cases in which attempts were made to enforce it. When the Earl of Bath[97] seizes £400 from a family on the ground that the members are his villeins, and is pursued by them

---

[92] R.O. *Misc. Bks. Land Rev.*, vol. 220, fol. 220, Brisingham (Norfolk) 1589: "Alice Bartram, the widow of W. Bartram, the lord's villain by blood, took by surrender of said William for term of life on 4 Feby., remainder to Roger Bartram, lord's villain by blood." Holkham MSS., Titleshall Documents, Terrier of Godwick, 1508: "Also five roods of the Prior in the hands of Thomas Frend, native."

[93] Among the 742 customary tenants on the manors belonging to the Earl of Pembroke surveyed in 1568 there appears to be 7 *nativi domini*, *i.e.* villeins by blood, viz., 1 at Washerne (Wilts), 2 at Stooke Trister and Cucklington (Somerset), 4 at Chedeseye (Somerset), of whom one has been manumitted.

[94] *Selected Records of Norwich* (Tingey), vol. vi. p. 180: "Robert Ryngwoode brought in a certain indenture wherein Lewis Lowth was [bound] to hym to serve as a prentys for seven years. And Mr. John Holdiche cam before the Mayor and other Justices and declared that the said Lewis is a bondman to my lord of Norfolk's Grace, and further that he was brought up in husbandry untyl he was xx year old. Whereupon he was discharged of his service."

Note the way in which Statute law is used to compel the agricultural labour which the vanishing jurisdiction of lord over serf is ceasing to be able to enforce.

[95] Roxburghe Club, *Surveys of Manors of William, First Earl of Pembroke*, Manor of Chilmerke: "Johannes Reve tenet per indenturam totum illud capitale messuagium excepta et omnino reservata omnia wardas, maritagia fines ... nativos," &c.

[96] Russell, *Ket's Rebellion in Norfolk*, p. 49: "We pray that all bond men may be made free, for God made all free with his precious blood shedding." The German peasants in the articles drawn up at Memmingen in 1525 demanded the abolition of serfdom "since Christ hath purchased and redeemed us all with his precious blood." The Christian appeal is a common one; see below.

[97] Selden Society, *Select Cases in the Court of Requests*, John Burde and another v. The Earl of Bath. The quarrel dragged on from 1535 to 1544, when the plaintiff's goods were restored. (In 1551, however, when all bad landlords were raising their heads, his house and cattle were again seized.)

for nine years from one court to another, or when a lord[98] of a manor is compelled by a royal commission appointed for the purpose of investigating the matter, to repay the value of the beast taken from a man who is proved by the court rolls to be his villein, and the latter, having received it back, declines to stop proceedings unless he be paid heavy compensation in addition, one must see rather a proof of the practical disappearance of villeinage than of its survival. Its occasional enforcement is clearly regarded as something outrageous; it is a freak of arbitrary despotism, which has hardly more historical significance than the seizure of the Derby winner as a copyhold heriot would have at the present day. Public opinion, even the opinion of those engaged in estate management, condemns such attempts unreservedly, and when they come to the ears of the authorities they strain the law on the side of the bondmen.

This change from servile to free labour, begun some two centuries before, and virtually completed in the reign of Elizabeth, is a high landmark in the development both of economic and political society. It is a long step towards modern industrialism on the one hand and the modern all-inclusive state on the other. By sapping the organisation of society on the basis of tenure, and thus making room for the more elastic relationships of the wage-contract, it prepared the way for new methods of production and for the growth of new centres of economic power. The refusal of the courts to allow that the lord of a manor had, *qua* lord, a theoretical right to dispose of the persons and chattels of his unfree tenants, meant the final triumph of the common law in regions with which for four centuries after the Norman Conquest it had not dared to interfere. Henceforward, while the German peasant is driven afield to gather snails and wild strawberries for his lord, is plundered and harried and tortured without hope of redress, his English brother is a member of a society in which there is, nominally at least, one law for all men. His liberty may be more in shadow than in substance, yet the shadow is itself an earnest of greater things. To us who know the misery of many of the poorer classes in the sixteenth century the boast that "if any slaves or bondmen come here from other realms, so soon as they set foot on land they became so free of condition as their masters," may read like a bitter mockery. But it is something that the boast should be made, and when England is confronted with the greatest moral issue of the modern world, that boast will stand her in good stead.[99] She owes some

---

[98] *Ibid.*, Netheway *v.* George, 1534. For other cases see Selden Society, *Select Cases in the Court of Star Chamber*. Carter *v.* Abbot of Malmesbury (vol. i., 1500), and Selby *v.* Middlemore (vol. ii., 1516–1522). Mr. Leadam's remarks (int. cxxix.) show that a man who was legally a villein might be economically very prosperous: "Thomas Carter ... was charged 40 marks for his enfranchisement. He kept a man-servant. He rode on horseback. He gave a feast to celebrate his freedom. He was even on friendly terms with the gentlemen of the Abbot's household." See also Savine, *Trans. Royal Hist. Soc.*, vol. xvii. Lord Stafford actually tried to seize the Mayor of Bristol and his brother as bondmen!

[99] Hargreave's speech in Somersett's case (1771–1772, Howell, *State Trials*, xx.) is based largely on precedents drawn from villeinage: "Though villeinage itself is obsolete ... those rules, by which the claim of it was regulated, are not yet buried in oblivion.... By a strange progress of human affairs the memory of slavery expired now furnishes one of the chief obstacles to slavery attempted to be revived.... The law of England, then, excludes every slavery not commencing in England, every slavery, though commencing there, not

acknowledgment to the nameless serfs who fled from farm and homestead, till villeinage, in spite of the law, bled gradually to death.

Having said so much we must hasten to guard ourselves, by adding that the final disappearance of serfdom in this country neither involved any radical conversion of opinion, nor prevented the classes who depended solely on their labour from being, on occasion, cruelly oppressed. It would be a mistake to see in the attitude of the governing classes towards villeinage a symptom of humanitarian feeling for the rights of a helpless class, such as prompted the emancipation movement of the last century. How little humanitarianism influenced economic policy in relation to those who were too powerless to be dangerous, is shown by the sanguinary statutes relating to the destitute, and in particular by the extraordinary legalisation of slavery in the Act[100] of 1547, by which a confirmed vagrant might, when captured, be made a bondman for life. Nor must we think of the disappearance of legalised serfdom as effecting a great improvement in the lot of the ordinary wage-worker. Those who benefited by it were not so much the workers for wages, as the landholding peasants. The wage-labourer, who was tied to his parish by the Statute of Artificers almost as completely as the serf had been by the custom of the manor, can hardly have seen much difference between the restrictions on his movement imposed by the Justices of the Peace and those laid on him by the manorial authorities, except indeed that the latter, being limited to the area of a single village, had been more easy to evade.

Even if we confine our attention to the landholding peasants, to whom the advantage (for they were quick to seize it) was certainly real enough, we may doubt whether they did not lose almost as much by the intrusion into agriculture of competitive commercial forces as they gained by the final disappearance of a claim which had always been held in check by the custom of the manor, and which, since the ravages of the Great Plague, had been steadily circumscribed by commutation. The truth is that the sharp antithesis drawn by modern commercial societies between serfs and the free labourers on whose slowly straightening backs our civilisation is uneasily poised, and emphasised as though it marked a line between hopeless oppression and unqualified liberty, requires to be supplemented by categories derived from a wider and more tragic range of experience than was open to our forefathers. There are more ways of living "at the will of a lord" than were known to Glanvill and Bracton, and the utility of the contrast in the sphere of legal analysis does not save it from being but a thin abstraction of the countless forms of tyranny which spring from the world-old power of one human being to use another as his tool. That dependence on the uncontrolled caprice of a master whom one hates to obey and dare not abandon, which, by whatever draperies it

---

being ancient and immemorial. Villeinage is the only slavery which can possibly answer to such a description, and that has long expired by the death or emancipation of all those who were once the objects of it. Consequently there is now no slavery which can be lawful in England."

[100] 1 Ed. VI., c. 3. Possibly, however, the penalty of bondage was regarded as a step towards greater leniency, as the punishment of "incorrigible rogues" had hitherto been death.

may be veiled, is still the bitter core of serfdom,[101] is compatible with the most diverse legal arrangements; with wage labour as with forced services, with tenure by a competitive money rent as well as with tenure by personal obligations, with freedom of contract as well as with inherited status, with protection by the national courts as well as with its absence.

When we turn over the pages in which the writers of the sixteenth century declare that bondage is contrary to "the Christian religion which maketh us all in Christ breathren, and in respect of God and Christ *conservos*,"[102] and congratulate themselves on its disappearance, we must not doubt their sincerity, but we may envy their inexperience. We must remember that a condemnation of villeinage was quite compatible with a policy of great severity towards the wage-labourer, and was in fact not unconnected with it, since the latter had almost everywhere stepped into places and functions formally held by the bondman. Villeinage disappeared in England earlier than on the continent of Europe, not for the ethical reasons given by Fitzherbert and Smith and Norden, but because the growth of a commercial organisation of agriculture had made its maintenance both useless and impossible. The intellectual conversion did little more than follow on the economic change to make a virtue of necessity. The personal rightlessness of the villein and the hateful incidents of villeinage, such as chevage, merchet, and leyrwite, had had their utility in the fact that they kept him at the disposal of the manorial authorities as an instrument of agriculture. With the substitution of hired labour for the cultivation of the demesne by the services of bond tenants, their maintenance lost its attractiveness. No employer wants to retain a permanent staff, if there are "hands" whom he can take on and put off at pleasure. Villeinage ceases but the Poor Laws begin.

Much more important than this difference of legal status are differences in the tenure by which customary tenants hold their lands. Under the name of customary tenants are grouped together all holders of lands which pass by surrender and admission in the court of the manor, and which are subject to the custom of the manor as evidenced by the records of the court. But not all these lands are held by exactly the same title. Some are held by copy of court roll according to the custom of the manor, on the terms set out on a copy of the entry of admission. Others are held without a documentary title, and are often said to be occupied at the will of

[101] More's remarks on the lot of the wage-workers of his day have a refreshing note of reality. The Utopians are "not to be wearied from earlie in the morning to late in the evenninge with continuall worke, like labouringe and toylinge beastes. For this is worse then the miserable and wretched condition of bondemen. Whiche nevertheless is almooste everywhere the lyfe of workemen and artificers, saving in Utopia" (More, *Utopia*, Pitt Press Edition, pp. 79–80).

[102] Smith, *De Republica Anglorum*, Lib. III., ch. 8. See also Fitzherbert, *Surveying* (1539): "How be it, in some places the bondmen continue as yet, the which me seemeth is the greatest inconvenience that now is suffered by the law." Norden, *The Surveyor's Dialogue* (1608): "Which kinde of service and slavery, thanks be to God, is in most places of this Realme quite abolished and worne out of memory.... Truly I think it is a Christian parte so to do [*i.e.* manumit bondsmen], for seeing we be nowe all as the children of one father, the servants of one God, and the subjects of one king, it is very uncharitable to retain our brethren in bondage, sith, when we were all bond, Christ did make us free."

the lord, or at the pleasure of the lord, or by grant or permission of the lord or of the court, their essential feature being that the tenant does not possess any instrument recording the transaction, but has, if necessary, to appeal to the records of the court or even to its mere memory.

One must hasten to add, however, that these classes are not mutually exclusive. A copyholder is a tenant at will, though qualified by the addition of the words "by copy of court roll according to the custom of the manor." It not seldom happens that in rentals and surveys he is simply described as a tenant at will, and that the fact that he has a copy is not recorded. A tenant at will is usually (though not always) a customary tenant, and, when he is, he can appeal to the custom with as good a right as a copyholder, though of course the fact that his title is not in his own keeping may prejudice him if the manorial authorities want to get rid of him. "All[103] copyhold land," it was said, "is commonly customary, but all customary land is not copyhold," and one may accept the statement with the reservation that "commonly" must not be taken to mean "always," for it is quite usual in parts of England for land which by no stretch of imagination can be called customary land, for example, part of the lord's demesne, to be let by copy of court roll. The fact that "tenant at will" was sometimes used as a compendious phrase for "copyholder," and that both are sometimes described simply as "customary tenants" without further definitions, makes it impossible to offer any accurate estimate of the relative number of those holding by copy and those holding at will. It may, however, be of interest to give an analysis of the entries as they appear in a group of manorial documents. It is as follows[104]: —

**TABLE III**

| | Total | "Copyholders" | "Customary Tenants" | "Tenants at Will" |
|---|---|---|---|---|
| Northumberland | 436 | 362 | 45 | 29 |
| Lancashire | 451 | 295 | 156 | ... |
| Staffordshire | 272 | 170 | ... | 102 |
| Leicestershire | 311 | 157 | ... | 154 |
| Northamptonshire | 355 | 253 | 93 | 9 |
| Norfolk | 596 | 536 | 45 | 15 |
| Suffolk | 146 | 53 | 82 | 11 |
| Wilts and Somerset | 817 | 786 | ... | 31 |
| Hampshire | 251 | 251 | ... | ... |
| Ten other manors in the south of England | 158 | 87 | 45 | 26 |
| Total | 3793 | 2950 | 466 | 377 |

---

[103] Norden, *The Surveyor's Dialogue*. He continues: "For in some places of this Realme Tennants have no copies at all of their lands or tenements, or anything to show for that they hold, but there is an entry made in the Court Books, and that is their evidence."

[104] See Appendix II.

These figures, one must repeat, are merely a summary of the entries in surveys and rentals. Probably they underestimate the number of copyholders, as we know that copyholders were sometimes entered as tenants at will or as customary tenants for the sake of brevity, while it is not probable that tenants at will who had not got copies were often written down as copyholders. One may suspect that this, rather than any difference of custom, is the explanation of the relatively small number of those who are returned as copyholders in Lancashire, Staffordshire, Leicestershire, and Suffolk. Still, these figures do show the enormous preponderance of copyholders among the customary tenants, and show it all the more certainly if the number of copyholders is to be taken, as is probable, as the minimum. And this agrees with what we know from the incidental references of the writers of the time. Of 1000 tenants on the great ecclesiastical manor of Scrooby in Nottinghamshire "the most part" were said by Archbishop[105] Sandys in 1582 to be copyholders. Harrison[106] in 1587 spoke of copyholders as those "by whom the greatest part of the realm doth stand and is maintained." At the beginning of the seventeenth century Coke[107] could say that the third part of England consisted of copyhold. Copyholders, it is true, are far from being all of one type; for the essence of their tenure is that it depends on the custom of the manor which varies from place to place, and when we come to consider how far they have security against eviction these differences are of crucial importance. Still, in spite of the varieties of copyhold tenure, it is useful to know that to the bulk of the population in the sixteenth century landholding meant holding by copy of court roll according to the custom of the manor. No account of the agrarian changes can stand for a moment which does not give full weight to the fact that, in most parts of England, the copyholders greatly outnumber all other classes of tenants.

The numerical predominance of the customary tenants and among those of the copyholders, together with the disastrous effects upon them which are ascribed by most of our authorities to the agrarian changes of the sixteenth century, makes a somewhat detailed examination of their position essential. In particular it is important to try to bridge the gap between the agricultural system of the sixteenth and that of the thirteenth and fourteenth centuries, out of which it emerged, and of which it continued to bear unmistakable traces. The problem is really a twofold one, partly legal and partly economic. First, what was the legal nature of copyhold tenure, and how did it arise out of mediæval villeinage? Secondly, there is the question, which for us is more important, of the type of agriculture which prevailed among the mass of the people. The economist wants to know whether the customary tenants were large cultivators or small, whether they included considerable capitalists and mere cottagers or whether their holdings were of a fairly uniform pattern, whether they farmed mainly for subsistence or for the market, whether they lived entirely by tillage or were pasture farmers as well, whether they were tied down by custom or showed any signs of being influenced by the

---

[105] Archbishop Sandys to Queen Elizabeth, Saturday 24 November to 4 December, 1582 (quoted by E. Arber, *The Story of the Pilgrim Fathers*, pp. 61–64).

[106] Harrison in *Elizabethan England* (Withington), p. 120.

[107] Quoted by Nasse, *The Land Community of the Middle Ages* (Ouvry's trans.). I have not been able to trace the reference.

agricultural innovations of our period.

Of these two questions the first has been investigated much more thoroughly than the second. We shall return to it later in considering how far the copyholder had security of tenure, and enjoyed legal protection against the lord who wished to evict him. But we may say at once that we accept in substance the argument of those who hold that most copyholders are the descendants of villeins holding villein land, that copyhold tenure is, in fact, villein tenure to which the courts from the end of the fourteenth century have gradually extended their protection, and that the puzzling differences between the position of one group of copyholders and another are due to differences in manorial custom which were followed and upheld by the courts. This not only is the traditional view, in the sense of being that which is implied in the insistence of contemporaries that copyhold originated in base tenure, and that copyholders were tenants "whom the favourable hand of time hath much enfranchised,"[108] but also seems to be that which best fits the situation of the copyholder as we find it in the sixteenth century.

This line of development is suggested, though it is not proved, by the mere preponderance of copyholders. In looking for the antecedents of so numerous and widely spread a class we can only find them in the tenure of the mass of the people in the thirteenth and fourteenth centuries, that is in villein tenure. Further, we do not find in villein tenure any such fundamental distinction between customary tenure which was protected and base tenure which was not, as has been sometimes postulated as an explanation of the qualified legal security possessed by copyholders 200 years later. On the contrary, the tenure of the villeins is marked by the same variety of customary conditions as appears in that of the copyholders, with the difference that, when once copyhold has taken root, these customs are enforced by the courts. The same conclusion is borne out by the survival of ancient formulæ among the terms by which the conditions of the copyholders are recorded in the surveys. It is quite common for copyholders in the sixteenth century to be described as occupying "bond"[109] or "native" land; sometimes one finds a whole list of them set down under the rubric "holding[110] native lands by copy of court roll." The last thing, of course, which occurred to the writer of these entries was any legal theory as to the origin of copyhold tenure. All he was concerned to do was to describe the holdings in the way which was most precise and left least room for possible disputes. Clearly, he must have had it in his mind that lands which in his day were let by copy of court roll were lands which were known generally in the village as bond lands, and which in earlier documents were described as being occupied in villeinage.

---

[108] Norden, *The Surveyor's Dialogue*.

[109] *E.g.*, R.O. Rentals and Surveys Gen. Ser., Portf. 27, No. 32, Dunstall (Suffolk): "Bond land held by copy of court roll, 13s. 4d. Of holders of 3 bond pightells, 5s. 4d." MSS. of Earl of Leicester at Holkham, Tittleshall Books, No. 62, Langham Hall (Norfolk): "Redditus assissæ native tenentium. ... John Rose per copiam, 4d." R.O. Rentals and Surveys Gen. Ser. Portf. 14, No. 70, Barton (Staffs.): "T. Collinson 1 messuage ¼ virgate land de bond ... by copy 2 Hen. viii."

[110] MSS. of Earl of Leicester at Holkham, Billingford and Bintry MSS., No. 9, Foxley: "Native tenentium per copiam rotuli curiæ."

One may approach the question in another way, by looking at the circumstances of those exceptional manors on which the tenants at will are more numerous than the copyholders, and which are instructive just because they represent a variation from the general type. A case in point is the Manor of Knyghton in Wiltshire. On the majority of the manors held in that county by the Earl of Pembroke the copyholders are far the most numerous class, and on some they are the only class, among the customary tenants. At Knyghton,[111] however, there are no copyholders; all the customary tenants hold at the will of the lord, and when one examines the position and methods of agriculture more closely, one finds that they display several signs of being in other respects more antiquated and conservative than is the case in other parts of the same country; for example, all the holdings are either virgates of twenty-four acres or some fraction and multiple of a virgate, which is not at all common on other Wiltshire manors, and implies an unusual approximation to the conditions of the peasantry two centuries before. Is it unreasonable to conclude that this is a case of arrested development, and that Knyghton is a manor on which the tenants at will have never turned into copyholders, because for one reason or another it has lain outside the main stream of agricultural development?

The connection with copyhold tenure of some of the characteristic obligations and disabilities of villeinage points in the same direction. In spite of the general commutation of services into money payments, which Mr. Page's statistics show to have taken place before the middle of the fifteenth century, one still finds the attenuated records of labour rents surviving for many generations after the direct management of the demesne by manorial officials has been abandoned, and passing with the rest of the farm equipment to the farmer who takes it on lease. In Norfolk and Suffolk they seem indeed to have disappeared almost altogether, which is what one would expect in view of the fact that those counties were the Lancashire and West Riding of the period, and no doubt, even when labour services were still exacted, the farmer relied mainly upon hired labour. But it would be a mistake to regard the tenants' works as everywhere so trifling as to be of no economic importance. Often, it is true, they are inconsiderable. At South Newton,[112] for example, though the uncertainty which had been one of the marks of villeinage still survived among the copyholders in the shape of the duty of "gift carriage," the transport of such timber as was wanted to the lord's house at Wilton, the purely agricultural services were unimportant, and the tenants of every yardland had only to mow the farmer's meadow and to carry his hay. At Cuxham,[113] in Oxfordshire, on the other hand, the authorities were still getting twenty-eight boonworks in autumn from the copyholders at the end of the fifteenth century. On a Northumbrian[114] manor belonging to Tynemouth Priory down to the dissolution of the monasteries "every tenant did lead to the castle in the prior's time one load of hay,

[111] Roxburghe Club, *Surveys of Manors of William, First Earl of Pembroke.*

[112] Roxburghe Club, *Surveys of Manors of William, First Earl of Pembroke.*

[113] Merton Documents, 5902.

[114] *Northumberland County History,* vol. viii., p. 220 (one may add that in parts of Northumberland the labourers are still called "bondagers"; Mr. Clay tells me that in the Calder valley farmers still use "daywork" as a unit for measuring fields). See also *Calendar of Proceedings in Chancery, temp. Eliz.,* D. d. 2, 44, for a suit by a farmer to recover services due from tenants.

mow three several dayworks of hay, rake one daywork and sheare three severall dayworks in the corn in harvest every year." At Washerne,[115] in Wiltshire, the copyhold tenants' labours were in 1568 still quite an important affair: each holder of one virgate of twenty acres "shall plough three half acres for the lord's winter seed and shall harrow them, and also the aforesaid tenants shall wash and shear the lord's sheep ... and further each of them shall mow one acre of meadow ... and gather hay thence and prepare it.... Each of the said tenants shall reap one acre of wheat and he must bind the crop and carry it. Also each of them shall reap one acre of barley." On a Lancashire[116] manor in 1628 every plough hand is obliged to do two days' work in the year with a team on the demesne, and two days with a labourer. Such elaborate obligations as appears at Washerne are, it is true, the exception. But they show that in the middle of the sixteenth century there were still backwaters where the remnants of agricultural services were a not inconsiderable burden; and if their comparative lightness marks the progress from villeinage to a wage system, their survival as clearly shows that villeinage was the pit from which copyhold tenure was digged.

More striking still, perhaps, is the persistence of disabilities of another kind. The old marks of personal bondage, chevage, merchet, leyrwite, liability to tallage, and the rest have almost disappeared. But traces of them are still found clinging to the copyhold tenants. Copyholders pay a fixed sum to be free of tallages.[117] They pay salt silver instead of the salt with which they had once been obliged to toil to the lord's manor-house; they are forced to act as the lord's reeve, and collect his rents, heriots, and strays. In one curious instance one finds something very like a tallage[118] being taken at the beginning of the seventeenth century, though of course that is not what it is called. The tenants are simply collected and told that they must help the lord to pay for an estate which he has bought, by giving him three years' rent apiece, that, if they do, no more gifts will be demanded during his lifetime, and that, if they do not, he will refuse to renew holdings as they fall in. Even merchet, the most hateful of all the incidents of villeinage, is something more than a mere memory. As late as 1620 the tenants of Holt[119] in Denbighshire thought it worth while to point out to the crown surveyor that "they are freed from payment of any sum of money upon the marriage of their daughters," and even in 1654 Leyrwite and childwite were still being paid by the heiresses of cop-

---

[115] Pembroke Surveys.

[116] *Chetham Society Miscellanies,* vol. iii.

[117] Pembroke Surveys, Estoverton and Phipheld: "Tenentes de Estoverton reddunt annuatim pro pannagio et tallagio ... ivs." For salt silver, *ibid.,* South Newton. For liability to serve as Reeve, *ibid.,* Paynton.

[118] *Chetham Society Miscellanies,* vol. iii.: "I would wish you to call the tenants first all together and to signify unto them that my father and I have gone through with Mr. Ireland for Warrington, and the summe we are to give is above £7000; and this was done making no doubt that towards it every one of them being tenants would by their assistance enable us to finish it.... If they faile in this, they may provoke us to sharp courses, especially mee, who have had a purpose to take the third part of every living as it falls."

[119] Wrexham Free Library, *Ancient Local Records,* vol. ii. MS. transcript by A.N. Palmer, "Survey of the Town and Liberty of Holt."

yhold tenants on some of the Warwickshire[120] manors.

It will not, therefore, be surprising to find that the humble origin of copyhold tenure has left marks upon it in other ways as well, and, in particular, that though the copyholder is not without legal protection when the lord tries to get rid of him, that protection is often of a somewhat shadowy and ineffective kind. His title is a customary one, and mighty as custom still is, it has for centuries been growing gradually weaker. Its weakening is at once an advantage and a disadvantage to the peasantry. It relieves them of odious obligations and leaves them greater room to push their fortunes. It lowers a protecting barrier and exposes them to the dissolving forces of competition.

---

[120] Savine, *Quarterly Journal of Economics*, vol. xix.

# CHAPTER II

## THE PEASANTRY

### (a) The Variety of Conditions

When one turns from what legal historians have said on the origin and development of copyhold tenure to consider the economic position of this class of tenants, one finds oneself in a region of much greater uncertainty. The legal historian may speak of the copyholders as constituting, in spite of minor differences, a fairly well-defined class. The economic historian cannot. He finds, on the contrary, the widest difference between the economic conditions of tenants holding their land by copy of court roll, not only, as would be expected, in different parts of the country, but on the same manor. In the thirteenth century to say that a man is a villein tells us something at least about his economic position, at any rate when the general features of the manor on which he is a villein are known. He will probably have a standard holding of a virgate or half-virgate; he will have rights in the common meadow land and in the common waste; he will do work on the lord's demesne. In the sixteenth century tenure is no clue to economic status, and to say that a man is a copyhold tenant tells us nothing at all about the extent of his holding or the sort of husbandry which he pursues. The vast majority of copyhold tenants are peasants, men who make a toilsome living from their land with the help of their families and a few hired servants. But in England by our period the line between class and class has ceased to coincide with differences of title; if copyhold tenure is born of a humble stock, yet it has risen so much in the world that the upper classes are not ashamed to hold out a hand to welcome it; and among copyholders are found the names not only of many small freeholders, but also of gentlemen and knights.[121]

Among the peasants who form the bulk of the population there is, again, the greatest diversity. Sometimes the copyholders are simply emancipated villeins, who have commuted most of their services, and who hold by copy instead of at the will of the lord, but whose economic condition has hardly changed at all. Thus in Northumberland[122] the holdings of the copyholders on several manors reflect very accurately the distribution of land between the bondage tenants in the thir-

---

[121] *Crondal Records*, edited by Baigent, Part I., p. 159; the Crondal customary of 1567. Among the copyholders appears a knight and four gentlemen.

[122] *Northumberland County History, e.g.* Surveys of High Buston (vol. v. p. 208); Acklington (vol. v. p. 372); Birling (vol. v. p. 201), and figures of eight townships in Tynemouthshire, vol. viii. p. 230.

teenth and fourteenth centuries; the holdings have grown slightly in size, but they have apparently a more or less continuous individual existence from the earliest times. In parts of Wiltshire,[123] on the other hand, though not in all parts, there is no possibility of establishing any connection between the virgate and semi-virgate of the fourteenth century villeins and the acreage held by the copyholders two hundred and fifty years later; both in size and number the holdings are markedly different. In Norfolk and Suffolk ancient class divisions have often been obliterated altogether, and bond and free lands are interlaced in the holdings of the customary tenants in quite inextricable confusion.

Again, there is the greatest variety in the methods of agriculture.[124] Everywhere among the copyhold tenancies arable land predominates to an extent which is in marked contrast to the frequent preponderance of pasture land on many of the demesne farms. But to some tillage seems to be their sole livelihood, while others are very considerable sheep-farmers. Some are cultivators on quite a big scale, well outside the Board of Agriculture's interpretation of a "small-holder" to-day, with 80, 90, 100, or even 200 acres of land. Often they are better off economically than many freeholders, and when Harrison and Sir Thomas Smith classify[125] copyholders in general with "day labourers and poor husbandmen," they must surely have been either speaking loosely, or else thinking not of their economic but of their legal position. But others hold only 5, 10, 15, or 20 acres, so that arithmetical averages of the size of their holdings are very little guide to the real distribution of land. Yet it would not be true to say that such inequality is universal, for in the same county one finds some manors on which the holdings seem all to be cut to a regular standard pattern, and others where the variety of size is almost infinite, while in the North striking divergences of area seem to be as much the exception as they are the rule in the South and the East. On some manors, again, the copyhold tenants have enclosed land and hold much in severalty; on others nearly all of it lies in the open fields. Some have extensive rights of common, while on other manors such rights are non-existent, or are too insignificant to be recorded by surveyors.

In fact the impression given by the surveys is that of a condition of things which is very far from being stationary, but in which, on the contrary, much shifting of property and many changes in the methods of cultivation have been going on, and in which the legal position of the peasants is no guide at all to their economic characteristics. The task of finding a manor to serve as a pattern and standard for the rest, which is hard enough in the thirteenth century, is a sheer impossibility in the sixteenth, and the student works with a deep sense of the danger of sacrificing fidelity to simplicity of statement.

### *(b) The Consolidation of Peasant Holdings*

But difficult as it is to reduce to any order the very diverse economic conditions

---

[123] Roxburghe Club, *Surveys of the Lands of William, First Earl of Pembroke.*
[124] See below, pp. 105–115.
[125] Smith, *De Republica Anglorum*, Lib. I., c. 24. Harrison, *Elizabethan England* (edited by Withington), p. 13.

of the customary tenants at the beginning of the sixteenth century, the task, at any rate in outline, has got to be faced. And this involves a short account of movements which take us some way back into the Middle Ages. No one can understand the contrast between the conditions of the Irish peasantry in 1850 and their condition to-day without knowing something of the agencies which have been at work in the interval, of the Fair Rent Courts, the Congested Districts Board, and the Land Purchase Acts; no one can appreciate the changes which are taking place in rural France without having taken at any rate a glance at the position of the peasantry before the Revolution, and at the Code Napoleon. Certainly the substantial alteration which overtook agrarian relationships in many parts of England between 1500 and 1640 is unintelligible if it is regarded as a wave suddenly appearing in a calm sea, a revolution by means of which commercial relationships of sometimes an almost modern elasticity developed quite rapidly in village communities of an almost mediæval immobility. To understand the agrarian problem of the sixteenth century we must know the sort of framework on which the new forces worked, and the sort of tendencies of which they were the continuation.

Moreover, the history with which we are concerned is primarily the history of the peasants as landholders, and only secondarily the history of their personal condition. Generalisations about the disappearance of villeinage and the substitution of hired labour for the working out of rents in labour services do not help us much here. Speaking broadly, it is no doubt true that, in spite of the survival of many vestiges of the old order, wage-labourers are as normally the means of cultivating the demesne at the end of the fifteenth century as servile tenants are at the end of the thirteenth. But significant as this change is for the history of the wage-earning classes, it does not by itself seem to throw much light on the characteristic features of the sixteenth century problem, the substitution of large tenancies for small, the displacement of small holders, and the undermining of the customary routine of the open field village. Certainly the two movements are connected; equally certainly that connection is not a direct or obvious one. The change in the personal condition of the peasantry is not by itself the key to changes in the use and distribution of property. Why should it be? In Prussia the abolition[126] of villein services in 1807 was carried out by a decree which had as its object not a diminution, but an increase, in the number of small tenants; and it is not self-evident that an alteration in the method of cultivating the lord's demesne must have produced changes in the disposition of the customary holdings in fifteenth and sixteenth century England.

The very variety in the economic conditions of the peasantry which makes generalisation so difficult is, however, itself a significant feature, because it is in marked contrast with the comparative uniformity which existed among great masses of them in the thirteenth and fourteenth centuries. It suggests that even in agriculture custom has to some extent been broken down by commercial enterprise, and that commercial enterprise has had the natural result of accentuating inequality in the possession of property. It warns a student of the agrarian changes of the sixteenth century that he has not only to explain the way in which the small

[126] Edict of October 9, 1807, Clauses 10, 11, 12. See Cobden Club, *Systems of Land Tenure in Various Countries*: Morier's Essay on Germany.

cultivator lost ground then before the large estate, but also how it was that his economic position differed in many cases so much from that of the villein of two hundred years before, and that it may very well be that the answer to the latter question will throw light upon the former.

Let us put ourselves in the position of a jury catechising some "aged man" about the year 1500, catechising him not about boundaries, or rights of common, or manorial customs, but about the general changes in the distribution of property in his village. If surveys and court rolls may be trusted, there is one thing that he could hardly fail to tell us, and that is that for as long as he can remember there has been a great deal of buying and selling of land by the customary tenants, a great many changes in occupancy, and on the whole a tendency for those changes to result in the concentration of several holdings in fewer and larger tenancies. "Virgates which in grandfather's time," he would say, "used to belong to A., B., C., and D. now belong to A. alone. Men who used to occupy one holding each, now occupy two or three; when they cannot buy they lease, and some have bought so much that they sublet part of their holdings to others. Indeed there is not much sense in talking about virgates or half-virgates at all. Once each of them had a separate holder; once Durrant's shottes belonged to Durrant, Gunter's mead to Gunter, Parry's croft to Parry, Hawkins' meade to Hawkins, Woolmer's lande to Woolmer, Blake's tenement to Blake. To-day, though the old names remain, they are no guide to the families holding the land. Frankling has bought Durrant's and Gunter's and Blake's, Vites has bought Parry's, while Pynnole's and Pope's and Hawkins' and the rest of Blake's holdings have all passed into the hands of Blakewell."[127]

One thing at any rate is clear. If frequent changes of occupancy point to a free land-market, then such a free land-market has existed for a long time among the customary tenants; and if a keen demand for land among the peasantry is a proof that small men are thriving, and see their way to thriving still more by adding to their properties, then there is a good deal of this healthy land hunger in English villages before the age of the Tudors. We read to-day of how the French peasant will pinch himself and his family to add a few acres to his little estate, and we take it as an indication that small cultivation has a firm root in France, and that rural life is on the whole enterprising and prosperous. Certainly such a state of things is in marked contrast with the stagnation prevailing in the lower ranges of village society in countries where great estates pass almost intact from generation to generation between the tall palings of family settlements, with the small man, who would get land if he could, staring helplessly through the bars. Now, at any rate in the fifteenth century, England belonged very markedly to the first type, not to the second; to the type where there is much buying and selling of land in small plots by small cultivators, not to the type where land is locked up and rarely comes into the market, rarely at any rate into a market where it can be bought by the small peasantry. This mobility of land is of much significance when we come

[127] The instance is taken from a map of the manor of Edgeware now in the All Souls muniment room. The map was made in 1597. But many earlier examples can be found of land being known by the name of one of its early holders, long after it had passed into the possession of some one else.

to consider the breaking down of customary rules before the forces of competition, and the formation of great estates out of the holdings of the customary tenants. Let us consider it in more detail, first from the point of view of the changes in the economic basis of rural life which it produces, and secondly from the point of view of the process by which those changes were brought about. We will for the present leave on one side the demesne farm and the land held on lease, and look only at the customary land which forms the backbone of the copyholders' estates.

The first source of information to which we turn consists of the surveys and rentals, in which the holdings of the tenants are set out in detail. To those accustomed to the picture of village life contained in the records of the thirteenth and fourteenth centuries, the surveys of the fifteenth and sixteenth centuries present certain features which at once arrest attention. For one thing, there is a much greater inequality between the holdings of different customary tenants on the same manors than is usually found among the holdings of virgators and semi-virgators two centuries before. For another thing, some of their holdings are very much larger than anything we find belonging to the same class of tenants at an earlier date; occasionally, indeed, they can only be described as enormous, running into 150 or 200 acres of land; often they amount to 80 or 90. In the third place, the number of customary tenants is, on the whole, much smaller than it was 200 years before, and that even on manors where there has been an increase in the area cultivated by them. The latter fact is significant, and we shall return to it later. But before doing so, let us ask the meaning of the growing inequality in the holdings of the customary tenants and of the great increase in the size of some among them.

Great as is the variety of conditions visible on a thirteenth century manor, it is on the whole true to say that this variety usually conforms to a rough rule or principle. One can find on the same manor families whose holdings differ very largely in size, from the 25 to 40 acres occupied by the holder of a virgate, the 12 to 16 acres of a semi-virgator, to the 2 or 3 acres or less occupied by a cottar. But normally each individual holds much the same amount of land as other individuals of the same class; one holder of a virgate has about as much as another holder of a virgate, one holder of half a virgate about as much as his fellow, one cottager about as much as another cottager. There are in fact different grades, but for each grade there is what may be called a standard area of land, a unit of agrarian organisation, and though that standard area varies a good deal in different parts of the country it is usually fairly easy to discover what it is on any one manor. Outwardly, at any rate, village life is organised, and the distribution of property is settled in the main by the authority of custom, rather than by commercial forces acting directly upon the tenants.

Now after the middle of the fifteenth century it is common to find quite a different condition of things from this. There are, it is true, manors where holdings preserve their primitive equality down to the very end of the sixteenth century, especially manors in backward parts of the country, where the influence of commerce has been little felt; especially also manors where the demesne farm, instead of being leased, has been retained in the hands of the lord. But in the South of England these are the exception. The rule is that with regard to the area held by the customary tenants there is no rule at all. On the same manor copyholders may be cultivating anything from a quarter of a virgate to two, three, four, or even more virgates; if their holdings are expressed in acres they may be holding anything from 1 acre to 100 or 150. Economically, indeed, customary tenants are often not a class at all, if the essence of a class is common characteristics and a similarity of economic status, though in the face of certain dangers they will act as one. On many manors the nature of their tenure is the only common link between them, and the nature of their tenure is compatible with the greatest economic variety.

This variety is most noticeable when we examine a large number of manors one by one, since, when the figures of many different manors are added together, their distinctive features are liable to be concealed in the aggregate. Still, to get some idea of the scale on which the peasants carried on their agriculture, it is perhaps worth examining the following table[128] of the holdings of 1600 odd customary[129] tenants on fifty-two manors.

This table enables us, in the first place, to make a comparison between the economic positions of groups of tenants in different parts of England. It will be seen that the "predominant rate"—what we may call the predominant acreage— varies considerably. In Wiltshire it is between 20 and 25 acres, and, including the next two columns, 36 per cent. of all the tenants hold something between 20 and 35 acres. In Northumberland the predominant acreage is between 30 and 35, and nearly one half the tenants, 41 per cent., hold between 30 and 40 acres. Elsewhere the most common holding is a good deal smaller. In Lancashire (if we omit the cottagers, nearly all of whom come from one manor) the predominant acreage is between 10 and 15 acres, though a great many persons hold between 5 to 10 acres. In Staffordshire the largest group of tenants is that holding under 2½ acres, and more than one-half of them hold less than 10 acres. In Norfolk and Suffolk the same state of things obtains, but in a more pronounced form. Little emphasis need be laid on the large number of cottagers there, nearly all of whom are found on a single semi-urban manor, that of Aylsham. But it is clear that the mass of the peasantry in those counties are very small holders indeed. When the cottagers are left on one side, 22 per cent., about one-fifth, of the landholders have under 2½ acres; 54 per cent., more than one-half, have under 10 acres. It is fortunate for them that Norfolk and Suffolk are the home of the woollen industry.

In the second place, let us notice a fact which is more relevant to our immediate purpose. That fact is the great variety in the scale of landholding obtaining between different tenants in the same part of the country. In this matter, again, some counties present a marked contrast to others. In Northumberland the uniformity in the size of the holdings of the tenants is much more marked than the variety. About two-thirds of them appear in the four columns representing holdings from 30 to 50 acres. Only six hold more than 50, and though on one manor there are ten tenants holding less than 2½ acres, there are, apart from these, comparatively

---

[128] For the sources from which this table is constructed, and its defects, see Appendix II..

[129] On three small manors I have included some tenants who may possibly be freeholders or leaseholders.

few holding under 25 acres. On all the manors which have been examined in this county there is, in fact, a regular standard holding in the sixteenth century, which varies from 30 to 45 acres on different manors, but which on the same manor varies hardly at all. But Northumbrian agriculture is always several generations behind that of the South and East, and when we turn to Wiltshire, or to East Anglia, or to the nine manors given at the bottom of the table, we find a condition of things in which there is much greater irregularity. The line extends farther at both ends than it does in Northumberland. There are more individuals and fewer clusters. The grouping of holdings round certain standard patterns is much less marked. If we look at all the manors together, we find that the four most populous columns contain almost exactly one-half (49.1 per cent.) of the whole population, exclusive of cottagers without land. In Northumberland the corresponding columns contain two-thirds, in East Anglia, Lancashire, and Staffordshire rather less, on the nine manors in the South and Midlands about one-half, in Wiltshire a little over one-third. Again there are more large holders and more very small holders in the South and East, than there are in Lancashire and on the Northumbrian border. In Lancashire and Northumberland 4.4 per cent. of the tenants, exclusive of cottagers, have holdings of more than 50 acres. In Suffolk and Norfolk the corresponding figure is 8.5 per cent., in Wiltshire 16.9 per cent., on the nine other manors 14 per cent.

**TABLE IV**

Column Key

| | | | | | | |
|---|---|---|---|---|---|---|
| A | Total Number of Tenants | K | 35 and under 40 Acres. | U | 85 and under 90 Acres. |
| B | Cottages or Houses with or without Gardens. | L | 40 and under 45 Acres. | V | 90 and under 95 Acres. |
| C | Under 2½ Acres. | M | 45 and under 50Acres. | W | 95 and under 100 Acres. |
| D | 2½ and under 5 Acres. | N | 50 and under 55 Acres. | X | 100 and under 105 Acres. |
| E | 5 and under 10 Acres. | O | 55 and under 60 Acres. | Y | 105 and under 110 Acres. |
| F | 10 and under 15 Acres. | P | 60 and under 65 Acres. | Z | 110 and under 115 Acres. |
| G | 15 and under 20 Acres. | Q | 65 and under 70 Acres. | A' | 115 and under 120 Acres. |
| H | 20 and under 25 Acres. | R | 70 and under 75 Acres. | B' | 120 and over. |
| I | 25 and under 30 Acres. | S | 75 and under 80 Acres. | C' | Uncertain. |
| J | 30 and under 35 Acres. | T | 80 and under 85 Acres. | | |

| | A | B | C | D | E | F | G | H | I | J | K | L | M | N | O | P | Q | R | S | T | U | V | W | X | Y | Z | A' | B' | C' |
|---|---|---|---|---|---|---|---|---|---|---|---|---|---|---|---|---|---|---|---|---|---|---|---|---|---|---|---|---|---|
| Ten manors in Northumberland | 96 | … | 10 | 1 | 2 | 1 | 3 | 1 | 12 | 27 | 13 | 10 | 10 | … | … | 1 | 1 | 2 | 1 | … | 1 | … | … | … | … | … | … | … | … |
| Four manors in Lancashire | 168 | 38 | 14 | 19 | 29 | 35 | 7 | 4 | 7 | 7 | 2 | … | … | 2 | … | … | 1 | … | … | … | … | … | … | … | … | … | … | 1 | 2 |
| Three manors in Staffordshire | 103 | 8 | 21 | 16 | 14 | 6 | 10 | 11 | 3 | 1 | 2 | 2 | 2 | 2 | … | 1 | 1 | … | … | … | … | … | … | … | … | … | … | 1 | 2 |
| Two manors in Northamptonshire | 255 | 30 | 53 | 24 | 22 | 22 | 13 | 22 | 5 | 10 | 3 | 7 | 2 | 5 | 2 | 7 | 2 | 2 | 2 | 2 | … | … | … | … | 2 | … | … | 4 | 14 |
| Three manors in Leicestershire | 129 | 13 | 17 | 6 | 6 | 8 | 3 | 3 | 5 | 1 | 10 | 7 | 8 | 7 | 7 | 6 | 2 | 4 | 1 | 2 | 1 | 1 | 2 | … | … | … | 1 | 1 | 7 |
| Five manors in Suffolk and eight manors in Norfolk | 391 | 52 | 77 | 40 | 69 | 28 | 26 | 19 | 14 | 5 | 9 | 4 | 2 | 4 | 7 | 3 | 3 | 1 | 1 | 1 | 1 | … | 1 | … | 2 | 1 | … | 4 | 17 |
| Seven manors in Wiltshire and one manor in Somersetshire | 156 | 3 | 5 | 7 | 12 | 8 | 7 | 27 | 16 | 14 | 10 | 12 | 5 | 7 | 2 | 4 | 3 | 4 | 1 | 2 | 1 | … | 2 | … | … | … | … | … | 4 |
| Nine other manors in the South of England | 366 | 23 | 58 | 27 | 52 | 29 | 31 | 16 | 22 | 12 | 11 | 10 | 13 | 3 | 6 | 7 | 6 | 3 | 5 | 4 | 4 | 1 | 2 | 4 | … | 1 | 1 | 7 | 9 |
| Total, twenty-two manors | 1664 | 167 | 255 | 140 | 206 | 137 | 100 | 103 | 84 | 77 | 60 | 52 | 42 | 28 | 26 | 29 | 18 | 17 | 11 | 11 | 8 | 2 | 7 | 4 | 4 | 2 | 1 | 18 | 55 |

In the non-commercial, non-industrial North there is something like economic equality, something like the fixed equipment of each group of tenants with a standard area of land which is one of the first things to strike us in a mediæval survey, and, as we shall see later, manorial authorities for a long time insist on that rough equality being maintained, because any weakening of it would disorganise the old-fashioned economy which characterises the northern border. In the industrial East and South this uniformity existed once, but it exists now no longer. Wiltshire is humming with looms; Norfolk and Suffolk are linked to the Continent by a thousand commercial ties, and will starve if the clothiers lose their market. The mighty forces of capital and competitive industry and foreign trade are beginning to heave in their sleep—forces that will one day fuse and sunder, exalt and put down, enrich and impoverish, unpeople populous counties and pour Elizabethan England into a smoking caldron between the Irish Sea and the Pennines; forces that at present are so weak that a Clerk of the Market can lead them and a Justice of the Peace put a hook in their jaws. It is natural that mediæval conditions of agriculture should survive longest in the North. It is natural that they should survive least where trade and industry are most developed, and where men are being linked by other bonds than those of land tenure. But we must not comment until we have examined the text more closely. We would only draw attention to the contrast between the South and the North, to the contrast also between the great diversity in the size of the peasants' holdings in the sixteenth century, and the much greater uniformity two or three hundred years before.

This contrast gives a clue to certain features of village life which are distinctive of our period, and at the risk of wearying the reader one may illustrate it from the circumstances of particular manors. At Cuxham,[130] in 1483, there are, in addition to tiny holdings of a few acres or of fractions of acres, holdings of one-quarter of a virgate, of half a virgate, of one virgate, of four virgates. At Ibstone[131] in the same year there are two tenants at will holding one virgate each, one tenant holding five tofts and three crofts, while the rest hold little except cottages and gardens. At Warton[132] in Lancashire, there are in the reign of Henry VIII., in addition to various holdings expressed in terms of acres, four holdings of half a bovate, two of three-quarters of a bovate, seven of one bovate, two of one and a quarter bovates, four of one and a half bovates, four of two bovates, one of two and a quarter bovates, one of three bovates. At Barton[133] in Staffordshire, in 1556, the typical holding is one virgate of 24 acres. But though this forms the nucleus of the copyholders' properties a good many of them have acquired so much extra land, and a good many apparently have parted with so much of the land which they once held, that though 24 acres is still the predominant holding, the majority of the tenants hold something more or something less than this. At Byshopeston,[134] in 1567, there are men holding half a virgate, two virgates, three virgates, four virgates, six

---

[130] Merton Documents, Rentale de Cuxham (Nos. 5902 and 5905).

[131] Merton Documents, Rentale de Ibston (No. 5902).

[132] R.O. Rental and Surveys, Gen. Ser., Portf. 19, No. 7, f. 79–87.

[133] R.O. Rentals and Surveys, Gen. Ser., Portf. 14, No. 70.

[134] Roxburghe Club, *Surveys of Lands of William, First Earl of Pembroke*.

virgates. At Knyghton[135] there are holders of anything from a half to two and a half virgates.

Looking at this grouping of holdings, one is tempted at first sight to say that the virgate has ceased to be a unit of open field tillage, and has become merely a common form, an idea which is laid up in the minds of surveyors, and which is produced automatically, even when it corresponds to nothing in the fluid world of agriculture. This, however, would be an error. On the contrary, the conservatism[136] of rural arrangements is such that yardlands, bovates, virgates, and oxgangs, continue to do duty in circumstances which seem quite incongruous, and to be used, not only in theory, but in practice, to apportion rights over arable, meadow, and pasture, long after holdings have been redistributed in such a way as altogether to destroy the former equality of shares. On the Leicestershire manors of Barkby[137] and Kibworth[138] holdings were set down in terms of yardlands in 1636, though the condition of things in which a yardland or half yardland formed one tenant's holding had long since given way to one in which the smaller holders occupied a few acres and the wealthier 2½, 3, and 3½ yardlands. Still, though the continuance of these measures even into the eighteenth century should be noted, there is no reason why we should use them, and the modern reader will perhaps get a better idea of the growing heterogeneity in the economic conditions of the customary tenants if the distribution of their property is expressed in terms of acres.

Our first example comes from Malden[139] in Surrey. It shows on a small scale the tendency towards concentration of property in larger parcels. In 1452 there were on that manor one holder of 24 acres, three holders of 16 acres, two holders of 15 acres, and families holding 10, 8, 6, 5, 2 acres respectively. That 16 acres had been the normal holding is fairly obvious; it is obvious also that though this normal holding is still traceable, it is on the way to being obliterated. Later specimens of a similar kind come from Ashfield[140] in Suffolk and Ormesby[141] in Norfolk. In 1513 there were on the former manor tenants holding 7, 10, 15, 21, 22, 36, 37, 45, 107, 121 acres, and all intermediate sizes. On the latter, in 1516, the holdings were much smaller, but they were still more various in area, ranging from 2 to 31 acres. One or two of the Wiltshire and Somersetshire manors surveyed for the Earl of Pembroke in 1567 offer examples of the reverse state of things in which the tenants' holdings were all cut out to a standard pattern. At Washerne,[142] for example, a manor where the demesnes were not leased but retained "in the hand of the lord," nearly all the copyholders had exactly 20 acres each. But this is an exception

[135] *Ibid.*

[136] The inconvenience of reckoning in yardlands is noticed by a writer in the seventeenth century: "The tax of land is after the yardland; a name very deceitful by the disproportion and inequality thereof, the quantity of some one yardland being as much as one and a halfe or two in the same field, and yet there is an equality of taxes" (Joseph Lee, *A Vindication of a Regulated Enclosure*, 1656).

[137] Merton Documents, MS. book labelled Kibworth and Barkby, 1636.

[138] *Ibid.*

[139] Merton Documents, Rental of Malden.

[140] R.O. Rentals and Surveys, Gen. Ser., Portf. 14, No. 85.

[141] *Ibid.*, Portf. 22, No. 18.

[142] Roxburghe Club, *Surveys of Lands of William, First Earl of Pembroke*.

which proves the rule. At Estoverton[143] there were some tenants holding 69, 48, 38 acres of arable, and others with 12, 10, 9, 3, and 2 acres. At Donnington[144] there were holders of 63 and 52 acres in the fields and holders with only 8 or 9 acres. At South Brent[145] the divergence between large and small customary tenants is more striking still. One occupies about 90 acres, several others over 50, while the vast majority hold less than 30 acres in holdings which are hardly ever of the same size. At Crondal[146] we find in 1567 exactly the same inequality in the area cultivated by different tenants, exactly the same combination of very large with very small holdings. Taking one tithing only of that manor—that of Swanthrop—we are met by tenants holding 112, 104, 66, 58, 47, 44, 30, 27, 25, and 3 acres. Finally, let us take two extreme instances. They are drawn from the closing years of the sixteenth century; but their inclusion may be justified by the fact that they reveal in a pronounced form the tendencies which we have seen at work elsewhere a century and a half before, and that they offer a peculiarly clear example of larger customary holdings formed out of the aggregation of several smaller ones, since the names of the previous tenants are stated by the surveyor. On the two Middlesex manors of Edgeware[147] and Kingsbury[148] all relics of the state of things which had presumably existed there, as on other manors, two or three centuries before, the state of things in which there were groups of men holding virgates or half virgates, has disappeared so entirely as to leave no traces behind. On the former the thirty-eight copyholders occupy holdings of almost any size between 1 rood and 130 acres; out of the 722 acres of copyhold land as much as 254, a little over one-third, are in the hands of two large tenants. On the latter there is, *mutatis mutandis*, the same story; out of the twenty-seven copyholders thirteen hold less than 15 acres, eight hold more than 30, and of those eight two hold more than 100 acres apiece.

These examples are drawn from 12 different counties.[149] Let us see more exactly what they suggest. They suggest that, quite apart[150] from any movement on the part of lords of manors to throw the holdings of the customary tenants into large farms and to evict their holders, quite apart from any external shock such as was given to the organisation of village life by the change from tillage to pasture on the part of lords and their farmers, there has been going on an internal change in the relation of the customary tenants to each other. So far we have been concerned only with the result of that change, not with the process by which it is brought about. The result, as evidenced by the surveys, is the consolidation of several holdings, or parts of holdings, into fewer and larger tenancies, the appearance of a class

[143] Roxburghe Club, *Surveys of Lands of William, First Earl of Pembroke*.

[144] *Ibid.*

[145] *Ibid.*

[146] *Crondal Record*, Part I. (Baigent), pp. 210–221. Customary of 1567.

[147] All Souls Documents, Map and Description of the Manor of Edgeware (1597).

[148] *Ibid.*, Map and Description of the Manor of Kingsbury (1597).

[149] Similar examples could be adduced from Northamptonshire and Leicestershire, were it worth while, *e.g.* at Duston in Northants in 1561 there were tenants holding 2 virgates, 1¾ virgates, 1½ virgates, ½ virgate, ¼ virgate (R.O. Rentals and Surveys, Portf. 13, No. 23). At Desford in Leicestershire, *temp.* Hen. VIII., one finds the same division and aggregation of virgates (R.O. Rentals and Surveys, Duchy of Lancs., Bdle. 6, No. 7).

[150] See below, pp. 72–75.

of well-to-do peasants by whom such larger tenancies are held, and a widening of the gap between the most prosperous and least prosperous. Customary tenants hold 3 or 4 virgates, 80 or 90 or 100 acres, and their holdings are composed of holdings and parts of holdings which formerly belonged to several different tenants. Customary tenants even become the landlords of other customary tenants. At Yateleigh[151] one copyholder has as many as twenty sub-tenants, and it is not at all uncommon for the surveyors of the sixteenth century to record the names both of owners and occupiers in estate and field maps. There can hardly be a clearer proof of the re-arrangement of property which has been going on among them than the fact that some of them hold more land than they can cultivate themselves and sublet it to smaller men, who become their sub-tenants.

May one not say, in fact, that by the beginning of the sixteenth century the rough equality which had once existed between the holdings of different groups of customary tenants is fast disappearing, and that by the middle of that century it has, in some parts of the country, disappeared altogether? The village community is often no longer made up of compact groups of holders with more or less equal holdings, more or less equal rents and services, more or less similar economic positions. Even as early as the time when the great agrarian changes which contemporaries summed up under the name of "enclosing" begin to produce legislation on the part of governments and riots among the peasantry, its appearance of a systematic adjustment of property and obligation is already far on the way to disappearance. Its members still hold shares in the open fields, and are still bound by a common routine of cultivation, save in so far as that routine has been undermined in the ways to be described below. But it is easy to be deceived by the external shell of organisation into thinking of village life at the end of the fifteenth century as being much more homogeneous than it really was. After all there are shareholders and shareholders. There is very little similarity in economic interest or social position between the artisan who buys a £5 share in a Bolton spinning-mill and a capitalist who invests £5000 in the same concern. There was hardly more, one may suspect, between the copyholder who cultivated a few acres and the copyholder who held 100 or 200 acres and sublet part of his holding to a poorer neighbour, though the lands of both were intermixed, though both held of the same manor, though both were nominally bound by the same custom. This comparison says more than we mean; for, with few exceptions, the inequality in the holdings of the peasantry revealed by the manorial documents is not so great that it cannot be spanned by enterprise and good fortune. Looking back from a world in which the mass of mankind have no legal interest in the land which they cultivate or the tools which they use, what strikes the modern reader most in the sixteenth century is not the concentration of property, but its wide distribution. Nevertheless, even in these petty rearrangements of holdings there is a meaning. They are the beginning of greater things. To appreciate their importance we must obliterate from our minds our knowledge of later developments, and regard them as the innovation which they are. We must remember that they are the economic foundation of a prosperous rural middle class.

---

[151] *Crondal Records, loc. cit.*

### (c) The Growth of a Land Market among the Peasants

If the surveys were our sole source of information it would not be easy to say how this regrouping of holdings has been brought about. Even the surveys, however, do not leave us quite in the dark. They suggest that it has taken place very largely through the play of commercial forces within the ranks of the customary tenants themselves, through the eager purchasing of land which we noticed as one feature of rural life at the close of the Middle Ages, and through the growth of a cash nexus between individuals side by side with the rule of custom. This is a factor in the break up of the mediæval condition of landholding upon which sufficient emphasis has perhaps not always been laid. The pre-occupation of the writers of the sixteenth century with the special problem of their own day, when the existence of a class of well-to-do copyholders was taken as something needing no explanation, and their decay before the growth of the great leasehold estate occupied the attention of all interested in agricultural problems, caused the significance of the development of these thriving peasants to be forgotten in the agitation and regrets which accompanied their depression, and naturally concentrated interest on the changes introduced by lords and great farmers, through which that depression was mainly caused. In every age prosperity is taken as a matter of course, and, in defiance of all experience, mankind reserves its surprise for distress.

But the special phenomenon of the growth of large customary tenancies which we have been considering can hardly be explained except as a result of enterprise among the tenants themselves. The piling up of customary holdings in the hands of one individual is quite a different thing from the adding of customary holdings to the demesne which the lord retained or leased to a farmer. It means a transference of property, but a transference not from a customary tenant to the lord or the lord's farmer, but from one customary tenant to another. It suggests that before the "enclosing movement" of the sixteenth century brought its crop of evictions, economic forces had long been at work to break up the village community into large holders and small. When in 1452 John Blackman, copyhold tenant of Maiden,[152] holds Keyser's, Key's, and Skinner's tenements, it can only mean that Keyser, Key, and Skinner have parted with their tenements to John Blackman. The lord may have put pressure upon them to sell, but the customary land is not diminished, it is simply rearranged; the result is not an addition to the manorial demesne, but the appearance of a copyhold tenant with a great deal more land than his neighbours. The cases in which the existence of more than one survey of the same manor enables us to contrast the condition of the customary tenants at different dates make it quite clear that this aggregation of holdings was a well-marked movement which went on quite apart from any encroachment by manorial authorities on the customary land. Some time between 1340 and 1454 two virgates at Castle Combe,[153] which at the earlier date were in separate hands, have been formed into one holding. And naturally, the later we come, the more marked the change which we find. At Aspley Guise[154] in 1275 the forty customary tenants each held almost exactly

[152] Merton Documents, Rental of Maiden, 1496.

[153] *History of Castle Combe* (Scrope).

[154] For information as to Aspley Guise I am indebted to the kindness of Dr. H.G. Fowler of Aspley Guise, who has allowed me to see the material which he has collected for

half a virgate. In 1542 one finds among the tenants at will and copyholders three occupants of the original half virgate, one tenant with 30 acres, two tenants with 60 acres each, three tenants with 75 acres each. These large holdings have plainly been formed by the aggregation of half virgates in fewer hands and into parcels of two, three, four, and five half virgates apiece. This case is a very clear one, because nearly all the holdings are multiples of the original standard, even the rent being calculated from this basis.

Elsewhere the aggregation of small customary holdings into large is equally marked, but it has not been carried out with such a nice regard to the maintenance of the original units. In the tithing of South[155] Newton, part of the Manor of South Newton in Wiltshire, there were in 1315 seven holders of a virgate, each of whom occupied 23 acres, seventeen holders of half a virgate with 12 acres each, and eight cottagers. When the manor was surveyed in 1567 the customary tenants, though fewer in number, cultivated a good deal more land than they had two and a half centuries before, so that there is no question of their holdings having been merged in the demesne. But the land was very differently distributed between them. Of the ten copyholders then remaining only one held the original virgate. Of the rest there were holders of 59, 65, 80, and 96 acres, of 7, 13, and 15 acres, and of various acreages between these wide limits. The symmetry of the earlier arrangement has entirely vanished. Instead of a cluster of small cultivators organised in three well-defined layers, we have a chain stretching from a mere cottager up to a petty capitalist. A very similar change has taken place on the Manor of Crondal.[156] If one compares, for example, the arrangement of holdings on the tithing of Swanthrop in 1287 and 1567, one finds that the rough symmetry which existed at the former date has altogether disappeared by the latter. In 1287 there were eight persons holding virgates, seven holding half virgates, two holding quarter-virgates, and four whose holdings are not expressed in virgates. By 1567 all this has been altered. There are tenants holding 100, 66, 58, 47 acres; there are three with less than 10 acres, and there are five with holdings of various sizes between these limits, but in no case reducible to any common measure. How could such a transformation come about, unless, as was suggested above, there was much buying and selling of land, much rudimentary commercialism inside and behind the decent cloak of routine which seems to be spread over our villages? Is not this explanation forced upon us when we examine the holdings of the larger peasants and find them made up of pieces bought from one and leased from another, pieces taken from the waste or from the lord's demesne or from the common pasture? And if it is correct, does it not point, on the one hand, to a good deal of enterprise among the small holders, and since enterprise can hardly exist without a certain level of prosperity, to a good deal of prosperity; and, on the other hand, to movements which in time are likely to dethrone custom altogether and put competition in its place?

To these questions we shall return later. But happily we are not restricted to inferential argument for our knowledge of these internal changes in the economy of village life before the sixteenth century. We have the court rolls of manors, and a history of the manor.

[155] Roxburghe Club, *Surveys of Lands of William, First Earl of Pembroke* (Straton).
[156] *Crondal Records* (Baigent), pp. 111–116, and 210–222.

the court rolls are full, from a very early date, of transactions which show how the state of things which has been described was being brought about. In examining the evidence which they offer of the shifting of property among the peasantry we shall have to go some way back, and we shall do well to begin with a distinction and a warning—a distinction between the legal framework of rural life and its economic tendencies, and a warning that we shall have to deal with a somewhat tiresome mass of detail, which the general reader can avoid by turning to the summary at the end of this chapter.

In the picture of the mediæval manor which is usually offered us the features which receive most emphasis are its systematic apportionment of works and services, its regulation by binding customary rules, its immobility and imperviousness to competitive and commercial influences; in short, its character as an organisation in which even the details are settled by custom. In the "typical manor," as it appears in some accounts, the main lines are drawn with almost photographic sharpness. There are the free holders on the free land, the bond tenants each with his virgate or half virgate of bond land, and the officers and servants of the lord, a system the parts of which are knit together by the lord's need of extracting labour services to cultivate his demesne. Now that the internal economy of a thirteenth century manor displays to a very remarkable degree the authority of custom in all its arrangements is not, of course, denied; and it is specially proper to emphasise it when we are contrasting it with modern agriculture, or when we are regarding it from the standpoint of law. But this is only one aspect of it, and if we assume that the economic relationships between the different members of it always followed the same grouping and ran on the same lines as the legal ones, we are likely to ascribe to them a simplicity and a hard and fast character which, we may be quite sure, they never possessed in real life, and to miss those very innovations which throw most light on economic development.

True of such development early rentals and surveys show little trace. But let us remember the purpose for which they were prepared. The manorial officials were concerned with getting in an income, not with supplying information about the methods of agriculture or the cross-relations between one tenant and another, except in so far as they affected the manorial revenue. The source of the income was the holding, not the holder; or, rather, it did not matter to them who the landholder was, whether he was one individual or another, or whether he was a partnership of half-a-dozen individuals, provided that the land, however held, yielded the customary services and payments. The nearest analogy would be an apportioned tax which a Government divides between different localities, each locality having to raise a certain sum, but making its own arrangements as to what individuals shall pay. It is the virgate which pays rents, which mows the lord's meadow, reaps the lord's fields, carries the lord's messages, pays a stoup of honey and a churchshot of white corn; and as long as the meadow is mowed and the message carried, the question what individual holds the virgate is quite a subsidiary one for the bailiff, and one which the tenants can arrange among <u>themselves much</u> as they please. Each half virgate at Cuxham[157] has got to do two

[157] Merton Documents, No. 5902, Rental of Cuxham, 1483: "Johannes ... pro uno messuagio et una virgata terræ et dimidia xxiiis. et 6 precaria in autumno vel 2s.... Thomas Lee,

boonworks or pay 4d. But the manorial economy is not at all disturbed by the fact of one tenant holding not half a virgate, but a virgate and a half; for he has to do, or pay some one else to do, six boonworks and pay 2s. if he does not. A half-hide at Bramshot[158] has to make half-a-dozen different payments in money and kind; but there is another to prevent John, Stephen, Roger, and William clubbing together to work it and arranging the payments among themselves as they please.

Clearly in these circumstances a rigid classification of holdings by the manorial authorities is quite compatible with a great deal of diversity in the arrangements made with each other by the holders, and we are likely to miss a good many innovations if we look at the manor only through the eyes of officials and as a revenue-producing concern.[159] We must no more expect to get from them an exhaustive account of the exact individuals at any one time using the land, or of the scale on which farming is carried on by the peasants, than we expect the shareholders' list of a limited company to tell us who has the spending of the dividends. The shares stand in A.'s name, but the interest may go to A.'s married daughter. The holding stands in the name of Thomas in the books of the manor, but it may be that part or all of it is worked by Walter. To put the case in another way, to the lord and his steward a manor is primarily a business, a business on which various obligations can be imposed and from which various profits can be extracted. But it is also a village community consisting of peasants whose economic relations are by no means exhausted in the interest which the lord takes in them as part of its stock, and who have economic dealings which are important when we begin to inquire into changes in the distribution of peasant property. The number of the holdings and the amount of payments and services may remain quite unaltered, and yet at the same time if one individual begins to acquire several shares his property will grow at the expense of other persons. Precisely because it is new, the appearance of such small capitalists is not readily traceable in the stereotyped forms used by the manorial officials. Precisely because it is new, it is of the greatest economic significance. It shows what may be called, by contrast with later developments, the old agrarian régime, producing the new type of well-to-do peasant who is one of the protagonists in the class struggles of the sixteenth century.

And this upward movement is no mere matter of conjecture. That behind the stiff legal framework of the manorial organisation there was a tendency for property to pass into the hands of the more prosperous tenants, and that there was a Rector ecclesiæ ibidem pro uno tofto ... et una virgata terræ 18s. et 4 precaria in autumno vel 16d."

[158] *Crondal Records* (Baigent), p. 96, Rental of 1287: "Johannes filius Fabri, Stephanus Draghebreck, Rogerus de Hallie, et Willelmus le Hart ... tenent j dimidiam hidatam terræ. Reddendo inde per annum 5s. ad festum S. Mich. et xixd. de Pondpany et ad festum Beati Martini viii gallinas de chersetto, et ii gallinas contra Natale, et x ova contra Pascha, et facient in omnibus omnia sicut Willelmus de Haillie." P. 125: "William, son of Gonnilda, and Galfrid Levesone, John, son of Matilda, and Emma, a widow, hold one virgate of land containing 27½ acres on paying and doing as the said Robert of Estfelde." There are many similar entries.

[159] Vinogradoff, *Villainage in England*, pp. 250–251: "The general arrangement admitted a certain subdivision under the cover of an artificial unity, which found its expression in the settlement of the services and of the relations with the lord."

sort of primitive commercialism even at a time when commercial ideas had little influence over the methods of agriculture, becomes evident if we examine the elements out of which the small properties of the fourteenth century are composed. The gradual formation of a class of wealthy peasants took place in three ways, through the buying up by well-to-do men of parts of their neighbours' properties, through the colonising by villages of the unoccupied land surrounding them, and through the addition to the customary holdings of plots which had at one time been in the occupation of the lord, but which, for one reason or another, he found it more profitable to sell or lease to his tenants. Even before the end of the thirteenth century it is by no means unusual to find land changing holders pretty rapidly both by transfer and by lease. The customary land passes in the manorial court; the outgoing tenant surrenders it, and the incoming tenant is formally admitted by the steward. When a peasant leaves the manor or dies without heirs, the other tenants offer a sort of small land-market, and bid for his land or part of it to add to their own. Hence holdings or fractions of holdings change hands with some frequency at the court customary, the well-to-do, who can afford to take more land, offering the lord an increased rent to obtain a share in a holding the possession of which has for some reason lapsed. In the court rolls of the Lincolnshire manor of Ingoldmells,[160] for example, there are many such transfers, six sales occurring in successive courts held in 1315 and 1316. At Crondal,[161] in 1282, a tenant has for some reason given up his holding; the rest of the community dart on it like minnows on a piece of bread; and it is at once split up among as many as ten other tenants, who find sureties for the continuance of the normal services. At Hadleigh,[162] in 1305, a tenant sells part of his land to be built upon. At Castle[163] Combe, in 1367, a villein enters by licence of the lord on two virgates of land and a separate pasture.

Such examples of what may be called petty land speculation could be multiplied almost indefinitely, and point to a good deal of mobility in rural society even in the thirteenth and early fourteenth centuries. At the same time one can see signs of relationships of a more complicated character tending to establish themselves between the tenants, and breaking up the symmetry of the manorial arrangements. There is a marked tendency for holdings not to remain intact but to be split up among different holders. Sometimes this takes place in the ordinary course of transference from father to son. The virgate held by the former is divid-

---

[160] *Ingoldmells Court Rolls* (Massingberd), October 1315 to June 1316.

[161] *Crondal Records* (Baigent), pp. 152–153. Court Roll of 1282. "Hugh Sweyn gives to the lord 15d. that he may be able to hold 2½ acres of arable land of the tenement formerly Richard Wisdom's, paying therefor yearly 15d. of rent: sureties for the services being Gilbert Swein and Roger Carter." Nine other tenants take fractions of Richard Wisdom's holding in the same way.

[162] *Victoria County History of Suffolk*, "Social and Economic History" (Unwin). Professor Unwin has some suggestive remarks on similar developments in other parts of the county.

[163] *History of Castle Combe* (Scrope), p. 162: "Johannes Pleyslede, nativus domini, cepit de domino unum messuagium et duas virgatas terrae tenendas in bondagio, secundum consuetudinem manerii ... Reddit etiam annuatim sex denarios pro quadam pastura vocata le Hatche, et pro via ad eandem."

ed, for example, into two cotlands, each of which is held by one child,[164] or the heir to a holding divides it with his mother.[165] More frequently one is left to infer the actual process of division from the way in which the Rentals describe holdings as being occupied by groups or partnerships[166] of tenants, who share the land between them, each being responsible for a part of the rents and services owing from the virgate. Such an arrangement does not imply that there is any partnership in actual cultivation, any partnership in the modern sense of the word. It means, on the contrary, that the different parts of the holding are divided among several different cultivators, and that its apparent unity is quite artificial, simply a fiscal expression to enable the authorities to see that it renders its share of payments and services.

Again there is much leasing and sub-letting of land by the more prosperous of the customary tenants. Like labourers who hold allotments to-day, they often find it convenient to hire extra land and at the same time to let out parts of their own holdings, which may be inconveniently situated, or hard to work, or for some other reason not worth retaining. Thus in Lancashire the Clitheroe[167] court rolls show many fines being paid in the early fourteenth century for permission to "tavern," that is simply to lease, land. In 1351 there are several tenants on the manor of Sutton[168] in Hampshire who have leased cotlands from the larger customary tenants. At Crokeham on the neighbouring manor of Crondal[169] we hear as early as 1287 of one tenant paying 12d. for his holding "through the rents of" another customary tenant, who stands as an intermediate landlord between him and the manorial authorities. On this manor, indeed, sub-letting of land proceeded very far, and had created by the middle of the sixteenth century exactly the result which one would have expected, the existence, namely, of a considerable number of subtenants holding land from the copyholders and known by the name of Hallmote[170]

[164] *Crondal Records* (Baigent), p. 129, Rental of Dupehale (Dippenhall) 1287: "Edmunde de Bosco and William de Bosco hold 2 cotlands which were formed out of one virgate of land which Adam de Bosco formerly held."

[165] *Ibid.*, p. 153: "Margery Palmer comes and surrenders into the hands of the lord a virgate of land with a house in Crondal, and Galfrid her son comes and gives to the lord 6s. 8d. to have seizin thereof, upon this condition, that the said Margery have the third part, and two pieces more, of the aforesaid tenement, for the term of her life."

[166] *Crondal Records* (Baigent), p. 117, Rental of Yateleigh, 1287: "John de la Perke and Thomas Squel hold one virgate of land containing 22 acres, on payment therefor of 2s. 10d. on the Feast of St. Michael and 7½ for Pondpany, and one stoup of honey, and 75 eggs, and shall perform all services like Thomas Kach.... Walter le White and Osbert de la Knelle hold one virgate of land containing 29½ acres.... Roys de Pothulle and John le White hold one virgate of land containing 29 acres."

[167] *Court Rolls of the Lordships, Wapentakes, and Demesne Manors of Thomas, Earl of Lancaster* (edited by W. Farrer). Halmote of Colne, 1323: "Thomas le Harper for taverning 3 acres of land, 6d. Roger ... for the same of 2 acres of land, 4d.," and *passim*.

[168] *Crondal Records* (Baigent), p. 140: "John Thomas holds a messuage and a 'ferdell' of land, excepting one cotland and a perch.... Thomas le Freyn holds of the above a cotland and a perch."

[169] *Ibid.*, p. 134: "William de Suche gives to the lord 12d. yearly, to be allowed to hold 6 acres through the rents of Hugh of Wyggeworthale."

[170] *Crondal Records* (Baigent), pp. 159–383. Customary of 1567. The name does not

tenants. Nor is mere subtenancy the most elaborate of the arrangements which arise among these Lilliputian capitalists. The peasants deal in land, and naturally they employ land agents to act as brokers for their bargains. When "Robert Bagges surrenders one bovate of villein land into the hands of the lord for the use of Symon Clerk, and the same Symon forthwith surrenders the aforesaid bovate to the lord for the use of William Flaxman, and William Flaxman pays 12d. to enter thereupon,"[171] may we not say that we have the whole machinery of land speculation, seller, middleman, and client, complete?

So far we are on safe ground. But it is not easy to describe the sort of conditions in which this petty commercialism, this emergence of peasants richer and more prosperous than their fellows, takes place. Clearly it implies the existence of small stores of capital, of some surplus over the consumption of the current year, which its fortunate possessors can use as a starting-point for further acquisitions; nor ought this to surprise us, for the usurer who traffics in his neighbours' misfortunes by lending money or corn at exorbitant rates, is by no means an unfamiliar bugbear in the mediæval village. Clearly, again, we must not look for some single *primum mobile* to explain how such small capitals could be brought into existence. With all its apparent homogeneity the manorial population had, from the beginning of things, included people some of whom were in so much better a position than others for building up considerable properties as to make it no matter for astonishment that, as time went on, they should improve their advantage and attract more than their share of any increase in wealth which might take place. The appearance in the fourteenth century of a rural middle class is, indeed, much less remarkable than the extreme slowness of its development in the more backward parts of the country. For one thing, even the strictest equalisation of shares could not prevent the holder of exceptionally fertile land from being better off than his less fortunate fellow. Since services and rents were based on the requirements of the demesne, with a view to their rough apportionment among all the peasants, and were not adjusted, like modern competitive rents, so as to sweep away the surplus arising on superior sites, the occupants of the latter could build up, under the ægis of custom, the nucleus of a very considerable property.[172] For another thing, the mere fact that the village was subordinated to a lord, who exploited it

necessarily imply subtenancy in any way, the Hallmoot being simply the court of the manor. At Yateleigh one copyholder, Richard Allen, held about 263 acres, of which about 126 were held from him by 21 subtenants (pp. 258–265 and 378–379).

[171] Footnote in *The Rebellion of Wat Tyler*, by Petruschevsky (Russian), p. 210: "Ricardus Flaxman qui de domino tenuit in bondagio unum messuagium et II. bovatas terræ et xvi acras terræ de Forland quæ quondam fuerunt Johannis Colyn ad terminum xx. annorum ex dimissione prædicti Johannis per licenciam curiæ, venit hic et reddidit in manus domini prædictas duas bovatas terræ et acras di' terræ et prati ad opus Willelmi Dolynes deduct' prædicto messuagio." Duchy of Lancaster Court Rolls, Bdle. 32, No. 307, and *ibid.*, p. 211: "Robertus Bagges redd' in manus domini 1 bovatam terræ in bondagio ad opus Symonis Clerk Tenend 'sibi et suis, etc. Et idem Symon instanter redd' in manus domini prædictam bovatam terræ ad opus Willelmi Flaxman sibi et heredibus suis secundum consuetudinem manerii, et dat ad ingressum xiid." Duchy of Lancaster Court Rolls, Bdle. 33, No. 324: "Instanter" is remarkable.

[172] See below, pp. 115–121.

by means of officers and servants, supplied village society with an upper layer of people who had larger opportunities than the mass of the peasantry for improving their position. Stewards, bailiffs, and greaves were frequently rewarded for their services with grants of land for which only a nominal rent was asked, and of course the most obvious way of using their advantage was further to increase it by adding to their properties. In a somewhat similar position to these were the peasants who were let off easily because their labour was not needed for the lord's estate. It is quite a mistake to think of the mediæval villager as a man pinned down to subsistence level by the economic pressure which grinds, as in a mortar, the poorest classes in modern society. Of course individuals were cruelly oppressed, and when the harvest failed whole communities, as in India to-day, must sometimes have been blotted out at a blow. But the whole story of the extraordinary upward movement which took place among the peasantry in the fourteenth and fifteenth centuries is unintelligible, unless we admit that the legal rightlessness of the villein was, in fact, quite compatible with a good deal of economic prosperity. His liability to the manorial authorities, though in law unqualified, was in reality a liability limited, on the one hand, by the rule of custom, and, on the other, by the fact that he worked, not for an ever hungry world-market, but for a by no means insatiable local demand. Since services were adjusted to holdings, not to holders, a family of five or six persons usually did not send more than one or two to work on the lord's estate, and the remainder had opportunities for economic advancement, which necessarily became greater as the growth of population made the weight of the lord's requirements less exacting.[173] Moreover, the rudimentary specialisation of industrial employments, which can plainly be seen going on in the villages of the fourteenth century, brought into existence the man who was half peasant, half artisan or tradesman, and who could employ the money which he made in trade to carry on his husbandry on a larger scale than his neighbours. Such, for example, were the smiths, carpenters, turners, shoemakers, tailors, butchers, walkers, websters, and shearmen, who appear so constantly in Poll Tax returns.[174] When a weaver is able, though a villein, to leave 3000 marks to his heirs,[175] the village capitalist has plainly come upon the scenes. Nor must we forget that, however self-contained some manors may have been, there were others whose proximity to a chartered town or to a seaport acted as a magnet to draw rural conditions out of the rut of custom. Among the serfs who bought permission to emigrate, there were some who, having made money as town craftsmen, strayed back to their "villein nest," and acquired considerable properties with their hardly amassed wealth, like the Italian or Austrian peasant of to-day, who, after years spent in the sunless tenements and restaurants of New York, returns at last to be the envy of Calabrian and Tyrolese villages. From several sides at once, therefore, from those who socially rank above the mass of the population, from the peasant who combines trade and husbandry, from the enterprising serf who sets out to make his fortune at a distance, forces are at work to build up the considerable holdings that are the basis of

[173] See *E.H.R.*, vol. xv. pp. 774–813; Vinogradoff's review of Page's *The End of Villeinage in England*.

[174] Powell, *The Revolt in East Anglia*, Appendix I.; and Putnam, *The Enforcement of the Statute of Labourers*, pp. 80–81.

[175] Scrope, *History of the Manor and Barony of Castle Combe.* p. 233.

the well-to-do peasantry of the future.

But while these causes were always operating on individuals, the most potent influence in forming a class of prosperous peasants was, no doubt, the spread of commerce and its reaction on agriculture. Its effect is shown by the fact that it is just in those parts of the country where trade is most highly developed, and where, therefore, the use of money and the growth of wealth encourage speculation of all kinds, that the commercialising of landed relationships, and the appearance of a middle class, arises earliest and spreads furthest. The change is specially noticeable in the Eastern counties, which, from an early date, are the home of industry. Examples of the extreme variety and irregularity in the holdings of the customary tenants on the manors of Suffolk in the sixteenth century, which we have already contrasted with the arrangements in the backward parts of the country such as Northumberland, begin to make their appearance at a very early date in that county of fisheries and manufactures. At Hadleigh,[176] where the woollen industry has set money in circulation, the processes both of splitting up the customary holdings, and of letting two or three of them to a single tenant, is conspicuous at the beginning of the fourteenth century, and has completely altered the distribution of property which existed a century before. At the little fishing village of Gorleston[177] at the end of the thirteenth century each of the former tenancies was divided up among several tenants, sometimes three or four, sometimes eight or ten, and once as many as twenty. At Hawstead, in the same county, the free tenants have let off part of their holdings and added to them by leasing additional land in its place. In short, whenever trade becomes a serious factor in rural life, one finds a very general tendency for new arrangements of land to grow up side by side with the customary holdings, which are the backbone of the manor, because it is from them that the lord extracts his services for the cultivation of the desmesne. As long as the necessity for labour services continues, the number of holdings does not undergo any appreciable alteration, but the number of holdings ceases to be a guide to the number of holders.

It is clear that the organisation of the manor is compatible with a good deal of shifting of property among the customary tenants, and that an alteration in its arrangements begins at a comparatively early date, without any external shock and through the desire of such tenants as can afford it to buy and lease land from other tenants who are less well off. If such a tendency were at all general, it would explain the gradual aggregation of larger holdings into fewer hands, and the appearance of considerable inequality in economic status among members of the village community whose legal position was the same. Sometimes, indeed, the authorities of the manor think that the process is going on too fast, that tenants have forgotten that, though they deal in land as though it were their own, it is really the lord's, and that they must not jeopardise the rents and services which he expects from it by alienating it without his permission. Sometimes a day of reckoning comes, when "tenants having more than one customary tenement" are "to show cause why they should not be excluded from the other tenements but one,

---

[176] *Victoria County History of Suffolk*, Unwin's article on Social and Economic History.
[177] *Ibid.*

unless license be granted them."[178] But in view of the multitude of transactions which come before us, we can hardly doubt that licence was nearly always granted if the purchaser or lessee was thought by the steward to be substantial enough to make the land do its duty,[179] and that tenants who wanted to buy and sell, lease and let, had very little opposition to expect from the lord or his steward.

After all the picture is one which we ought not to have any difficulty in understanding, if once we get rid of the idea, born of our melancholy modern experience, that the buying of land in small parcels is for the small man the road to ruin, a luxury in which none but the well-to-do can afford to indulge. We have all heard much of the iniquities of the English system of land transfer, and have contrasted its cumbersomeness, its expense, its uncertainty, with the facilities for buying small plots offered by methods like those of France, where sales and mortgages are entered in a public registry, which any one has the right to inspect. But we need not look to the Continent or the British Dominions to see a market for real property working freely and smoothly. In our period by far the most general form of tenure was one customary tenure or another, and whatever the disadvantages of customary tenure may have been—and they were many—they had one great compensating advantage. Customary holdings could be transferred easily, cheaply, and with certainty, by surrender and admission in the court of the manor. Since there was no doubt that the freehold was in the lord, there was no expensive investigation of titles to eat up the prospective profits of the purchaser, and the Court Rolls offered a record, one is tempted to say a register, of the nature of the interest which a tenant had had in any holding from time immemorial. Of course the adjustment of the respective claims of lords and tenants raised very knotty problems, and these will be examined later. But, as long as they were in abeyance, the fact that peasant holdings could be transferred so readily contributed to the breaking up in the regularity of manorial arrangements, to the passage of land from one family to another, and to the formation of larger properties out of small.[180]

Such petty transactions among the peasantry were not, however, the only way in which substantial peasant properties came into existence. In addition to the

[178] *Merton Documents*, "A table of the Matters, Orders, and Customs Conteyned in Severall Courts of the Manor, 1563": "Daye given to all ye tenants of ye manor to remove and expell their undertenants by Michaelmas that shall be in ye yeare 1563, upon paine of every delinquent forfeiting 20s." "Daye given to the aforesaid tenants having above one customary tenement to be here at ye next court to shew," etc., as above. See the Customary of High Furness quoted below, p. 101; also Hone, *The Manor and Manorial Records*, pp. 177–178, Court Rolls of Payton, Oxon.: "And the aforesaid Laurence Pemerton, in his life time, substituted Walter Milleward as his subtenant ... contrary to the custom of the Manor without license; therefore let him have a talk thereon with the King's officer before the next court."

[179] This is the meaning of entries of two names as "sureties" when land changes hands. See *Crondal Records*, Court Rolls of 1281 and 1282, *passim*.

[180] Since writing the above I have seen that the same view of the advantages of copyhold (the descendant of villein) tenure is taken by Dr. Hasbach, who quotes an eighteenth century writer to the effect that copyhold as compared with freehold land had the advantage of "the greater certainty of its title and the cheapness of its conveyance" (Hasbach, *A History of the English Agricultural Labourer*, pp. 72–73).

transference of land from one tenant to another there were other causes working to produce much the same results. The first was the continuous taking in of plots of waste land by tenants who got permission from the manorial authorities to make encroachments upon it. The second was the abandonment of the system of cultivating the demesne by the labour rents of the tenants. Long before the enclosing of the common waste by lords of manors and farmers had become a very serious grievance—that it was a grievance at an early date is proved by the Statute of Merton[181]—one finds arrangements being made for bringing unused land under cultivation. Sometimes this movement goes on on a very large scale indeed; the Abbey of St. Albans gets a licence from the King in 1347 to "improve its wastes aforesaid and to grant and let them for their true value to whomsoever of their tenants comes to take them"[182] and about the same time 500 acres of waste in the forest of High Peak[183] are let by the Crown to three tenants, much to the disgust of the neighbouring commoners. Usually the encroachments on the waste take place piecemeal. The process by which piece after piece was clipped off it and added to the tenants' holdings is shown very clearly in Rentals and Court Rolls. Occasionally it goes on without sanction; a tenant surreptitiously draws into his holding an extra piece of land for which he pays nothing, and is only found out when he has occupied it for some time. But this is rare, for such encroachments are a source of profit to the lord, both in the payment made for the original permission to make them and in the rent coming from them, and the steward is therefore careful that they should be made through the court and entered in detail on the rolls of the manor. Thus at Ashton-under-Lyne,[184] in 1422, both freeholders and customary tenants had made large intakes of wood and waste and were paying for some of them as much as 13s. 4d. and 10s. The Halmote Court of Colne[185] in 1324 shows many tenants paying a few pence for acres and half acres of waste. At Yateleigh,[186] in 1287, almost every one of the fifty-three customary tenants held, in addition to

---

[181] 1235, c. 4. One may remark, however, that the power which a single freeholder had had before 1235 to prevent the breaking up or enclosure of common pastures, even when he had more than was sufficient for his own beasts, was a genuine hardship for the lord, for other freeholders, and for the customary tenants; see the remarks in Pollock and Maitland (*History of English Law*, vol. i. p. 612).

[182] *Gesta Abbatum Monasterii St. Albani*, vol. iii. pp. 120–121, quoted by Petruschevsky, *op. cit.*, pp. 179–180.

[183] *Victoria County History*, Derbyshire, vol. ii. p. 170.

[184] Glover, *History of Ashton*, p. 355. "Richard the Hunte ... for an intake 3d. ... Thomas of the Leghes for the one half of the intake in Palden Wood 13s. 4d. The same Thomas of the Leghes for an intake besyde Alt Hey 10s."

[185] *Court Rolls of the Lordships, etc., of Thomas, Earl of Lancaster* (Farrer). Halmote of Ightenhill, 1324, January 18: "John de Briddeswail for entry to half an acre of waste in Habrincham, 6d., for the same yearly, 2d." Same court, May 7, 1324.: "Richard le Skinner for entry to 4 acres of waste in Sommerfordrod, 6d., for the same yearly, 6d.," and *passim*. In the north of England there seems to have been very much colonising of the waste, perhaps because original settlements were small. See Turner, *History of Brighouse, Rastrick, and Hipperholme*, pp. 66–67, and *Trans. Rochdale Literary and Philosophical Society*, vol. vii., Rochdale Manor Inquisition.

[186] *Crondal Records* (Balgent), pp. 116–120, *e.g.* "Robert, son of Peter de la Pierke, holds one acre of encroachment land on paying 4d."

his land in the open fields, land taken from the waste amounting in the aggregate to 37 acres, while some possessed no land at all except that which they had thus reclaimed. In the tithing of Aldershot,[187] on the same manor, one tenant held 52 acres in encroachments. At Crokeham[188] another held 63½ acres in addition to the standard half virgate of customary land; another, at Southwood,[189] 16 acres.

The process of nibbling away the waste was, in fact, very general, and was a natural and inevitable one. The lord gained by leasing part of it to be broken up and cultivated, while, so long as sufficient land was left for grazing, the tenants gained by getting land which they could add to their holdings, and on which the growing population could settle. It must be remembered that the area under cultivation was everywhere an island in an ocean of unreclaimed barrenness which cried out for colonists.[190] In the Middle Ages land was abundant and men were scarce; the land wanted the people much more than the people wanted the land. Moreover, with the simple methods of cultivation prevailing, the number of persons which a villein's holding could maintain was strictly limited, and the tendency to "diminishing returns," with the consequent difficulty of maintaining a growing population on the same area, must have come into play very soon and very sharply. Surveyors[191] appreciated this, and pointed out on some manors that unless the tenants' holdings were enlarged they could not make a decent living and, what was more important to the authorities, could not perform the customary services. It is not surprising, therefore, to find that at a comparatively early date the manorial population began to overflow the boundaries of the customary land and to occupy the waste, with the result that the area under cultivation grew, in some cases, enormously.[192] We can hardly be mistaken in supposing that this was

[187] *Ibid.*, pp. 123–127.

[188] *Ibid.*, pp. 131–134. "Richard Wysdon holds half a virgate of land containing 16 acres.... The same holds 63½ acres, which were in his ancient occupation, and were found to be over and above his said virgate, and (included) in many encroachments."

[189] *Ibid.*, pp. 122–123: "William of Southwoode holds 16 acres of encroachments and other detached pieces."

[190] Thorold Rogers (*Agriculture and Prices*, vol. i. p. 34: "Not much less land was regularly under the plough than at present") thinks otherwise. But (i.) modern agriculture has many ways of using land besides keeping it "under the plough"; (ii.) we know that in the eighteenth century large tracts now cultivated were barren heaths, and it is difficult to believe that these had been cultivated in the Middle Ages.

[191] See below, p. 189. The instances there quoted are later than the period with which we are now dealing, but as they mostly come from Northumberland, a very conservative county, they are perhaps to the point.

[192] *e.g.* at South Newton in Wiltshire (see p. 74), tithing of Swanthrop in Crondal, where the area of the tenants' holdings was in 1287 about 360 acres, and in 1567 about 607 acres, and tithing of Crondal, where the area of the tenants' holdings was in 1287 about 181, and in 1567 about 284. But these figures are not altogether satisfactory; and sometimes one finds a reduction, *e.g.* at Dippenhall (from about 287 acres at the earlier date to about 275 at the later date). The plague relieved the pressure of population, and thus removed one incentive for breaking up the waste; on the other hand, it left the survivors much better off, and thus more able to increase the scale of their husbandry. But until we know much more about the growth of population we shall not make much of general comparisons of this kind.

the chief cause of the remarkable difference in the amount of land which strikes one when one compares some of the surveys of later and earlier dates. In any case the result was to increase the opportunities possessed by the more prosperous tenants, who could afford to rent additional land, of adding to their holdings, and thus to produce a growing inequality in the distribution of property among them.

If the instances which have been given above are at all typical of the state of things on many manors, the economic rigidity of rural life in the thirteenth and early fourteenth centuries must have been a good deal less than is often suggested. The legal forms are stiff and unchanging, but the life behind them is fluid, and produces all sorts of new combinations and arrangements which make legal forms a better index of what was a hundred years before than of what at any moment is. In particular one finds considerable movement going on before the Great Plague. The more fully manorial records are explored, the more difficult does it seem to generalise about the effects of that great catastrophe. One cannot say that it was the beginning of the commutation of labour services into rents, for on some manors they were partially commuted before it, and on some they were not entirely commuted till nearly two centuries later. One cannot say that the leasing of the demesne was due to the Plague; for where the labour supply was small, parts of it were leased already,[193] and after the Plague the authorities of different manors met the crisis in different ways, sometimes beginning by letting the demesne only to return later to the older system. It may be suggested, however, that its influence has been somewhat exaggerated by those authorities who would have us regard it as the watershed of economic history. No doubt the Great Plague was the single most important event in the economic history of the fourteenth century, just as the Irish famine of 1846 was the single most important event in the economic history of Ireland in the nineteenth century. But neither the Irish famine nor the Plague had the effect of sweeping economic development on to wholly new lines. What they both did was enormously to accelerate tendencies already at work. The customary tenants were buying and leasing land from each other before the Plague, and before the Plague some lords were leasing out their demesnes, but on a small scale. After the Plague the death of many holders and the poverty of many survivors caused land to come into the market on a vastly greater scale and at a cheaper rate, with the result that the aggregation of holdings, the beginnings of which have been described as above, proceeded with vastly increased rapidity. That this was the case immediately after the Plague is shown by the familiar entries[194] as to the transference of holdings which have lost their cultivators in the Court Rolls. The movement seems to have continued, however, long after the immediate effects of the Plague had passed away, and to have resulted on some manors in the fifteenth

[193] *e.g.* at Hadleigh in 1305 (*Victoria County History*, Suffolk, Unwin's article); at Crondal in 1287 (*Crondal Records*, p. 110); at Ormsby in 1324 (Massingberd, *History of Ormsby*).

[194] *e.g.* Scrope, *Castle Combe*, p. 164. Court Rolls of 1357: "Johannis filius Johannis Payn venit et finem fecit cum domino per 12d. pro ingressu habendo in illo messuagio et virgata terræ quæ Johannis le Parkare quondam tenuit.... Et dictum tenementum concessum est ei ad tam parvam finem eo quod dictum tenementum est ruinosum et decassum; et existebat in manu domini a tempore pestilentiæ pro defectu emptorum." Massingberd, Ingoldmells Court Rolls for years 1349–1352. Gasquet, *The Great Pestilence*. Page, *The End of Villeinage in England*.

century in something which might almost be called free trade in land. One finds a readiness to buy and sell customary holdings which belies the idea of the manor as a rigid organisation in which little room was left for changing contractual arrangements, and one finds also the natural result of the rising commercialisation of land tenure in the grouping of several holdings under one tenant, in the appearance of the practice of some tenants sub-letting lands to others, and in general in the passing of property from the economically weak to the economically strong, which naturally does not go on rapidly till there is a market in which they both can meet.

At the same time by the beginning of the fifteenth century another force of great importance was beginning to operate. The increase in the size of the customary tenants' holdings, and the growth of a class occupying much more land than the ordinary villein tenancy, was brought about not only by encroachment on the waste and the aggregation of holdings, but also by the transference to the tenants of that part of the manorial land which has been the lord's demesne. The process by which the demesne ceased to be cultivated by villein labour, and became frequently an area subject to the more elastic arrangements of leasehold tenure, has been often described, and we shall have to return to it later in speaking of the development of the large capitalist farm. Here it is sufficient to point out that, the abandonment of the primitive system, by which the tenants worked out their rents in labour on the demesne, had two consequences which are of great significance in the development of the villein into the prosperous peasantry of the fifteenth and early sixteenth centuries.

In the first place, it meant that one great force making for equality between the holdings of different tenants was removed. The system which gave each customary tenant on a manor what may be called a standard holding was surely an artificial one, in the sense that it bears the mark of deliberate arrangement, and is not one which would tend to be established by the play of economic forces. As we have seen, economic forces did begin to impair it at an early date. Its persistence is more remarkable than its disappearance, and why had it persisted? Partly, no doubt, because the idea that each full household should be equipped with a standard holding was part of the original organisation of the village community, upon which the feudal superstructure had been imposed, and which it used as a machine for grinding out its revenue. Partly also through the needs of that superstructure itself. As the tenants were the instruments by which the demesne was cultivated, and as the demesne could not be cultivated unless the tenants were adequately equipped with the means of livelihood, the rough equality which existed between their holdings, though arising from the communal arrangement of village life, and not deliberately imposed from above, had, nevertheless, been, in fact, a quite necessary condition for the working of the lord's private estate. A settled relation between holdings and services was a convenience to the manorial authorities, and in this sense the work done on the demesne was a force tending to keep the tenants' holdings fixed, as it were, on a scale which did not easily allow of much variation.[195] When the demesne ceased to be cultivated by labour

[195] The view that the equality of holdings was the creation not of the communal needs of the peasantry but of deliberate arrangement by the authorities, seems to be untenable in face of the evidence of early records showing that freeholders as well as the servile

services, what had been from the point of view of the manorial officers, though not from that of the villagers, the chief practical reason for maintaining equality between the different holdings disappeared, and the inequality which economic forces were tending to produce developed more rapidly.

In the second place, when labour rents were commuted into money, the demesne was often added to the tenants' holdings, with the result of still further destroying their symmetry, by the opportunity which was given to men with money to buy up parcels of land. This movement went on so unobtrusively that its significance is liable to be overlooked. In reality, however, it was a change of very great importance, scarcely less important than the decay of villein services and disabilities which was the other side, the personal as contrasted with the agrarian side, of the same break up of the old system of cultivation. One must remember that the lord's demesne formed a very large part of a great many manors, often no doubt the most fertile and desirable part. One may recall again that there are other European countries in which the sharp distinction between the demesne and the holdings of the peasants was maintained in full mediæval vigour almost to our own day. In Prussia,[196] for example, a Royal Decree, the Decree of 1807, was needed to break it down, and to allow the land held by lords of manors to be bought by the small cultivator. What the partial obliteration of this line meant in fourteenth and fifteenth century England was that a great deal of land, land on which the peasantry, one would suppose, had often turned covetous eyes, was thrown into the market for families who could afford it to buy and lease, that for a century or so after the Plague great estates were being broken up into small, instead of small being consolidated into great, that for a century or so the land market turned in favour of the small man as much as it afterwards turned against him.[197]

Of course the leasing of the demesne was not universal; nor, when it was leased, was it always divided up among the tenants. Often it was transferred *en bloc* to a single farmer, and became the nucleus of the large leasehold farm whose management we shall examine later. Sometimes it was first divided up and later consolidated again, with results disastrous to the interests which had grown up upon it. But the existence in the sixteenth century[198] of many small demesne tenancies is a proof that a common way of treating it was to divide it up among

---

peasantry held roughly equal shares (see Vinogradoff, *Villainage in England*, Essay II., chap. iv. and chap. vi). On the other hand, the apportionment of services to holdings tended to stereotype the existing arrangement. A late example which displays both elements, that of authoritative pressure and that of communal organisation, is supplied by the Customary of High Furness (R.O. Duchy of Lancs. Special Commissions, No. 398): "As heretofore dividing and portioning of tenements hath caused great decay, chiefly of the service due to her Highness for horses, and of her woods, and has been the cause of making a great number of poor people in the lordship, it is now ordered that no one shall divide his Tenement or Tenements among his children, but that the least part shall be of the ancient yearly rent to her Highness of 6s. 8d." See below, p. 101.

[196] Edict of October 9, 1807, Clause 1.

[197] Compare a document, *temp.* Hen. VIII., quoted by Gonner, *Common Land and Enclosure*, p. 155 n., which states that whereas landlords at one time could not find tenants, now the case is altered and tenants want landlords.

[198] For the use of the demesne in the sixteenth century see below, pp. 200–213.

the peasants; and if we cast our eyes back over the records of the fourteenth and fifteenth centuries we can find many examples to show how such a state of things was brought about. Sometimes small plots of the demesne are leased for terms of years. At Tykeford, in 1325,[199] the surveyor found that 48 acres of demesne which were then in the hands of the lords used to be leased to the tenants. The bailiff's accounts of the manor of Amble[200] in Northumberland show that in 1328 "the forlands" were let out to the bondage tenants, and in 1337 four of the latter got leases of from 2 to 4 acres of demesne at Acklington.[201] In 1436 at Ambresbury[202] 2 carucates were leased to various tenants for a term of years, as well as 8 acres of meadow and 400 acres of pasture; and at Winterborne[203] 2 carucates, 6 acres of meadow, and 300 acres of pasture were leased in the same year. But in the fifteenth century the leasing of the demesne was constant, and there is no need to multiply examples which can be found in almost every survey of the period. Where the land was not leased it was quite usual for it to be held by copy. This was a common practice in the fifteenth century in the south-west of England. The surveyor[204] who, in 1568, gave an account of six manors in the Western counties, found that in all of them the Barton or demesne had been split up among the customary tenants for very many years and was held by them as copyholders. The same thing happened on the manors of the Earl of Northumberland, where the tenants' holdings were increased by pieces taken from the lord's demesne and divided equally among them. It happened at South[205] Newton in Wiltshire, where in 1567 a good deal of the Barton land was held by the tenants, who were copyholders, on the same terms as the rest of their customary holdings; at Stovard,[206] and Childhampton,[207] and Estoverton,[208] where the customary tenants held "Bordland." Very probably those pieces of the demesne which on some manors were held by copy of Court Roll, had originally been let on lease in the way described above. The difficulty of distinguishing them was very great, since normally they would lie in the open fields scattered among the strips which formed the customary holdings, in such a way that the movement of a balk obliterated the difference. It is not surprising, therefore, that in spite of the efforts of the lord's officials, they should constantly have lost their identity. The remarkable thing is that they retained it so often, and that surveyors were able to pin down a couple of acres among 30 or 40 others as not being, like the rest, customary land, but as having at one time, perhaps several generations before, been parts of the lord's demesne which it is "good to revyve and keep in memory that it should not hereafter decay, but that at all tymes it may

---

[199] Dugdale, *Monasticon*, vol. v., Survey of Tykeford.

[200] *Northumberland County History*, vol. v., Amble: "4s. 8d. de forlands dimissis diversis tenentibus." "4 acres leased by the Prior for 8 years to Roger at 8d. per acre."

[201] *Ibid.*, vol. v., Acklington.

[202] Hoare, *History of Wiltshire*, Hundred of Ambresbury.

[203] *Ibid.*

[204] Humberstone, *Topographer and Genealogist*, vol. i. p. 43. See below, pp. 208–209.

[205] Roxburghe Club, *Surveys of Lands of William, First Earl of Pembroke* (Straton).

[206] *Ibid.*

[207] *Ibid.*

[208] *Ibid.*

be devyded from the customarye."[209]

With these words, so suggestive of the blurring of lines which in previous ages were sharply drawn, we may pause to consider where we stand. Our argument has aimed at showing the large changes which have taken place in the position of the peasantry as landholders before the agrarian revolution of the sixteenth century begins. We have not been able to give any quantitative measurements of the developments. But we have seen enough to understand the direction in which economic forces are setting. The substitution of hired labour for villein services, and the formation of a middle class of considerable landholders out of the occupiers of virgates and semi-virgates who formed the bulk of the population on most mediæval manors, are changes which have taken place quietly and which have nothing sensational about them. But the growth of relationships based on a cash nexus between individuals, which they both imply, has effected a very real alteration in rural conditions, an alteration which is in a small way like that occurring to-day when the discovery that a quiet village possesses mineral wealth or is a convenient holiday resort puts money into circulation there, causes farming lands to be cut up into plots which are bought by the savings of speculative tradesmen, and adds a new tangle of commercial relationships to the slowly moving economy of village life. Speculation in land on a small scale begins among the more prosperous villeins at an early date, as the inevitable result of an increase in prosperity and of the land hunger of a growing population. It is immensely accelerated through the impetus which the plague, by emptying holdings of their occupants, gives to the formation of something like a land market, and the result is that the holdings of the more fortunate grow and the holdings of the less fortunate diminish. As a consequence, there is in many fifteenth century villages the greatest variety in the economic conditions of the peasantry. Except where commercial forces have been held in check by the remoteness of the township from centres of trade, or where the needs of the manorial authorities oblige them to resist any subdivision of holdings for fear it should lead to the loss of services, the comparative uniformity characteristic of their holdings in the thirteenth century has disappeared, and the equality in poverty of the modern agricultural labourer has not yet taken its place. Though the old Adam of economic enterprise seems to be banished by the insistence of stewards and bailiffs that holdings which are responsible for certain works shall be treated as an indivisible unity, he sneaks back, even in the mediæval manor, in the shape of agreements among the peasantry, agreements which break that unity up by way of exchange, of sale, of leasing, and sub-letting. By the end of the fifteenth century the different elements in rural society are spread, as it were, along a more extended scale, and there is a much wider gap between those who are most, and those who are least, successful.

Taken together these changes mean, on the whole, an upward movement, an increase in the opportunities possessed by the peasantry of advancing themselves by purchasing and leasing land, more mobility, more enterprise, greater scope for the man who has saved money and wishes to invest it. They mean that custom and authority have less influence and that class distinctions based upon tenure

[209] *Topographer and Genealogist*, vol. i., Survey of the Manor of Whitforde in the County of Devon.

are weakened. But the upward curve may turn and descend; for they imply also a tendency towards the dissolution of fixed customary arrangements and of the protection which they offer against revolutionary changes, a tendency which in the future, when great landowners and capitalists turn their attentions to discovering the most profitable methods of farming, may damage the very men who have gained by it in the past. In the next two chapters we shall glance at the first point, and pause at greater length upon the second: first, the economic condition of the mass of the peasantry before the great agrarian movements of the sixteenth century begin; secondly, the signs of coming change which may react to their disadvantage. We shall try to maintain the standpoint of an observer in the early years of the sixteenth century. But economic periods overlap, and Northumberland is still in the Middle Ages when Middlesex is in the eighteenth century. So we shall not hesitate to use evidence drawn from sources that are in point of time far apart.

# CHAPTER III

## THE PEASANTRY (CONTINUED)

### *(d) The Economic Environment of the Small Cultivator*

It was the argument of the previous chapter that the fourteenth and fifteenth centuries saw the emergence from the mass of manorial tenants of a class of wealthy peasants who bought and leased their neighbours' lands, added to their property parcels taken from the waste and demesne, and by these means built up estates far exceeding in size the normal villein holding. The change from labour services to money rents left the peasantry with time for the management of larger holdings, and the spread of a money economy increased their means of acquiring them. Cheap land and easy transfer favour the movement of property from one man to another. In the manorial courts transfer was easy, and, especially after the Great Plague, land was cheap. It is not necessary to take sides in the much debated question of the economic conditions of the fifteenth century, in order to hold that, on the whole, such changes made the greater part of it a period of increasing prosperity among the small cultivators. To support this view one could quote Fortescue's[210] proud description of the well-being of the common people. One could point out that in the dark days in the middle of the sixteenth century the peasants themselves looked back to the social conditions of the reign of Henry VII.[211] as a kind of golden age, and clamoured for their restoration. One could cite a good many examples pointing to an upward movement. Large estates are left at death by men who are legally villeins. Villeins, especially in the eastern counties, buy up freehold land and found considerable properties. A bond tenant in Lincolnshire marries into a knight's family. Bond tenants are found leasing the manorial demesne in one block and farming estates of several hundred acres. Nor must we forget that the peasants of the sixteenth century are often very substantial people, and that even when the taint of personal villeinage is still upon them.

But isolated instances of this kind, suggestive though they are, are not likely to carry conviction unless they agree with what we know of the general economic

[210] Fortescue on the Governance of England (Plummer), chapter xii.: "But oure commons be riche, and therefore thai give to thair kynge, at somme times quinsimes and dessimes, and ofte tymes other grate subsidies."

[211] Russell, *Ket's Rebellion in Norfolk*, p. 48 foll.; see passage quoted below, pp. 335–337. For the sentences immediately following, see Scrope, *History of the Manor and Barony of Castle Combe*, p. 233: "A serf ... is said to have left at his death in 1435 chattels estimated at 3000 marks or £2000." Massingberd, Ingoldmells Court Rolls, int. xxix.; Davenport, *History of a Norfolk Manor*, p. 53.

situation. Economists who live after the days of Samuel Smiles will hesitate before they base optimistic conclusions as to the conditions of any class on cases of good fortune among individual members of it. We should be false to the spirit of our period if we did not recognise that the economic ideal of most men, an ideal often implied though not often formulated, was less the opening of avenues to enterprise than the maintenance of groups and communities at their customary level of prosperity. We shall have hereafter to speak of the changes which overtook the English social system in the course of the sixteenth century, in so far as they were connected with changes in the methods of agriculture and of land tenure. Before we do so we may pause for a moment to look at the village of the later Middle Ages as a social and economic unit.

The foundation of its whole life is the possession by the majority of households of holdings of land. Land is so widely distributed that the household, all of whose members are entirely dependent for their living upon work for wages, is the exception. Though this cannot be statistically proved, it is rendered almost certain by several converging lines of evidence. Turn first to the table on pp. 64 and 65, which sets out the acreage of the customary tenants' holdings. It will be seen that, when all the counties represented are grouped together, the tenants who have only cottages form less than one-tenth of the total number. In East Anglia and in Lancashire the proportion, it is true, is considerably higher; but these counties are exceptions to the general rule, and the cottagers usually have gardens, which, if they do not amount to the minimum of four acres laid down by the Act of 1589, are nevertheless not infrequently of one or two acres in extent. If we may trust these figures, the typical family has a small holding of from two and a half to fifteen acres. Our second line of evidence quite falls in with this conclusion. It is clear from the tone of legislation that the class of workers who depend solely on a contract of service is in sixteenth century England not very large. Elizabethan[212] legislation provides expressly for the needs of farmers by empowering Justices of the Peace to apprentice unoccupied youths to husbandry, and to set the unemployed to work in the fields. Even in the middle of the seventeenth[213] century, when a strong movement has been at work for one hundred and fifty years in the opposite direction, there are complaints from pamphleteers that men who should work as wage-labourers cling to the soil, and in the naughtiness of their hearts prefer independence as squatters to employment by a master. Such comments throw a flash

---

[212] Statute of Artificers, 5 Eliz. c. 4.

[213] See below, pp. 277–279, and *Hist. MSS. Com.*, Cd. 784, pp. 322–323. Presentment by the grand jury, Worcestershire, 1661, April 23: "We desire that servants' wages may be rated according to the statute, for we find the unreasonableness of servants' wages a great grievance, so that the servants are grown so proud and idle that the master cannot be known from the servant except it be because the servant wears better clothes than his master. We desire that the statute for setting poor men's children to apprenticeship be more duly observed, for we find the usual course is that if any are apprenticed it is to some paltry trade, and when they have served their apprenticeship they are not able to live by their trades, whereby not being bred to labour they are not fit for husbandry. We therefore desire that such children may be set to husbandry for the benefit of tillage and the good of the Commonwealth." See also Britannia Languens (1680) for remarks on the scarcity of labour even at the end of the seventeenth century.

of light on the way in which the peasants regard the alternatives of wage labour and landholding. Sometimes they themselves give us a glimpse into their mind on the matter. They tell us how they face that most fundamental of economic problems, the Achilles' heel of modern civilisation, the problem of so arranging their little societies that as many persons as possible may enter life with some material equipment for self-maintenance in addition to their personal strength and skill. Here is an extract from a customary of the Lancashire manor of High Furness[214] drawn up in the reign of Elizabeth:—

"As heretofore deviding and porcioning of tenements hath caused great decay, chiefly of the service due to her Highness for horses and of her woods, and has been the cause of making a great number of poor people in the lordship, it is now ordered that no one shall devide his tenement or tenements among his children, but that the least part shall be of ancient yearly rent to her Highness of 6s. 8d., and that before every such division there shall be several houses and ousettes for every part of such tenement."

This seems a hard rule. Will it not result in the creation of a body of propertyless labourers employed by a small village aristocracy? That danger is appreciated, and is dealt with in the clauses which follow:—

"If any customary tenant die seized of a customary tenement, having no son but a daughter, or daughters, then the eldest daughter being preferred in marriage shall have the tenement as his next heir, and she shall pay to her younger sister, if she have but one sister, 20 years ancient rent, as is answered to her Majesty; and if she have more than one sister she shall pay 40 years ancient rent to be equally divided among them....

"For the avoiding of great trouble in the agreement with younger brothers, it is now ordered that the eldest son shall pay to his brothers in the form following:—If there is but one brother, 12 years ancient rent; if there are two brothers, 16 years ancient rent to be equally divided.

"If there be three or more, 20 years ancient rent to be equally divided.

"Whereas great inconvenience has grown by certain persons that at the marriage of son or daughter have promised their tenement to the same son or daughter and their heirs, according to the custom of the manor, and afterwards put the tenement away to another person; it is ordered that whatever tenements a tenant shall promise to the son or daughter being his sole heir apparent at the time of his or her marriage, the same ought to come to them according to the same covenant, which ought to be showed at the next court."

The motive of the first rule is a mixed one. Its object is partly to obviate the risk that the Crown, which is lord, of the manor, may lose its services if holdings are too much subdivided, partly to prevent the appearance of a class which has too little land for a living. The motive of the other rules is to ensure that the custom of primogeniture, which obtains among the customary tenants on this manor, shall not result in the creation of a propertyless proletariat. Holdings are not to be divided. But the payment to other members of the family of a sum ranging from

[214] R.O. Duchy of Lancaster, Special Commissions, No. 398.

about one-half to more than the whole of their capital value is made a charge upon them, and with that money they can purchase land elsewhere, or take, like the French peasant girl, a considerable *dot* to their husbands. Sue,[215] the daughter of Old Carter, the rich yeoman, whose security for the marriage-portion "shall be present payment, because Bonds and Bills are but Tarriers to catch fools, and keep lazy knaves busy," was a match for whom gentlemen's sons were willing enough to compete.

These groups of from ten to a hundred households which constitute the ordinary village of southern and middle England, form small democracies of property holders, who are of course under the authority of a lord, but whose subjection does not prevent them from exercising considerable control over the management of their own economic affairs, nor impose any effective bar on those individuals who have the means and capacity to advance themselves. We can watch them arranging[216] the course of agriculture, deciding when the pastures at Wolsyke and Willoughbybroke are to be "broken," imposing fines on those who encroach on the several pasture land, throwing open the Pesefield on Holy Thursday to the village horses, shutting them out of Street headlands for fear of the "stroyinge of Korn," making charitable provision for gleaners who cannot work, punishing those who ought to work but in their depravity would rather glean. We can observe how the wide distribution of land gives an opportunity to a humble family to better itself by judicious husbandry and well-calculated purchases. True, the peasant's land is no longer held in approximately equal shares as generally as it had been in the thirteenth century. The growth of a money economy, the withdrawal of the levelling pressure of villeinage, the growth of population, has in the more progressive parts of the country left a gap into which individualising commercial forces wind themselves in the way which has already been described. But these changes are important mainly as precursors of more extensive innovations. As yet they have done little more than make tiny breaches in the wall of custom. They have enabled individuals to rise from the general level into positions of comparative affluence. They have not proceeded so far as to enable the successful to exercise a decisive direction over the economic affairs of their fellows. Though Northumberland is exceptional in the way in which down to the very end of the sixteenth century it preserves its system of standardised holdings, it is none the less true that all the petty land speculation, whose operations we have traced above, has not the effect of producing any very large changes in the distribution of property. If, when compared with its condition two hundred years before, the village of our period shows remarkable irregularity, it offers precisely an opposite aspect to the observer who compares it as it is then with its condition two hundred years later. The gaps which have appeared between the holdings mark the disintegrating influence of economic enterprise; but they are gaps which enterprise can span, and the graduation of holdings from the two or three acres of the humblest to the fifty or sixty acres of the most prosperous, together with the abundance of unoccupied land, supplies a kind of staircase along which in the country the younger

---

[215] See Dekker's *The Witch of Edmonton*. I have ventured to assume that in this play "yeoman" is used in its wide non-technical sense.

[216] See *e.g. Hist. MSS. Com.,* Cd. 5567, pp. 106–107, and below, pp. 159–162.

son can travel from the position of a labourer to that of a small holder, as he does in the towns from apprentice to master-craftsman. From this point of view the characteristic *morcellement* of holdings, so bitterly denounced by economists who, like Arthur Young, approached the problem from the point of view of the large farmer, was a positive advantage. It meant that land could be bought and sold, as it were, retail. It meant that the labourer could begin with one strip of land of half an acre, and add other strips to it as he worked his way up. It meant that even the humblest peasant usually had some live-stock of his own; for even the smallest customary holding usually carried with it rights of common. Such conditions are, of course, no safeguard against poverty. No doubt there were plenty of people like Widow Quin, whose "leaky thatch is growing more pasture for her buck goat than her square of fields."[217] But they are a safeguard against destitution, and indeed against any complete loss of independence.

Let us turn to a part of England where something like the open field system survives to this day, and ask the inhabitants what they think of it. In the so-called Isle of Axholme there are still common fields with intermixed strips. Here is the evidence[218] which a body of labourers there sent into a Select Committee of Parliament in 1899: "We, the undersigned, being agricultural labourers at Epworth, are in occupation of allotments or small holdings, varying from two roods to three acres, and willingly testify to the great benefit we find from our holdings. Where we have sufficient quantity of land to grow two roods each of wheat, barley, and potatoes, we have bread, beans, and potatoes for a great part of the year, enabling us to face a long winter without the dread of hunger or pauperism staring us in the face." One of the tests by which the economic prosperity of a community may be measured is its success in preventing the appearance of a residual population, which cannot fit itself into the moving mechanism of industry without ceaseless friction and maladjustments. In most villages before extensive evictions begin that mechanism moves very slowly; property is widely diffused, and the residuum must have been small. That there was often distress through bad harvests and pestilence is certain. But was there much of the economic helplessness, more terrible than physical distress itself, which is the normal lot of most of the propertyless wage-earners of the modern world? We hesitate to say. Hesitation on such a point may perhaps be counted to our peasants for righteousness.[219]

---

[217] Synge, *The Playboy of the Western World.*

[218] Quoted by Slater, *The English Peasantry and the Enclosure of Common Fields*, pp. 58–59. He remarks "a labourer ... begins with one 'land,' then takes a second, a third, and so on," and quotes Mr. Haggard's statement that the "Isle of Axholme ... is one of the few places ... in England ... truly prosperous in an agricultural sense."

[219] Customs like those of High Furness, together with the complaints as to the scarcity of agricultural labour, make one reflect on a fundamental question of economics, viz., the average age of marriage and its relation to the distribution of property and organisation of industry. It is well known that the age of marriage is influenced by (among other things) the age at which maximum earning power begins, *e.g.* to-day it is lower for the unskilled labourer than for the artisan, for the former reaches his prime earlier than the latter; lower for the artisan than for the professional man, because the latter takes longer than the former in getting together a practice or rising from a low initial salary. The difference is not primarily due to differences of thrift or foresight as between different classes, but to the fact

that the deferring of marriage, which is prudent in (say) a lawyer, who does not reach his full earning power till thirty-five or later, is imprudent in (say) an engineer who has all the experience he needs at twenty-six or twenty-seven, and still more imprudent in the labourer, who reaches his full earning power at twenty-one or twenty-two, and in whom it falls off rapidly after he has passed the prime of life. When a large number of agricultural and industrial workers (in the sixteenth century probably a majority) were small landholders or small masters, did the fact that they had to wait for the death of a parent to succeed to their holding, or (in towns) for the permission of a guild to set up shop (*i.e.* to reach their maximum earning powers) tend to defer the age of marriage? If the possibility of this being the case is conceded, ought we to connect the slow growth of population between 1377 and 1500 (on which all historians seem to be agreed) with the wide distribution of property, and ought we to think of the considerable increase in the landless proletariate which took place in the sixteenth and seventeenth centuries as tending in the opposite direction? In the absence of statistics we cannot answer these questions. But I am inclined to argue that they are at any rate worth investigation. (i) Contemporary opinion shows that in the eyes of sixteenth century writers the problem of population was a problem of underpopulation. The prevalent fear is "lack of men" for military purposes. Starkey's Dialogue speaks of it as "a consumption of the body politic," and suggests as remedies to allow priests to marry, to forbid gentlemen to employ more serving men than they are able to "set forward" to matrimony (on the ground that "men whych in service spend theyr lyfe never fynd means to marry"), to endow with a house and a portion of waste land at a nominal rent persons who marry, to exempt from taxation all persons who have five children and less than a hundred marks in goods, to tax bachelors 1s. in the pound, and give the proceeds to "them which have more children than they be wel abul to nurysch, and partely to the dote of poor damosellys and vyrgins" (Part II. p. 8). Hales (p. lv. of Miss Lamond's introduction to *Commonweal of England*) speaks of depopulation in a similar strain, as also does Harrison forty years later. There are some complaints as to excess of population in 1620 (see below, pp. 278–279), but these do not become general till the very end of the seventeenth century (see Defoe, *Giving alms no charity*). (ii) The position of a son who acquires a holding when his parent dies is analogous to that of an apprentice who cannot set up as a master till given permission by the proper authorities. It is quite plain that in the eyes of the ordinary man in the sixteenth century one of the advantages of a system of compulsory apprenticeship was that it prevented youths marrying at a very early age. *E.g.* an Act (2 & 3 Philip and Mary) forbids the admitting of any one to the freedom of the city of London before the age of twenty-four, and enacts that apprentices are not to be taken so young that they will come out of their time before they are twenty-four. The reason alleged for this rule is the distress in the city of which "one of the chief occasions is by reason of the overhasty marriages and over soon setting up of householdes by the young folke of the city ... be they never so young and unskilful." A petition of weavers states (*Hist. MSS. Com.*, C.D. 784, p. 114): "Whereas by the former good laws of their trade no one could exercise the same until he had served an apprenticeship for seven years and attained the age of twenty-four, now in these disordered times many apprentices having forsaken parents and masters ... refuse to serve out their time, but before they are eighteen or twenty years old betake themselves to marriage." One may contrast the extraordinary reduction in the age of marriage of the people of Lancashire brought about by the early factory system, with its armies of operatives who had nothing to look forward to but the wages earned immediately on reaching maturity (Gaskell, *Artisans and Machinery*, 1836, and *The Manufacturing Population of Great Britain*, 1833), and compare the results usually ascribed to the wide distribution of landed property in France. See also the remarks of Slater on the effect of the eighteenth century enclosing (*The English Peasantry and the Enclosure of the Common Fields*, p. 256), and Hasbach, *History of the English Agricultural Labourer*, pp. 120 n. 138–139, 178. Young ascribed "a great multiplication of births" to

In the second place, let us examine the use which the peasants make of their holdings. Modern writers tell us that among the conditions necessary to the prosperity of a class of small holders the most important are a wise choice of the kind of farming to be pursued, a sound organisation of credit, cheap marketing, and rural bye-employments to back agriculture. Modern writers who are not English would probably add a tariff on imported agricultural produce. In our period the type of cultivation pursued by the large farmer was undergoing rapid changes. That of the peasantry was hardly a matter of choice. It was dictated by the necessity, under which most villages still lay, of being largely self-supporting in the matter of corn supplies, a necessity recognised and crystallised in the customary routine of village husbandry. The preponderance of arable farming among the peasantry is illustrated by the table[220] on page 107, which should be contrasted with that given on pages 225–226.

The figures in this table do not pretend to complete accuracy. But they indicate the distribution of land between different uses with sufficient correctness to show the sort of agriculture followed by the small holder of our period. They prove unmistakably that his standby was the grain crops grown on the open fields.[221] Students of rural conditions will be quick to recognise the contrast which the picture offers to the economy of the modern small holder. In our own day the breaking up of large farms into smaller tenancies has proceeded furthest in those parts of the country which are most suitable for pasture. The occupier of a holding of less than 70 or 80 acres usually relies mainly on stock farming in one form or another, and on the growing of vegetables and fruit. Corn-growing he leaves to much larger men, and, when he does grow grain, he does so mainly to provide fodder and straw for his beasts. In the sixteenth century almost exactly the opposite was the case. In so far as the large farmer with 200 or 300 acres can be said to have had a specialty, it was not corn-growing but sheep and cattle grazing. The small man relied mainly, though not entirely, upon tillage, and though, even in his case, pasture farming assumed increased importance as the century went on, grazing was chiefly a supplement to arable farming. To this statement there are of course certain exceptions. Though villages where the customary tenants hold more pasture than arable are rare, they are not unknown, and occasionally one finds one

---

the fact that "the labourer has no advancement to hope" (*Suffolk*, 1797, p. 260); Duncombe, "The practice of consolidating farms ... tends to licentiousness of manners" (*Herefordshire*, p. 33). A witness before the Select Committee on Emigration, 1827, stated, "The labourers no longer live in farm houses as they used to do, where they were better fed and had more comforts than they now get in a cottage, in consequence there was not the same inducement to early marriage" (*qu.* 3882). In the absence of direct statistical evidence all we can say is (i) that when persons look forward to entering on property or setting up as small masters their point of maximum earning power is later than it is when they can earn the standard rate of the trade at twenty-two or twenty-three; therefore (ii) that the average age of marriage is likely to be higher in a society composed largely of small property owners than in one composed largely of a propertyless proletariate.

[220] See Appendix II.

[221] It must be remembered, however, that there was pasture on the one field which every year lay fallow, and that the amount of this does not appear in the figures given below.

where large numbers of tenants of the most diverse economic conditions, with pasture holdings ranging from 6 to 100 acres, have no arable at all. Sometimes such an arrangement is to be accounted for by the fact that a part of the demesne lands of the manor, which happens not to be suitable for tillage, has been divided up among the population of younger sons and labourers who have no holdings in the open fields. In the neighbourhood of considerable towns, again, there was a market[222] for vegetables and dairy produce which gave an impetus to this side of agriculture, and the home counties poured butter and cheese, fowls, eggs, and fruit into London, as France and the Channel Islands do at the present day. Still, to speak broadly, the small holder of the sixteenth century, unlike the small holder of the twentieth, was before all things interested in arable farming, and interested in rights of pasture chiefly as a necessary adjunct to it.

**TABLE V**

| Manor (excluding houses, orchards, garths, &c.). | Total Area. | | | Arable. | | | Meadow. | | | Pasture. | | |
|---|---|---|---|---|---|---|---|---|---|---|---|---|
| | ac. | ro. | po. | ac. | ro. | po. | ac. | ro. | po. | ac. | ro. | po. |
| Four in Northumberland and one in Lancashire | 1730 | 3 | 13¼ | 1533 | 2 | 32¾ | 98 | 1 | 6⅛ | 98 | 3 | 14 |
| Seven in Wiltshire and one in Dorset | 3963 | 3 | 0 | 3636 | 3 | 0 | 124 | 3 | 32¾ | 202 (in close plus considerable rights of pasture not expressed in acres). | | |
| Four in Midlands (Bedford, Leicester, Northants, Stafford) | 2092 | 3 | 2 | 1670 | 2 | 17 | 167 | 3 | 32 | 254 | 0 | 33 |

Corn-growing in England has been for the last hundred years a branch of farming so completely surrendered to the large capitalist, that it is not easy to realise a state of things in which the typical corn-grower was a man with less than 60 acres, and a man who could make a good living from a holding of that size. To understand the economics of his position we must think away the conditions which have in the last century made it intolerable. Or rather we must think away all except one. That one was the perennial problem of agricultural credit. In this matter, certainly, the poorer among the peasantry suffered as their successors all over the

[222] Camden Society, Norden, Speculum Britanniæ, Part I., Intro.: "And these commonly are so furnished with kyne that their wives twice or thrice a week conveyeth to London mylke and butter, cheese, apples, pears, frutmentye, hens and chickens, baken, and other country drugs ... and this yieldeth them a large comfort and relief."

world suffer to-day. They were apt to be in the grip of the moneylender. Cheap land, as the modern colonist knows, is of little avail to the man who has not the capital needed to stock it, and to carry over the interval between harvest and harvest, when his receipts fall off but his expenses continue. In the endless arguments which took place on the ethics of moneylending at a later date, it was a common complaint that village financiers drove a hard bargain with the peasants whom misfortune compelled to resort to them. In a backward village the only man with capital to lend might be the local corn-dealer, brewer, or maltster, the large farmer who held the lord's demesne, or the lord of the manor himself and his agent. Like an American farmer in the grip of an "elevator," the peasant who wanted money for his crops had often to sell them to a dealer[223] who gave a ridiculously low price for them, and then made an enormous profit by holding them till the price of corn rose, or by sending them to a market where there was a scarcity. Lords[224] of manors, it was said, helped their tenants out of temporary difficulties by advancing them small sums, and then used their advantage to screw extra labour on the demesne out of them. Manor courts[225] in the Middle Ages had fined villagers for usury, but one may suspect that these were capitalists too potent for them to control, and one does not wonder at the headshakings of the prudent Fitzherbert over the man whose method of farming compels him to be a borrower. The form which charity and co-operative effort took points in the same direction. Hospitals[226] and monasteries advance money to buy seed. Well-to-do men aid their relatives by stocking their farms for them. Gilds[227] make loans of cattle and sheep, and the last legacy of a philanthropic parson to his parishioners is money with which to buy a cow for the poor. How far the charitable and corporate organisation of loans succeeded in keeping the small cultivator out of the clutches of the usurer, and how far the dissolution of the monasteries and the confiscation of part of the Gild lands deteriorated their condition by placing them more at his mercy, are questions which deserve consideration but which we have not sufficient evidence to answer.[228] In forming any estimate, however, of rural conditions, the hand to

[223] See *The Death of Usury or the Disgrace of Usurers*, 1594: "It is a common practice in this country, if a poore man come to borrow money of a maltster, he will not lend any, but tells him, if he will sell some barley, he will give him after the order of fore-hand buyers; the man being driven by distresse sells his corn far under foote, that when it comes to be delivered he loses halfe in halfe, oftentimes double the value. I have heard many of these fore-hand sellers say that they had rather allow after 20 pounds in the hundred for money, than to sell their fore-hand bargaines of corn. These are most extreme usurers."

[224] *A Discourse upon Usurie*, by Thomas Wilson, 1584: "A lord doth lend his tenants money, with this condition that they shall plough his land, whether doth he commit usurie or no? I do answer that if he does not pay them for their labour, but will take the benefit of their labour for the use of his money, he is an usurer."

[225] *Hist. MSS. Com.*, Cd. 2319, p. 27: "Juetta ... is a usuress, and sells at a dearer rate for accommodation."

[226] *Hist. MSS. Com.*, Cd. 7881, p. 129, St. Saviour's Hospital gives "20d to a poor man to buy seed for his land."

[227] *Victoria County History*, Suffolk, "Social and Economic History": "The gild let out in one year 8 cows and 4 neats at 19d. each." For the parson's cow, see *Hist. MSS. Com.*, Cd. 784, p. 46.

[228] On the subject of the monasteries see Gasquet, *Henry VIII. and the English Monas-*

mouth economy of the poorer peasants, and their consequent helplessness in the face of any unexpected catastrophe, such as an unusually bad harvest, a cattle plague, and (in the fifteenth century) the destruction of crops by civil disturbances, must not be forgotten. In that age less capital was needed to stock a holding than in our own, but it was scraped together with even greater difficulty. On the very eve of the dissolution of the monasteries there were some remote manors where "Money was so scantie that coigned leather went bargaining between man and man,"[229] and where corn rents were substituted for money because the tenants had no money in which rent could be paid.

On the other hand, before the great agrarian changes of the sixteenth century began, and in those parts of the country which were least affected by them, the economic environment was in other respects favourable to the class of which we have been speaking. As far as corn-growing is concerned, *petite culture* flourishes most readily when the methods of production are primitive and trade little developed. It is not necessary to point out that, in the sphere of production, the conditions which have given its present tremendous advantage to large-scale corn-growing are the fruit of the last century, and that in our period there were neither machinery nor expensive manures to require the outlay of large capital, and to make arable farming almost a branch of factory industry. Moreover, there is reason to believe that the growth of prosperity among the peasants had been accompanied by an improvement in the technique of cultivation. Not to mention the part which they took in enclosures, of which we shall speak later, there were, at any rate by the beginning of the seventeenth century, certain exceptional parts of the country where it was said[230] that in good years from thirty-two to eighty bushels of grain were raised to an acre, instead of the ten which Walter of Henley had thought a fair return in the thirteenth. We may believe this or not as we like; probably we should discount it by at least one-half. But even the average peasant, who could not possibly make his land perform these prodigies, was buttressed by the natural protection of unpassable roads, which tended to make every village, even almost every landholding family, more or less self-sufficing in the matter of food supplies. A highly organised corn trade is as unfavourable to the existence of small corn-growers as a wide market is to the small master-craftsman, because it sets a premium upon the qualities needed for business management—qualities often quite different from those needed for effective farming—and thus (in the absence

---

*teries*, chap. xxii., and *passim*.

[229] For reference see below, p. 198, n. 2.

[230] Norden, *The Surveyor's Dialogue*. He is speaking of parts of Somersetshire. "Now I say if this sweet country of Tandeane and the western part of Somersetshire be not degenerated, surely, as their land is fruitful by nature, so doe they their best by art and industrie ... they take extraordinary pains in soyling, plowing, and dressing their land.... After the plough there goeth some 3 or 4 with mattocks to break the clods ... they have sometimes and in some places foure, five, six, eight, yea tenne quarters in an ordinary acre." For Walter of Henley's figures see Maitland, *Domesday Book and Beyond*, pp. 437–438. Gregory King at the end of the seventeenth century estimated the average yield "in a year of moderate plenty" at a little more than 11 bushels (Rogers, *History of Agriculture and Prices*, vol. v. pp. 92 and 783). I quote Norden not as giving what was general, but to show what it was thought could be done.

of co-operation) plays into the hands of the capitalist, who buys and sells in bulk and can pick his market. To the mass of the peasantry in our period the commercial side of agriculture offered no problem, because for the mass of the peasantry it did not exist. The wealthier among them, it is true, did grow corn for the market, and sent their supplies far afield through the hands of middlemen, much further sometimes, if we may believe contemporaries, than Customs Officials should have allowed. In certain parts of England rudimentary industrial specialisation had made a regular corn trade a necessity. In Norfolk,[231] for example, where manufactures and agriculture had drawn apart to an extent unknown elsewhere, a rough local division of labour was concentrating the woollen industry in that part of the country most suitable for grazing, and was bringing together a huge population of wage-earners, who depended for their food supplies on the grain produced by the "tilth masters" in "the champion part of the country," and whose needs baffled the traditional policy of trying to prevent corners by checking the transport of corn. But down to the very end of the eighteenth century, and still more under the Tudors, there was a large body of small landholders who pursued their way undisturbed by market fluctuations because they grew wheat almost entirely for subsistence. To a foreign observer[232] English agriculture in the reign of Henry VII. seemed "not to be practised beyond what is required for the consumption of the people." Between the two extremes of capitalist farmer and hired labourer, the poles between which the needle of the Government's policy as to prices uneasily oscillates, there stands the man whose family consumes the product of his land, and who rarely puts his small supplies on the market, because, if he tries to do so, "he loseth[233] the labours of himself, his horse and carte, and husbandry at home," and "is in hazard to pay deare for a place to chamber it till the next market day." Such a man, if entirely occupied in tillage, did little more than supply the wants of his own household; if a sheep farmer as well, he worked up the wool in his own home in the manner enjoined on thrifty housewives by Fitzherbert. From the point of view of national welfare his security was purchased by the distress in which the difficulty of moving corn supplies involved the wage-earner. The constant local famines of the sixteenth and seventeenth centuries should remind us that the more self-sufficing a country's agricultural economy, the narrower the margin there is likely to be between the landless classes and starvation. But with them for the present we are not concerned, and if we confine our attention to the landholding peasantry we can see that to them the backwardness of trade was a positive advantage. The risk of spoiling good farming by ineffective marketing was not one which faced the small holders of our period.

Moreover, in estimating the causes which in the fifteenth century favoured a growth in their prosperity, we should not overlook that it was a period in which commercial policy encouraged the corn-grower. In the series of compromises which were struck between the interests of the farmer and those of the consumer the scale during the greater part of it was tilted in the direction of the former, and when success had caused his holding to grow to a size which made trade in

---

[231] *Original Papers of the Norfolk and Norwich Archæological Society*, 1907.
[232] Camden Society, 1857, *An Italian Narration of England*.
[233] *Original Papers of the Norfolk and Norwich Archæological Society*, 1907.

grain inevitable, he dealt in a market which the Government tried to turn in his favour. That section of the industry which supplied the market obviously gained by freedom of export and by import duties upon foreign wheat, though the fact that England was largely a corn exporting country made the latter less important than the former. From 1437 to 1491 free export of wheat was permitted, subject to the obligation to obtain an export licence when prices in the home market rose above a certain point. In 1463 the same policy was carried furthur, and an Act was passed restricting its importation. Such a commercial[234] policy was no doubt adopted mainly in the interests of the great landed proprietors. But that the prosperity of the small cultivators was to some extent bound up with the Government's encouragement of corn-growing can hardly be doubted. Competent observers in the sixteenth century gave its abandonment by the Tudors as one cause of the subsequent decline in the condition of the peasantry, and a return to it as one remedy for their distress.

If the peasantry were favoured in the fifteenth century by a state of things in which the small corn-grower's position was still unshaken, did they not also gain by the beginnings of industrial expansion and by the pasture farming that accompanied it? That a man who was mainly dependent upon tillage might also be a grazier upon a considerable scale, is shown by the following table of the animals kept by the customary tenants on six[235] manors in the south of England.

| I. | II. | III. | IV. |
|---|---|---|---|
| Manors. | Customary Tenants. | Sheep kept by Customary Tenants | Other Beasts (minimum) |
| 6 | 112 | 7440 | 793 |

One must not, of course, forget that a certain number of beasts were indispensable to arable farming. Perhaps one-third or one-half the cattle in column IV. should be written off as simply part of the corn-grower's necessary equipment. The sixteenth century small holder, who keeps plough beasts, is no more a grazier on that account than his twentieth century successor, who uses his grain for fodder, is a corn-grower. But, when this has been remembered, we may perhaps allow these figures to remind us that in the agriculture even of the small man there was room for considerable diversity, and that in the fifteenth and sixteenth centuries it was probably much more diversified than it had been two centuries before. So much is said in the writings of our period of the harm done by the great grazier, that we perhaps do not always sufficiently realise that the customary tenants both then and long before were often themselves graziers on a considerable scale. They raise stock, and are interested in the woollen trade as well as in the corn-growing. Ultimately, when time enough had elapsed for the profitableness of sheep farming to supply lords of manors with a motive for clearing away interests which interfered with the formation of sheep runs, the movement for laying

[234] See below, p. 197.

[235] Roxburghe Club, *Surveys of Manors of William, First Earl of Pembroke; cf.* R.O. *Land Rev. Misc. Bks.*, 182, fol. 1, Rental of the late Priory of Launde (Leicestershire, 1539), where there are tenants paying for common pasture for about 430 sheep.

down land to pasture did result in evictions and rack-renting. But, looking at the fifteenth century as a whole, may we not say with some confidence that the growth of the woollen industry must have brought increasing prosperity to many villages? Though it is not till almost the last decade that complaints of enclosing become sufficiently clamorous to attract the attention of the Government, the spread of woollen manufacturers into rural districts was going quietly on throughout the whole century, and benefited the peasants both by the lucrative bye-employment which they offered to both sexes, and by the alternative to arable farming which the demand for wool supplied in the shape of sheep-grazing. The large number of sheep kept by the customary tenants of many manors in the south of England, and the increase in the complaints as to the over-stocking of commons contained in the Court Rolls of the fifteenth century, show that they were not slow to seize the opportunity, and that the great pasture farms, which aroused the indignation of More and Latimer, had their precedent in the small flocks of thirty or forty sheep which had long been run by the peasantry upon the common wastes or pastures. It would seem that, as so often happens, the new departure was first made on a small scale by small men, and chat it was not until some time had elapsed that its wholesale adoption by large capitalists plunged them in distress. The movement towards pasture-farming as a special branch of agriculture is one that proceeds gradually for a hundred years, before the demand for wool becomes sufficient to produce the body of capitalist graziers whose interests come into sharp collision with those of the peasantry.

But after all, the profits arising from favourable economic circumstances may be of very little advantage to the mass of cultivators. They may simply be handed on to the landlord in the shape of increased rents. At a time when, both in Ireland and Scotland, rents are being fixed by public tribunals, we are not likely to forget that the profitableness of agriculture has no necessary connection with the prosperity of tenants. Trade may be increasing, and the return from the land may be growing, and yet those things may profit the farmers and peasants very little, unless they have some security that they will not see them drained away in increased payments for their land. It is important, therefore, to consider how far rents were competitive and how far they were customary, how far the tenants held the surplus due to economic progress, and how far it passed to the landlord.

Some light is thrown on the general situation by the following table[236]:—

**TABLE VI**

| Manor. | Rents. | | | | | | | | | | | |
|---|---|---|---|---|---|---|---|---|---|---|---|---|
| | 1295–1308 | | | | | | | | | 1568 | | |
| 1. South Newton. | £13 | 19 | 3½ | | | | | | | £14 | 4 | 8 |
| | 1347 | | | 1421 | | | 1485 | | | 1628 | | |
| 2. Ingoldmells | £61 | 9 | 4 | £71 | 10 | 3 | £72 | 6 | 8 | £73 | 17 | 2 |
| | 1287 | | | | | | | | | 1567 | | |

---

[236] For the sources and defects of this table see Appendix II..

| | £ | s | d | £ | s | d | £ | s | d | £ | s | d |
|---|---|---|---|---|---|---|---|---|---|---|---|---|
| 3. Crondal | £53 | 7 | 0 | | | | | | | £103 | 2 | 8¾ |
| | | 1351 | | | | | | | | | 1567 | |
| 4. Sutton War-blington | £5 | 17 | 4¾ | | | | | | | £8 | 10 | 4 |
| | | 1295 | | | | | | | | | 1542 | |
| 5. Aspley Guise | £7 | 8 | 4 | | | | | | | £10 | 5 | 10 |
| | | 1248 | | | 1567 | | | | | | 1585 | |
| 6. Birling | £9 | 2 | 6½ | £14 | 9 | 4 | | | | £14 | 9 | 4 |
| | | 1352 | | | 1478 | | | 1567 | | | 1580 | |
| 7. Acklington | £18 | 13 | 2 | £19 | 13 | 11 | £19 | 13 | 5 | £20 | 0 | 5 |
| | | 1483 | | | | | | | | | 1505 | |
| 8. Cuxham | £9 | 9 | 3 | | | | | | | £8 | 9 | 3 |
| | | 1483 | | | | | | | | | 1600 | |
| 9. Ibstone | £4 | 8 | 10 | | | | | | | £3 | 15 | 0½ |
| | | 1483 | | | 1567 | | | 1585 | | | 1702 | |
| 10. High Buston | £3 | 12 | 0 | £3 | 12 | 0 | £3 | 12 | 0 | £12 | 0 | 0 |
| | | 1539 | | | | | | | | | 1608 | |
| 11. Amble | £22 | 14 | 6 | | | | | | | £16 | 0 | 5 |
| | | | | "The reign of King Henry VII." | | | | | | | 1529 | |
| 12. Malden | | | | £4 | 9 | 10 | | | | £4 | 6 | 7 |
| | | 1527 | | | 1588 | | | | | | 1607 | |
| 13. Kibworth | £23 | 6 | 7 | £26 | 15 | 1 | | | | £19 | 14 | 5 |
| | | 1304–5 | | | 1348–9 | | | 1373–4 | | | 1461 | |
| 14. Standon | £21 | 17 | 3 | £23 | 8 | 0 | £23 | 2 | 2½ | £33 | 3 | 3½ |
| | | 1317–8 | | | 1445–6 | | Henry VIII. | | | | | |
| 15. Feering | £29 | 10 | 9½ | £32 | 14 | 10 | £16 | 2 | 6½ | | | |
| | | 1321 | | Henry VI. | | | 38–39 Henry VI. (1460) | | | | | |
| 16. Appledrum | £7 | 0 | 11 | £10 | 11 | 6 | £13 | 14 | 10½ | | | |
| | | 1357 | | | | | | | | | 1501 | |
| 17. Minchin-hampton | £41 | 14 | 4 | | | | | | | £41 | 19 | 9 |
| (works) | £4 | 18 | 0 | | | | | | | | | |
| | | 1280 | | | 1441 | | | 1547 | | | | |

| | £ | s | d | £ | s | d | £ | s | d | |
|---|---|---|---|---|---|---|---|---|---|---|
| 18. Langley Marish | £20 | 16 | 5½ | £24 | 0 | 0 | £45 | 3 | 5¾ | |
| | Henry VI. | | | 1521 | | | James I. | | | |
| 19. Lewisham | £8 | 11 | 7 | £23 | 1 | 6½ | £90 | 3 | 3 | |
| | Edward III.(?) | | | 15th century(?) | | | James I. | | | |
| 20. Cuddington. For terms of Easter and Michaelmas | £6 | 4 | 2¾ | | | | | | | |
| (for whole year) | £12 | 8 | 5½(?) | £15 | 16 | 7 | £9 | 19 | 8¾ | |
| | 1314–15 | | | 1386–7 | | | 1484–5 | | | |
| 21. Isleworth (Michaelmas) | £21 | 16 | 10 | £23 | 3 | 10¼ | £18 | 18 | 0 | |
| | 1207–15 | | | | | | 1607 | | | |
| 22. Wootton (free and customary tenants) | £9 | 11 | 2 | | | | £13 | 19 | 0½ | |
| | 1271 | | | | | | 1547 | | | |
| 23. Speen | £6 | 13 | 9¾ | | | | £17 | 4 | 2 | |
| | 1303–4 | | | 1314–15 | | | 1478–9 | | | |
| 24. Schitlington | £29 | 13 | 0½ | £30 | 4 | 10 | £58 | 11 | 9 | (exclusive of ferm of land and ferm of manor). |
| | 1383–4 | | | 1474–5 | | | 1519–20 | | | |
| 25. Cranfield (rent of vill including ferm of lands) | £68 | 15 | 2 | £63 | 19 | 10¼ | £72 | 2 | 1¾ | |
| | 1325–6 | | | | | | 1482–3 | | | |
| 26. Holywell | £12 | 18 | 2 | | | | £22 | 7 | 8 | |
| | 1536 | | | | | | 1803 | | | |
| 27. Farleigh | £4 | 9 | 9 | | | | £4 | 15 | 5 | |

It will be seen that, in spite of some considerable increases, many rents were comparatively stationary during long periods of time. Moreover, in all probability, they were more stationary than is suggested by the statistics given above. For at the earlier dates there were works the value of which usually does not appear among the money rents. As time went on, more land was brought under cultivation and the demesne was leased; and though an attempt has been made to exclude the latter factor, it is not always possible to do so with certainty. The later figures, therefore, are, if anything, a more exhaustive account of the tenants' burdens than the earlier, and the small difference which exists between them on several manors is for this reason all the more remarkable.

These figures, it will be said, if they prove anything, prove too much. Do we not know that one of the grievances of the peasantry in the sixteenth century was the rack-renting of their holdings? Have we not the evidence of Fitzherbert, Latimer, and Hales to prove it? To these questions one must answer that it is certainly true that lords of manors did make a strenuous effort to get from their tenants increased payments for their holdings, and that the success which in many cases they achieved was one great cause of the decline in the condition of the peasantry. The matter, however, is not so simple as it appears. In respect of their liability to be competitively rented, some parts of the lands of a manor stood on a different footing from others; and again, fixed rents of customary lands were quite compatible with movable fines. An attempt will be made in subsequent chapters[237] to illustrate both the rack-renting of those parts of a manor where the rent was least controlled by custom, and the upward movement of the fines charged on the admission of tenants to their holdings. These figures of stationary or almost stationary rents must not, therefore, be taken as giving a full account of the relations between the customary tenants and the manorial authorities, as though there was no other way in which the latter could compensate themselves. Subject to this qualification, however, they do indicate that, at any rate on the customary holdings which formed the kernel of the manor, there is for a very long period little rack-renting. They suggest that the tenants' payments have a fixity which would make Arthur Young tear his hair. They fall in line with the statements of authorities like Fitzherbert and Norden as to the difficulty experienced by the manorial officials in forcing up rents of assize, that "are as in the beginning, neither risen nor fallen, but doe continue always one and the same." And this fixity of rents is a factor in the prosperity of the peasantry which can hardly be over-estimated. When not neutralised by exorbitant fines, it means that any surplus arising on the customary tenements as the result of growing trade, or of the fall in the value of money, or of improved methods of agriculture, anything in fact which is in the nature of economic rent, is retained by the tenants. Secured by the custom of the manor, as by a dyke, against the competitive pressure which under modern conditions transfers so much of the fruits of progress into the hands of the owners of land and capital, they enjoy an unearned increment which grows with every growth in economic prosperity, and have an interest in their holdings almost similar to that of a landlord who is burdened only with a fixed rent-charge like the English land tax. One of the best established generalisations of economics, ground into the English people by thirty years of misery, is that the effect of agrarian protection is to make a present to landlords. But agrarian protection itself wears a different complexion when the rise in rents which it produces is not transferred to a small and wealthy class of absentee owners, but retained by thousands of men who are themselves cultivating the soil.

Lest such a picture should seem to be drawn too much in the spirit of the

---

[237] See below, pp. 139–147 and 304–310.

economic theorist, let us make its meaning more precise by pointing out that the retention of the unearned increment by copyhold tenants was a fact of which the manorial authorities were perfectly well aware, and the results of which they were sometimes at pains to estimate arithmetically by setting side by side with the actual rent paid the rent which the holdings would fetch if put up to competition. Four examples may be given. At Amble,[238] in 1608, the surveyor gives the rent of the customary tenants as £16, 0s. 5d., and "the annual value beyond rent" as £93, 4s. 4d. On the great manor of Hexham[239] in the same year the rents of the 314 copyhold tenants amounted to £126, 4s. 8¼d.; the "value above the oulde Rentes" was £624, 4s. 1d. In the various townships of the manor of Rochdale[240] part of the land was rack-rented. But a great deal of it was held at payments which left the tenant a substantial margin between the rent which he paid to the king and the letting value of the land, a margin which varied from 2d. an acre in parts of Wardleworth, to 6d. an acre in parts of Wardle, 8d. an acre in Walsden, and 10d. an acre in Castleton. On the manor of Barkby[241] in Leicestershire the difference was still more striking. The rents paid by free and customary tenants together amounted in 1636 to £11, 8s. 7½d.; the value of their holdings was put by the surveyor at £215, 1s. 6d. And, of course, the fact that these rentals come from the very end of the sixteenth, and the beginning of the seventeenth, centuries, makes the evidence which they offer of the inability of manorial authorities to insist on copyhold rents keeping pace with the rising value of land, when they had every motive to enforce such correspondence if they could, all the more significant. For a century they have been screwing up rents wherever they can, and here are tenants, who, as far as rents go, put 6d. in their own pockets for every 1d. they give to the landlord. Let us repeat that these figures, striking as they are, would, if taken by themselves, give a misleading impression of the position of the copyhold tenants. Even when the lord of a manor cannot break the barrier opposed by manorial custom to a rise in rents, he may be able to dip his fingers in the surplus by raising the fines charged on admission; he may be all the more exacting in screwing the last penny out of those holdings where the rent is not fixed by custom. But though we must not forget the other side of the shield, though the very fixity of rents on many manors should make us scrutinise other conditions very carefully, we must not forget either that a tenant whose rent is unaltered for 200 or 250 years, a tenant who, after a period of sweeping agrarian changes in which a bitter cry has gone up against the exactions of landlords, is paying a fifth, or a sixth, or even an eighteenth of what could be got for his holding in the open market, is a tenant whom most modern English farmers would envy. Whatever his other disadvantages he has at any rate

---

[238] *Northumberland County History*, vol. ii.

[239] *Ibid.*, vol. iii. pp. 86–94. On this manor at the time of the survey, though the distinction between the old rent and the "cleare yearly value above the old rent" was noted, the latter seems to have been tapped by a rise in rents ("cleere improved rent above the ould rent").

[240] *Rochdale Manor Inquisition*, 1610, by H. Fishwick (*Trans. of the Rochdale Literary and Scientific Society*, vol. vii.).

[241] Merton Documents, MSS. Book labelled "Kibworth and Barkby, 1636." For another illustration of fixed copyhold rents, see Maitland, *English Hist. Review*, vol. ix.: The History of a Cambridgeshire Manor.

one condition of prosperity. He will not be eaten up by rack-renting. No wonder that such a man can accumulate capital and buy up land to add to his holding. No wonder that he can sublet parts of it at a profit. No wonder that in the day of agrarian oppression the wealthier peasantry stands stubbornly against it, that they can carry cases from one court to another, and that there are manors where they boast that "20[242] of them would spend 20 score pounds" in fighting an unpopular landlord. On the whole, the individual cases of enterprise and prosperity among the customary tenants of the fifteenth century do fit into the view that the economic environment was favourable to the peasantry. They may be regarded as symptoms, not exceptions.

Here, perhaps, we should stop. What manner of men these were in that personal life of which economics is but the squalid scaffolding; what stars threw for them their beams on that tremendous whirlpool of religion and politics into which Europe was plunging, we cannot say. Of the hopes and fears and aspirations of the men who tilled the fields which still give us in due season their kindly fruit, we know hardly more than of the Roman plebs, far less than of the democracy of Athens. Yet these men too had their visions. Their silence is the taciturnity of men, not the speechlessness of dumb beasts.

That the peasantry as a class were no politicians was a natural consequence of the position which they had occupied throughout the Middle Ages. On a small number among them, in the Eastern counties a large number, the State had for centuries showered duties and obligations with a lavish hand, and the freeholders, though they must often have cursed the tediousness of suit of court, and jury service, and Parliamentary elections, turned that tiresome discipline to good account in the days when the Stuarts had contrived to make politics to thousands of heavy-handed obstinate people throughout England a matter not only of money but of conscience. The non-participation of the bulk of the peasantry in the same large interests was not due to poverty, for often the copyholders were wealthier than the freeholders who listened to Pym and Hampden on that first great election campaign in 1640, and left their farms to fight for King or Parliament. Nor was it due to timidity or lack of spirit, for, as we shall see later, they frequently asserted themselves in the course of the sixteenth century in their own characteristic way of agrarian strikes.[243] It was rather that the centre of their interests and their social horizon were different. The freeholders from an early date had been brought into contact with the chief institutions of the organised political state. Since the twelfth century they had been protected in their holdings by the courts, and had learned through that cunning procedure which was the fruit of Henry II.'s[244] sleepless nights, that though often one cannot do much with the law, one can do even less without it. Since the thirteenth century they, along with their social superiors, had

---

[242] Quoted, Leadam, "The Security of Copyholders in the Fifteenth and Sixteenth Centuries" (*English Historical Review*, vol. viii. pp. 684–696). The case in question was that of the inhabitants of Thingden *v.* John Mulsho.

[243] See below, pp. 329–331.

[244] Bracton, f. 164 b.: "Succuritur ei per recognitionem Assisæ novæ dissesinæ multis vigiliis excogitatam et inventam" (quoted Pollock and Maitland, *History of English Law*, vol. i. p. 125 n.).

returned members to Parliament, and had acquired that facility in grumbling at taxation which is the beginning, though not, as is so commonly supposed, the end, of political wisdom. Thus they became a body in whose eyes the Law, Parliament, the State, loomed up, though for ages dimly enough, as a big something which it is well to have on your side, something which requires, like the new fangled arquebuses, to be carefully handled, something which, if neglected, may give you a surprising shock, but if treated with proper respect may teach manners even to your landlord. Of course your first duty is to him. You ride and fight for him readily enough as your fathers did. But still, you do it because you have said you will, not because he has said you shall, and though London lawyers are a pack of knaves, it is good to know that the law will, if necessary, make him see the difference.

But the freeholders have been for centuries a privileged class, and those of the peasants who are copyholders, a far more numerous body, are in a very different position. Your fathers were villeins, who hung on the words of the upstart manorial officials, who "had no right to know at night what they should do on the morrow,"[245] who never had the bitter satisfaction of grumbling that they got no return for the wages paid to the knights of the shire, who had no redress from the King's Courts if threatened with eviction. Of course you are not in the same position now. Your blood has been purged of the servile taint for generations. The lawyers have been competing for your business, and so the Court of Chancery has invented a new procedure to protect you in your holding. "When thieves fall out...." Still, it is better to run no risk of offending your superiors, for the law is a chancy thing, and your title (you keep the copy under lock and key and refuse to show it to the new surveyor lest he should twist it into meaning what it doesn't) is none too clear.[246] Deep down in your mind, beneath the prosperity of to-day, there are dim memories of old, unhappy, far-off things, and your shoulders slouch at their recollection. *Weh dir dass du ein Enkel bist!* The bailiff has invented a pedigree as long as your arm to prove that your great-grandfather was a villein, and had no business to have bought his freedom for the preposterous reason that the money with which he bought it was the lord's all along. The toadying beast is even trying to curry favour by saying that your copyhold is for life only, and that your fine is uncertain. True, there are plenty of ancient inhabitants who will swear in the manor court that your family has lived in the village before the present lord was ever heard of. But it is easy to bully and cajole them into silence. Were not Walter and Hugh turned adrift, "weeping bitterly," because money had to be found to pay the young lord's debts? As a copyholder, then, you are much less conscious of the State than if you are a freeholder, because in the matter which interests you most, the security of your holding, you have for centuries had no dealings with the State at all. Your idea of Government is a vague reverence for a King who sits far away in Westminster with a crown on his head and his judges about him, and who gov-

[245] Bracton, Lib. iv. cap. 28, f. 208.

[246] *Northumberland County History*, vol. iii., Pt. V., pp. 86–104, Survey of Hexham (1608): "Their fines they pretend to be certain, viz. one year's rent at everye change of tenant, but not herritable. They have there, for certaine, very ancient evidences and Court Rolls, but they woulde not show them unto us, nor any of their coppies." See also Appendix I. No. IV.

erns his kingdom as a good lord—not like yours—governs his manor. For the rest you are a non-political animal, who take little interest in affairs of State, because in the past the State has taken so little interest in you. When your fathers made London tremble in the great days of 1381 (you can see from your hay-stack the hill where they were hanged, hanged "like dogs"[247]) what they demanded was fair rents and freedom from villein services. When you went out with Ket in 1549 you asked the same, and, untaught by their experience, you begged that the King would see that you had the fair play which his Justices of the Peace, who are your landlords, will never allow you.[248] When King and Parliament come to blows, you curse both impartially, remain neutral as long as you can, and only turn out when they begin driving the village beasts. Your sentiments are pithily expressed in the motto which a local wit has devised for the village banner: "If you take our cattle, we will give you battle."[249]

If, however, the peasantry are on the whole uninterested in the larger problems of government to which the world has agreed to confine the word politics, this is not because they are incapable of self-help, or destitute of any conception of public expediency. It is because the framework of their lives has for ages been different from that of the freeholders, because the centre round which their social interests revolve is even more localised than it is to the freeholders, because what matters to them most is not the law of the land but the custom of the manor. We shall have hereafter[250] to discuss the vexed question of the legal position occupied by the copyholders in the sixteenth century. But we may pause for a moment to point out here the decisive part which custom had played, and still played in our period, in moulding the lives of the mass of the peasantry, because unless this is firmly grasped we cannot understand their mental horizon. It is the custom of the manor which gives them their social environment and their conception of public order. The commonest name for all those who hold neither freely nor by lease is "customary tenants," men whose title is rooted in custom. When the courts begin to interfere to protect copyholders, they introduce that sweeping innovation under the guise of enforcing customary conditions. They do not say "copyholders can be evicted." Nor do they say "copyholders cannot be evicted." They say, "Tell us what the custom of your manor is, and if it is one which does not seem to a plain man too unreasonable, we will enforce it." When tenants and landlords fall out, it is always to custom that the tenants appeal. When the peasants ask the Government for assistance, they do so by demanding the observance of their "old customs."

Let us look at the custom of the manor more closely. The phrase has, of course, misleading suggestions for modern ears. We tend to think of custom as some-

---

[247] *Hist. MSS. Com.*, Part VII., pp. 49–50 (1596): Some information concerning those intending the rebellion in Oxford.... "And Steer said that there was once a rising at Enscombe Hill by the commons, and they were persuaded to go down and were after hanged like dogs. 'But,' said he, 'we will never yield, but will go through with it!'"

[248] See below, pp. 334–337.

[249] Warburton's *Rupert*, iii., 118 (quoted Gooch, *English Democratic Ideas in the Seventeenth Century*, p. 112).

[250] See below, pp. 287–310.

thing indefinite and inconclusive; something which is not, like the law (we speak of what should be), the embodiment of reason; something which fetters progress and is the opposite of freedom; something which is mere habit, and very likely a "bad habit" at that. All this is true in a sense. It is the way in which in the sixteenth century an enterprising landlord looks at the custom which ties his hands. But it is not the way in which it is regarded by the peasants. The custom of the manor does not mean to them a mere feeble acquiescence in existing conditions, mere inertia. It is not a negative, but a positive thing. It is no more inconsistent with progress to observe the custom, than it is inconsistent with progress to keep out of gaol by observing the law. For the custom is simply the law of the village. Like the main rules of the common law, it comes down from a dim age that is beyond the memory of man. Like law it is enforced by a court, the court of the manor. Like law it can be altered (and in some respects and on some manors often is altered to meet the new conditions of our period) by the proper authority, which again is the court of the manor. Of course it is not law in the fullest sense. From one stand-point it is the antithesis of law, the law of the King's Courts, which, till the end of the fourteenth century, has taken no cognizance of the customary tenures, though since that time the Court of Chancery, by intervening to enforce the custom of the manor in respect of copyholds, has been breaking down the opposition. Still, for the mass of the peasantry, even in the sixteenth century, custom is a bigger, more important, thing than the law of the national courts. It is with custom that the first decision will lie.

Again, the custom of the manor is not at all a vague or indefinite thing. That it reposed partly on the Court Rolls, partly on the memory of ancient inhabitants, we can see from the frequent appeals which are made to both of them. But it certainly is no mere nebulous tradition. On the contrary, it is often most rigorous in its precision. It lays down boundaries and numbers stocks and stones. It adjusts and readjusts agricultural arrangements. It enters into the details of social life with a bold hand. Let us reflect, to take an example, on the customs of High Furness, parts of which have been quoted above. Here we have a whole village agreeing about matters which do not at first sight seem, like the use of pastures or the fixing of boundaries, of a specially public character. The term on which a man's property is to be distributed among his descendants, this, if anything, one might expect to be left to his own discretion, once the succession of an heir to maintain the rents and services due from the holding had been provided for. The rules quoted above go much further than this. They settle exactly what proportion of a man's proper-ty is to go to his different children, male and female, from the eldest down to the youngest. Imagine a Parish Council to-day distributing the wealth of deceased pa-rishioners with the object of seeing that the whole of the younger generation shall obtain some kind of start in life, and you will have an analogy to what is done by the prudent men of High Furness.

Or take another example, where the points handled are of a somewhat differ-ent kind. Here are the customs of the manor of Bushey,[251] as set out in 1563 by twenty customary tenants in response to an inquiry by the lord: —

[251] I take them from the MSS. Court Rolls of the Manor of Bushey, kindly lent me by the late Miss Lucy Toulmin Smith.

"In primis to the fyrste article we saye that no copyholder at the tyme of his death dying seased of twoo copyholdes hathe paid any more than one quycke heriott by the tyme of any remembrance, or before, to our knowledge.

"Item to the seconde we saye that the lorde oughtte to have the second beste for hys herryott and the heyer the beste.

"Item to the thyrde we saye that the copyholder that doth surrender his copyholde ought not to paye any herryott upon the surrender of his copyholde except yt be in extreme of deathe.

"Item to the fourth we saye that lords of the mannor have never demanded nor any copyholder payde any more for their ffyne than one yere's rente of the lande.

"Item to the fyfth we saye that the widdowe upon the deathe of her husbande shall have the thyrde parte of the rente of the lande, but not the thyrde part of the lande except yt be surrendered to her by her husbande.

"Item to the syxth we saye that the copyholder may sell hys underwoode and stocke upp by the roote the same wytheout lycense of the lorde.

"Item to the seventh we saye that the copyholder may fell tymber for reparacion or otherwyse to sell the same to hys use and profyt; so hathe yt byn used by our tymes and by all tyme beyond the memory of man.

"Item to the eytthe we saye that the copyholder may make a grante of hys copyholde for three yeres wythoute the lord's lycense, and the lorde to take nothing for the same.

"Item to the nineth we saye that the tenants maye take surrender bothe within the manor and without the manor.

"Item to the tenth we saye that we cannot answer for that we knowe not every man's lande.

"Item to the eleventh we saye that every copyholde is not heryottable.

"Item to the xiith we knowe not where the Courte Rolles, Rentals, or customaryes of the manor are remayning or in whose custodye.

"Item to the xiiith we saye that we knowe not of any deutyes or rentys withdrawn from the lordshippe.

"Item to the xiiiith we saye that we never knewe nor hearde any heryott payde for freeholde at the dethe of the freholder.

"Item to the fyfteneth we say that the freholder hathe never payde relief at alienacion, but at deathe only.

"Item to the xvith we saye that a copyholder dying his heir being wythin the age of xiii yeres the custody of the body and lande oughte to be comytted by the lorde to the nexte of the kyn to whom the inheritance may not dyscende."

In themselves these customs are not in any way remarkable, except perhaps for the uniform favour which they show to the interests of the tenants. They might be paralleled from those of scores of other manors. What is worth noticing is the precision of the rules laid down. The relations between the lord and the tenants are settled with the definiteness of a sort of great collective bargain.

It would be going beyond the scope of this essay to enter upon the large question, on which so much learning has been expended, of the respective parts played in manorial origins by the communal organisation of villagers for the purpose of self-government in their agrarian affairs, and by the authoritative pressure of superior authorities for the purpose of using the village as the basis of a financial and political system. But one may point out that facts such as have been quoted above in illustration of the rule of custom cannot easily be fitted into any theory which regards the economic arrangements of the manor as the result simply of a system imposed from above, and which treats the customary rights of the peasants as the outcome of concessions made by lords from time to time in their own interests, the revocation of which involved no larger difficulties than necessarily surround the alteration of practices sanctioned by long use. However much the organisation of village life may have been stereotyped by the pressure directed upon it by the desire of the manorial authorities to extract rents and services on an unvarying plan, one cannot trace it altogether to its subordination to such external forces, because the custom of the manor acts as a restriction which impedes the free action of lords themselves and their agents, even when they are most anxious to break through its meshes. This is seen more clearly perhaps in the sixteenth century than in earlier periods, for the very reason that the sharp collision of interests between lords and tenants makes it more possible to distinguish those parts of manorial custom which represent the economic interests of the tenants, from those which represent the power of the manorial authorities imposed upon them. Under the latter heading would fall the rules as to heriots and reliefs, rules forbidding waste, rules requiring tenants to pay "for the rushes which they gather on the lord's common,"[252] or to perform the surviving remnants of labour services, while a rule such as that of High Furness, forbidding the division of holdings to such an extent as to prevent the discharge of services or the obtaining of an adequate living by the occupier, may be regarded as a compromise in which the interests of both lord and tenant receive consideration. Under the former may be placed the custom which fixes rents, and, on some fortunate manors like Bushey, fixes fines to be paid on admission, sanctions the sub-letting of copyholds and the felling of timber, and allots rights of pasture to each arable holding. Not all of these, of course, stand upon the same footing of importance. The right to cut wood is much less essential than the right to graze cattle. But some of them, at any rate, like rights of common pasture, seem to be bound up with the very existence of the village as an agricultural community, and all of them are dictated by the interests of the peasants in protecting themselves against encroachments, as clearly as are those of the first type by the desire of lords to make the manor a source of profit to themselves. It is scarcely possible to account for the obstacles put by manorial customs in the way of changes which would benefit the lord and be detrimental to the tenant, except on the supposition that they are rooted in something more indestructible than the mere concession of privileges which long use has solidified and hardened; some-

---

[252] Aldeburgh, *temp.* Henry VIII., R.O. *Misc. Bks. Treas. of Receipts,* vol. clxiii. See Appendix I., No. II.

thing which can only be found in the fact that they are an essential part of the life of the village, to which the lord himself, as a condition of extracting revenue from it, is almost bound to conform.

This brings us to our original point, the way in which the whole social environment of all the tenants, except the freeholders, who do not need the protection of custom, and the leaseholders,[253] who cannot get it, is dependent upon the custom of the manor. Fraught with modern associations as it is, the phrase "collective[254] bargain" is perhaps the nearest we can get to expressing what the custom of the manor means to the peasants themselves. Of course it is much more than this. The custom has the sanction of immemorial antiquity. The phrase "time out of mind" is no mere piece of idle rhetoric. The stable self-perpetuating conditions of economic life create a sort of communal memory, in which centuries are focussed. There were villages where, in the reign of Elizabeth, the effects of the Great Plague[255] were still dimly remembered. But regarding the matter from the point of view of the practical working of village life, we shall not be far wrong if we think of the peasants as a body of men who are more or less organised, and of the custom as a system of common rules which regulates the relations between them and the lord. And it is evident that the custom of the manor, at any rate in our period, is a safeguard of the tenants' interests rather than of those of the manorial authorities. It is not only that the changes which followed the Great Plague have set the peasants free from the most irksome customary restrictions, but, further, that, in the sixteenth century, it is the lord who wants to make innovations and the tenants who resist them, and that it is therefore the latter who stand to gain most by clinging to custom. The custom sets up a standard by which encroachments can be opposed, by which the village as a whole can put a solid barrier in the way of change, by which blacklegging (in the shape of one man taking a holding over the head of another) can be prevented. Competitive forces have, it is true, been gradually undermining custom, and by the sixteenth century an increasing number of tenants have the terms on which they take their holdings settled by the higgling of the market without reference to any authoritative rule. Nevertheless, as far as the copyholders, who are the kernel of the manor, are concerned, competition is held in check by the fact that, on certain fundamental matters, there is a common understanding between the peasants, which is recognised by the lord himself. The manorial authorities cannot bargain with the tenants one by one. They have to deal with the villagers as men who are "organised," who are members of a society, who know what they have to expect in the way of heriots and rents and fines, and who will be supported by village opinion in resisting innovations. On occasion the

---

[253] Some copyholders, who held land which was not "customary land" but part of the demesne or the waste, were not protected by custom either: for a discussion of this point see below, pp. 293–294.

[254] See below for an example from Crondal, p. 295.

[255] MS. Transcript by A.N. Palmer of "The Presentment and Verdict of the Jury for the Manor of Hewlington," 1620 (Wrexham Free Library, *Ancient Local Records*, vol. ii.): "Which decay (as by the ancient records appeareth) did growe by reason of the great mortalitie and plague which in former tymes had been in the reign of Edward III., and also of the rebellion of Owen Glendower and trouble that thereupon ensued."

peasants will strike. On occasion they will force their landlord to arbitration.[256] One might almost say that the customary tenants are trade unionists to a man. Again, who shall determine what the custom is? The court rolls will throw light on certain points, and occasionally we find lords appealing to them successfully in order to upset the tenants' claims. But on many matters there is no guide but tradition; the exponents of tradition are the ancient inhabitants; the lord has to ask them to expound it, as he does the tenants of Bushey. Can we doubt that this was a powerful check on autocratic action on his part? Lords come and go. But the custom of the manor endures, and probably loses nothing in the telling.

If, then, we ask what the custom means to the peasantry, we must think not of the "forbidding, stale, and meagre ways," which is what the word custom too often suggests in the twentieth century, but of the phrase "ancient customs and liberties," which is so common in the charters of Boroughs. The custom of the manor is a body of rules which regulates the rights and obligations of the peasants in their daily life. It is a kind of law. It is a kind of freedom. And since it is the custom which most concerns the mass of the peasantry, it is not the state, or the law, but the custom of the manor which forms their political environment and from which they draw their political ideas. They cannot conceive the state except as a very great manor. Their idea of good government is the enforcement of an idealised customary.[257]

Having said this we can say little more. There is no standard by which we can measure civilisation, and if we knew more than we do, the village life of the sixteenth century—and England is all villages—would still be a mystery to us. Yet, before returning to the humbler task of examining economic conditions, we may perhaps summarise the sort of impressions formed of the peasants by those who knew them in their own day, impressions no doubt as misleading as a traveller's sketches of modern England, yet, like a traveller's sketches, possessing a certain value, because they show the points which an intelligent outside opinion selects for emphasis.

One is encouraged in one's belief in the comparative prosperity of a large number of the peasantry in the earlier sixteenth century by the comments which the writers of the periods pass upon it, even after a decline has already begun. The picture we get is of an open-handed, turbulent, large-eating and deep-drinking people, much given to hospitality and to merriment both coarse and refined; according to modern standards very ignorant, yet capable of swift enthusiasm, litigious, great sticklers for their rights, quick to use force in defence of them, proud of their independence, and free from the grosser forms of poverty which crush the spirit. The latter feature strikes everybody. Foreign visitors[258] notice with amazement the outward signs of wealth among the humbler classes. English writers, though their tone becomes sadder and sadder as the century proceeds, are never

[256] *Victoria County History of Gloucestershire,* Social and Economic History, p. 146. For agrarian strikes see below, pp. 329–331.

[257] See below, pp. 338–340.

[258] Harrison in *Elizabethan England* (Withington), p. 114, quoting one of "the Spaniards in Queen Mary's days." "These English have their houses made of sticks and dirt, but they fare commonly so well as the king."

tired of boasting of it. Even in the eighties of the sixteenth century, when many of the peasants are much worse off than they had been a hundred years before, Harrison, though he paints in dark colours the ruinous effects of the agrarian changes, describes their hearty life with good-humoured gusto. "Both the artificer and the husbandman are sufficiently liberal and very friendly at their tables, and when they meet they are so merry without malice, and plain without inward Italian or French craft and sublety, that it would do a man good to be in company among them.... Their food consisteth principally of beef and such meat as the butcher selleth. That is to say, mutton, veal, lamb, pork. In feasting also the latter sort, I mean the husbandmen, do exceed after their manner, especially at bridals, purifications of women, and such odd meetings, where it is incredible to tell what meat is consumed and spent, each one bringing such a dish, or so many with him, as his wife and he consult upon, but always with this consideration that the lesser friend shall have the better provision." The peasants themselves have a good conceit of their position, and all unmindful of the whirligig of time and its revenges, contrast it with that of their class in France, where women labour like beasts in the fields, where men go in wooden shoes or no shoes at all, where the people drink water instead of ale, eat rye bread and little meat, and have not even the heart, like honest Englishmen, to rob the rich who oppress them, and that in the most fertile realm in all the world;[259] "Caytives and wretches, lyvyng in lyke thraldome as they dyd to the Romaynes, and gevynge tribute for theyr meat, drinke, brede, and salte, which for theyr wayke personayges and tymorous hartes I may compare to the pigmies who waged battayle against the Cranes, so that I dare let slip a hundred good yeomen of England against five hundred of such ribaldry."[260] Apart from the utterances of these good Jingoes, stray glimpses show us a people which not only is materially prosperous, but is also bold in action, and can produce men of high moral ardour. In the twentieth century the rural population is a bye-word for its docility. Its ancestors in the sixteenth were notorious for their restiveness. Hales, who knew and loved them, makes one of the characters in his dialogue[261] suggest that men at arms should be used to put down the disturbances made by them and by the unemployed weavers, only to answer, through the lips of another, that to call in the military will be the best way to make them riot all the more:—"Marie, I think that waye wold be rather occasion of commotions to be stirred than to be quenched, for the stomakes of Englishmen would never beare that, to suffer such injuries and reproaches as I knowe suche (*i.e.* the men at arms) use to do to the subjects of France."

These humble people have their idealisms. They produce martyrs for the new religion and for the old, Lollards who suffer persecution for upholding the Wy-

[259] Fortescue, *On the Governance of England*, chaps. iii. and xiii. The Scots, he thinks, are only one degree less faint-hearted than the French. "Thai ben often tymes hanged for larceny, and stelynge off good in the absence off the owner theroff. But ther hartes serve them not to take a manys gode, while he is present, and woll defende it."

[260] Coke, *Debate of Heralds*. See also the quotation, Froude's *Henry VIII.*, vol. i. chap, i., from a State Paper of 1515: "What comyn folke in all this world may compare with the comyns of England, in riches, freedom, liberty, welfare, and all prosperity? What comyn folke is so mighty, so stronge in the felde, as the comyns of England?"

[261] *The Commonweal of this Realm of England* (Lamond), p. 94.

cliffite tradition in the quiet villages of Buckinghamshire, Catholics who follow
Aske in that wonderful movement of northern England, the last of the crusades,
in 1536, or fall in Devonshire thirteen years later before the artillery of Herbert.
Nor are they altogether cut off from the springs of learning. For at the beginning
of the sixteenth century the upper classes have not yet begun to covet education
for themselves sufficiently to withhold it from the poor. Bequests[262] show that the
sons of well-to-do peasants may have been among those godly yeomanry whom
Latimer[263] described as once, in happier social conditions than those amid which
he preached, frequenting the older universities, and the records of some sixteenth
century grammar-schools tell a similar story. Among the first twenty-two names
on the register of Repton[264] there are five gentlemen, four husbandmen, nine

[262] *Victoria County History*, Berkshire, ii., 208. In 1558 a yeoman leaves his son a portion of land worth £10 a year "for his keepinge and learninge in Oxford for five years nexte."
On the same page there is a case of a man described as a "yeoman" who is tenant by copy
of Court Roll.

[263] Latimer's *Sermons*. The first sermon preached before King Edward, March 8, 1549
(Everyman Series, p. 86): "We have good statutes made for the commonwealth, as touching commoners and enclosures; many meetings and sessions; but in the end of the matter
there cometh nothing forth. Well, well, this is one thing I will say unto you; from whence
it cometh I know, even from the devil. I know his intent in it. For if ye bring it to pass that
the yeomanry be not able to put their sons to school (as indeed universities do wondrously
decay already); I say ye pluck salvation from the people and utterly destroy the realm. For
by yeomen's sons the faith of Christ is and hath been maintained chiefly." See also *A Supplication of the Poor Commons* (E. E. T. S.): "This thing causeth that suche possessioners as
heretofore were able and used to maintain their own children ... to lernynge and suche other
qualities as are necessary to be had in this Your Highness Royalme, are now of necessitie
compelled to set theyr own children to labour, and al is lytle enough to pay the lorde's rent,
and to take the house anew at the end of the yere." The children of yeomen had no doubt
been educated mainly for the Church, and some attained high position (*Surtees Society*, vol.
lxxix. pp. 263–264, for the son of a yeoman becoming a Bishop, and vol. li. No. 53, the son
of a yeoman becoming subdeacon of York, vol. lxxix. pp. 176–177, for a yeoman's son sent
to school for fifteen years). But in the fifteenth century this was not always so, v. Leach,
*Educational Charters*, p. 41, for a school founded in Yorkshire, a county which "produced
many youths endowed with light and sharpness of ability, who do not all want to attain the
dignity and elevation of the priesthood, that these may be better fitted for the mechanical
arts and other concerns of this world." A case of hostility to the education of the poorer
classes based on the idea that education should be reserved for "gentlemen" is given *ibid.*
p. 470, where the notorious Lord Rich and other gentlemen argue "as for husbandsmen's
children, they were more meet ... for the plough and to be artificers than to occupy the place
of the learned sort. So that they wished none else to be put to school, but only gentlemen's
children." Cranmer retorted, "Poor men's children ... are commonly more apt to apply their
study than is the gentleman's son delicately educated ... the poor man's son by painstaking
will be learned, when the gentleman's son will not take the pains to get it, ... wherefore if the
gentleman's son be apt to learning let him be admitted; if not apt, let the poor man's child
being apt enter in his room."

[264] *Repton School Register*, 1564–1910. One of the husbandmen kept his boy at school
for ten years. The average school life of the sons of seven yeomen was between six and sev-
en years; one stays for twelve years, going to school at five and staying till seventeen. If one
may judge by the attitude of most modern parents ("I went to the mill when I was ten, and
why shouldn't Tommie?"), these men must have been pretty comfortably off.

yeomen, two websters or weavers, a carpenter, and a tanner.

But by that time much had changed, and for seventy years before these documents begin the peasantry in many parts of England had had sterner things to think of than the schooling of their children.

# CHAPTER IV

## THE PEASANTRY (CONTINUED)

### *(e) Signs of Change*

So far attention has been concentrated upon those phenomena which suggest that, before the great agrarian changes of the sixteenth century begin, there has been a period—one may date it roughly from 1381 to 1489—of increasing prosperity for the small cultivator. We have emphasised the evidence of this upward movement which is given by the growth among the peasantry of a freer and more elastic economy. We have watched them shake off many of the restrictions imposed by villeinage and build up considerable properties. We have seen how the custom of the manor still acts as a dyke to defend them against encroachments, and to concentrate in their hands a large part of the fruits of economic progress. In the century from the Peasants' Revolt to the first Statute against Depopulation, in spite of the political anarchy which disfigures it, there is, as it seems to us an interval between one oppressive régime and another, between the leaden weight of villeinage and the stress and strain of the gathering power of competition. In that happy balance between the forces of custom and the forces of economic enterprise, custom is powerful, yet not so powerful that men cannot evade it when evasion is desired; enterprise is growing, yet it has not grown to such lengths as to undermine the security which the small man finds in the established relationships and immemorial routine of communal agriculture.

There is, however, we need hardly say, another side to the picture, and to that other side we must now turn. We must examine again from another point of view some of the ground over which we have already travelled, and we must modify the opinions which we have formed by bringing a fresh range of facts into perspective. The piecemeal changes which have been going on in the internal organisation of so many manors look forward as well as back, and are of significance as throwing light on the larger innovations of the later period. For one thing, they mean the appearance among the customary tenantry of persons who are in a small way capitalists, and who supply a link between the great farmer of the sixteenth century and the agricultural organisation of earlier periods. The emergence out of the mediæval peasantry of prosperous cultivators, occupying two or three times as much land as their grandfathers, is a proof that holdings of a considerable size can be managed successfully, and the farmers of the demesne are often drawn from among them. For another thing, the inequality which has appeared among the holdings of different tenants implies the growth of a state of things in which innovations in the customary methods of agriculture are much more likely to be made than they were when all the tenants were organised in fairly well-defined classes. The smaller among them are still practising subsistence farming when the larger are producing on a considerable scale for the market, are acquiring capital, are extending their holdings, are even becoming landlords themselves. There arises therefore a divergence of agricultural methods and economic interests between them, which is quite compatible with the fact that both large and small tenants stand in the same legal relationship to the lord of whom they hold. The enterprise which the former show in their dealings with land and in encroaching on the routine of manorial cultivation cannot fail to have a powerful influence in preparing the way for the individualistic movement which sweeps over agriculture in the sixteenth century, and from which the peasants, as a class, suffer so severely. The freedom with which parcels of land change hands must inevitably weaken the connection between the family and the holding, and result in leaving the least successful without any land at all. The difficulty of maintaining a peasant proprietary without restricting the alienation of land is one which is familiar to modern Governments, and there is clear evidence[265] that, even before the evictions of the sixteenth century began to attract attention, a decline in the number of customary tenants was brought about on a good many manors by the mere process of the

---

[265] I am inclined to think that an investigation of the manorial records of the fifteenth century would show a considerable decrease in the number of customary tenants, not as a result of evictions, but simply as a consequence of one man buying out another and forming one larger holding out of two or more smaller ones. The evidence for this is as follows: (1) When several holdings pass to one man there must be a diminution unless more land is brought under cultivation. Such an agglomeration of holdings has been shown to be very frequent. (2) A comparison of fifteenth and sixteenth century surveys with those of an earlier date shows a marked diminution in the number of customary tenants (a) before complaints as to enclosure become loud, and on manors where there is no trace of enclosing by lords or large farmers; (b) on manors where more land is cultivated by the customary tenants than at an earlier date. Thus at Haversham there were 52 tenants of all kinds in 1305, 35 in 1458, 14 in 1497 (*Victoria County History*, Gloucestershire, vol. ii. pp. 61–62). On six Northumbrian manors, where there is no sign of evictions on a large scale, there were 82 customary tenants in 1294, and 37 in 1567, and where intermediate surveys enable one to narrow the limiting points, one finds that there has been a considerable diminution before the end of the fifteenth century. On the four tithings, of South Newton, Childhampton, Stovord, and Little Wishford, which made up the manor of South Newton, customary tenants numbered at the beginning of the fourteenth century 32, 7, 13, 13, and in 1567 10, 3, 7, 1, the average holding having grown from 10½ to about 43 acres (Roxburghe Club, *Pembroke Surveys*). At Sutton Warblington there were in 1351, 28 customary tenants, and in 1568 there were 7, while the average acreage of each tenant's holding had increased enormously (*Crondal Records*, Baigent). At Dippenhall and Swanthrop, two tithings of the manor of Crondal, the customary tenants numbered 40 in 1287, 24 in 1568, while the average size of their holdings had risen from between 18 and 19 to just under 35 acres. At Aldershot the number of customary tenants during the same period fell from 48 to 37 (*ibid.*). Such figures are of course full of pitfalls. In the North border warfare reduced the population, and the effects of the Great Plague have to be considered. The great growth in the size of holdings does, however, suggest that a diminution in the number of customary tenants may have occurred without any encroachments being made by lords on the customary land, and merely through one tenant buying up the land of another.

well-to-do buying up the poorer men's holdings.

Such movements prepare the way for greater changes: petty capitalism is naturally followed by capitalism on a larger scale. It is surely at first sight somewhat surprising that the noticeable upward movement in the condition of the rural population, which coincides with the disappearance of villeinage and the growth of copyhold tenure, should have been followed by the marked depression which all observers agree to have occurred in the following century. Why should a class which has displayed such remarkable signs of vigour and enterprise find such difficulty in holding its own? An answer to this question cannot be given till after a consideration of the new causes at work in the sixteenth century. But may it not be that their position had to some extent been undermined by the very changes which at first improved it, and that the enterprise of the larger customary tenants, while it added to their prosperity as long as they led the way in it, tended to weaken the customary relations and the customary methods of agriculture which had protected the small man, and to leave him at the mercy of competitive forces which he could not control? Such an undulating line of development, in which the small producer gains temporarily from the expansion of markets and improved technical methods which ultimately rob him of his independence, can be paralleled from the later history both of agriculture[266] and of manufacturing industry. It seems to us to offer a thread which connects the capitalist farmer of the sixteenth century with the prosperous peasantry of the fifteenth. When there is much buying and selling of land among the peasantry, much colonising of new plots taken from the waste and the demesne, we should expect to see the influence of competition beginning to override that of custom; we should expect to see the paring away of communal restrictions to make room for individual arrangements of a more elastic nature. In the remainder of this chapter we shall approach this problem by considering two movements—the growth at an early date of competitive rents on those parts of manors where custom was weakest, and the enclosing of land by customary tenants themselves. The former offers a precedent for the rack-rents and excessive fines of which so much is heard in the sixteenth century, the latter at once an analogy and a contrast with the enclosures carried out by lords of manors and capitalist farmers, which we shall discuss in Part II.

### (f) The Growth of Competitive Rents on New Allotments

The development of competitive rents is a subject which must always possess a peculiar fascination for the historical economist, inasmuch as the distribution of wealth depends to no small degree upon the manner in which the surplus gains wrung from nature are shared between different classes. The wealth which, under a régime of great estates and leasehold tenure, accrues to a tiny body of landlords, is, in a community of small freeholders, retained by the cultivating tenant, and, when the tenure of land is such that custom sets a barrier to a rise in rents, is

[266] Thus the yeomen seem to have increased in prosperity at the end of the eighteenth and in the early nineteenth century (though at the same time large classes of agrarian workers were suffering terribly), because the rise in prices made corn-growing a gold-mine. The collapse came probably after 1815 (see Johnson, *The Disappearance of the Small Landowner*, chap. vii.).

divided between owner and occupier in a way which prevents the former from absorbing the whole advantage of superior sites, or the latter from being reduced to working for bare wages of management. The causes which determine the allocation of rents must always be of crucial importance for an understanding of economic conditions, and any change which augments them, diminishes them, or varies the degree to which different classes participate in them, is likely in time to produce a substantial alteration both in the economic configuration of society and in the possession of social privileges and political power. In modern times, it is true, the enormous area from which food-stuffs are drawn, and the relatively small space upon which manufacturing industry can be concentrated, has made the differential payments accruing to the landowner from varieties of soil and situation almost trifling compared with the surpluses drawn from finance and manufacturing industry by the infra-marginal capitalist and entrepreneur. Such "quasi-rents" are, however, a comparatively modern phenomenon. In our period the basis of wealth was land, and a crucial question is that of the manner in which incomes drawn from land were determined. We have seen that in the sixteenth century custom still ruled the payments made by most of the copyhold tenants. But at that time there were many complaints of rack-renting, and though we must leave till later an inquiry into their justification, it will help us if we take a glance at the new forces, which, even in the Middle Ages, were beginning to operate on the margin of cultivation.

The gradual extension of cultivation over the waste lands surrounding the village fields, and the not infrequent addition of parts of the lord's demesne to the tenants' holdings, was obviously the occasion, as it took place, of a number of new agreements between the payer and receiver of rents, which might or might not repeat the conditions of existing contracts. When new land was broken up for tillage an attempt seems in some cases to have been made by the manorial authorities to assimilate its treatment, as far as payment was concerned, to that of the existing customary holdings. The basis of the rent paid was a comparison between the areas of the encroachments and the ordinary holding of a customary tenant; the payment was so many ploughlands'[267] worth, and sometimes the corresponding services were extracted from them. On the other hand, the mere fact that the land was new land, which did not come into the original scheme of manorial finance and organisation, tended to make it the point from which new relationships could spring. For one thing, it was the natural starting-point for the process of substituting money rents for labour. When the customary holdings offered a sufficient supply of labour for the cultivation of the demesne, the manorial authorities naturally preferred to take the payments for additional land in the shape of money rather than in services of which they already had sufficient. Services are sometimes exacted for the new encroachments, but they are the exception; and the assimilation of the payments for these new holdings to those made for the customary holdings

---

[267] *Crondal Records* (Baigent), p. 132–133, Rental of 1287: "The same Hugh holds certain encroachments on payment of 3 ploughlands' worth, 3 hens, and 3d. at the said term." "Emma of Wyggeworthhall ... holds certain encroachments on payment therefor 11s. 6d. and one ploughland's worth." These documents throw much light on the whole process of the extension of cultivation over the waste.

was either not seriously attempted or was unsuccessful. One can quite understand that, even if the lord wanted labour services from those parts of the waste which were broken up and added to the cultivated area, he might not be able to get the improvements made on the old terms. Quite apart, therefore, from the process of commutation, the growth of money rents developed as a natural accompaniment of the growth of population.

The second point is more important. It is that the rents paid for the new holdings taken from the waste differed from such money payments as were made for the customary holdings, in that they were not to the same extent dominated by custom, but were to a much greater extent influenced by competition. This contrast is the tiny seed of great changes, and may be illustrated by an example drawn from the south of England at a comparatively early date. At Yateleigh,[268] one of the tithings of the manor of Crondal, the absorption of the waste by the customary tenants went on with great rapidity even in the thirteenth century, and in the rental drawn up by the steward in 1287 we find the rents and services paid for the customary holdings and the rents paid for the encroachments set down side by side. The latter fall into a definite scheme which can be picked out at a glance. With a very few exceptions the rent charged for an acre of land taken from the waste is always 4d., and this is the basis for all other payments for the varying portions of waste occupied by the tenants. A two acre piece pays 8d. For a piece of 9½ acres the payment is still about 4¼d. per acre, the awkward sum of 3s. 4½d. The rents and services of the customary holdings, however, cannot be reduced to any such simple and uniform plan of adjusting rent to acreage. In the first place all of them, whatever their size, are liable to an initial charge of 9½d., called "Pondpany." In the second place there is only the roughest correspondence between the amount of land held by a tenant and the payment which he makes. A holding of 22 acres pays 2s. 10d., but so does a holding of 32 acres, while one of 29 acres pays 2s. 2d. Holdings of 12½, of 16, and of 18½ acres all make exactly the same payment of 2s. In short, though it would not be quite true to say that the payment made bears no relation to the size of the holding, the relation which it bears is not at all definite and precise. It is a general relation applying rather to groups of holdings roughly marked off from others by broad differences in extent, not to individual holdings. There is no standard price per acre at all, such as appears in a modern land market, and such as exists for the land taken from the waste.

What is the reason of this remarkable contrast between the rents of pieces of land lying quite near to each other and held by the same tenants, which causes the payment for one set of holdings, the encroachments, to be adjusted uniformly to the area held, and the other, the customary holdings, to be rented apparently without any economic plan at all? The answer is that the payments for the encroachments and the payments for the customary holdings, if they are both to be called rents, are rents of very different kinds. The payments made for the customary holdings are not based directly on the economic value of the land, but on the value of commuted services, and all the holdings, though of unequal size, are liable to much the same services. All make a general payment of 9½d., because that sum

---

[268] *Crondal Records* (Baigent), pp. 116–120.

is the value of some payment in kind or service which they had made before the money payment took its place. Holdings of 32 acres and 22 acres, just as holdings of 12½ and 18½ acres, make the same payments, because the labour rents had been only very roughly adjusted to the size of the holdings, and these payments are commuted labour rents, not rents fixed by putting up an acre for leasing and taking what can be got for it. It is of course quite true that services and the size of holdings were connected, and that therefore the money rents which took the place of services and the size of holdings were connected also. But the connection is rough, arrived at by apportioning between holdings the labour services needed to cultivate the demesne, without distinguishing precisely differences of a few acres in the size of different holdings, and the subsequent money rents are not adjusted to the acreage because they express the roughness of the original apportionment.

Now clearly these considerations did not apply to the rents paid for the encroachments which were taken from the waste. The greater part of them had never been liable to labour services at all. Each acre stood by itself, as it were, as simply a piece of cultivatable land of a certain area, not part of a complex on which certain obligations had been imposed. Each, therefore, gets a market value, based on what will be given for it, much sooner than does the land making up the customary holdings, which are not exposed to the levelling influence of the market because they are bound together by their place in the social organisation of the manor. Hence it is on this land, the land leased piecemeal from the waste by tenants who were prosperous enough to afford the extra outlay, that one gets the appearance of something like true competitive rents, because it is here that commercial influences have freest play and are least checked by their subordination to custom. In the same way, when the tenants at Brightwalton[269] do the full quota of work demanded, the rent of their customary holdings is abated accordingly. But not so the rent of the new land which was once part of the waste: in fixing its rent the lord is not checked by any collective sense on the part of the village community; he has a free hand and will make the best bargain he can.

Thus, at a very early date, a fringe of leasehold land forms itself round the manor in addition to the ordinary customary holdings. Because it is on the margin of cultivation the initial rent is low, and because the land is leased the rent can be raised. Exactly the same thing applies to the leasing of the demesne, and sometimes even to the land which one tenant hires from another, because here also the element of competition enters to adjust rents in accordance with supply and demand and with little regard to the influence of custom. When the greater part of the demesne is still cultivated by the labour of villeins, and only small plots are leased to the tenants by way of experiment, the bailiff balances one method against the other, and recommends the resumption of the land which "would pay better

---

[269] Camden Society, 1857. Rental and Custumal of the Manor of Brightwalton. Under the heading virgators it is said, "If they do the full day's work set out above each of them ought to have his rent reduced 12d." Under the heading of villeins holding assarted land it is said, "Be it known that no customary tenant shall have any reduction of rent of the lands which he holds by way of assart or in the common of Greeneholt for any office or work to be done for the lord."

in the hands of the lord."[270] On some manors, it is true, demesne land seems to have been merged inextricably in the customary holdings, and to have been held later, like them, by copy of court roll.[271] But the manorial authorities were anxious to keep it separate precisely because it was recognised that if kept separate it could be let at a competitive rent. Thus the charter which was granted to the little borough of Holt[272] in Denbighshire, in 1413, provided that the tenants should pay for "every burgage 12d., for every curtilage 12d., for every acre of land belonging to their free burgages 12d., and for every acre of land which was wont to be of the lord's demesne two shillings." And though, during the confusion of the following century, much of the rent appears not to have been collected, the Crown, of whom the burgesses hold, does not forget that a high rent was due from the demesne, and one hundred and fifty years later requires them to bring up their payments for it to the level fixed in 1413. At Castle Combe, in the middle of the fifteenth century, one finds the steward of the manor watching the land market with a view to getting the best price that he can for the demesne, and speculating whether "any man will ferme the parkis and the conyes at any better price above X marks than yt ys now."[273] The same tendency towards competitive rents can be seen equally well in the case of the land leased by one tenant from the holdings of others, which for one reason or another have been surrendered to the lord. Thus at Mildenhall,[274] in 1381, a villein pays for his land nearly 1s. 6d. an acre, a very high rent, which is at once explained when it is seen that his holding consists of pieces of land held on a ten years' lease from the holdings of five or more other tenants. Elsewhere one can almost see the bidding up of rents going on. For what else can happen when the demesne lands of a manor are leased to four tenants who, in turn, make their profit by leasing them again to the other tenants,[275] or when a villein pays £6 to enter on two acres of arable land,[276] or when land is worth 3s. 6d. an acre after the rents and services have been discharged from it to the lord,[277] so that the holder

[270] Camden Society, *Inquisition of the Manors of Glastonbury Abbey*, Brentmarsh, 1189. A tenant holds "1 acre de terra arabili in dominico, utilius esset quod esset in manu domini."

[271] *e.g.*, on the Devonshire, Somerset, and Cornwall manors surveyed by Humberstone *temp.* Phil, and Mary (*Topographer and Genealogist*, vol. i.).

[272] MS. Transcript by A.N. Palmer of the Survey of the Manor of Holt, 1620 (Wrexham Free Library, *Ancient Local Records*, vol. ii.).

[273] Scrope, *History of the Manor and Barony of Castle Combe*, p. 258 (1440—1550).

[274] *Victoria County History*, Suffolk. I quote the writer's remarks in full. "The bailiff's accounts for the manor begin in that very year [1381], and the one striking feature in them is the system of leases which appears to have gradually displaced other kinds of tenure since the time of the pestilence. A few are for forty years, but most are for ten or six years.... The land so leased is not mainly demesne land. It belongs largely to villein tenements that have fallen into the lord's hands, and the process of consolidation described had already taken place at Mildenhall. The land held by John Kelsynd on a ten years' lease includes, for example, '3 acres of Frere's, Hayward's and Willway's tenement in Bradinhawfield, 1 acre of Holmes' tenement in Suttonfield, 5 acres of Zabulo's tenement in one piece at Lambwash,' and the rent of the whole 22 acres is 31s. 1d., or nearly 1s. 5d. an acre, an extremely high rent for land not stated to be meadow or pasture."

[275] Scrope, *History of the Manor and Barony of Castle Combe*, p. 203.

[276] Massingberd, *Ingoldmells Court Rolls*, Introduction, p. xxx.

[277] *Ibid.*

who cares to sublet can reap a substantial profit on the difference?

The truth is that, at any rate by the middle of the fifteenth century, the rents of different parts of a manor are being settled on quite different principles. They are not all customary rents, as they tended to be at an earlier date, nor are they all competitive rents, as they tend to be to-day. The latter are growing because of the improved economic position of the tenants, which enables them to hire or purchase land over and above their customary holdings, and their growth has been greatly accelerated by the enormously increased opportunities for land speculation which were offered when the Great Plague brought thousands of acres into the land market. It is in the demand put forward by the men of Essex in 1381,[278] "that no acre of land, which is held in villeinage or serfdom, may be had at a higher rent than 4d.," rather than in the reference to the already decaying labour services, that there is a warning of troubles to come. But long after that, as we have already seen, a great deal of land is still held by rents which are customary and little influenced as yet by the play of competition. We have, in fact, what is almost an illustration of modern theories of rent, with this difference, that though the condition of competitive rents being charged appears as the margin of cultivation is lowered, custom at first prevents the owners of land from taking advantage of their position and asking the full competitive rents from the holders of the superior sites, so that part of the surplus is for a long time enjoyed by the tenants. Such a state of things is clearly a precarious one. When the tenements of Hugh and Thomas are being rack-rented there will obviously be a strong temptation to cause Walter's to follow suit, and if the custom is a barrier to a rise in rents, but not to a rise in fines, to make heavy fines do on the latter what high rents do on the former. If it had been given to our peasants to happen on some monstrous mediæval Ricardo, would they not have wondered how long such an intermingling of payments fixed by custom and payments fixed by competition was likely to continue, and have foreseen, what actually occurred in the sixteenth century, an attempt, though not always a successful attempt, to force up the payments for customary holdings to something like the maximum which the condition of agriculture would allow? They would have said:—"This fellow fears not God, neither regards he man. He is a usurer, a great taker of advantages, an oppressor of his neighbour. We will beat him, and put him in our stocks, and maim his cattle. Nevertheless in the bottom of his foul mind there is some glimmering of sense, and we will give heed to his warning. The devil brings it, but it may be that God sent it. The Court shall recite our good customs once more, and our young men shall look to their bows. Weapon bodeth peace."[279]

[278] Stubbs, *Constl. Hist.*, vol. ii. p. 479, n. 5.

[279] The word "usury" denoted in the Middle Ages and in the sixteenth century not merely exorbitant interest on a loan, but any oppressive bargain, including the raising of prices, the beating down of wages, and the rack-renting of land (see *e.g. A Discourse on Usurie*, by Thomas Wilson, 1584). The phrase "a great taker of advantages" comes from a complaint by the people of Hereford against an unpopular divine who lent money at interest and rack-rented land (*S. P. D. Eliz.*, cclxxxvi. Nos. 19 and 20), and the phrase "weapon bodeth peace" from an account of an agrarian dispute in Lancashire—it is the sort of grim joke that stubborn and humorous people would appreciate—in *L. and P. Henry VIII.*, vol. xiii., Pt. II., p. 535. "On Sunday night Wheateley sent his daughter to bid him to come to

## *(g) The Progress of Enclosure among the Peasantry*

While competitive conditions are creeping forward on those parts of the village lands which have been most recently taken in, even more momentous changes are occurring on the customary holdings themselves. By the end of the fifteenth century we are walking through fields that are being cut up with the hedges which give the dullest English landscape the trim beauty of a garden. For a century and a half, while in the great world the new state rises on the ruins of the Middle Ages, while Tudors give way to Stuarts, and Stuarts browbeat and are browbeaten by ever more impatient Parliaments, in courts customary and sometimes in noisier assemblies not without arms, we shall be discussing whether those hedges are to stand or fall. The great enclosing movement has begun.

Like most great economic changes it has begun quietly and for a long time men are doubtful whether it is a great change at all, and, if it is mischievous, in what exactly the mischief consists. Nor indeed does the mass of the population, who feel the new conditions most, ever become quite clear on this point. Events are too various and move too swiftly for them. They see that great men enclose with little regard to the interests of their poorer neighbours. They curse them for their enclosures,[280] and believe with the faith of an age which has re-discovered the Bible, that they, like greedy Ahab, the father of enclosers, will be cursed. When the encloser should call on God to witness his deed the devil's name starts to his lips. His cattle are struck by lightning, and his children do not live to reap the fruits of his iniquity. But the peasants enclose themselves, and though they feel the

Parson's Close to mow Mr. Tempest's meadow there. Had heard that whoever should mow the meadow should be beaten off the ground, and sent to ask if he should bring a weapon. Wheateley sent word again 'howe weapon boded peace, therefore bring his weapon with him.' Brought his bow and shafts."

[280] For the popular attitude towards enclosures see below, pp. 313–340, and Leland (quoted Hone, *The Manor and Manorial Records*, p. 117): "The Duke of Buckingham made a fair park by the Castle of Thornbury, Gloucestershire, and took very much fair land in, very fruitful of corn, now fair lands for coursing. The inhabitants cursed the Duke for those lands so enclosed." I cannot refrain from quoting the following passage (*Topographer and Genealogist*, vol. iii): "To the Right Honble. House of Parliament now assembled, the Humble Petition of the Mayor and Free Tenants of the Borough of Wootton Basset in the Countie of Wilts, Humble sheweth to this Honourable House" [that their common has been seized and enclosed by the lord of the manor, who] "did divers times attempt to gaine the possession thereof by putting in of divers sorts of cattle, in so much that at length, when his servants did put in cowes by force into the said common, many times and present upon the putting of them in, the Lord in his mercy did send thunder and lightning from heaven, which did make the cattle of the said Francis Englefield [the lord of the Manor] to run so violent out of the said ground, that at one time one of the beasts was killed therewith; and it was so often that people that were not there in presence to see it, when it thundered would say, Sir Francis Englefield's men were putting in their cattle into the land, and so it was, and as soon as those cattle were gone forth, it would presently be very calm and fair, and the cattle of the towne would never stir, but follow their feeding as at other times, and never offer to move out of the way." For the allusion to invoking the devil, see Moore, *The Crying Sin of England*, &c. It was said that the grantees of monastic estates died out in three generations (Erdeswick, *Survey of Stafford*, ed. Harwood, p. 55). The same was said of enclosers (Moore, *op. cit.*).

difference between one sort of enclosing and another, they are simple men who cannot make the matter plain to lawyers and commissioners, and when things reach a certain point they will fight it out.

In every age there are words which are sufficiently definite to become a battle-cry, and yet which contain so many shades of meaning and are susceptible of such varying interpretations, that those who seem to differ most profoundly really differ because they are using the same word to express quite different ideas. Such a word was enclosing. For many years it was a burning question—with statesmen, with preachers, with the mass of the peasantry. But those who tell us exactly what it meant are few, and they tell us hardly more than is sufficient to show that it meant several different things in different connections. The picture of enclosure which carried Ket's followers against the walls of Norwich was that immortalised two centuries later in Goldsmith's "Deserted Village"; a vision of village cornfields turned into dreary expanses of pasture, where sheep grazed amid ruined homesteads and cattle were stalled in the mouldering churches.[281] When the scientific agriculturists of the age eulogised enclosures, they thought of a more orderly and productive cultivation arising in place of the intolerable "mingle mangle" of the open fields. The Levellers, who in the seventeenth century carried on the agitation against enclosure, had no objection to such as took place "only or chiefly for the benefit of the poor."[282] The panegyrists of enclosing like Fitzherbert and Norden denounced[283] lords who made enclosure an occasion to rack-rent and depopulate. The Justices of Nottinghamshire[284] complain to the Government that enclosure drives people into the already overburdened towns, but they are careful to explain

[281] See the ballad of Nowadays (1520):

> "Envy waxeth wonders strong,
> The Riche doth the poore wrong,
> God of his mercy sufferith long
> The Devil his workes to worke.
> The Townes go downe, the land decayes;
> Of cornefeldes playne layes,
> Gret men makithe now a dayes
> A shepecote in the Church.

> The places that we Right holy call
> Ordeyned ffor Christyan buriall
> Off them to make an ox-stall
> These men be wonders wyse;
> Commons to close and kepe,
> Poor folk for bred to cry and wepe;
> Towns pulled down to pastur shepe,
> This ys the newe gyse."

[282] "The Leveller's Petition" (Bodleian Pamphlets, 1648, c. 15, 3, Linc.).

[283] Fitzherbert, *Surveying*: "I advertise and exhort in God's behalf all manner of persons, that ... the lords do not heighten the rents of their tenants or cause them to pay more rent or a greater fine. A greater bribery and extortion a man cannot do than upon his own tenants, for they dare not say him naye, nor yet complain." Norden, *The Surveyor's Dialogue*, Book III.: "Lords should not depopulate by usurping enclosures, a thing hateful to God and offensive to man."

[284] *Victoria County History, Nottinghamshire*, vol. ii. p. 282.

that enclosures of less than five acres in size improve agriculture without depopulating the country. The Government itself under Elizabeth sets its face against the enclosures which produce evictions, but nevertheless expressly sanctions the exchanging of strips, which is desired chiefly in order that small enclosures may be made.[285] In this phase of the eternal quarrel between the plain man and the technical expert both the technical expert and the plain man were right, and needed only a definition to unite against the avarice and oppression which snatched a golden harvest from their confusion. It is the tragedy of a world where man must walk by sight that the discovery of the reconciling formula is always left to future generations, in which passion has cooled into curiosity, and the agonies of peoples have become the exercise of the schools. The devil who builds bridges does not span such chasms till much that is precious to mankind has vanished down them for ever.

One such distinction, however, we must draw at once. Enclosure is usually thought of in connection with the encroachments made by lords of manors or their farmers upon the land over which the manorial population had common rights or which lay in the open arable fields. And this is on the whole correct. This is what the word would have suggested to nine men out of ten in our period: this aspect of the movement was the most rapid in its development and the most far-reaching in its effects. But there was another side to it which was at once earlier in point of time and productive of quite dissimilar results. There is abundant evidence to show that the open field system of agriculture, with its intermingled strips and its collective, as opposed to individual, rules of cultivation, was undergoing a gradual dissolution from within even before the larger innovations of great capitalists gave it a shock from without. At the very time when the peasantry agitated most bitterly they were often hedging and ditching their own little holdings and nibbling away fragments of the waste to be cultivated in severalty. It is, of course, true that the effect of enclosure by the lord of a manor or large farmer was usually very different from that of enclosure by the customary tenants. The latter was a slow process of attrition, which went on quietly from one generation to another, often no doubt after discussions in the manorial court. The former was frequently an invasion. But though their social effects were dissimilar, from a technical point of view they were both part of the process through which cultivation at the discretion of the individual was substituted for cultivation in accordance with common customary rules. Enclosing by lords and large farmers was not so much a movement running counter to existing tendencies, as a continuation on a larger scale and with different results of developments which in parts of England were already at work. Great changes are best interpreted in the light of small, and it will therefore be worth our while to look shortly at the sort of enclosing which was being carried out by the peasantry themselves.

First, one may review briefly what is told us by those who wrote on the technique of agriculture. Fitzherbert[286] and Hales in the sixteenth century, Norden

[285] 39 Eliz. c. i.

[286] Fitzherbert, *Book of Husbandry*. Norden, *op. cit.*: "One acre enclosed is worth one and halfe in common." *Commonweal of this Realm of England*, p. 56. Lee, *A Vindication of a Regulated Enclosure*.

and Lee in the seventeenth, make it quite plain that, apart from enclosures carried out by lords of manors, a movement is going on among the tenants which is also known by the name of enclosure. It has as its object the formation of compact fields out of the scattered strips, and the substitution of closes surrounded by hedges for rights of grazing over the common pasture, meadow, and waste. It has as its effects a great increase in the output of wheat, opportunities for better grazing and stock-breeding, and a consequent rise in the value of land; the improvement being partly due to psychological[287] reasons, to the fact that a man who has a free hand will put more labour into the land than one who is fettered by customary rules, partly to technical causes such as the better draining and cleaning of land which the enclosure of arable ground makes possible, the greater security offered against damage done by straying cattle, the improvement in the quality of pasture when it is no longer liable to be eaten bare by the beasts of a whole township. The method by which such a change takes place is re-allotment. The construction of hedges—enclosing—is simply the machinery by which the new lines of demarcation between one man's land and another's are drawn and kept firmly in their place; and though the word *enclosure* gives a vivid picture of the alteration which is produced in the appearance of the country, *re-allotment* or *redivision* of land describes much better the process by which it is brought about. The ideal form of it is described by Fitzherbert.[288] All the landlords in a village must come to an agreement that their tenants should exchange their holdings with each other. An exact statement of the area of land in tillage and pasture held by each tenant must then be made. When this has been done, every man is "to change with his neighbour, and to leye them (*i.e.* the acres, which were formerly scattered) together, and to make him one several close in every field, to leye them together in one field and to make one several close for them all; and also another several close for his portion of his common pasture, and also his portion of his meadow in a several close by itself, and all kept in several both winter and summer. And every cottager to have his portion assigned to him according to his rent." Such enclosure does not, it is contended, interfere unfairly with any one's vested interests. It makes a spatial rearrangement of property, but it does not alter its economic distribution. It does not result in evictions or depopulation. It simply converts rights exercised jointly over a larger area into rights exercised individually over a smaller one. The map is dissolved into scattered pieces, but it is put together again; and when it is put together all the pieces are still there. The tenants part with shares in the common fields, meadows, and pastures, to get smaller fields, meadows, and pastures to themselves. The latter are more valuable than the former. What is lost in extension is gained in intension.

But this account is an ideal one, a description of the most excellent way, not necessarily a description of what is being actually done. For that we must turn to the surveys. In the picture of agriculture which is given by the surveyors one can see the open field system of cultivation at almost every stage of completeness and disintegration at different places. On many manors there is hardly any sign

---

[287] *Commonweal of this Realm of England*, p. 49: "That which is possessed of many in common is neglected of all."

[288] Fitzherbert, *Surveying*, chap. xl.

of the scattered strips, which make up the individual tenant's holding, coalescing into compactness, hardly any sign of encroachments upon either the common pasture or the meadow or the waste. Elsewhere one finds that though the bulk of the land still lies in the open fields, and though the greater part of the meadow and pasture is undivided, a considerable proportion has been enclosed by the tenants and is held in severalty. Elsewhere one finds the common meadow split up and the arable enclosed, the arable enclosed and the waste unenclosed, or all of them enclosed more or less completely. It would be of great interest and importance to determine the relative preponderance of enclosure by the tenants in different parts of the country, and to see how far the districts where this type of enclosure by consent had been commonest were identical with those where the reports of the Royal Commissions of the sixteenth and seventeenth centuries show that depopulating enclosures made least way. Very probably it would be found that the latter movement went on least rapidly where the former had proceeded furthest, and that where the tenants themselves had from an early date substituted enclosed for open field husbandry, as apparently they had in Kent, Essex, Cornwall, and parts of Devonshire[289] they had least to fear from that kind of enclosure which was accompanied by encroachments on the part of manorial authorities, and which seems to have produced most dislocation in the Midlands and Eastern counties. But this is a suggestion which our material is too scanty either to confirm or disprove. Enclosure by consent did not cause popular disorder; and therefore we cannot say, taking the country as a whole, how far enclosure on the part of the bulk of the smaller tenants had proceeded. We can only give cases which show that on some manors it had advanced very far, and which bear out the evidence of the writers on agriculture as to there being a well-defined movement away from open field husbandry on the part of the peasants themselves, without attempting to determine its extent or its geographical distribution.

Look, first, for example, at the picture given by the Commission of 1517. Thanks to Mr. Leadam,[290] we are able to say what the average acreage of the enclosures in each county represented was, what proportion of the enclosures was due to lords of manors, lay or ecclesiastical, and what proportion was due to the tenants. Now it is generally, though not universally, true that the enclosures reported to this Commission fall into two main types. The first consists of considerable enclosures carried out mainly by lords of manors. The second consists of smaller enclosures carried out mainly by other classes. Thus the five districts where the average size of the enclosures made is largest are Cambridgeshire, Gloucestershire, Yorkshire North Riding, Yorkshire West Riding, Yorkshire East Riding, where it is 129, 96, 84, 77, 62 acres respectively, and in these the proportion of the enclosures which is due to the lords of manors is high also—72 per cent., 52 per cent., 79 per cent., 92 per cent., 64 per cent. Contrast with the position in these counties that obtaining in Berkshire, in Salop, and in London and its suburbs. In Berkshire the average size of an enclosure is 32 acres, in Salop 18, in London 10, and in these districts the

---

[289] *Commonweal of this Realm of England*, p. 49. *Victoria County History*, Essex. I am inclined to say "almost certainly" rather than "very probably" (see below, pp. 167 and 262–263.

[290] *Trans. R. H. S.*, New Series, vol. vi., and *The Domesday of Enclosures*.

lords play a much smaller part in enclosing. They are responsible for 42 per cent. of the acreage enclosed in Berkshire, 12 per cent. of that enclosed in Salop, 3 per cent. of that enclosed in the vicinity of London. Does not this suggest that in parts of the country — we cannot yet say what parts — there is much small enclosing by small men?

Turn next to the story told by the surveys. Though Wiltshire is on the whole a country of recent enclosure, there was a certain amount of several farming on the part of the customary tenants on the Wiltshire manors in the middle of the sixteenth century. Out of 4128¼ acres held by them on eight manors the surveys show that 202¼ acres lie in closes.[291] This is a very small proportion, only 5 per cent., and suggests that on most of them the holdings lay in the open fields, and that, as a general rule, the common utilisation of meadows and pastures still obtained. On one, however, as much as 132 acres out of 1103, or just under 12 per cent, were enclosed, and at best these are minimum figures which do not accurately represent how far the movement had gone; for, though a surveyor would not describe unenclosed land as enclosed, he might very well class enclosed land with other land of the same description, for example as meadow or pasture, and omit to state that it was occupied in severalty. On some Staffordshire[292] manors again there are similar tentative beginnings of enclosure, and a similar impossibility of determining its actual extent. Then, too, there are manors where the greater part of the land still lies in the open fields, but where enclosure has proceeded a little further. At Salford,[293] in Bedfordshire, eight of the tenants have enclosed about 51 acres, which they hold separate from, and in addition to, their holdings in the open fields, in amounts varying from 2 to 17 acres. At Weeden Weston,[294] in Northamptonshire, the three largest tenants (apart from the farmer of the demesne) hold "in several ground enclosed" 28 acres. In addition to this, part of the manor called "the mere land," the exact nature of which is obscure, has been broken off and split up among all the fourteen tenants, some holding only 2 or 3 acres, others holding 15 or 20 acres. Finally, as examples of manors where enclosure by the customary tenants was carried furthest, we may take those of Edgeware[295] and Kingsbury in Middlesex. From the admirable maps of these two manors, which were made in 1597, no one could even guess that the open field method of cultivation had ever existed there. The land of each of the numerous tenants lies in fields, often quite small fields, which are separated from each other by hedges. Instead of the "spider's web" of the older method we have the irregular chessboard of modern agriculture.

[291] Roxburghe Club, *Surveys of the Manors of William, First Earl of Pembroke.* The manors are South Newton, Washerne, Donnington, Knyghton Estoverton and Phiphelde, Wynterbourne Basset, Byschopeston, and South Brent and Huish (the last in Somersetshire.) The manor where most is enclosed by the customary tenants is Donnington.

[292] *e.g.*, R.O. Rentals and Surveys, Gen. Ser., Portf. 14, No. 70, Barton (3 & 4 Ph. and Mary): "J. Whiting ... 1 close of 7 acres by copy ... J. Whiting ... ½ virgate ... 1 intake of 2 acres by copy."

[293] All Souls' Maps (survey on back of map of Salford).

[294] *Ibid.*, Weedon Weston.

[295] *Ibid.*, Edgeware and Kingbury. All these four instances come from the last decade of the sixteenth century.

These instances tell us nothing of the origin, extent, or distribution of the movement which they represent. They are useful merely as offering concrete specimens of enclosure on the parts of free and customary tenants, which confirm what is told us by the surveyors. There was certainly a well-defined trend away from the methods of common field agriculture taking place in the course of the sixteenth century and before it on the part of the peasantry. We can, however, go further than this; and premising that in the infinite variety of rural conditions in different parts of the country any classification must be somewhat arbitrary, we can distinguish two main elements in the movement.

In the first place there is among the tenants on some manors something like a deliberate movement towards the substitution of "several" for open field husbandry. This was a change which occurred almost spontaneously when the economic interests of the majority of tenants were pushing in the same direction, and can be seen affecting both pasture, meadow, and arable holdings. The Commission[296] of 1517 found that in certain places land had been enclosed neither by individual landlords, nor by individual tenants, but by "the village," and the manorial documents give us a clue to what such entries mean. In the surveys of the sixteenth century we not infrequently find that meadows and pastures which were originally occupied in common have been split up among the tenants, so that each has the exclusive occupation of a few acres, the share which each tenant takes being proportioned more or less exactly to his holding of arable in a manner which precludes the idea that the change can have taken place by piecemeal individual encroachments, or in any way except by an intentional redistribution of land, in which the interests of all the tenants received consideration.[297] Such a division of meadow and pasture is paralleled by cases in which the re-allotment of arable holdings is carried out both by freeholders and by copyholders almost exactly in the manner prescribed by Fitzherbert. Thus at Ewerne,[298] in Dorsetshire, the customary tenants got permission from the lord to make enclosure on the open fields; appointed persons to "extend and tread them out," and then united the dispersed strips into compact holdings, so that "the more part of the manor was enclosed, and every tenant and farmer occupied his land several to himself." At Mudford, in Somersetshire, the tenants were found by the surveyor in 1568 to be contemplating the same step. A similar course was taken in the early seventeenth century on several Northumbrian manors, of which Cowpen[299] may be taken as

---

[296] *e.g.* Whitecote (Salop) 40 acres, and at Wyndeferthing (Norf.) 25 acres are enclosed by the *villata* (see Leadam, *Trans. Royal Hist. Soc.*, New Series, vol. vi.).

[297] Roxburghe Club, *Surveys of Pembroke Manors*. At Washerne nineteen out of twenty-one customary tenants held separate pieces of meadow and pasture, the largest 7½ and the smallest 3½ acres, but usually almost equal. At Donnyngton, twelve out of thirty-two customary tenants had pieces of land "extractum de communia." R.O. Rentals and Surveys, Duchy of Lancaster, Bdle. 3, No. 29, Agarsley (Staffs., 1611).; here the pasture appears to have been divided up among the copyholders, but there are considerable inequalities in their shares.

[298] *Topographer and Genealogist*, vol. i.

[299] *Northumberland County History*, vol. ix. In this case enclosure was carried out by the freeholders. But the procedure is similar to that at Ewerne. The allusion to "justice and right" shows what the reason for the intermixing of strips had been.

a typical example.

The procedure followed by the freeholders of that township was to get their land surveyed by an expert, to divide it into two great portions, and to agree that each man should have an allotment in one or other of the two divisions proportionate to the holding which he had occupied in the open fields, due regard being had to the quality as well as the acreage of each holding, "so that some have not all the best ground and others all the worst, but that each man have justice and right." Such instances may prove to be exceptional in the sixteenth century; it is our impression that they were, and that the attempts which the peasantry made to overcome the difficulties associated with the open field system of cultivation more often took the form of individual exchanging of strips, than of a formal agreement to abandon one method of cultivation and to adopt another. But, even though exceptional, they are of some interest as offering complete examples of changes which have been going on more generally on a smaller scale and in a less systematic manner. They afford a striking contrast to the enclosing by the manorial authorities which we shall examine in a future chapter, and offer an analogy to the enclosures which were carried out in the eighteenth and nineteenth centuries. They resemble the latter in being a deliberate attempt to make a clean sweep of the old system of open field agriculture. They differ from them in being the outcome of voluntary agreement among the tenants, not of legislation.[300]

---

[300] We know why lords wanted to enclose much better than we know why tenants wanted to enclose. Here is a petition from a freeholder (*Northumberland County History*, vol. v. undated): "To the Right Honourable Earl of Northumberland, William Bednell ... gent., humbly prayeth: That where the said village of Over Buston is held in common ... it would please your good lordship to consent that partition may be made of the same, and that also there may be convenient exchange of the arable lands lyinge in the common fields there to be rateable reduced into severall by the same partition for the reasons under-written.

"First, for that the common and pasture of the said village lying open, unfenced upon the common and fields of Wordon and Bilton, wherein are many tenants and great number of cattle, the profits of the same are continually by them surcharged, and your lordship's tenants prevented.

"By reason hereof divers quarrels and variances have happened, and daily like to ensue between the tenants of both towns, by chasing, rechasing, and impounding of their cattle damage fezant, which cannot be kept out but by perpetual staffherding, to the great charge of your honour's poor tenants.

"Your lordship's tenants being four in number, unprovided to keep able horses by reason of the want of convenient pastures and meadow, may be enabled by this particion for that purpose.

"Inclosure would greatly strengthen the said village, and your lordship's tenants, against the incursions of Scotts and foren ryders, which otherwyse, lying open, cannot be defended by the number there, who are forced to watch generally together every night, to their great charge and endurable toil.

"This breeding betterment to the soil and ease to your lordship's tenants will augment your honour's revenue there, avoid forren commoners, prevent contentions, enable your lordship's tenants to do your honour their requisite service, and bind your orator to pray that your lordship live long in happy state."

Much more general, however, than enclosure by agreement of the whole township, is the enclosure which takes place through the initiative of individual tenants, who, without any common agreement as to a policy of enclosure being reached by the village community as a whole, make sporadic encroachments on the common pasture or waste, and consolidate their arable holdings by exchanging strips with their neighbours. Our best information on the first point is obtained from the manorial court rolls. The court was the guardian of the customary methods of cultivation. How far it could maintain them against a lord or his farmer who wished to break them down, and how far it was merely his mouthpiece, is a difficult question, which we need not at present discuss. Certainly it did occasionally uphold the common rule of the township even against the lord; certainly the mere fact that when that rule is uncertain the lord refers the matter to the court in the form of a series of questions which it is to answer, gave the tenants the opportunity of building up a kind of case law which can hardly have failed to act as a brake upon arbitrary action by the manorial authorities. But however impotent it may often have been when confronted by an enclosing lord of the manor, its rules set very effective limits to the discretion exercised by tenants in their agricultural arrangements, and it checked enclosing by individuals for several reasons. It was of the essence of the open field system of tillage, and of the joint use of common meadows and pastures, that unauthorised encroachments by a single tenant should be an inconvenience to his neighbours. If made on the arable, they might interfere with the customary rotation of crops, and would certainly diminish the area of land available for the village cattle on the fallows and after harvest. If made on the common waste, they threw the village economy into confusion by upsetting the arrangements under which each holding could place so many beasts to be grazed there. "It is both law and reason," wrote a surveyor grieved by such aggression on the part of a large tenant, "that every tenant of like land and like rent have like portion in all things upon the common pasture."[301] The court, as the upholder of manorial custom, was occupied with discovering and checking breaches of it. On manors where there was not sufficient grazing land to allow of each tenant pasturing as many beasts as he pleased, it fixed "the stint" which each was allowed to turn out on the common. It decided whether rights of pasture were confined to old tenements or whether they could be extended to cottages recently erected. It made rules as to what fields should be sown with what crops. It would fine a man "for refusing to consult his neighbours touching the common affairs of the township."[302]

Such action does not, of course, necessarily imply any highly developed communal organisation of village life. When four householders to-day bring an action against a fifth who has interfered with "ancient lights," they act simply as individuals who are temporarily united in defence of a common interest, and when a court customary fines a man for over-stocking the common pasture, it is possible to argue that there is no more in its action than the temporary alliance of individuals to suppress a nuisance. Yet such a view of the matter is incomplete. The common interest is there in both cases; but in the case of the village community

---

[301] *Northumberland County History*, vol. v. The Surveyor of Buston (1569).
[302] *Ibid.*

it is a permanent, not merely a passing, ground for co-operation; and if we must take to heart the warnings given by some legal historians not to see communism where there is only joint action, we must also insist that common action, which is in effect communal action, is quite possible without those who act either possessing, or feeling the need of possessing, any definite status.[303] It is perhaps not too presumptuous to suggest that the very precision with which the lawyer applies his keen analysis of juristic conceptions to remove the misconceptions of the lay mind, is sometimes an obstacle to the understanding of forms of organisation created by the daily routine of men quite unversed in the law. An employers' association or a trade union to-day in an industry which is not highly organised is, during two-thirds of its life, a mere collection of individuals. But in an emergency it can show very effectively that it is the organ of a common will. It is surely rather hard to deny the peasantry some measure of corporate management of common interests because they cannot answer questions as to the legal nature of a corporation, because they do not express their communal arrangements by the use of terms of art which they would not have understood. The economist, at any rate, will look at practice rather than theory. He will be inclined to doubt whether the villagers were any clearer as to the basis of their associated action than the mass of trade unionists were between 1875 and 1906. But he will see that, like trade unionists, they do in fact habitually act together and act effectively for the regulation of their common interests. No doubt such action was often mere adherence to a customary rule. But it is possible again to draw the antithesis between custom and organisation too sharply. After all custom does not work by itself. Especially in times of change, like the sixteenth century, it only works in so far as men make it work. On some manors it is frequently changed by the court, and clearly, when it is changed, we have not automatism but deliberate action.

But the power of a rule is not recognised till it is broken, and it is just these collisions between the plan of cultivation upheld by the court and the interests of individual tenants, which show how prevalent are the small enclosures made by the latter. They begin very early and are increasingly frequent throughout the fifteenth century. Let us make the picture more precise by giving one or two instances. In 1405 some customary tenants at Forncett[304] are fined 2s. 2d. because "they have made enclosures of their lands within the manor against the custom of the manor, on account of which action the tenants of the manor are not able to have their common there." In 1418 the court at Castle[305] Combe presents that three tenants "have sown the common fields and kept them several without the licence of the lord, when they ought to be common, to the common damage." At Ingoldmells,[306] in 1437, the court impounds the sheep of some tenants who have "entered upon the fields of Burgh and occupied the common there, where they have no common." At Coventry[307] from the middle of the fifteenth century, and at

---

[303] For references to the discussion on this point, see below, p. 244.

[304] Davenport, *History of a Norfolk Manor*, p. 80.

[305] Scrope, *History of the Manor and Barony of Castle Combe*, p. 236.

[306] Massingberd, *Ingoldmells Court Rolls*, p. 276.

[307] M.D. Harris, *Coventry Leet Book*, vol. ii., pp. 445, 456, 510, and elsewhere.

Southampton[308] throughout almost the whole of the century and a half following, continuous war was waged by the Court Leet against those who "oppressed the common" by over-stocking it with more than their authorised quota of beasts. Yet, in spite of elaborate and ever-changing regulations which were made as to the number which any person might place upon it, in spite of bye-laws requiring them to be delivered personally or through a servant into the charge of the town herdsman, ruling off aged animals which were past work, and imposing heavy fines on offenders, the constant references in the documents of the sixteenth century to pieces of land which are held by customary tenants in severalty show that this sporadic individualising of part of the manorial area had to a great extent broken down the customary routine of cultivation, even on manors where no extensive enclosures were carried out by the manorial authorities.

So far we have spoken of the encroachments by tenants on the common pasture. The growth of several occupation could occur there with less disturbance than on the arable holdings, because, if the pasture was a large one, the clipping off of a corner might leave the other tenants with more than was sufficient for their cattle. But enclosure made by one tenant on the open arable fields created a disturbance which was immediate and obvious. Indeed, if his holding lay in scattered strips, separated from each other by the strips of his neighbours, how could he enclose at all? He would at once come into collision with their demand that his holding should lie open for grazing purposes after harvest. Moreover, even from his own point of view, enclosure could hardly pay, for he would have to put hedges round each of 30 or 40 or 50 acre and half acre plots. One would expect, therefore, that individual tenants would be slow to undertake the hedging and ditching of their arable holdings; and this expectation is on the whole confirmed by the impression which one gets from the surveys and from the accounts of contemporaries.[309] On the tenants' arable land enclosure has not proceeded by the middle of the sixteenth century as far as on their pasture and meadow. Yet, even in this matter, the tendency is perhaps to exaggerate the stability of agricultural conditions. Even on the arable fields themselves individual tenants set themselves to overcome the obstacles in the way of enclosure, and they do so in the only way they can, by attempting first of all to consolidate their strips into larger holdings. This tendency is revealed most clearly by the open field maps. The picture of mediæval agriculture, to which Mr. Seebohm has accustomed us, is one in which holdings were made up of strips which lay scattered over the open fields at a considerable distance from each other. In the sixteenth century this condition of things survived in its entirety on many manors and partially on most. But, side by side with it, there is going on a process by which the strips coalesce into larger bundles, so that one tenant's pieces of land, instead of being far apart, very often lie next to each other, forming blocks of several acres. Those who make maps show the change by putting brackets round the

---

[308] Hearnshaw, *Court Leet Records of Southampton, passim, e.g.* 1551: "Thomas Betts and Thomas Fuller continue to oppress the common with sheep, therefore they are fined 8s. each" (p. 21).

[309] *e.g. The Commonweal of this Realm of England*, p. 56: "And weare it not that oure grounde lieth in the common fieldes, intermingled one with another, I thincke also oure fieldes had been inclosed, of a common agreement of all the townshippe, longe ere this time."

contiguous strips.[310] Written surveys, instead of describing parts of holdings with the words "lying between the land of A and the land of B," call attention to the new condition of things, which is still sufficiently unusual to deserve remark, with the words "lying together."[311] Sometimes in the maps one finds twelve or twenty strips bracketed as belonging to one man; sometimes the surveys state that 16 or 20 acres lie together. But even 10 acres is a big field, quite big enough to repay the cost of hedging and ditching. When sufficient strips have become contiguous to form a close of this size one great obstacle to enclosure has been removed. Unity of cultivation has been added to unity of ownership. The difficulty that enclosure will probably, though not necessarily, mean the exclusion of the other tenants' beasts after harvest still remains. But an individual tenant will no longer find enclosure impossible if he can persuade his neighbours to acquiesce in it. In fact he does sometimes persuade them, and in the midst of fields which are still open one finds here and there blocks which have been enclosed.

Nor can we doubt that this process of forming strips into blocks took place through deliberate action on the part of tenants, though we need not assume that the probability of its leading to enclosure was always foreseen. The amalgamation of the scattered parts of a single holding had sufficient advantages to commend it without any further change, and enclosure may often have been an afterthought. How could this amalgamation come about? It would naturally take place by a process of exchange[312] between tenants. As we have seen, the tenants were from an early date buying and selling, leasing and sub-letting, parts of their holdings. What could be more reasonable than that in doing so they should have regard to the situation of the plots which they acquired, and so arrange their bargains as gradually to substitute a few larger blocks for many scattered strips? This hypothesis (for it is only a hypothesis) receives a certain amount of confirmation from a curious fact to which attention was called for the first time by Professor Unwin.[313] It occasionally happens that we find the very tenants who sell and let part of their holdings are buying and leasing parts of other holdings from their neighbours. Thus, at Gorleston,[314] in Suffolk, a customary tenant sublets about half his holding of 12 acres to as many as eight other persons, and at the same time acquires plots of land from another eight holdings himself. At Crondal[315] Richard Wysdon adds enormously to his half-virgate by encroachments, and at the same time sublets 2½

----

[310] See opposite, the map of part of Salford.

[311] Merton Documents, No. 5209, Rental of Ibstone (about 1600): "Item, Thomas Skott holdeth ix acres as it is estymed lieinge together in Tillage." "John ... holdeth 16 acres of Lande lieinge together in Redfield."

[312] Exchanges are not uncommon, *e.g.* Roxburghe Club, *Pembroke Surveys*, Manor of South Brent and Huish: "Note that the same Thomas with leave of the Court has exchanged the said acre lying near Appleworth with John Moore, customary tenant of the lord, for one acre lyinge in Holmefield." Mr. Kolthammer has called my attention to a case (Ashford Court Rolls, 1605), in which a tenant gives up a number of half acre strips lying between the lands of another, and receives in exchange some strips of the latter which lie between his own.

[313] *Victoria County History*, Suffolk, Social and Economic History.

[314] *Victoria County History*, Suffolk, Social and Economic History.

[315] *Crondal Records* (Baigent), pp. 134, 149, 152, 154–155.

acres to Hugh Sweyn. Henry Simmond enters on land belonging to the same Richard Wysdon, and in turn transfers 8 acres of his holding to Matilda Huthe. What is relevant to the question in these transactions is not the mere sub-letting and selling of land. That, as we have seen, was common enough. The noticeable thing is that the same tenant who surrenders part of his holding acquires part of the holdings of other people. After the transactions are completed he holds about as much land as before, only it is differently arranged. May it not be that the desire that it should be differently arranged was one of the motives of the double transaction, and that in this way he sought to substitute for his dispersed strips a compacter and more manageable holding? Is he not like a shareholder who sells out Canadian Pacifics and invests in Consols, in order to have his property more directly under his own eye? At any rate such an explanation would account for the undoubted fact that in the sixteenth century holdings are much more compact than they are in the thirteenth century. But whether it is correct or not the growth towards compactness is a fact, and a fact which makes possible the enclosure of holdings in the open fields.

It is plain from these and similar instances that there was a well-defined movement from the fourteenth century onwards which made for the gradual modification or dissolution of the open field system of cultivation, and that it originated not on the side of the lord or the great farmer, but on the side of the peasants themselves, who tried to overcome the inconvenience of that system by a spontaneous process of re-allotment, sometimes, but not always, in conjunction with actual enclosure. On one manor it proceeded by the piecemeal encroachments of individuals, on another by the deliberate division of the common meadow or pasture, on a third by the voluntary exchanging by tenants of their strips so as to build up compact holdings, on a fourth by the redistribution of the arable land. It was a spontaneous movement in the sense of being initiated by the tenants and not merely forced upon them. The economic, as distinct from the legal, arrangements of the village community were much less rigid than some of the books about it would suggest. The open field system of cultivation was, in fact, already in slow motion in several parts of England, when the impact of the large grazier struck it, enormously accelerated the speed of the movement, and diverted it on to lines which were new and disastrous to the bulk of the rural population.

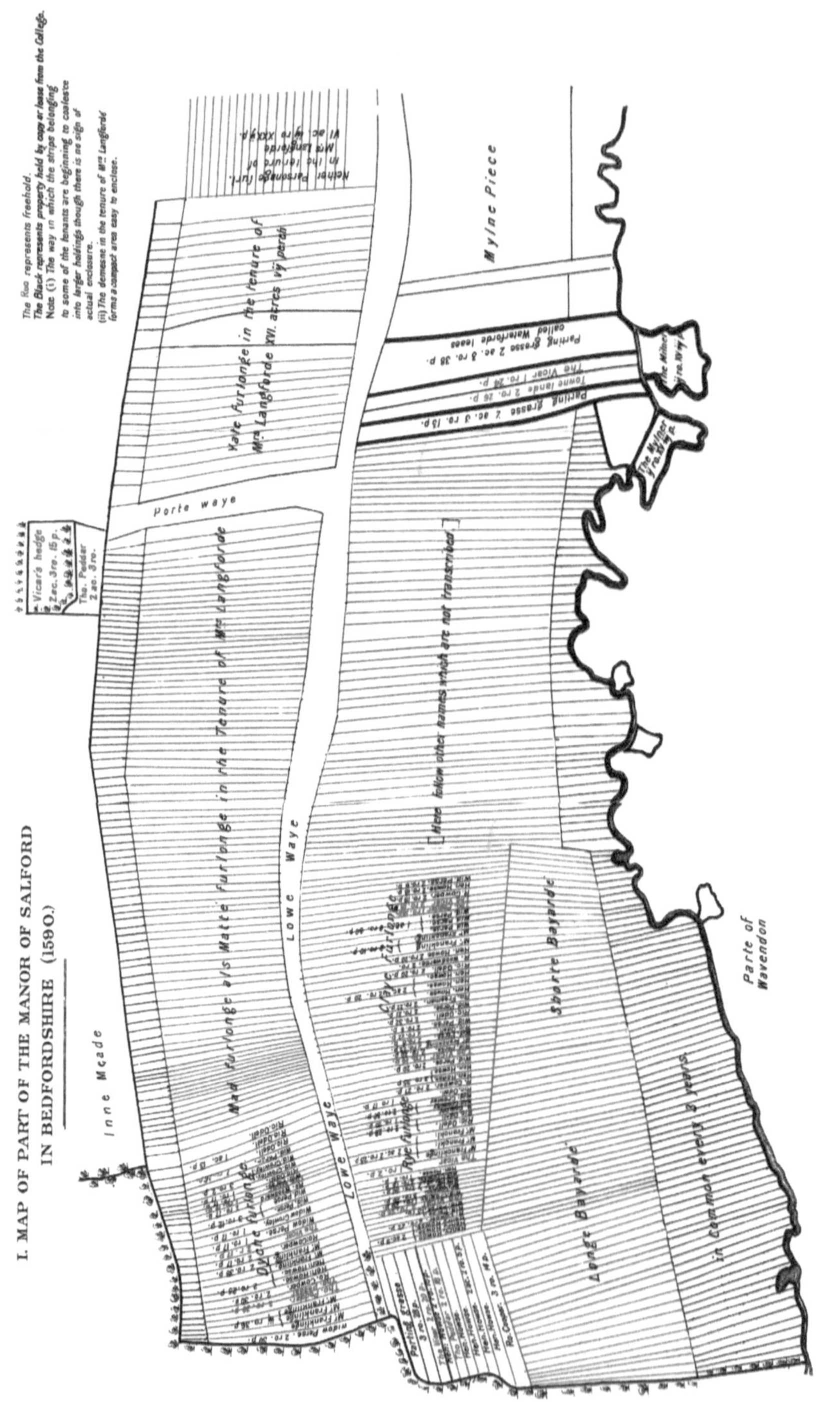


Map of Part of the Manor of Salford, in Bedfordshire (1590)

*The Red represents freehold.*

*The black represents property held by copy or lease from the College.*

*Note (i) The way in which the strips belonging to some of the tenants are beginning to coales'ce into larger holdings though there is no sign of actual enclosure.*

*(ii) The demesne in the tenure of M^rs Langfordé forms a compact area easy to enclose.*

This aspect of the enclosures, though not overlooked by contemporaries, has perhaps hardly received the emphasis which it deserves from modern writers. For one thing, a recollection of it explains certain apparent contradictions, the difference in the views expressed by different writers in the sixteenth and seventeenth centuries as to the social effect of enclosures, the disagreement between Mr. Leadam and Professor Gay as to whether enclosing was or was not usually followed by conversion to pasture, the strange statement of Hales[316] that "the chief destruccion of Townes and decaye of houses was before the beginning of the reigne of Kynge Henry the Seventh." The latter remark can hardly have been true of the great and sudden evictions which caused rioting and depopulation, and evoked the long series of statutes which begin in 1489. It may well have been a curt summary of the impression produced by a century of gradual consolidation and piecemeal enclosures carried out by the smaller cultivators. It would seem, again, to be the case that while landlords usually enclosed with the object of putting sheep where men had been, the tenants of customary holdings enclosed simply for the sake of better arable farming, or for the more convenient employment of meadow and pasture land. That is why Hales could make himself detested by landlords as the chairman of the only effective committee of Somerset's ill-starred Enclosure Commission, and at the same time say that certain kinds of enclosure are "very beneficiall to the commonweal." That is why Fuller and Moore a century later could damn enclosure in one sentence and qualify their verdict in the next. That is why Moore's numerous critics could repudiate his aspersions with some acrimony, and nevertheless admit that "when townes are in the hands of one or few men ... enclosure doth produce depopulation."[317]

---

[316] "The defence of John Hales agenst certyn sclaundres and false reaportes made of hym" (Appendix to Miss Lamond's introduction to *The Commonweal of this Realm of England*, p. liii.). Two things make the effect of the fifteenth century enclosures obscure. First, the pamphlets on popular grievances which begin in the sixteenth century were hardly possible before the general use of the printing press. Second, in the sixteenth century people appealed to the Tudor government for protection because it was strong enough to give it. In the fifteenth century there was no Government to preserve order, let alone protect the poorer classes. Even if there were, therefore, extensive enclosures producing depopulation, we might very well hear little of them. But, while confessing ignorance, I think Hales' statement compatible with the view expressed above and on page 138, note 1, that the fifteenth century was a time when the consolidation of holdings was going forward slowly through the small speculations of the peasants.

[317] *A Vindication of the Considerations concerning Common Fields and Enclosures* (Pseudonismus).

For another thing, the prevalence of small enclosures suggests that the view of those who represent the agriculture of the period as needing a violent shock to rouse it from a state of intolerable inefficiency can only be accepted with considerable qualification. We know that by the middle of the sixteenth century in certain counties, notably Kent, Essex, and Devonshire, the common field system of cultivation was already the exception and not the rule. We know, too, that though in parts of these counties its absence may have been due to differences in the original forms of settlement and clearance, it had elsewhere disappeared within historical times. We may conjecture that the reason why it decayed sooner in Kent and Essex than elsewhere was the fact that the neighbourhood of those counties to London and the sea, and to the commercial routes from the Continent, caused the influence of commerce and of a money economy to be felt there sooner than in the Midlands, with the natural result of accelerating economic and agrarian changes, and that in the examples quoted above we have the same process of individualisation in the method of agriculture going on quietly elsewhere in a way which would sooner or later have brought about a similar result to that which had already occurred in those two progressive districts. At any rate these rearrangements suggest a good deal of adaptability among the tenants who carried them out, and not the condition of organised torpor which some writers profess to find in the unenclosed village. That communal cultivation was incompatible with swift change may be granted. Of that fact its survival into almost our own day is a sufficient proof. That it prevented improvements altogether must be denied; and though no doubt to large farmers and impatient surveyors the petty operations of the smaller tenants seemed intolerably dilatory and wasteful, the student who looks at them in an age which has some experience of economic revolutions may well doubt whether rapid technical progress cannot be bought too dear, and regret that the gradual movement towards more rational methods of farming on the part of the small man was so soon overtaken by one over which the small man could exercise no effective control. Now, as then, land agents shake grave heads at the wastefulness of sacrificing the well-ordered dignity of a great estate to the encouragement of undercapitalised, untidy, higgledy-piggledy small holdings, and prove by arithmetic that the labourer has more comforts for less work. Now, as then, in those countries where the peasant tradition has not died altogether away, the unreasonable creature prefers starving on land which is his own, though it be but a tiny patch where he sweats from dawn to dark.

If it be objected to the view which we have taken of the slow spread of enclosure among the peasantry that they were notoriously opposed to enclosing, we must answer by repeating that there was nothing inconsistent in approving one kind and detesting another. After all there is no curse attached to landmarks, but only to the man who removes his neighbour's. Even in an open field village no one had a conscientious objection to fences in general; it all depended on where the fences were put. The object of enclosure was to shut in, or to shut out, or to do both. The villagers were not unwilling that an agreement should be reached whereby each man should shut his own beasts in a close of pasture, and shut out the beasts of other people from his arable after harvest. On the contrary, it was sometimes a grievance[318] that enclosure was not allowed. What they objected to was that one man should exclude others without compensation from rights of pasture or from their arable holdings. Moreover, provided that enclosure took place by consent, the advantages of it were overwhelming. When the superior[319] value of enclosed over unenclosed land was so marked that the former was sometimes assessed to subsidies at a higher rate than the latter, a man who, like many of our tenants, had money to spend on timber, would naturally wish to enclose. The growth of pasture farming by large graziers turned the minds of the smaller tenants in the direction of enclosing for themselves, because this, paradoxical though it may seem when the outcry against enclosure is remembered, was the most obvious way in which they could protect themselves. The explanation is that the system of open field cultivation and of common pasturage made it peculiarly easy for one large shareholder to ruin the rest by letting his cattle stray at large over the common, and even by encroachments on his neighbour's strips. Its underlying principle had been the apportionment of rights on a basis which was settled by the custom of the manor, as opposed to the acquisition by individuals for themselves of such rights as they could obtain by economic power, or by the accumulation of capital. This was the meaning of the strict allotment of grazing privileges by the establishment of a stint which each tenant, or rather each tenement, was not to exceed. The limitation to the capital which a man could acquire in the shape of stock—cattle and sheep—was practicable as long as that capital was small. When it became large, as in the sixteenth century it did, it was too powerful to be dammed up by the rules as to cultivation enforced in the manorial court, and the outward sign of this was the failure of the latter to prevent the "overcharging" both of the common waste, and of the common pasture formed by the field after harvest, with the beasts of the large grazier. Hence in some places the enclosing of pasture or arable was used by the tenants as a way of protecting themselves: at Mudford the

[318] *Topographer and Genealogist*, vol. i., Survey of Whitford: "I woulde wish that the same [the common] were divided among the tenants yielding some small rente ... the poore men with dyligence and labour woulde soon convert yt to amendement, and alter the nature thereof, but the ritche men will not consent to that, for yt is as good to them as theire several grounde or pasture. The poore are not able to store yt with cattle, nor to use the commodytie as they might do if welth woulde serve them. But the rytche do consume their own parts and their neighbouris also: and that is the cause they will not consent to the enclosure and partition thereof."

[319] There is interesting documentary proof of the statements of surveyors. Warwickshire MSS. Quarter Sessions Records, Michaelmas, 1636: "Fforasmuche as this Courte is informed that Overhinton (?) in this countie consists of 30 yardlands, of which 22 are enclosed and 8 yardlands thereof residue in the possession of Thomas [surname illegible] do lie in the common fields, and whereas the same 8 yardlands lyinge in the comon fields have been heretofore rated equally and proportionablie in all levies with thother yardlands, the said 22 yard of inclosed land being worth xx [pounds], for every yardland and the seid other 8 yardlands being worth but after the rate of x the yardland, it is ordered that the said 8 yardlands shall from henceforth pay in all levies but after the rate of x pounds for every yardland and the said 22 yardlands after the rate of xx pounds for every yardland, unless the owners of the said 22 yardlands shall att the next sessions uppon convenient notice hereof to them given shewe cause to the contrarie." The Justices do not understand the taxation of unimproved land.

tenants, at Newham and Tughall the surveyor in the interests of the tenants, at Southampton the Leet jury, were anxious[320] for enclosing, in order that the weak barriers which the custom of the manor offered to the farmers' or to neighbouring villagers' depredations might be supplemented by a strong quickset hedge. What damaged the smaller tenants, and produced the popular revolts against enclosure, was not merely enclosing, but enclosing accompanied either by eviction and conversion to pasture, or by the monopolising of common rights. When some of the tenants became large capitalists, what the rest lost by surrendering common rights might be more than compensated by the security which they thus obtained of grazing their own beasts undisturbed on a smaller area.

At the same time, though voluntary enclosing by the peasants was partly a symptom of the overshadowing of small property by large, it was much more than this, and was due partly to a change in their methods of agriculture, and partly, perhaps, to a genuine progress in the technique of cultivation. This is indicated by the enthusiasm of the expert opinion of the period for "several" holdings, and by the qualified praise of discriminating critics like Hales.[321] As we have seen above, there were parts of England—for example, "the sweet country of Tandeane," described by Norden—where cultivation was quite intensive in character, and intensive cultivation naturally gave an impetus to the individualising of arable holdings. Again, the advantage to the cattle breeder of "several closes and pastures to put his cattle in, the which would be well quicksetted, hedged, and ditched,"[322] was a commonplace. It has been already pointed out that on many manors of Southern and Eastern England the customary tenants were sheep farmers on a considerable scale. The adjustment of common rights must always have involved some difficulty: the fixing of so many head of beasts to each tenement was obviously a rough and ready arrangement based on the idea that the holding in the arable fields was the backbone of a man's substance, and that therefore it might properly be taken as a standard by which his rights of pasture and common could fairly be measured. The problems which arose could be imagined, even if they were not described for us at some length: "Where fields lie open and the land is used in common, he that is rich and fully stocked (up to the limit allowed) eateth with his cattle not his own part only, but also his neighbour's who is poor and out of stock. Besides that, it is an ordinary practice with unconscionable people to keep above their just proportion ... those who have consciences large enough to do it will lengthen their ropes, or stake them down so that their horses may reach into other men's lots."[323] As long as the great bulk of the customary tenants relied for a

[320] See *Topographer and Genealogist*, vol. i., for Mudford; for Newham and Tughall, *Northumberland County History*, vol. i.; for Southampton, Hearnshaw, *Court Leet Records of Southampton*.

[321] *The Commonweal of this Realm of England*, p. 49: "I meane not all inclosures, nor yet all commons, but only of such inclosures as turneth commonly arable lands into pastures; and violent inclosures, without recompence of them that have right to comen therein; for if land weare severallie inclosed, to the intent to continue husbandrie thereon, and everie man, that had Right to Common, had for his portion a pece of the same to himselfe enclosed, I thincke no harme but rather good should come thereof, yf everie man did agre theirto."

[322] Fitzherbert, *Book of Husbandry*.

[323] Pseudonismus, 1654, *Considerations concerning Common Fields and Enclosures*.

livelihood mainly on the subsistence farming of the arable land, these practical difficulties were probably not felt very keenly, because the comparatively few beasts which were kept could pick up a living without overcrowding each other. But when the raising of stock became almost as important as the cultivation of arable, the demand for more pasture and for better pasture grew enormously, and in the face of the competition for it the strict maintenance of the customary stint became more difficult. On manors where 150 or 200 sheep were kept by almost every tenant the motive either to enclose surreptitiously and in defiance of the custom of the manor, or to divide and enclose meadow and pasture by agreement, must have been extremely strong. Ought we not to ask why the open field system survived so long, rather than why it partially disappeared in the sixteenth century?

We may now summarise the argument of this part of our work. The manor, as we see it from the middle of the fourteenth century onwards, is not the rigid, motionless organisation which it is sometimes represented as being. Though it is governed by custom, custom leaves room for the growth of commercial relationships on the extending fringe of new land over which the village spreads; for the withdrawal by the villagers of part of their holdings from the common scheme of open field husbandry, the division of meadows and pastures, the exchanging of strips, the formation of closes like those represented in the map on the opposite page, which a man can use as he pleases and over which the customary routine of agriculture has no authority. This side of the enclosing movement, more properly described as redivision and reallotment than as enclosure, develops earliest in those parts of the country which, owing to their geographical position, are particularly exposed to the dissolving forces of trade and of a money economy. But with the improvement in the condition of the peasantry and the growth of pasture farming it spreads far afield, and by the middle of the sixteenth century, quite apart from the large changes introduced by lords of manors and capitalist farmers, it has effected a considerable alteration in the methods of agriculture even of the more stationary inland counties. Such piecemeal alterations are a gradual process; they are not regarded unfavourably by the peasantry; and a balance between their tentative individualism and the rule of communal custom is preserved by the action of the manorial court. They are to be carefully distinguished from the sweeping innovations of the sixteenth century, which alone deserve the name of an Agrarian Revolution. But they are closely connected with that revolution. For by making a breach in the walls of custom they bring us to the edge of two great problems, the growth of competitive rents, and the formation of large pasture farms out of the holdings of evicted tenants.

We have spoken at length of the prosperity of the peasants, because it is necessary to appreciate it in order to sympathise with the point of view from which they and their contemporaries regarded the agrarian problem. But evil days are coming upon the rural middle classes. Indeed they have already come. There is by this time much anger against depopulating landlords, much talk of the good customs of Henry VII., much murmuring lest men be brought to that slavery the Frenchman be in. We must leave the light and follow them into the shadow.

**Part of the Manor of Edgeware, in Middlesex (1597)**

*Note. This Map illustrates enclosure carried out by individual ten-ants on their own holdings. Such enclosure is not accompanied by the merging of several holdings in one great farm, and therefore does not cause evictions. It is commended by those who condemn evictions and conversion of arable to pasture. (vide. The commonweal of England. The second Dialogue F. 29.)*

# PART II
# THE TRANSITION TO CAPITALIST AG-RICULTURE

"The earth is thine, O Lord, and all that is contained therein; notwithstanding thou hast given the possession thereof to the children of men, to pass over the time of their short pilgrimage in this vale of misery. We heartily pray thee to send thy holy spirit into the hearts of them that possess the grounds, pastures, and dwelling places of the earth; that they, remembering themselves to be thy tenants, may not rack and stretch out the rents of their houses and lands; nor yet take unreasonable fines and incomes, after the manner of covetous worldlings; but so let them out to other, that the inhabitants thereof may be able to pay their rents, and also honestly to live, to nourish their families, and to relieve the poor: give them grace also to consider that they are but strangers and pilgrims in this world, having here no dwelling place, but seeking one to come; that they, remembering the short continuance of their life, may be content with that is sufficient, and not join house to house and field to field, to the impoverishment of others, but so behave themselves in letting out their tenements, lands, and pastures, that after this life they may be received into everlasting dwelling places; through Jesus Christ, our Lord. Amen." *—A Prayer for landlords, from a Book of Private Prayer, authorised and set forth by order of King Edward VI.*

"Nowe if I should demand of the gredie cormoraunts what they thinke should be the cause of sedition, they would saie:— 'The paisent knaves be too welthy, provender pricketh them. They knowe not themselves; they knowe no obedience; they regard no lawes; they would have no gentlemen; they would have al men like themselves; they would have all things commune. They would not have us master of that which is our owne. They will appoint us what rent we shall take for our grounds.... They will caste down our parkes, and lay our pastures open.... They will compel the King to graunt theyr requests.... We wyll tech them to know theyr betters. And because they would have all in common, we will leave them nothing,'" *—E. E. T. S., Crowley, The Way to Wealth.*

# CHAPTER I
## THE NEW RURAL ECONOMY

### *(a) Motives and Causes*

A common view of social development regards it as the outcome of irresistible causes working towards results which can be neither hastened nor averted, and treats the fact that events have followed a certain course as in itself an indication that no other course was possible. Whatever is has always been implicit in the past; the established fact rules by the divine right of being the only possible dynasty, and no scope is left for pretenders to contest or acts of settlement to alter its legitimate title. It is not surprising that such a theory should be peculiarly popular in interpreting economic history. On their frontiers even the most different forms of social organisation shade into one another. Each generation naturally sees in a strong light those regions of the past which reproduce the features with which it is familiar, and overlooks the existence of wide Hinterlands whose general features are quite different. Since important classes, like important individuals, find it difficult to believe in the truthfulness of any picture where they do not occupy the greater part of the canvas, they insensibly encourage a conventional interpretation of history, which lends an air of respectable antiquity to the legal and economic arrangements which favour them and which they favour, by treating such arrangements as an essential characteristic of civilisation itself. In reality, however, it is only by dragging into prominence the forces which have triumphed, and thrusting into the background those which they have swallowed up, that an appearance of inevitableness is given to existing institutions, which satisfies the desire to see them as links in an orderly chain of unavoidable sequences. Useful as the conception of a continuous development is, it can easily be carried too far. It is carried too far when it causes us to forget that a small alteration in the lie of the land might have caused the stream to take quite a different channel, and that the smoothly flowing waters of the plain are the outcome of a series of crises in the higher regions, where the spur of a mountain or a cleft in the rocks might easily have diverted their course into other directions. If we must talk of social evolution, we ought to remember that it takes place through the action of human beings, that such action is constantly violent, or merely short-sighted, or deliberately selfish, and that a form of social organisation which appears to us now to be inevitable, once hung in the balance as one of several competing possibilities.

Certainly the possibility that economic changes should have followed a quite different line from that which they actually have can hardly fail to strike the student of agrarian history. The facts, as we read them, do not lend unqualified support to the idea that the growth, at the expense of the little landholders, of great estates cultivated by hired labour was the inevitable result of irresistible forces, or that the new agricultural régime was a necessity on account of the sluggishness of the old. To an observer of agrarian conditions living about the year 1500, who looked back over the conditions of the last century, all the possibilities must have seemed to point in the direction of a continuous improvement in the condition of the peasantry. It is evident that the growth of prosperity among the small cultivators was leading from the beginning of the fifteenth century to the gradual consolidation of holdings, to keen competition for the use of land, and to increasing individualism in the methods of agriculture. Though the movement caused a diminution in the number of landholders, the diminution was very gradual. It was not the result of a sudden revolution affecting large numbers of tenants simultaneously; and even those who regarded enclosing with hostility were favourable to the process of gradual redistribution, which did not violate vested interests or cause any sensational disturbance. The appearance of the country would have changed, and the methods of cultivation would have improved. But there would have been no great cause at work to displace the peasantry from the soil, with the rapidity which entailed hardship, until a much later period than we are now considering. Obviously, however, it was not these slow internal changes in the manorial organisation which impressed observers. On the contrary, though they are noticed by the writer who took a scientific interest in agricultural questions, they are hardly mentioned by the majority of commentators on the life of the period, who were interested not in the technique of agriculture but in the social results of changing methods. What aroused their alarm and produced rioting and legislation was, as every one knows, a movement the distinctive feature of which was that it was initiated by lords of manors and great farmers, "the Graziers, the rich buchars, the men of law, the merchants, the gentlemen, the Knights, the Lords,"[324] in short by the wealthiest and most powerful classes, and that it was carried out frequently against the will of the tenants, and in such a way as to prejudice their interests.

As the small capitalist prepared the way for the great, the two movements were connected, and the simultaneous development of both of them explains the rather puzzling mixture of approval and criticism which is to be found in the comments of observers upon enclosing. But their economic and social results were very different. No doubt the incipient movement in the direction of reorganising national life on the basis of industry involved a breach with the customary methods of agriculture, which must in any case have caused a certain degree of dislocation. The development of the textile manufactures, which for two centuries were the chief source of English wealth, could not have taken place without the production of cheap supplies of raw material, and the growth of the towns was dependent on the saving of labour from agriculture. But in such changes the element of time—the speed at which the transition takes place—is all important, because upon it depends the feasibility of social readjustments to meet the new situation. The slow breaking up of the open field system, though it changed the methods of cultivation, might quite conceivably have effected only such a gradual diminution

---

[324] Crowley, *The Way to Wealth* (E. E. T. S.).

in the number of the small farmers, as to make the absorption into industry of those displaced comparatively easy. In so far as the changes of the sixteenth century were a social revolution, and not merely a gradual development, this revolution was the result not only of technical advances, but of the concentration of landed property and the development of new relationships between landlord and tenant. It is to the second of the two movements that we must now turn.

The new agrarian arrangements which we shall have to consider are called by the name of enclosure, and we will discuss later what exactly enclosure means in this connection. But there are enclosures and enclosures, and we shall do well to begin by drawing some distinctions. In the first place, then, the enclosing movement that will occupy us in this chapter has very little resemblance to the enclosure which we have considered in the last. It is carried out by great men, not by small. It proceeds wholesale, not piecemeal. It does not consist in many little cultivators rearranging their holdings by purchase, or sale, or agreement, but in one great proprietor or his agent consolidating small holdings into great estates. The new arrangements are imposed rapidly and with a high hand from without. They do not arise gradually from within through the spontaneous development of the peasants' needs and resources.

Again, the new movement bears very little resemblance to the rearrangements introduced by lords of manors, which, from an early date, have gone by the name of enclosing. Such rearrangements have not been few. People have talked about enclosing long before they have begun to lament enclosures. Not to mention the encroachments on the waste evidenced by the Statute of Merton, one finds the word "enclosure" used in the thirteenth and fourteenth centuries to describe a variety of agreements made between lords whose lands were contiguous, or between lords and their free tenants, by which, instead of the parties concerned using a given area in common as their pasture, each surrenders his right of access to part of it, and obtains in return the right to use another part in severalty. The Abbot of Malmesbury[325] and the men of Niwentone come to an arrangement with Walter of Asselegge and the men of that village, whereby the monastery agrees to follow the customary routine in cultivating the land lying between Niwentone and Asselegge, and not to common on the marsh at Cheggeberge, getting in return exclusive rights of pasture over another marsh, and over the east field of Niwentone. The Abbot and Monastery of St. Peter's[326] of Gloucester make an agreement with Lord Thomas Berkeley whereby the former are "to have and hold in severalty and enclose and approve at their will" certain lands lying in Southfield "so that the said Thomas and his free tenants may not ... claim or demand common, but be

---

[325] *Registrum Malmesburiense*, vol. ii. pp. 220–221: "Quod ... dictus abbas de Malmesburia non debet de cetero colere terram de Niwentone ... nisi antiquitus consueverat coli. Et quod dictus Walterus de Asselegge habebit mariscum suum de Cheggeberge quietum a communia hominum de Niwentone. Dicti vero abbas et conventus Malmesburia habebunt mariscum suum iacentem ex Orientali parte stratæ publicæ quæ vocatur Fos quietum et exceptum a communia hominum de Asselegge. Habebunt etiam ... campum Australem in Niwentone quietum et exceptum a communia hominum de Asselegge. Omnes vero aliæ terræ ad dictas villas pertinentes ... erunt in pastura communi."

[326] *Historia et Cartularium Monasterii Gloucestriæ*, i. 147–149.

excluded from it for ever," and in return covenant that the latter may "enclose and approve their lands in all parts of the summit of the Pike of Coveleigh." Similar arrangements are made between the Abbot of Glastonbury[327] and a neighbouring landowner, between the Abbot of Cerne[328] and Robert of Bloxworth, and between the City of Coventry[329] and the master and brethren of the Trinity Gild of that town.

Whether it is a chance that such agreements seem to occur with special frequency in the records of religious houses we cannot say. It is possible that the perpetual character of a corporation made exclusive enjoyment at once more desirable and more feasible; a great abbey, like St. Peter's of Gloucester, could pursue a continuous and far-sighted policy, and wait more than a generation to see the results of its experiments. Nor is it possible to understand the motives for such arrangements without information as to local conditions which is not easily obtainable. Sometimes the object was simply to protect land used for agriculture against the depredations caused by the game of a hunting landlord. Sometimes it would seem to have been to allow of a variation in the methods of agriculture, for example the sowing of a piece of land which could not be sown as long as several persons had right of pasture over it. Occasionally it was simply to realise an obvious convenience dictated by the lie of the land, each party gaining more by the exclusive use of pasture lying near to him, than he would lose by surrendering rights of common over that part which lay at a distance. Two points, however, are worth noticing. The first is the use of the word "enclosure." Arrangements which go by the name "enclosure" are made at a very early date by the manorial authorities, and the latter would have been very much surprised to be told that they were inaugurating an agrarian revolution. The second is the character of these enclosures. They are in every way different from those which produced discontent in the sixteenth century. Though they affected the routine of cultivation they did not imply any abandonment of arable farming. Since they were carried out mainly by an exchange of rights they did not prejudice the tenants. Further, the disputes of which they were sometimes the result were not disputes between the lord of a manor and his tenantry, but between the lord and tenants of one manor and the lord and tenants of another, the ground of the disagreement being the difficulty of adjusting rights of common over the debatable land which must often have lain between two manors, and the division of interests being, as it were, a vertical, not a horizontal, division. In fact, these early examples of enclosure throw light on the later movement only by way of contrast. What we meet in our period is not isolated innovations of this character, but a general movement spreading across England from Berkshire in the South to Norfolk and Lincoln in the North-East, and affecting especially the corn-growing counties of the Midlands, a movement which meant a great extension of pasture-farming, a violent collision of interests between the manorial authorities and the peasantry, and a considerable displacement of population. Clearly some new and powerful causes must have been at

[327] Hoare, *History of Wiltshire*, Hundred of South Domerham.

[328] *Hist. MSS. Com.*, Cd. 5567 (Report on the MSS. of Lord Middleton), pp. 61–62. This agreement was made in 1231.

[329] *Coventry Leet Book* (edited by Mary Dormer Harris).

work to account for it.

In the third place, the movement which goes by the name of enclosing in the sixteenth century has little similarity with the changes which proceeded under the same name from about 1700 to 1850, and which went on most swiftly in the reign of George III. It differs from them in method. In the eighteenth century Parliament is supreme. It is simply a committee of landlords and their hangers-on, and it makes Private Bill legislation a very easy method of getting enclosure carried out. In our period the Government, for reasons to be discussed later, sets its face against most kinds of enclosing, and such enclosures as are made are made in defiance of the law. It differs from them in motive. We must not prejudge the question whether the enclosures of our period were made mainly for pasture or for arable. But leaving this question on one side, we can point to certain broad contrasts. The ostensible motive of the eighteenth century enclosures is to improve the productive capacity of the land by spending capital upon it. This is the reason alleged when Private Bills are being promoted, and this is the aspect of the movement which causes it to be eulogised by the agricultural experts. Of course landlords were not philanthropists. As Mr. and Mrs. Hammond[330] have demonstrated, there were often very sordid motives behind their resounding platitudes on the advantage of throwing commons and small holdings into large compact estates, and, even when these were not too conspicuous, the interests of the smaller landholders were sometimes treated with the most outrageous injustice. Still the general nature of the movement was clearly in the direction of bringing under better cultivation land which had hitherto not been used to its full economic capacity. The price of foodstuffs after 1750 rose enormously, and the rise in prices offered a golden harvest to any one who would prepare land for producing larger supplies. The landlords of the eighteenth century did not merely enclose. They improved as well. Part of their increased rent rolls was interest on capital which they had invested for the purpose. Now in the sixteenth century there is very little trace of any movement of this kind. What improving is done, is done by the peasants themselves. There is no sign of the great proprietors making large capital outlays in order to render their estates more productive, except in the way of the trifling expenditure entailed by fencing, hedging, and ditching. They are by no means pioneers of agricultural progress. Enclosing is profitable to them not because it enables them to convert barren heaths into smiling corn-fields in the manner described by Arthur Young, but because it enables them to use the land as they please, to let it down to pasture when the price of wool is high, to employ few labourers on it instead of many, and, possibly, to add to their own estates part of their neighbours' holdings. They do not bring under cultivation land which would otherwise lie waste. On the contrary, very often they turn into a waste land which would otherwise be under cultivation. Whether the picture which represents the eighteenth century enclosures as the effort of an energetic and public-spirited class to overcome old-fashioned prejudices by applying the resources of science to agriculture is veracious or not, we need not now inquire. As far as the century and a half from 1485 is concerned it is altogether out of place.

---

[330] In their book, *The Village Labourer from* 1760 *to* 1832.

The changes which we are about to describe have at once a social and an economic reference. The former is the aspect which receives most attention from contemporaries. They lament the decay of the peasantry, the embittered relations between classes, the distress and discontent caused by the new agrarian régime. They are usually not much concerned with the economics of the situation. Economic issues are not yet separated from questions of personal and public morality. To find subtle reasons why it is unavoidable that a large number of persons should be impoverished seems to them very like condoning a crime. Some excuses only aggravate the offence, and if men are cursed with a neighbour who insists on fulfilling economic laws by raising prices or taking usury, they are less likely to discuss his conclusions than first to present him for breaking the statutes and then to break his head for his bad principles. So they judge the dominant movement by its fruits, and its fruits seem very evil. But to us the economic problem is the primary one. The occurrence of rapid changes in the structure of an old and stable society implies either some radical revolution in the basis of economic life, or some great change in men's conception of social expediency, or, what is most likely, an economic and a spiritual change occurring together. To understand its effect we must understand the sort of economic environment from which it springs.

In the first place, then, the age of the Tudors is a commercial age, and it becomes more commercial as the century goes on. No doubt it is only of certain classes and in certain relations of life that such a statement is true. The permanence of economic arrangements, which makes Froude declare that at the end of the fifteenth century the model of the upper classes was still the chivalry of the Arthurian legends, is seen still more strikingly among the artisans and peasants, and it is only very slowly and painfully that they are drawn into the net woven by the growth of capitalist trade. But it is with the classes who respond to the new movement that the power of the future, though not its graces, lies, and it is through the widening of the influence of commerce and commercial transactions that the economic developments most typical of our period take place. The age is a commercial one in the sense that much attention is given by Governments from the reign of Henry VII. onwards to fostering the conditions which promote trade and industry. This is not the place to discuss the meaning of Mercantilism or the truth of Bacon's[331] epigram that Henry VII. "bowed the ancient policy of this State from consideration of plenty to consideration of power." Though in the reign of Henry VIII. the State is almost a religion, one can easily exaggerate the influence of its interference even in that much governed age. Nevertheless no one who looks at the Statutes, or the Acts of the Privy Council, or the Domestic State Papers for the reigns of Henry VII., Henry VIII., and Elizabeth, can fail to realise that much of the time of Governments is occupied with devising measures which are intended to hasten industrial and commercial development. There is a settled habit of mind with regard to these matters which is quite conscious of its ends, though its means may often be ill-chosen. Every one is agreed that the encouragement of trade is the duty of the Prince.[332] There is a real popular demand for the intervention of the

---

[331] Bacon, *History of King Henry VII.*

[332] See *e.g.* Starkey's *England in the Reign of King Henry VIII.*, p. 173 (E. E. T. S.): "Ye, and though our cloth, at the fyrst begynnyng, wold not be so gud peradventure, as hyt

authorities, and they respond to it readily enough.

The age is a commercial one in the more fundamental sense that large economic changes are initiated by classes and individuals. Foreign trade grows enormously in the early years of Henry VIII., though certain branches of it suffer a temporary set back at the end of the reign.[333] The use of money, of which during the first quarter of the century there was a shortage, begins in the middle of it to spread throughout all classes. The industry which for the next three centuries is to be the chief manufacture of England becomes firmly established. Under the influence of widening markets, trade separates from trade.[334] Within single industries there is an increasing subdivision of labour; many links intervene between the group supplying the raw material and the group which hands the finished article to the consumer; a special class of capitalist entrepreneurs[335] appears to hold the various stages of production together, to organise supplies, and to find markets. Side by side with the development of manufacturing industry goes a development in the organisation of finance. In the woollen industry men buy and sell on credit. In tin-mining[336] and coal-mining[337] they sink shafts with borrowed capital. The first joint-stock[338] companies are established in the middle of the century with capitals of from £5000 to £20,000. There is a regular money market in London, there are bill brokers, arbitrage dealings between it and the Continent, adventurers who take advantage of the increasing fluidity of capital to speculate on the difference in the rates at which it can be borrowed in the Low Countries and in England. By the end of the century London has partially ousted Antwerp as the financial capital of Europe.[339]

In the second place, the social arrangements of England are such as to make it certain that this increasing activity will react almost immediately on agricul-

ys made in other partys, yet, in processe of tyme, I cannot see why, but that our men, by dylygence, myght attayne therto ryght wel; specially yf the Prince wold study thereto, in whose powar hyt lyeth chefely such thyngys to helpe." Also *The Commonweal of this Realm of England* (Lamond), and Pauli, *Drei Denkschriften*, &c.

[333] Schanz, *Englische Handelspolitik gegen Ende der Mittelalters*, Band II., "Zoll und Handelstatistik," pp. 1–156.

[334] Unwin, *Industrial Organisation in the Sixteenth and Seventeenth Centuries*.

[335] See *e.g.* the account of the East Anglian woollen industry in the *Victoria County History*, Suffolk (Unwin's article on "Social and Economic History").

[336] G.R. Lewis, *The Stanneries*, pp. 214–215, and quotations from Lansdowne MSS. 76, fol. 34, given there.

[337] *Hist. MSS. Com.*, Cd. 5567 (Report on the MSS. of Lord Middleton).

[338] W.R. Scott, *Joint-Stock Companies to 1720*, vol. ii.

[339] For a description of "The Exchange and What It is," see T. Wilson, *Discourse upon Usurie* (1584): his remark, "The second kind of bill ... may be called sicke and dry exchange, and is practised where one doth borrowe money abroad ... not meaning to make any real payment abroad, but compoundeth with the exchange to have it returned again," illustrates what is said above. See also Camden Society, *Dialogue or Confabulation of Two Travellers* (1580): "The said Hans had provided £10,000 for the Prince of Condy upon five in the 100 at interest, and if I would have the like he would help me unto it. Then I ... pondered what benefit it would be to me to let it out again at ten in the hundred to some nobleman in England." Down to about 1560 at any rate the English Government was constantly in the hands of foreign capitalists. See Gairdner, *L. and P. Henry VIII.*, and Burgon's *Life of Gresham.*

ture and on agrarian relationships. There have been countries where a sharp line has been drawn between trade and agriculture, where the landowner could not engage in trade without degrading himself, where the tradesman could not buy up the noble's land.[340] But this has never been the case in England. In that precocious island the Lombards had hardly settled in Lombard Street, when Mr. Pole's daughters discovered that the fine shades flourished their finest in country air, and there was a market for heiresses among the English aristocracy long before Columbus had revealed to Europe the Eldorado of the New World. From a very early date the successful merchant has bought dignity and social consideration by investing his savings in an estate. The impecunious gentleman has restored the falling fortunes of his house by commercial speculations, of which marriage into a merchant family, if not the least speculative, is not the least profitable. At the beginning of the sixteenth century both movements were going on simultaneously with a rapidity which was before unknown, and which must be explained as the consequence of the great growth of all forms of commercial activity. The rise of great incomes drawn from trade had brought into existence a new order of business men whose enterprise was not confined to the seaport and privileged town, but flowed over into the purchase of landed estates, even before the secularisation of monastic endowments made land speculation the mania of a whole generation. Great nobles plunged into commerce, were granted special trading privileges, and intermarried with the rising middle-class families who were often better off than themselves. In all ages wealth allies itself with wealth, and power with power. As soon as the appearance of rich merchant families creates a fresh and powerful interest in society, the old social system and the new[341] coalesce, and each learns from the other—the merchant how to make a display as a landed proprietor and a Justice of the Peace, the old-fashioned landlord how to cut down expenses and squeeze the utmost farthing out of his property in the best City manner. Even if the political and economic environment had remained unchanged, the mere formation of commercial capital and of a moneyed class could hardly have failed to work a slow revolution in agrarian relationships.

But the environment did not remain unchanged; and as a consequence, in economic affairs as in religion, the new order came, not gradually, but swiftly and with violence, sapping ancient loyalties, confronting with insoluble problems simple men who desired only to plough the land like their fathers, holding out to the privileged orders that prospect of suddenly increasing their wealth which is the most awful temptation from which any class can pray—if it will pray—to be delivered. On the side of politics a powerful motive for a change in the relations between landlords and tenants was supplied by the Tudor peace. In the turbulent days of the fifteenth century land had still a military and social significance apart from its economic value; lords had ridden out at the head of their retainers to convince a bad neighbour with bows and bills; and a numerous tenantry had

[340] *e.g.* Prussia before 1807.

[341] For examples see A. Abram, *Social England in the Fifteenth Century*, especially Part II., chap, ii., "The Rise of the Middle Class," and Plummer's *Fortescue*, p. 17. In the *Cely Papers* (Camden Society), p. 153, a correspondent of George Cely writes, "yowre sallys made withyn lesse than thys yere amountes above £2000 sterling."

been more important than a high pecuniary return from the soil.[342] The Tudor discipline, with its stern prohibition of livery and maintenance, its administrative jurisdictions and tireless bureaucracy, had put down private warfare with a heavy hand, and, by drawing the teeth of feudalism, had made the command of money more important than the command of men. It is easy to underrate the significance of this change, yet it is in a sense more fundamental than any other; for it marks the transition from the mediæval conception of land as the basis of political functions and obligations to the modern view of it as an income-yielding investment. Land-holding tends, in short, to become commercialised. The meaning of this movement is best understood if one compares with the South and Midlands those parts of England where to the very end of the sixteenth century the older conditions survived. The surveys of many Northumbrian[343] manors reveal throughout this period of rapid agrarian changes the continuance of a very primitive condition of things. The holdings of the customary tenants are often almost rigidly equal; there is hardly any change in their numbers; son succeeds father, and grandson succeeds son, with only the very slightest disturbance. The manorial officials, who in the South were cursed as the agents of evictions and rack-renting, were in the North much concerned with keeping tenants on the soil. At Acklington the tenants, writes Clarkson, "must be helped and rather cherished for service sake." At High Buston the holdings of the tenantry have been increased in order that "they should the better live and do their dutiful service to their Lord and master," and a freeholder is rebuked for action which results in curtailing the commonable area on the ground that "the tenants be but poor men and be not well horsed, as they are bound by their copies." At Tughall[344] the surveyor complains bitterly in 1567 that in time past, apparently a long time past, twenty-three tenants had been reduced to eight by "such as nothing regard his lordship's service, nor the commonwealth." To what are we to ascribe this permanence of tenure among the peasants, this exceptional solicitude for the maintenance of a numerous tenantry on the part of surveyors? Partly, no doubt, to the fact that Northumberland lay apart from the

---

[342] See the Paston Letters, *passim*; and also the account given in *Hist. MSS. Com.*, Cd. 5567 (Report on the MSS. of Lord Middleton), 142–145, of the marvellous doings of Sir Gylles Strangways in Dorsetshire as late as 1539; pp. 115–117 contain a similar case of private warfare from the year 1477.

[343] *Northumberland County History, e.g.* Amble (vol. v.), Acklington (*ibid.*), High Buston (*ibid.*), Birling (*ibid.*); vol. viii. p. 230, figures as to eight manors in Tynmouthshire. At Birling out of ten names which appear in the surveys of 1567, eight reappear in 1616; at Acklington, out of eighteen names, nine reappear; at High Buston, out of four names, four reappear in 1616 and two in 1702. But in parts of the county there were rapid changes at the end of the sixteenth and beginning of the seventeenth centuries; see below, pp. 257–258 and 260.

[344] *Northumberland County History*, vol. i. p. 350: "In the ancient tyme the fermor of the demaines had the charge of the tenants of the said lordship as bailiff, with the fee of £3, 0s. 5d. by year. Then was the town of Tughall planted with xi husbandmen well horsed and in good order, viii cottagers, iiii cotterells, one common smith for the relief and better aid of the said tenants and bailiff, being in number 23 householders, besides the demains, which are nowe by suche as nothing regard his lordship's service nor the commonwealthe brought to 8 farmers only, to the great decay of his lordship's service and discommodity of the said commonwealth."

main stream of commercial life, and was as yet little affected by the growth of the woollen industry. Mainly, however, it was the result of the military importance of a numerous tenantry on the Northumbrian border. In that wild corner which is neither England nor Scotland, English and Scots, Scroopes and bold Buccleughs, gnash their teeth at each other across the wan water of the Eden. In the long northern evenings about Lammastide moormen win their hay with axes in their belts and bows piled in the corner of the field, and customary tenants are bound by their copies to provide horse and armour, and to ride to the musters in person or by proxy. No wonder that while elsewhere landlords pore over their accounts of wool or timber, in Northumberland they should measure their wealth by the men whom they can bring out when the summons goes, and insist on feudal obligations with a rigour unknown in the South. When any night Scotch[345] raiders may come storming over the marches, any night the red cock may crow up to the very walls of merry Carlisle, a holding means not only a piece of land that grows wheat and feeds sheep, but a horseman in harness; and the dropping out of a holding, or its merging in that of some one else, results in the weakening of the force on which the peace of the border depends. As a consequence, there is nothing like free trade in land between the tenants, such as developed in the South under the forms of surrender and admission, and there is little incentive for the lord or his officials to get rid of them. Such an exceptional state of things comes to an end in Northumberland with the union of the two Crowns under James I., and its termination is the signal for an attempt to break down customary tenures on the part both of the Crown[346] and of private landowners.[347] But it survives a century longer on the border than it does elsewhere, and while it lasts it offers a standard by which may be measured the extent and significance of the change which is overtaking agrarian relationships in other parts of England, where commerce is more developed, and where, since a tenant can no longer serve his lord by fighting, a sheep may easily be more valuable than a man. With the development of a strong central Government the military strength of the great landlords was broken, though it blazed up in the Pilgrimage of Grace and in the rebellion of 1569, and as a consequence they turned their attention to getting the maximum economic return from the soil, or to adding to their social dignity by parks, instead of maintaining a large body of tenants upon it.[348]

[345] See *e.g.* the ballad of "Kinmont Willie," turning on an incident which occurred in 1596.

[346] *Cal. S. P. D. James I.,* vol. cxxxii., July 27, 1622. Letter to the Bishop of Durham to confer with the judges of Assize for the Northern Counties touching tenant-right or customary estate of inheritance claimed in those parts, ordering them to abide strictly by the King's Proclamation against tenant-right, or the holding of lands by border service, to countenance no claim founded thereupon, and to acquaint the tenants of his Majesty's pleasure therein, giving them no hope to the contrary. Apparently the instructions were not carried out, as in 1642 the Long Parliament was discussing the subject of the border tenures (Rushworth *Collections,* Pt. III., vol. ii. p. 86).

[347] See below, pp. 257–258.

[348] The effect of the Tudor policy on the land system is excellently described by Harrington in *Oceana,* and also in *The Art of Law-giving:* "Henry VII. being conscious of the infirmity of his title, yet finding with what strength and vigour he was brought in by the Nobility, conceived jealousy of the like power in case of a decay or change of affections.

The change meant an advance in civilisation among the upper classes, and a tightening of economic pressure upon the peasantry. The feudal seigneur had at his worst been a lawless tyrant, and at his best a despotic parent. But he had governed his estate as the sovereign, often the resident sovereign, of a petty kingdom, whose interests were roughly identical with his own; and though his depredations were a terror to his neighbours, his own tenants had little to fear from them, for his tenants were the force on which his very existence depended. In the new political conditions his occupation was gone, and his place was taken by two types of landed proprietor who were at once more peaceable and less popular. On the one hand, there emerges the landlord who is a laborious and acute man of business, and who sets about exploiting the material resources of his estate with the instincts of a shopkeeper and the methods of a land-agent. Of this kind are the Willoughbys[349] in the Midlands and the Delavales[350] in Northumberland. Often they are sheep-farmers. When their land is rich in minerals they sink coal-pits and mine for iron ore. The predecessors of the captains of industry of two and a half centuries later, they employ labour on a large scale, they open up trade across country by river, they higgle over port dues, they experiment with new inventions, they clear away without mercy any customary rights which conflict with their own. On the other hand, there are the gentry who buzz about the Court, regard London as the centre of the universe, and have periodically to be ordered home to look after the affairs of their country-sides by a peremptory mandate from the Government. When this type becomes prominent, in the reign of Elizabeth, it most commonly spends its time in the interminable pursuit of profitable sinecures, and in endeavouring to induce the City to believe that thrice-mortgaged estates are a gilt-edged

---

*Nondum orbis adoraverat Roman.* The lords yet led country lives; their houses were open to retainers, men experienced in military affairs and capable of commanding; their hospitality was the delight of their tenants who by their tenure or dependence were obliged to follow their lords in arms. So that, this being the Militia of the nation, a few noblemen discontented could at any time levy a great army, the effect whereof both in the Barons Wars and those of York and Lancaster had been well known to divers kings. This state of things was that which enabled Henry VII. to make his advantage of troublesome times and the frequent unruliness of retainers; while, under pretence of curbing riots, he obtained the passing of such laws as did cut off these retainers, whereby the nobility wholly lost their officers. Then, whereas the dependence of the people on their lords was of a strict ty or nature, he found means to loosen this also by laws which he obtained upon a fair pretence, even that of Population. But the nobility, who by the former law had lost their officers, by this lost their soldiery. Yet remained to them their estates, till the same Prince introducing the Statutes for alienations, these also became loose; and the lords, less taken (for the reasons shown) with their country lives, where their trains were clipped, by degrees became more resident at court, where greater pomp and expense by the Statute of Alienations began to plume them of their Estates" (Harrington, *Works*, 1700 edition, pp. 388–389).

[349] *Hist. MSS. Com.*, Cd. 5567 (Report on the MSS. of Lord Middleton), especially the entries relating to the development of the coal trade.

[350] *Northumberland County History*, vol. viii., p. 238, vol. ix. (under Cowpen). Robert Delavale apparently began life as an agent to the Earl of Northumberland, but he owned considerable property himself; in 1605 the whole of the lands of Cowpen were in his hands. He was an energetic encloser; see below, p. 260.

security. At its worst it produces Sir Petronel Flash,[351] a figure as typical of the sixteenth century as Squire Western is of the eighteenth. At its best it patronises the arts, sets sail for a new world of drama and romance, sighs over Vergil's Eclogues, and goes pricking, almost too graceful a chivalry, through the fairy kingdoms of Spenser. But the men of business, and the men of fashion, and the patrons of literature, are alike in being the symptoms of a new economic and political system, a system which has shorn landownership of the territorial sovereignty which had gone with it, broken down the personal relations of landlord and tenant, and, by turning agriculture into a business, has made it at once more profitable and less strenuous for the former, more exacting and less stable for the latter, than it had been when a lordlord was not only a drawer of rents but a local sovereign, a tenant not only a source of income but a dependent who was bound by a tie which was almost sacramental. "It was never a merry world since gentlemen came up"; "never so many gentlemen and so little gentleness"; "the commons long since did rise in Spain and kill the gentlemen, and since have lived merrily there"; such are some of the blessings the new landlords would hear from men who grumble to their mates between the spells of shearing sheep and mowing hay. Those who have watched the uncouth, rough-handed master of a backward industry, who has wrought among his workmen as a friend or a tyrant, blossom, under the fertilising influence of expanding markets, into the sedate suburban capitalist who sets up a country house in the second generation and sends his sons to Oxford in the third, and who scientifically speeds up his distant operatives through the mediation of an army of managers and assistant-managers and foremen, will not need to be reminded that economic changes which bring civilisation to one class may often be fraught with ruin to another. The brilliant age which begins with Elizabeth gleams against a background of social squalor and misery. The descendant of the illiterate, bloody-minded baron who is muzzled by Henry VII. becomes a courteous gentleman who rhapsodises in verse at the Court of Gloriana. But all that the peasants know is that his land-agents[352] are harsher. An Earl of Pembroke has been given immortality by Shakespeare. But the first of his name had founded the family on estates which had belonged to the Abbey of Wilton,[353] and by his exactions had provoked the Wiltshire peasants into rebellion. The Raleigh family—it was a Ra-

[351] See Marston's *Eastward Ho!*

[352] See the following extract (Lodge, *Illustrations of English History*, iii., 41). William Hammond to the Earl of Shrewsbury on the subject of raising money on the latter's estates from Palavicini, a moneylender: "Though his froward fortune hath made him unable to stand you almost in any steadde, hee hathe dealt with Mr. Maynard to aide him in the provision of this £3000 against the second of next month. He finds him very backwarde to disburse any money upon bond or any other security but lands; neither will he deal with lands in any way of mortgage for years or any long time, but only 2 or 3 months.... Yf, therefore, it stands with your honour's good liking to make a conveyance of Kingston to Sir Horatio ... after the rate of £7000 ... and withal to passe it in this absolute sort that iff the money then laid out by them for your Honour's use bee not repaid on May day next, that they fully enjoy and possess the lands as their owne.... Hee saith besides that his surveyors have certified him £500 will bee the most the lands will ever yeald yerely rent, without racking and oppressions, which are no course for suche meane men as they be to take."

[353] Roxburghe Club, *Surveys of Manor of William, First Earl of Pembroke*, Straton's introduction.

leigh's chance gibe at the old religion which set the West in a blaze in 1549—had endowed itself with a manor torn from the see of Wells,[354] as the Grenvilles had done with the lands of Buckland Abbey. The gentle Sidney's *Arcadia* is one of the glories of the age, and it was composed, if we may trust tradition, in the park at the Herberts' country-seat at Washerne,[355] which they had made by enclosing a whole village and evicting the tenants. The dramatists who reflect the high popular estimation of the freeholder[356] see nothing in the grievances of Mouldy and Bullcalf except the disposition of an ignorant populace to cry for the moon. Shakespeare's Cade, with his programme[357] of seven half-penny loaves for a penny, and the three-hooped pot that shall have ten hoops, is so far proposing only what an energetic mayor is quite prepared to carry out before breakfast. His crowning absurdity, which makes the stalls hiss and the pit cheer, is the promise that "all the realm shall be in common; and in Cheapside shall my palfrey go to grass." A few months after these words were printed Cade came to life in earnest. In the autumn of 1596 some Oxfordshire[358] artisans and peasants organised a revolt against "the gentlemen who took the commons," and from that year onwards to 1601 Parliament and the Council had their hands full of the question of enclosures. Men feel the contrast, even when it is only just beginning, and with natural inconsistency sigh for the old order even while they are glorifying the new. "Princes and Lords," wrote Henry VIII.'s chaplain[359] about 1538, "seldom look to the good order and wealth of their subjects, only they look to the receiving of their rents and revenues of their lands with great study of enhancing thereof, to the further maintaining of their pompous state; so that if their subjects do their duty therein justly, paying their rents at time affixed, for the rest they care not (as is commonly said) 'whether they sink or swim'"!

While the centralised government of the Tudors gave a new bias to the interests of landlords by stripping them of part of their political power, economic changes were hurrying the more enterprising among them into novel methods of estate management. In the situation which developed in the first fifty years of the sixteenth century they were exposed to pressure from two sides at once. They

[354] *History of the Parish of Wiveliscombe,* by Hancock. For Walter Raleigh and the revolt of 1549, see the dramatic account given by Holinshed. The incident is described in Froude's *Edward VI.* For the Grenvilles and Buckland Abbey see *Trans. Royal Hist. Soc.,* vol. vi. It ultimately came to Francis Drake.

[355] Straton's introduction to *Surveys of Pembroke Manors.*

[356] *e.g.* Heywood's *A Woman Killed with Kindness,* Act iii. sc. 1.

[357] *Henry VI.,* Part II., Act iv. scene 2. I am indebted for the reference to Professor Unwin. Part II. was first printed in 1595.

[358] *Hist. MSS. Com.,* MSS. of Marquis of Salisbury, Part III., pp. 49–50: "The attorney-general to Mr. Robert Cecil. Some information concerning those that intended the rebellion in Oxfordshire. Bartholemew Stere, carpenter ... was the first person of this insurrection. His outward pretence was to overthrow enclosures, and to help the poor commonalty, that were like to perish for want of corn, but intended to kill the gentlemen of that county and take the spoil, affirming that the commons long since in Spain did rise and kill the gentlemen in Spain and sithen have lived merrily there. After that he meant to have gone to London and joined with the prentices ... and it was but a month's work to overrun England."

[359] E. E. T. S., *England in the Reign of Henry VIII.,* p. 85.

stood to gain much if they adapted their farming to meet the new commercial conditions. They stood to lose much if they were so conservative as to adhere to the old methods. The explanation of the agrarian revolution most generally given by contemporary observers was that enclosing was due to the increased profitableness of pasture farming, consequent upon the development of the textile industries; and though a recent writer[360] has endeavoured to show that most of the land enclosed was used for tillage, and that therefore this explanation cannot hold good, there does not seem any valid reason for disputing it. The testimony of observers is very strong; they might be mistaken as to the extent of the movement towards pasture, but hardly as to its tendency; and with scarcely an exception they point to the growth of the woollen trade as the chief motive for enclosing.

Moreover, their evidence is confirmed by the proofs which we possess of the expansion of the woollen industry at the end of the fifteenth century. It is true that the figures collected by Thorold Rogers do not enable any satisfactory correlation to be made between the rise in wool prices and the progress of pasture farming. But they are statistically much too unreliable to upset the direct evidence of eyewitnesses, being based on various measures which are somewhat arbitrarily reduced to a supposed common standard, relating to many different qualities of wool, and being weighted in particular years by a preponderance of prices from particular counties which are sometimes clearly not typical at all. The figures of Schanz[361] as to the export trade in wool and woollen cloths, are a sufficient proof of the growth in the output of wool, and therefore in the growth of sheep-farming. They show that while the export of unmanufactured wool fell off in the sixteenth century, that of grey cloth grew enormously. In 1354 the export had been 4774½ pieces, from 1509 to 1523 it averaged 84,789 pieces a year, from 1524 to 1533, 91,394 pieces, from 1534 to 1539, 102,647 pieces, and from 1540 to 1547, 122,354 pieces, while in 1554 the total manufacture was estimated at 160,000 pieces of cloth and 250,000 pieces of hosiery. This expansion of the manufactured cloth industry was only the culmination of a growth which had been going on gradually for a hundred years. In 1464 the Flemish manufacturers[362] were complaining that their market had been invaded by English clothiers. Merchants like the Celys shipped enormous consignments of wool from the Cotswolds to the Continent.[363] The large number of sheep kept in England at the end of the fifteenth century was the amazement of foreigners;[364] and English buyers groaned over the high prices to which wool was driven by the competition of continental buyers.[365] The revolution in the technique of agriculture when sucked into the vortex of expanding commerce is, in

[360] See the discussion between Mr. Leadam and Professor Gay in *Trans. Royal Hist. Society*, vol. xiv., new series.

[361] Schanz, *Englische Handelspolitik gegen Ende des Mittelalters*, Band II., p. 18.

[362] Abram, *Social England in the Fifteenth Century*, p. 33.

[363] *Ibid.*, pp. 40–41.

[364] Camden Society (1847), *Italian Relation of England*.

[365] Camden Society (third series, vol. i.), *Cely Papers*. In 1480 the elder Cely writes: "I have not bought this year a loke of woll, for the woll of Cottyswolde is bought by the Lombardys" and in the following year, "Ye avyse me for to buye woll in Cottyswolde, bot it is at grate prise, 3s. 4d. a tod, and gret ryding for woll in Cottyswolde as was any yere this vii yere."

fact, simply an early, and, owing to the immobility of sixteenth century conditions, a peculiarly striking example of that reaction of widening markets on the methods of production, which is one of the best established of economic generalisations.

At the same time, the revolution was probably hastened by a change in commercial policy, which, while encouraging the export trade in woollen cloth, was after 1485 less favourable to the corn-grower. During the greater part of the fifteenth[366] century the Government was forced by the agrarian interests to allow freedom of export for grain except when prices reached a certain height, after which point an export licence was required. But the victory of Henry VII. produced a policy which was less influenced by the traditional object of helping the corn-growing landlords, and more favourable to commerce and the middle classes on which the new monarchy rested. In 1491[367] the export of grain, except with a special licence, was forbidden altogether, and in 1512 the prohibition was repeated by Henry VIII. Though the administration of such a policy must have been difficult, and its exact effect must be a matter of conjecture, the view taken by some contemporaries,[368] that it was a subordinate cause which stimulated the abandonment of old agricultural methods and caused a good deal of land to go out of cultivation, is at any rate intrinsically probable.

If the expansion of the woollen industry offered a fortune to those who adopted the new methods of estate management, the depreciation in the value of money threatened with ruin those who did not. The agrarian changes of the sixteenth century cannot be traced primarily to the revolution in general prices which all European countries experienced, because they had already proceeded some way before the full extent of the movement in prices became apparent. Throughout the fifteenth century the value of money, as far as can be judged from such statistics as we possess, was fairly stable, and, if anything, somewhat appreciated. During the first half of Henry VIII.'s reign there were complaints[369] of the scarcity of the metallic currency. On the very eve of the dissolution of the monasteries we find a religious house in Northumberland reversing the movement which had been going on for two centuries in most parts of the country, and actually commuting money rents into payments in kind,[370] on the ground that the tenants could not command

---

[366] Cunningham, *Growth of English Industry and Commerce*, Early and Middle Ages, pp. 447–448. The statute sanctioning export without licence when the price was below 6s. 8d. was 15 Hen. VI., c. 2, which was made perpetual by 23 Hen. VI., c. 5. 3 Ed. IV., c. 2, forbade the importation of foreign corn except when the price reached 6s. 8d.

[367] *Ibid.*, Modern Times, Part I., p. 85.

[368] *e.g. The Commonweal of this Realm of England*, pp. 54–60.

[369] See the whole question discussed in Schanz, *Englische Handelspolitik*, Band II., pp. 481–540.

[370] *Northumberland County History*, vol. viii. p. 232. In 1595 a dispute as to corn rents arose between the Earl of Northumberland and the Tynemouthshire tenants, the Earl insisting on payment by the Newcastle measure, the tenants demanding to pay by the Winchester measure, on the ground that they are so poor that "they are not able with horse, furniture, and geare to serve as their ancestors have done, as it appeared upon the late muster." Evidence given by an ancient yeoman before the Commission appointed to hear the case showed that the tenants had formerly paid in money, and that the change from money to corn had been introduced in the time of the last Prior for the sake of the tenants, not for the

the necessary coin. Such facts should warn us that England was far from being a single economic community, and that the effects of the cheap money penetrated into the more backward regions only very slowly indeed. Nevertheless, in the more advanced parts of the country, the tide turned soon after the beginning of the new century, though it was not till the fourth decade of it that it became a mill-race in which all old economic standards were submerged. The general course of the movement, so far as it affected commodities in general use, is set forth below. The figures are re-arranged from those supplied by Steffen,[371] whose work is mainly based on that of Thorold Rogers.

## TABLE VII

| | Wheat per Qr. | | Peas per Qr. | | Oats per Qr. | | Barley Malt per Qr. | | Oxen. | |
|---|---|---|---|---|---|---|---|---|---|---|
| | s. | d. | s. | d. | s. | d. | s. | d. | s. | d. |
| 1401–1450 | 5 | 9¼ | 3 | 2¾ | 7 | 9 | 4 | 3 | 16 | 5½ |
| 1451–1500 | 5 | 6¼ | 3 | 4¾ | 6 | 6¾ | 3 | 8 | 15 | 7½ |
| 1451–1500 | 6 | 10¼ | 5 | 1¾ | 9 | 4¾ | 4 | 5 | 22 | 9 |
| 1541–1582 | 13 | 10½ | ... | | 20 | 4¾ | 10 | 5 | 70 | 0¼ |

| | Sheep. | | Oxen. | | Hens. | Eggs per Qr. |
|---|---|---|---|---|---|---|
| | s. | d. | s. | d. | d. | d. |
| 1401–1450 | 7 | 6¾ | 2 | 1 | 2 | 5 |
| 1451–1500 | 1 | 10¼ | 8 | 3¼ | 2¼ | 5¼ |
| 1451–1500 | 2 | 10¼ | 10 | 0 | 3 | 9 |
| 1541–1582 | 6 | 4 | ... | | 4¾ | ... |

Though it would not be right, of course, to force these figures too far, as one cannot be sure that they are in all cases typical, the indication which they offer of a remarkable rise in prices beginning soon after 1500 is in all probability substantially correct. The result of this movement in dragging down the standard of comfort of the people has often been noticed, and need not be emphasised here. But it is important to observe that it had a very marked effect upon the traditional methods of agriculture, because it supplied landowners with a new incentive to squeeze the utmost possible income out of their estates. Since they were buying everything dearer, they were under a strong inducement to turn land to the most profitable use, and to revise all existing contracts which prevented an advance in tenants' payments. In the not unnatural confusion which surrounded the question of the cause of the general rise in prices, this aspect of the agrarian troubles failed very generally to be appreciated by contemporary writers, who were inclined to argue that the higher prices were due to the increased rents, instead of seeing that the increased rents were themselves the consequence of the increased prices. But

sake of the Priory.

[371] Steffen, *Studien zur Geschichte der Englischen Lohnarbeiter*, Band I., pp. 254–255 and 365–366.

it was emphasised in the middle of the century by the author of the *Commonwealth of England*,[372] and at the end of it by Gerrard de Malynes,[373] who puts the case with great power and perspicacity, though he perhaps may be thought to exaggerate the importance of the debasement of the currency. "Every man knoweth," he wrote in 1601, "that by reason of the base money coined in the end of the most victorious reign of King Henry VIII. all the forrain commodities were sold dearer, which made afterwards the commodities of the realm to rise at the farmers' and tenants' hands, and therefore gentlemen did raise the rents of their lands and take farms themselves and made inclosures of grounds, and the price of everything being dearer was made dearer though plenty of money and bullion coming daily from the West Indies.... If we require gentlemen to abate their rents, give over farms, and break up enclosures, it may be they would do so if they might have all their provisions at the price heretofore." Yet such a statement gives but a faint indication of the revolutionary effect upon agrarian relationships of the depreciation in the value of money. The modern reader, before whose eyes all economic standards are fluctuating from day to day, can hardly grasp the anarchy which it tended to produce in a world where values, especially land values, were objective realities which had stood unaltered for centuries together. The landlord sees his income slipping from him, though his estate pays as much as before. The tenant finds his landlord pressing for higher rents and fines, though the yield of the land has not increased. Yet neither desires anything but to remain as they were, and both are ignorant of the force which sweeps them out of the ancient ways. For, in the wholesome manner of the age, they ascribe all economic evils to personal misdemeanours, the unreasonableness of merchants, the covetousness of gentlemen, the extortions of husbandmen, and the real cause is an impersonal one, which carries them forward against their will, like men "thrusting one another in a throng, one driving on another."[374] It is easy to understand that it must have been difficult to maintain customary payments and traditional methods of agriculture against the screw which the rise in prices turned on the landowning classes. Agricultural experiments were in the air, and with experts explaining how to double the value of an estate by enclosure without prejudicing the tenants, it is not surprising that landowners, who saw their real incomes dwindling with the fall in the value of money, should have adopted the principle of their advice and neglected the qualifications.

## *(b) The Growth of the Large Leasehold Farm*

[372] *The Commonweal of this Realm of England* (Lamond), especially p. 81: "Knight: What sorte is that which youe said had greater loss thereby then those men had profitte? Doctor: It is all noblemen, and gentlemen, and all other that live by a fixed rent, or stipend, or doe not maner the grounde, or do occupie no byinge or sellinge.... He that maie spend £300 a yeare by such revennewes and fees, may kepe no better porte then his father, or anie before him, that could spend but £200. And so ye maie perceave, it is a great abatement of a man's countenance to take awaie the third part of his livinge. And therefore gentlemen doe so much studie the Increase of theire landes, enhauncing of their rentes, and so take farmes and pastures into theire owne hands."

[373] *A Treatise of the Canker of England's Commonwealth* (1601).

[374] *The Commonweal of this Realm of England* (Lamond), p. 100.

The changed situation created by these causes had the effect of producing a new policy on the part of landlords, which took different forms according to the circumstances of different localities, but which in the counties most deeply affected resulted in an increase in pasture-farming and in an upward movement in the payments made by tenants. The new régime seems to have affected first, as was natural, that part of their estates which was most entirely under their own control, and the disposal of which was least involved in other interests, namely, the manorial demesne. It is not altogether easy to construct a picture of the policy pursued by a typical enclosing landlord from the accounts of contemporaries, who were more interested in results than in the steps by which they were reached. According to some of them, lords in the sixteenth century were resuming into their own hands those parts of the demesne which had been let out, in order to supply their establishments with produce without having to rely on the markets when prices were rapidly rising. On some manors again, when the demesne was "in the hand of the lord," considerations which were not purely economic came into play; for example, one finds part of it being turned into a park, which was at once profitable as a means of grazing sheep, and prized for those motives of social amenity and ostentation which have done so much to make the English countryside the admiration of travellers, and so much to ruin the English peasantry. It was not seldom that the confiscated estates of monastic houses were converted into a pleasaunce or a deer-park by their new proprietors.

On the other hand, the manorial documents suggest that landlords were usually rather parties to changes in the methods of cultivation than themselves the agents who carried them out, because, at any rate in the case of the larger landowners, the demesnes were usually leased. The actual process of experiment and innovation took place on most manors through the instrumentality of the lessee.[375] The large farmer, who on many manors is foundmanaging the demesne, is much the most striking character in the rural development of the sixteenth century. His fortunes wax while those of the peasantry wane. Gradually he thrusts them, first copyholders and then yeomen, into the background, and becomes in time the parent of a mighty line, which later ages, forgetting poor Piers Plowman, whose place he has usurped, will look on as the representative of all that is solid and unchanging in the English social order. In our period he plays in the economics of agriculture the part which was played in industry by the capitalist clothier, and his position as the pivot of agrarian change is so important that it will repay close attention.

In the first place, then, it is clear that the foundation of the large farm was the

---

[375] This may seem inconsistent with the fact that in the statistics published by Mr. Leadam from the Inquisition of 1517 most enclosures in most counties are entered as made by lords of manors. I do not think, however, that this is necessarily so. When it is stated that a lord of a manor has enclosed and converted to pasture, it may very well be meant that his agent did so with his consent. *I.e.* the distinction would appear to be not between the lord and the lord's farmer, but between the manorial authorities (lord and farmer) and the rest of the landholders. The phrase used in the Berkshire returns, "converti permisit," indicates what I take to have been the most general, though not, of course, the invariable, course of events.

practice of leasing the demesne for a term of years, which was the normal way of disposing of it in the sixteenth century. In the reign of Elizabeth the distinction between the demesne and the customary tenancies still survived, and surveyors were at some pains to separate them in order to prevent the demesne being merged in the customary holdings. But the original meaning of the distinction had been almost obliterated; the demesne was no longer the centre of the manorial economy, as it had been when its produce maintained the lord's household, and the labour of the customary tenants, in spite of the survival of many services, no longer supplied the chief means of cultivating it. On the whole, it would be true to say that on ninety-nine manors out of a hundred the demesne was leased by the middle of the sixteenth century, and on the majority of them probably at a much earlier date. There are, of course, some exceptions. Certain manors the lord makes his headquarters, and there the home farm is retained in his hands, because it is required to supply his establishment. On other manors the demesne or part of it can no longer be distinguished from the holdings of the customary tenants, and is held by them by copy of Court Roll in the same way as the "customary land." In certain parts of England, again, the leasing of the demesne has not proceeded far, because the demesne has always been relatively unimportant. On several Northumberland manors, for example, the surveyor[376] could in 1567 find no demesne at all, either because it had all been divided up among the tenants, or because it had never existed. Nevertheless, in spite of these exceptions, a lease for a term of years to a farmer or farmers is the ordinary method of disposing of the demesne in the sixteenth century. This is proved in a very satisfactory way by the investigations of Professor Savine[377] into the disposition of the lands of monastic houses in 1534. After an exhaustive inquiry relating to several hundred manors he found that the cases in which the demesne was not leased were an insignificant proportion of the whole. An examination of smaller groups of manors tells the same story. Out of thirty-six[378] manors in Wiltshire, Somersetshire, and Devonshire surveyed for the Earl of Pembroke in 1568, it is possible to determine the use made of the demesne on thirty-two, and on twenty-nine of them it was leased. Of twenty-nine other manors examined at random at different periods in the sixteenth and early seventeenth century every one was in the same condition. There is no reason to distrust these instances on the ground that they may represent a development occurring too late in the century to be relevant to movements found in existence at the beginning of it, because in several cases where the history of a manor can be traced backwards, it is clear, as has been shown above, that the leasing of the demesne

---

[376] *e.g.* at Acklington (*Northumberland County History*, vol. v.), of which Clarkson the surveyor writes: "Neither is there any demaine lands or demaine meadows, but all is occupied together in husbandry"; at Birling (*ibid.*): "There is no demaine land or meadow, with all their husbandlands and meadows appertaining to the same"; apparently also at High Buston. Compare Vinogradoff, *Villainage in England*, p. 316: "Villages without a manorial demesne ... are found ... where the power of the lord was more a political than an economical one" (Norfolk and Suffolk, Lincoln, Northumberland, Westmoreland, &c.). For a manor where the demesne is kept in the hand of the lord in 1568 for the reason given above, see Roxburghe Club, *Surveys of Pembroke Manors*, Manor of Washerne.

[377] *Oxford Studies in Social and Legal History*, pp. 153–154.

[378] Roxburghe Club, *Surveys of Lands of William, First Earl of Pembroke*.

was quite common at least from the middle of the fifteenth century, and in parts of the country much earlier.

From the allusions made by contemporaries to the large farmer as one of the mainsprings of the changes of the period, one is disposed to look first at the demesne for the beginning of capitalist agriculture. Whether, however, the method of cultivating the demesne differed much from the cultivation of the customary holdings depended to a considerable extent upon the terms on which it was leased, and, in particular, upon whether it passed into the control of a single considerable tenant. It would be a mistake to think that the economic relationships which were established when the demesne ceased to be cultivated by villein labour were all of one type, or in particular that the demesne invariably passed into the hands of one holder. Mention has already been made of the practice of adding the demesne lands, or part of them, to the customary land held by copy of Court Roll, a practice which obviously resulted in maintaining in the hands of small cultivators land which might have gone to build up large properties.

Even when the demesne is leased it is not always leased to a single large farmer. In reality the surveys of the sixteenth century reveal two well-defined types of leasehold property subsisting on the lord's demesne, sometimes on neighbouring manors. The first type has as its distinctive feature that the lessees are a number, sometimes a very large number, of small farmers, who have been given allotments on the demesne and who hold them for various periods of years, sometimes for life only, sometimes for eighty, sometimes for ninety-two or ninety-nine, years. Many examples of this type of small leaseholder come from the west of England. Thus at Ablode,[379] in Somersetshire, before the demesne was leased out by St. Peter's to a large farmer in 1515, it had already been leased to seventeen of the customary tenants. At Paynton,[380] in 1568, the Barton land was held in small plots by fifty-one leaseholders, at South Brent[381] by eighteen. But examples of this arrangement are found all over England. At Higham Ferrers,[382] in Northamptonshire, the demesne has been divided among nine tenants; at Stondelf,[383] in Staffordshire, among thirty-one. At Shape[384] in Suffolk and Northendale[385] in Norfolk the demesnes are added to the holdings of the customary tenants. At Forncett,[386] in Norfolk, parts of the demesne are in the same way leased out in small parcels in the fifteenth century for gradually lengthening periods of years, though by the beginning of our period they seem to have been held by copy in the same way as the customary land. Elsewhere we get what appear to be variations of the same system, in the form of sub-letting or of joint-cultivation. At Castle Combe,[387] for example, the demesne lands were leased in 1454 to four tenants, "with the intention that they themselves

[379] *Historia et Cartularium Monasterii Gloucestriæ*, vol. iii. App., pp. 291–295.
[380] Roxburghe Club, *Surveys of Lands of William, First Earl of Pembroke.*
[381] *Ibid.*
[382] R.O. Rentals and Surveys, Portf. 13, No. 34.
[383] R.O. *Land Rev. Misc. Bks.*, vol. clxxxv., ff. 70–74.
[384] R.O. *Misc. Bks. Treas. of Receipts*, vol. clxiii., ff. 187.
[385] R.O. Rentals and Surveys, Roll 478, No. 3.
[386] Davenport, *History of a Norfolk Manor.*
[387] Scrope, *History of Manor and Barony of Castle Combe*, p. 208.

should let to farm to all the tenants of the lord some portion of those lands." On other manors groups of tenants seem to make themselves jointly responsible for the rent required. It was not an unknown[388] thing even at quite an early date for a whole village to come forward and make a kind of collective bargain with the lord as to the terms upon which they would take over the demesne lands, and when the leasing of the demesne became the regular practice townships sometimes stepped into the shoes of the bailiffs, and averted the entry of the large farmer by leasing the lands themselves, and making their own arrangements as to the way in which they should be utilised. One may suspect, indeed, that such action took place in a good many cases when the land was leased to many small tenants, as at Paynton and South Brent, even though the intervention of the township is not expressly stated. Sometimes, however, the communal character of the bargain is quite beyond doubt. For example, at Cucklington,[389] on the manor of Stooke Trister in Somersetshire, twelve tenants leased together at a rent of £8 for forty years a sheep house with 250 acres of land. At Chedsey,[390] in the same county, the whole of the demesne, which lay mainly in small parcels of one or two acres, was held in 1568 on a twenty-one years' lease by the tenants of the manor. At Caston,[391] in Norfolk, we find an entry of rent which is paid by "the inhabitants of the town of Scratby for certain lands occupied for their benefit." The phrase "town lands," which appears not infrequently[392] in the surveys and estate maps of the sixteenth century may perhaps be taken as indicating the same conclusion. In what way exactly we ought to interpret these arrangements—whether we should regard them as nothing more than a summary expression of the fact that all the tenants have severally rights over part of the estate, or whether we should conceive of them as implying some higher degree of corporate action than this, and as the outcome of a bargain struck with the lord by the village as a village, is an interesting and difficult question,[393] to which we shall recur later in speaking of rights of common. But we may mention two points which suggest that there is in them a certain element of practical communism to which legal historians sometimes do less than justice. The first is that we occasionally find certain tenants acting on behalf[394] of, one might almost

---

[388] Vinogradoff, *The Growth of the Manor*, note to chap. ii., Book III., p. 370, and his quotations from Maitland: "The villains of Bright Waltham ... constituted a community which held land, which was capable of receiving a grant of land, which could contract with the lord, which could make exchange with the lord."

[389] Roxburghe Club, *Surveys of Lands of William, First Earl of Pembroke*.

[390] Roxburghe Club, *Surveys of Lands of William, First Earl of Pembroke*.

[391] R.O. Rentals and Surveys, Gen. Ser., Portf. 12, No. 52, p. 10 d.

[392] See the map of part of Salford, p. 163, and compare R.O. Rentals and Surveys, Gen. Ser., Portf. 27, No. 32 (Lavenham in Suffolk): "Of Township of Tuddenham Free land foldcourse, 6s. 9d." *Ibid.*, Portf. 13, No 21 (Colly Weston in Northants): "The inhabitants for bushy ground paying two years 11s. Item, in every third year they pay nothing." At Wymondham (R.O. *Aug. Off. Misc. Bks.*, vol. ccclx., f. 91) one finds under the heading "Towne lands" 38 acres held by copy by the "feoffees of the Vill of Wymondham" (37 Eliz.) in Trust for the school.

[393] See references quoted below, pp. 244–253.

[394] *e.g.* Scrope, *History of Manor and Barony of Castle Combe*, p. 203. Extent of Manor, 1454: "Et notandum quod prædictae terræ dominicates cum pratis et pasturis supra specificatis dimittebantur ad firmam Ricardo Hallewey, Edwardo Yonge, Johanni Costyn,

say, representing, others. The second is that in some cases the demesne lands are divided among them in exactly equal[395] shares, so that, though every one has more land than before, the relative sizes of their holdings are unaltered. The last fact is a very striking one. It means, in the first place, that the new land has been allotted on some common principle and by some formal agreement. Clearly, if each tenant had bought as much land as he pleased, we should have had not equality but inequality. It points, in the second place, to the enduring strength of the ideas and interests underlying the system of agricultural shareholding which is characteristic of the mediæval village. We can understand a very primitive system of agriculture designed to secure each household the standard equipment needed to support it. But one would naturally suppose that at the end of the Middle Ages, when new land which had hitherto belonged to the lord was offered to the villagers, each would buy up as much as he could without regard to the interests of his neighbours. It is probable that in most cases, as in those quoted in Chapter III., this is what happened. But in some instances it is not. The old economic ideas which had governed the disposition of the ancient customary holdings are applied to the new land which the cessation of demesne cultivation by the lord throws into the market, and the villagers re-allot it on the old plan. Even in its decay the mediæval land system shows its vitality by meeting new situations with the ancient methods.

These small tenants were described as "farming the demesne," and their existence may perhaps mark a sort of half-way house in the evolution of the manorial demesne into the large leasehold farm. One may suspect that that development was not at all likely to take place rapidly in the circumstances of the fifteenth century. According to the generally accepted view the practice of leasing part of the demesne, though occurring at a very early date on manors where the labour sup-

Willelmo Gaudeby, et Edwardo Noorth, ea intentione quod ipsi dimitterent ad firmam omnibus tenentibus domini aliquas portiones dictorum terrarum secundum magis et minus pro earum cultura, et reddunt pro firma inter se cxiiis. viiid."

[395] R.O. *Land Revenue Misc. Bks.*, vol. ccxxi., fol. 1. Survey of Manor of Brigstock (Northants) 4, James I. Here the demesne is held by twenty-two tenants, each having 8 acres, 3 roods, and 1 acre of meadow. Mickleholme meadow (also demesne land) is held by five tenants, each having 1 acre. One finds on some Northumberland manors a growth in the size of customary holdings combined with the preservation of almost exact equality between them, which surely must be taken as proving that the increase in the area held grew, not by sporadic encroachments on the part of individuals, but by definite allotment on some communal plan. Thus at Birling there were in 1248 ten "bondi," each holding 30 acres or one husbandland; in 1498 nine holding 30 acres or one husbandland, and four holding one husbandland of 30 acres between them; in 1567 ten customary tenants, each holding 33 acres; in 1616 the average holding has risen from 33 to 42½ acres, but there is still substantial equality, the largest holding amounting to 44 acres, 3 roods, 3½ poles, and the smallest to 40 acres, 0 roods, 33 poles (I omit the facts as to the cottagers). In spite of two considerable additions to the land of the village, there is little change in the relative proportions of the tenancies. At Acklington there were in 1352 thirty-five bondage holdings of 16 acres each, of which nine were vacant (presumably on account of the plague). In 1368 these nine vacant holdings were let to the other tenants for herbage. In 1498 there were eighteen tenants, of whom seventeen held two husbandlands apiece (*i.e.* 32 acres) and one, one husbandland (*i.e.* 16 acres). *Northumberland County History*, vol. v.

ply was too small for it to be cultivated by the villeins, received a great impetus from the scarcity of labour which was produced by the Great Plague, and went on side by side with the gradual commutation of labour services into money rents. Of course one must not dogmatise about changes which took centuries to accomplish, and which developed at very different degrees of speed in different parts of the country. But the accounts of particular manors supplied us by surveyors bear out the view that the development of a class of small leaseholders took place as the result of the abandonment of the old system of cultivating the demesne by means of the works of the tenants organised under the supervision of the manorial officials. "The lorde departed his habitation and caused his officers to grant out parte of his landes to his tenants at will." "The medowes lying in Hinton were the lordes' severall meadowes, which nowe are divided among the tenants." "When the lorde departed his habitation, and granted out the demesnes, the part was delivered and letten to the use of the tenants." "One Sir John Taverney, Knight, dyd inhabit within the said mannor, and kept great hospitalitie, and occupied the demesnes in his own possession, which are large and greate, and now of late years granted out by copye for terms of lyves among the tenants." Such information, collected by a curious investigator[396] in the middle of the sixteenth century from the lips of aged peasants in the west of England, takes us back to a time when the leasing of the demesne was a comparative novelty. Is it surprising that the landlord who leased for the first time should prefer to do so on this small scale, should choose to grant plots of land piecemeal for short terms of years rather than to form a single farm? The practice was at first an experiment, an alarming departure from accepted methods undertaken only through dire necessity. A great catastrophe like the plague might make it profitable, but time would naturally elapse before it was done systematically and on a large scale. At the same time a class of farmers with sufficient capital to manage several hundred acres of land could not come into existence at once. The ordinary villein tenants, who were the first lessees on many manors, could hardly jump immediately from farming twenty or thirty acres to farming a whole estate, though those of them who as bailiffs had previously been responsible for managing the demesne, and who seem sometimes to have managed it as farmers for the lord, rather than as hired servants, were certainly in a better position to do so.

It would seem indeed that the question whether, when the sixteenth century began, the demesne lands of a manor were leased to many small tenants or to one or two large farmers, was decided largely by local and personal conditions, and may fairly be described as a matter of chance. When they lay in many scattered strips unified culture was impossible till they had been consolidated, and therefore there was no particular reason for leasing them to one tenant rather than to many; whereas, when they were from the start in two or three great blocks, it was obviously very improbable that they would be sub-divided. In those parts of the country where sheep-farming was less profitable than elsewhere one motive for introducing a single large farm was absent, while where the demesne had already been leased in small plots the manorial authorities might dislike to make an

---

[396] Humberstone, *Topographer and Genealogist*, vol. i. (surveys *temp.* Phil. and Mary of various manors belonging to the Earl of Devon).

abrupt change affecting many households disadvantageously. The general movement would appear, however, to have been in the direction of longer leases and larger tenancies. Thus Miss Davenport has shown that at Forncett the leasing of the demesne began[397] in small parcels and for short periods from the end of the fourteenth century, and gradually took place on a larger scale and for longer periods as the practice became more familiar. The earlier leases of the Oxfordshire manor of Cuxham[398] alternate between six and seven years in length, and it is not till 1472 that the College owning it appears to have granted a lease of as much as twenty years. Sometimes one can see the system of leasing small parcels to many little farmers, and that of leasing the whole demesne to one large farmer, coming into competition with each other. A case in point comes from Ablode[399] in Somersetshire. In 1515 the Abbot and Convent of St. Peter's, Gloucester, leased the whole manor of Ablode to a farmer for eighty years. But at the time when the lease was made the demesne lands and demesne meadows were already occupied by the customary tenants. Accordingly the covenant with the farmer provides that as soon as the other tenants' agreements terminate, he shall have the reversion of their lands to use as he pleases. Here the two types of demesne cultivation are seen merging into one another, with the result that the large farm is consolidated out of the small tenancies which preceded it.

At the beginning of our period these small demesne tenancies had already disappeared from many manors, if they had ever existed on them, and the normal method of using the demesne was to lease it to a single[400] large farmer, or at any rate to not more than three or four. In spite of the instances given above, in which the home farm and its lands were split up among numerous small tenants, most of the evidence suggests that the leasing of the demesne to a single farmer was as regular a way of disposing of it in the sixteenth century as its cultivation by manorial officials with the labour of villeins had been in the thirteenth. The very slow development of the large farm in certain parts of the country was due rather to the insignificance or absence of the demesne on some northern manors than

[397] Davenport, *History of a Norfolk Manor*, p. 57. When first leased in 1373 the demesne was leased as a whole, but this plan was abandoned. Early in the fifteenth century it was leased in small plots, at first for six or seven years, and then for twelve, twenty, or forty years. Finally parts of the demesne were granted to be held at fee farm.

[398] Merton Documents, Nos. 3100 (lease of 1361 for seven years), 3002 (lease of 1420 for seven years); 2856 (lease of 1424 for one year); 1874 (lease of 1472 for twenty years).

[399] *Historia et Cartularium Monasterii Gloucestriæ*, vol. iii. App., pp. 291–295. The words are "Sed bene licebit præfatis ... substituere tenentes ad eorum bene placitum in omnibus illis terris dominicalibus supradictis modo in manibus tenentium ibidem existentibus, cum reversio prædicta inde acciderit."

[400] Thus in 1535, on nineteen out of twenty-two manors owned by Battle Abbey, the demesne was farmed by a single tenant, on one by two, on one by three, while on one it was retained in the hands of the monks (*Oxford Studies in Social and Legal History*, vol. i.; *English Monasteries on the Eve of the Dissolution*, by A. Savine). On twenty-five manors out of thirty-two held by the Earl of Pembroke in 1568, the same unified management obtained (Roxburghe Club, *Surveys of Pembroke Manors*). Savine's remarks are to the point: "The lord of the manor seldom divided up the demesne into separate plots of land to be let to local tenants. Usually the demesne and its buildings, sometimes even together with the live and dead stock, passed into the hands of one farmer" (*ibid.*).

to the prevalence of any alternative methods of utilising it. The terms on which the farmer took over the land varied naturally in detail, but these differences are unimportant. In a few cases he holds it by copy. Normally he is a leaseholder, sometimes for life, more usually for a period of years ranging from twenty-one to eighty. Again the lessee's interest may be more or less inclusive. Sometimes only the demesne, including any customary works upon it of the tenants which may survive, is leased. Sometimes the lease includes the live-stock of the manor, which, or the equivalent of which, the farmer must replace at the end of his term. Sometimes the profits of the court are leased as well, though more usually they are reserved, together with any income from fines, to the lord. Sometimes there is an arrangement of great interest and importance by which the whole body of manorial rights, including the income from the courts, confiscation of straying beasts, and the rents of the customary tenants, are leased to the farmer, who thus becomes the immediate landlord of the other tenants.[401] The greater part of the farmer's rent is by the middle of the sixteenth century paid in money. But certain payments in kind[402] survive, and supply a link between the vanishing subsistence cultivation, and the growing commercial economy. Where money was scarce, tenants were sometimes allowed to pay in kind as a concession to their interests, and some landlords still found it convenient to receive part of their rent in grain, fowls, pigeons, fish, or a fat bull, a practice which on college estates lasted down to the very end of the seventeenth century. But the value of such payments was carefully calculated in terms of money, and they were the exception.

The growth of large farms had proceeded so far by the middle of the sixteenth century that in parts of the country the area held by the farmer was about equal to that held by all the other tenants. On some manors it was less; on others it was a great deal more. The average area of the large farmer's land in Wiltshire seems to have been about 352 acres, and it is not unusual to find manors where there are only two or three customary tenants, while on some there were none at all. Wiltshire no doubt must not be taken as typical of all other counties, as the acreage of the leasehold farms held by men who had capital to spend could so easily be increased by drawing in great tracts from the rolling stretches of Chalk Down. But elsewhere, though the acreage held by the farmer of the demesne is less, 170 or 150

[401] As at Knyghton in Wilts in 1568 (Roxburghe Club, *Pembroke Surveys*), where the holdings and rents of the customary tenants appear in the farmer's lease, *e.g.* "Walter Savage ad voluntatem tenet ut parcellam dicti manerii l close etc. ... et reddit 56s. ad manus dicti firmarii."

[402] Here is an example from a lease of 1562. The farmer pays "yearly to the lord for the aforesaid farm —

| | |
|---|---|
| 10 quarters of corn, per bushel, 12d. | £4 |
| 20 quarters of barley, per bushel, 8d. | 106s. 8d. |
| 10 quarters of oats, per bushel, 3d. | 26s. 8d. |
| 20 capons, per caput, 4d. | 6s. 8d. |
| 20 pigeons, per caput, 4d. | 6s. 8d. |
| 12 great fish called trouts, per caput, 3d. | 3s." |

(Survey of South Newton, *ibid.*).

acres, and though one or two of the larger copyholders control a great deal of land themselves, he is still, compared with the bulk of the customary tenants, a Triton among minnows. Arithmetical averages are, however, unsatisfactory, and a better idea of the scale on which the large farmer carried on business may be obtained from the following table:—

**TABLE VIII**

Column Key

| | | | |
|---|---|---|---|
| A | Under 50 Acres. | J | 450–500 Acres. |
| B | 50–99 Acres. | K | 500–549 Acres. |
| C | 99–149 Acres. | L | 550–599 Acres. |
| D | 150–199 Acres. | M | 600–649 Acres. |
| E | 200–249 Acres. | N | 650–699 Acres. |
| F | 250–299 Acres. | O | 700–749 Acres. |
| G | 300–349 Acres. | P | 750–799 Acres. |
| H | 350–399 Acres. | Q | 800–849 Acres. |
| I | 400–449 Acres. | R | 850–900 Acres. |

| | A | B | C | D | E | F | G | H | I | J | K | L | M | N | O | P | Q | R |
|---|---|---|---|---|---|---|---|---|---|---|---|---|---|---|---|---|---|---|
| Eighteen farms on sixteen manors in Norfolk | ... | 2 | 2 | 3 | 1 | ... | 3 | 1 | ... | 2 | 3 | ... | ... | ... | 1 | ... | ... | ... |
| Thirty-one farms on twenty-three manors in Wiltshire | 4 | 2 | 4 | 4 | 3 | 4 | 3 | ... | 2 | 1 | 1 | ... | ... | ... | ... | ... | 1 | 2 |
| Eighteen farms on thirteen manors in several counties | 2 | 3 | 3 | 1 | 3 | 2 | 1 | ... | ... | 3 | ... | ... | ... | ... | ... | ... | ... | ... |
| Total, sixty-seven farms on fifty-two manors | 6 | 7 | 9 | 8 | 7 | 6 | 7 | 1 | 2 | 6 | 4 | ... | ... | ... | 1 | ... | 1 | 2 |

It will be seen that if all the farms are grouped together, rather more than one half, thirty-seven out of sixty-seven, have an area exceeding 200 acres, and that the area of rather more than a quarter exceeds 350 acres. The figures must be read with the caution that they in some cases certainly underestimate the real extent of the land used by the farmer, as rights of common often cannot be expressed in terms of acres.

### *(c) Enclosure and Conversion by the Manorial Authorities*

When we turn from the agricultural arrangements described in previous chapters to examine these large farms, we enter a new world, a world where economic power is being slowly organised for the exploitation of the soil, and where the methods of cultivation and the standards of success are quite different from those obtaining on the small holdings of the peasantry. The advantage to the lord of the system of large farms, compared either with the retention of the demesne in his own hands, or with the leasing of it in allotments to small tenants, was obvious enough for its extension to be no matter for surprise. The utilisation of the produce of the demesne by the lord's household was unnecessary when markets were sufficiently reliable to offer a regular supply, and inconvenient when the landlord was an absentee. The division of the estate among small tenants meant the creation or maintenance of interests opposed to agricultural changes, and made it impracticable to vary the methods of agriculture to meet varying demands, except by the rather cumbrous process of a common agreement ratified in the manorial court. The leasing of the demesne to a large farmer got rid of those disadvantages. The lord was secured a regular money income, which was considerably higher per acre than that got from the customary tenants; and since the land was under the management of a single individual, who was sometimes equipped with a good deal of capital, it was much easier to try experiments and to initiate changes. When not only the demesne, but the whole body of manorial rights, was included in the lease, the property became of that most desirable kind, in which ownership is attenuated to a pecuniary lien on the product of industry, without administrative responsibility for its management.

Opportunities for new methods of cultivation were afforded by the leasing of the demesne to a single farmer, which would lead us to look at his holding as the place where agrarian changes were most likely to begin, and to start from that in order to trace the effect of these large properties on the small properties of the customary tenants. On the one hand, any wide development of leasehold tenure involves a certain mobility in rural society and a disposition to break with routine. There must be a market for land, which again implies that some class has accumulated sufficient capital to invest and has got beyond mere subsistence farming. It naturally arises either when new[403] land is brought into cultivation, or when the development of trade makes farming for the market profitable, or when changes are being introduced into the methods of agriculture, or when the value of land is uncertain (for example, when it is thought that it may contain minerals),[404] because in all these cases leasehold, being a terminable interest, enables the owner of land to adjust his rent to the tenant's returns. On the other hand, the landowner

[403] See pp. 139–147.

[404] See *Northumberland County History*, vol. ix., account of Cowpen, and *Victoria County History*, Lancashire, article on Social and Economic History. For the same reasons mills and fisheries were naturally the first parts of a mediæval manor to be leased for terms of years.

does not get the full advantage of the elasticity in rent and management that lease-hold tenure makes possible, unless the tenant is a man of some substance, who can spend capital in cultivating land on a large scale, in stocking a farm with sheep and cattle, in carrying crops until the best market is found, and in making experiments in new directions.

One can easily understand the reasons which favoured the large farm, if one reflects on the change in economic environment, the outlines of which have been already described. The most important economic cause determining the unit of landholding is the nature of the crop to be raised and the methods used in producing it; and the nature of the crop depends mainly on the conditions of the market. Now in the sixteenth century the market conditions were such as to leave room for a large number of small corn-growers, because trade was so backward that a great number of households farmed simply for subsistence. On the other hand, even in the case of corn-growing, the size of the most profitable unit of agriculture was increasing with the development of an internal corn trade—a development which is proved by the strenuous attempts which the Government made to regulate it through the Justices of the Peace; while in the case of sheep and cattle grazing on the large scale practised by the graziers of the period, there was obviously no question but that an extensive ranch, which could be stocked with several thousand beasts, was the type of holding which would pay best. That a class of capitalist farmers of this kind was coming into existence in the sixteenth century is indicated both by the complaints of contemporaries that small men find farms taken over their heads by great graziers, who have made money in trade; by the fact that the stock and land lease, a form of metayage under which the working capital was supplied by the landowner, had given way on many manors to the modern type of lease under which it is provided by the lessee;[405] and by the way in which one farmer would become the lessee of two[406] or more manors, a clear indication of the existence of wealthy men who had money to invest in agriculture. It was the substitution of such a class for the small leaseholders among whom the demesne had often been divided, and their appearance for the first time on manors where the demesne had been kept in the hands of the lord until it was leased to one large farmer, which gave a rapid and almost catastrophic speed to the tendency to enclosure which, as we have seen, was already going on quietly among the small tenants, because it meant the control of a growing proportion of the land by persons who had capital to spend, and who, since they held their farms by lease, not by copy, were under the pressure of competitive rents to adopt the methods of agriculture which were financially most profitable. This in itself was a new phenomenon, at least on the large scale on which it appeared in the sixteenth century. In modern agriculture one is accustomed to seeing the area sown with

[405] Owing to the advantages which the small holding has for dairy purposes (personal attention to cattle, &c.), it is still the custom in parts of the country, *e.g.* Devonshire, for the large farmers to sublet small dairy farms out of their holdings, and to supply the lessee with all the stock, including the cows and the cottage. See Levy, *Large and Small Holdings,* chap. ix.

[406] Several examples of this are to be found in the *Pembroke Surveys.* Contemporaries called it "the engrossing of farms."

any crop varying according to movements in the market price of the produce, so that on the margin of cultivation land is constantly changing its use in response to changes in the world's markets. But such adaptability implies a very high degree of organisation, and when farming was carried on mainly by small producers for their own households, the reaction of changing commercial conditions on the supply was much slower, and cultivation was to a much greater extent a matter of routine. It was the development of the large capitalist farmer which supplied the link binding agriculture to the market and causing changes in prices to be reflected in changes in the use to which land was put.

The tendency which we should expect to find represented most conspicuously upon the demesne farms is of course that enclosing of land and laying of it down to pasture, which is lamented by contemporaries. The word "enclosing," under which contemporaries summed up the agrarian changes of the period, has become the recognised name for the process by which the village community was broken up, but it is perhaps not a very happy one. Quite apart from the difficulties which it raises when we come to compare the enclosures of the eighteenth century, which were made under Act of Parliament, with those of the sixteenth century, which were made in defiance of legislation, it is at once too broad and too narrow to be an adequate description even of the innovations of the earlier period, too broad if it implies that all enclosures entailed the hardships which were produced by some, too narrow if it implies that the only hardships caused were due to enclosure. It selects one feature of the movement towards capitalist agriculture for special emphasis, and suggests that the hedging and ditching of land always produced similar results. That, however, was by no means the case. Enclosure might take place, as has been shown above, without producing the social disturbances usually associated with it, provided that it was carried out by the tenants themselves, and with the consent of those affected. The concentration of holdings and the displacement of tenants might take place without enclosure. On a desert island there is no need of palings to keep out trespassers; and a manor which was entirely in the hands of one great farmer was a manor where the maintenance of enclosures was almost unnecessary. At the same time the word does describe one of the external features which usually accompanied the agrarian changes. The general note of the movement was the emancipation from the rules of communal cultivation of part or all of the land used for purposes of tillage or pasture. The surface of a manor was covered with a kind of elaborate network of rules apportioning, on a common customary plan, the rights and duties of every one who had an interest in it. A man must let his land lie open after harvest; he must not keep more than a certain number of each kind of beasts on the common; he must plough when his neighbours plough, and sow when his neighbours sow. The effect of the growing influence of the capitalist farmer was to clear away these organised restrictions from parts of the manor altogether, and violently to shake the whole system. Enclosing was normally the external symptom of the change, for the practical reason that the simplest way of cutting a piece of land adrift from the common course of cultivation, or from the rules laid down for the use of the commonable area, was to put a hedge round it, partly to keep one's own beasts in, partly to keep other people's beasts out. The essential feature of the change was that land which was formerly subject to a rule prescribing the methods of cultivation became land which was used at the individual's discretion.

The agent through whom enclosing was carried out was usually the large farmer. When the farmer leased only the demesne lands, and the demesne lands lay in large compact blocks, not in scattered strips, he could naturally practise the new economy of enclosure upon them without colliding with any other interest, except in the cases where they were divided into several tenancies; while if steps were taken to get rid of the interests which the customary tenants had either in the open fields, in the meadows, or in the common, the land lost by them was normally added to the area which the farmer leased, and enclosed by him. In the surveys of the period one finds manors in every stage of the transition from open field cultivation to enclosure, and though such individual instances tell us nothing of the extent of the movement, they offer a vivid picture of what enclosing meant, and give the impression that enclosure had usually proceeded further on those manors where the farmer held the largest proportion of the land. The slowness of the movement towards enclosure on the holdings of the customary tenants has already been described. As a contrast to it one may look at the following table, which sets out the condition of things on some demesne farms:—

Table IX

| Number of Demesne Farms Examined. | No signs of Enclosure. | Under 5 per Cent. Enclosed. | 5 to 24 per Cent. Enclosed. | 25 to 49 per Cent. Enclosed. | 50 to 74 per Cent. Enclosed. | 75 to 99 per Cent. Enclosed. | 100 per Cent. Enclosed |
|---|---|---|---|---|---|---|---|
| 47 | 12 | 9 | 7 | 7 | ... | 4 | 8 |

These figures are not offered as any evidence of the absolute area enclosed in the counties represented. They may, however, perhaps be taken as an indication that the demesne farm was usually that part of the manor on which enclosure was carried out most thoroughly. Thirty-one of the manors included in the table are in Wiltshire and Norfolk, and where the conditions of things on the tenants' holdings can be compared with that obtaining on the demesne, it is almost always the case that the new economy has spread furthest on the latter. Neither in Wiltshire nor in Norfolk had enclosure by the peasants themselves proceeded very far in the latter half of the sixteenth century.

The conditions, however, on different manors varied so enormously that much weight cannot be laid on these figures, and it is both more important and more practicable to examine particular examples of the ways in which the large enclosed estate was built up. In the first place, then, one may say with some confidence that those parts of a manor which lent themselves most readily to enclosing were the waste, the common pasture, and the common meadow, while the enclosing of the farmer's holdings of arable land took place more gradually, less thoroughly, and with greater difficulty. Thus selecting from the manors tabulated above those in which the quality of the land enclosed is distinguished, and omitting those where it is merely stated to lie "in closes," one finds that partial or complete enclosure of the arable has been made on nine, of the meadow on eleven, and of the pasture on twenty, manors. The explanation of this is to be found by recollecting the characteristics of the organisation into which the farmer stepped. The arable land which formed the lord's demesne was often scattered, like the tenant's, in comparatively small plots over the three fields; unity of ownership did not by any means necessarily imply unified culture, and before these could be enclosed they had to be consolidated into fewer and larger blocks. Moreover, if the object of enclosure was conversion to pasture, it must be remembered that the enclosure of the arable implied a very great revolution in the manorial economy. A farm which was well equipped for tillage had barns, granges, agricultural implements, which would stand idle if the arable land was enclosed for pasture, and it was therefore natural that, as long as other land was available in sufficient quantities for sheep-farming, such land should be enclosed for the purpose, before the ordinary course of cultivation on the arable land was abandoned. The common meadows and the common wastes did not offer these obstacles to enclosure. Since the individualising tendencies of personal cultivation did not operate upon these parts of the village land, the method of securing equal enjoyment of them had not been, as in the case of arable, to give each household a holding consisting of separate strips scattered over good and bad land alike, but to give each holder of an arable share access to the whole of the pasture land. They were, therefore, usually not divided and scattered to anything like the same extent, and it was thus much easier for the rights of different parties over them to be disentangled, and for the land to be cut up and enclosed "in severalty." Hence, where the tenants are most numerous, and where there are fewest signs of change, the effect of the large farmer is often seen in the withdrawal of part of the common waste from communal use. If the growth of sheep farming made the small tenants anxious, as in many cases it did, to acquire separate pastures for their flocks, it can readily be understood that the large farmer, who had more to lose and more to gain, was likely to pursue the same policy unless checked by organised opposition. Normally the change seems to have taken place by converting the right to pasture a certain number of beasts in common with other tenants into the right to the exclusive use of a certain number of acres. Instead of the whole commonable area lying open to a number of animals "stinted" in a certain proportion among the commoners, the stint is abandoned, and the basis of allocation is found not in a fixed number of animals, but in a fixed area of land, which forms the separate common of the individual farmer, and which is naturally enclosed. Many examples of this division of commonable land are found in the surveys, especially in connection with the common waste of the manor, which enable us to trace the change from collective to individual administration. Thus, to give a few instances, at Winterbourne Basset[407] the farmer has all the meadow land except one half-acre, and a separate close of 140 acres on the downs, where he can graze nearly three times as many sheep as all the customary tenants.

---

[407] Roxburghe Club, *Surveys of Lands of William, First Earl of Pembroke.* The farmer has four closes of meadow amounting to 9 acres, one meadow of 2½ acres, one meadow of 7 acres, one meadow of 8½ acres. In addition to that and the hilly pasture, there is in his possession "unus campus noviter inclusus, qui aliquando seminatur, aliquando iacet ad pasturam," and which "olim sustentare potuit 900 oves et catalla non extenta."

At Knyghton[408] he has enclosed with a hedge part of the sheep's common, no sheep at all being kept by the customary tenants. At Massingham,[409] in Norfolk, where much of the demesne arable lies "in the fields," there is an enclosed pasture containing 123½ acres; and on another farm of 203 acres, which has apparently been formed out of the demesne, one finds 28 acres of arable "in the fields" and 65 acres of "pasture enclosed," the remaining 80 acres lying "in the sheep courses." The best picture of what the change meant is given by the two maps[410] printed opposite. In No. III. the meadow, save for a small piece used exclusively by All Souls, is common, each tenant presumably being allowed to place so many beasts upon it. In No. IV. the meadow has been divided up among the tenants, and instead of pasturing a limited number of beasts on the whole of it, each can pasture as many beasts as he pleases on part of it. It is not necessary to point out the significance of this change from the point of view of the social organisation of rural life. It means that communal administration of part of the land has been abandoned and its place taken by use at the discretion of the individual tenant.

---

[408] *Ibid.*, "De terra montanea unde pars includitur cum sepe iuxta Crowcheston continens per estimationem 100 acres, et custodire potest supra prædictam 900 oves." Sometimes it is expressly stated that the farmer alone is to have a certain pasture, *e.g.* at Chalke (*ibid*): "Et etiam dictus firmarius habet ibidem unum montem vocatum a Doune et bene cognitum est quia circumcinctum est per sepem et bundas, et custodire potest 600 multones quia nullus habet communiam in eo nisi firmarius solus, et continet per estimacionem 200 acres."

[409] R.O. Rentals and Surveys, Gen. Ser., Portf. 24, No. 4, f. 46 (*temp.* Hen. VIII.). "The fold course will carry 1800 sheep at £8 a hundred."

[410] In All Souls' Muniment Room.

## III. MAP OF PART OF THE MANOR OF MAIDS MORTON IN BUCKINGHAMSHIRE (1590.)

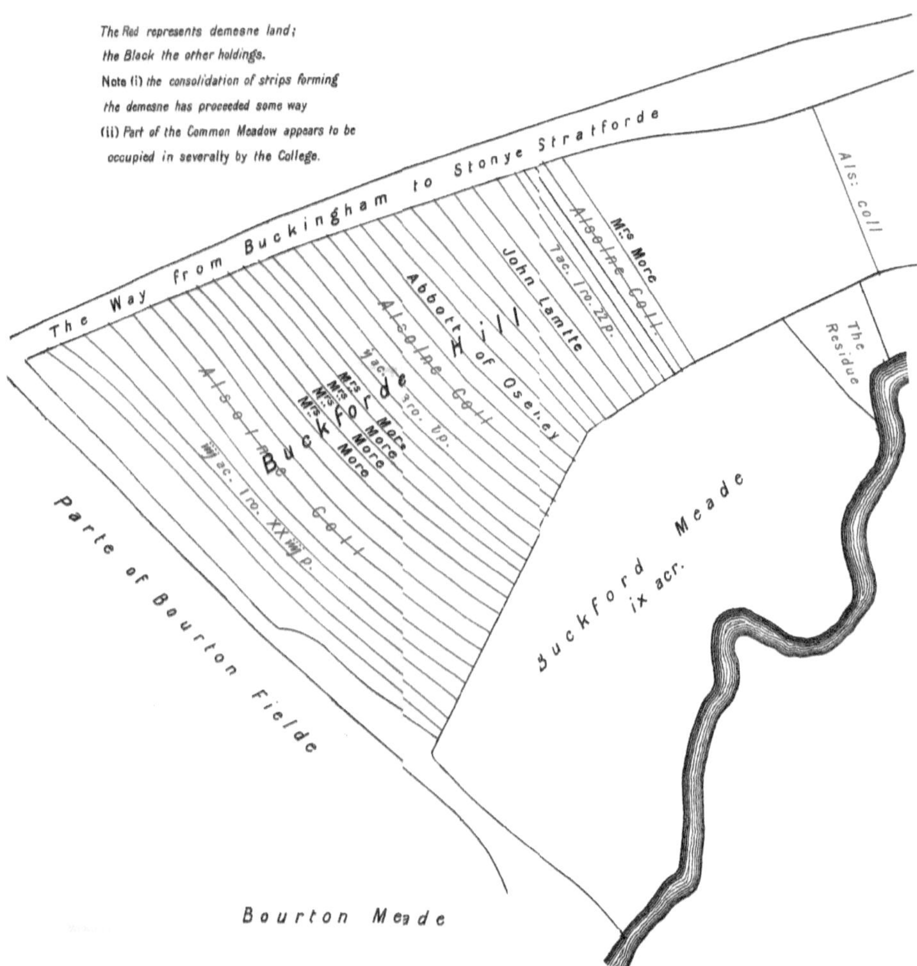


**Map of Part of the Manor of Maids Morton, in Buckinghamshire (1590)**

*The Red represents demesne land; the Black the other holdings.*

*Note (i) the consolidation of strips forming the demesne has proceeded some way*

*(ii) Part of the Common Meadow appears to be occupied in severalty by the College.*

IV. MAP OF PART OF THE MANOR OF CRENDON IN BUCKINGHAMSHIRE.
(ABOUT 1590.)

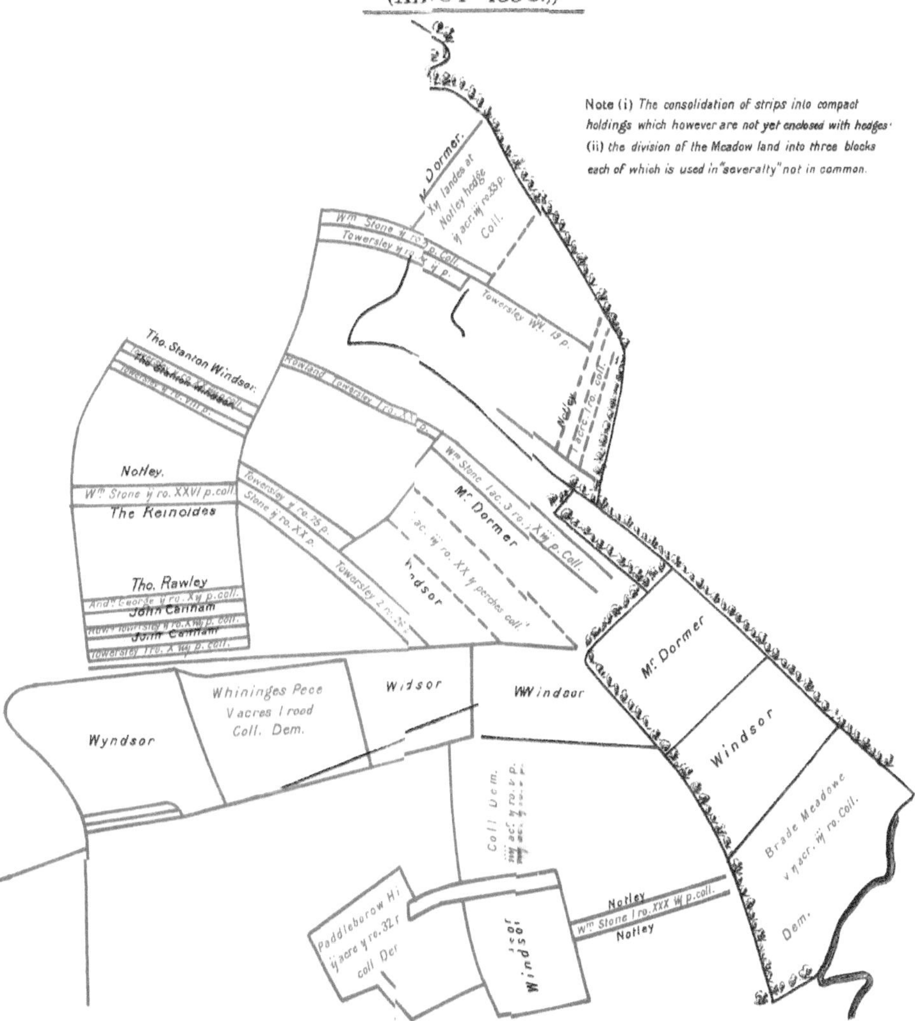


**Map of Part of the Manor of Crendon in Buckinghamshire (about 1590)**

*Note (i) The consolidation of the strips into compact holdings which however are not yet enclosed with hedges.*

*(ii) the division of the Meadow land into three blocks each of which is used in "severalty" not in common.*

But while the pasture ground and meadow offered special facilities for enclosure, there is abundant evidence that the farmer's arable land was also in many cases enclosed. On some manors the whole of the arable demesne lay together, and in that case there was no obstacle in the way of enclosing it. More usually it lay in three pieces, one block in each of the three great fields, and here again, when there was sufficient motive for enclosure, enclosure was easily practicable. The only arrangement which offered a really difficult problem was that in which it was divided into acre and a half strips scattered about the manor at a distance from each other. One finds cases in which such strips numbered several hundred, but the impression given by surveys is that, at any rate by the middle of the sixteenth century, such extreme subdivision was exceptional, and that the consolidation of holdings by means of exchange and purchase, which we have seen at work from an early date on the holdings of the customary tenants, had often proceeded so far on the demesne as to have rounded off the farmer's property into comparatively few large holdings. As an illustration of the first steps towards unification and enclosure we may take the manor of Sparham,[411] in Norfolk, which was surveyed about 1590. Here the 189 acres which compose the demesne, and which are leased to a farmer, are still much scattered. They lie in seventy different pieces, most of which are quite small, acres, half-acres, and roods. But even here there has been a considerable amount of consolidation, and it has been followed by the beginnings of enclosure. The 37½ acres of pasture lie in five pieces of 11, 9, 7, 5, 5½ acres, all of which have been enclosed. The arable is still intermixed with the strips of the other tenants in the open fields. But on the arable itself consolidation and enclosure are creeping forward. There are four strips lying together which comprise 6¾ acres. There is one enclosure, consisting of arable, wood, and meadow, and containing 17 acres. The neighbouring manor of Fulmordeston[412] offers an example of a state of things in which the same tendency has worked itself out to completion. The 742 acres leased by the farmer of the demesne are entirely enclosed. There are two woods comprising 50 acres. There is an enclosure of 250 acres, 35 perches, consisting of "Corne severall and Broome severall." There is a "great close" of 130 acres, 1 rood, "longe close" of 57 acres, 3 roods, "Brick kyll close" of 40 acres, 1 rood, "Brakehill close" of 24 acres, 1 rood, a field of 106 acres called Hestell, and another of 83 acres, 2 roods. But these different stages are best illustrated by maps[413] Nos. I., III., IV., V., and VI.

---

[411] MSS. of the Earl of Leicester at Holkham, Sparham Documents, Bdle. No. 5.

[412] *Ibid.*, Fulmordestone Documents, No. 59. Description of manor at bottom of map (1614).

[413] In All Souls' Muniment Room.

## V. MAP OF PART OF THE MANOR OF WEEDON WESTON IN NORTHAMPTONSHIRE (1590)

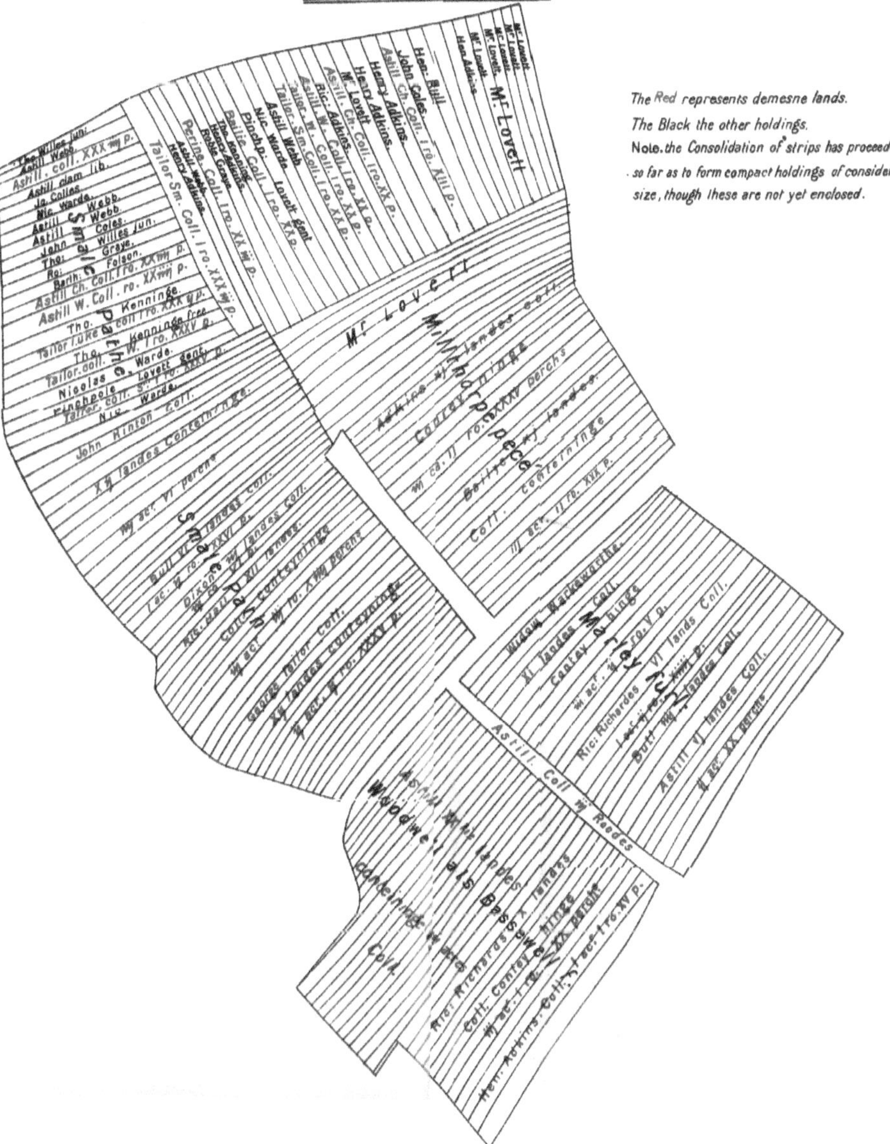



**Map of Part of the Manor of Weedon Weston, in Northamptonshire (1590)**

*The Red represents demesne lands.*

*The Black the other holdings.*

*Note. the Consolidation of strips has proceeded so far as to form compact holdings of considerable size, though these are not yet enclosed.*

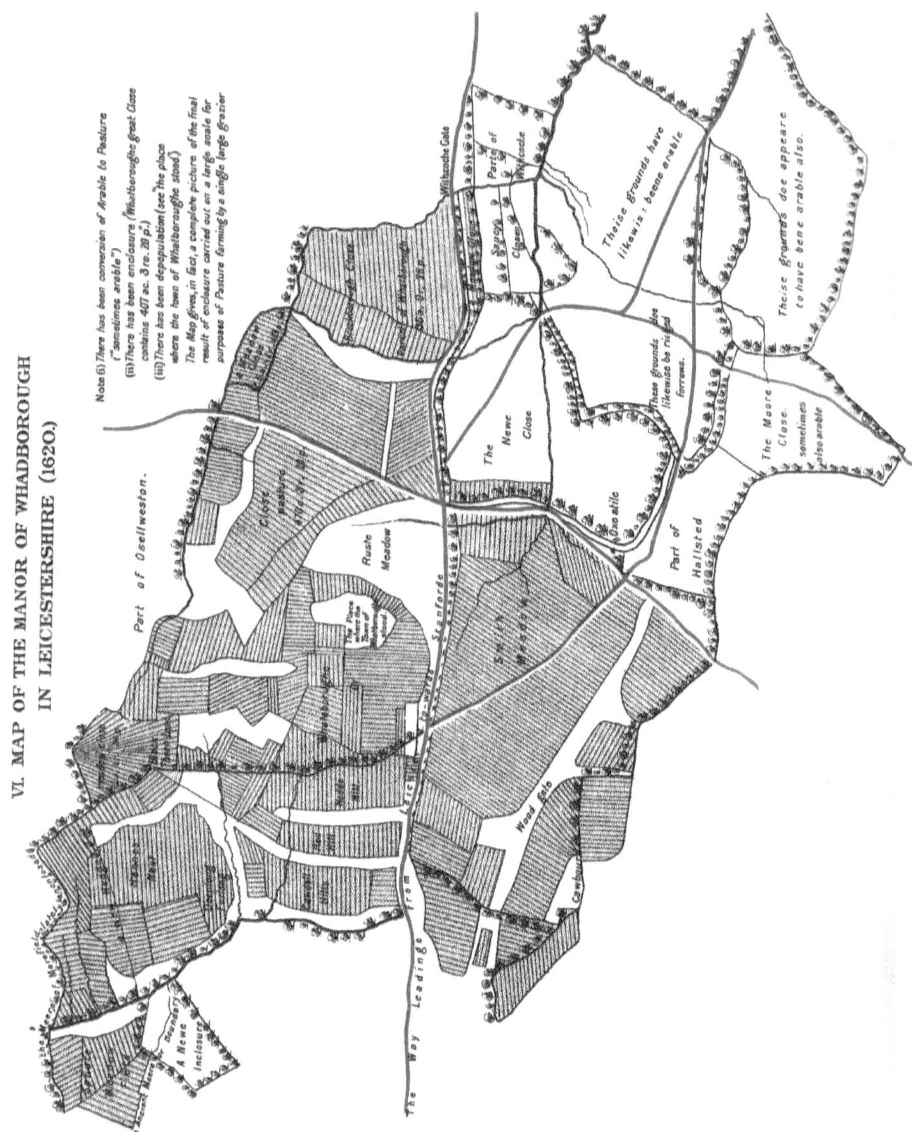



**Map of Part of the Manor of Whadborough in Leicestershire (1620)**

*Note (i) There has been conversion of Arable to Pasture ("sometimes arable")*

*(ii) There has been enclosure ("Whatboroughe great Close contains 407 ac. 3 ro. 20 p.")*

*(iii) There has been depopulation (see "the place where the town of Whatborough stood.")*

> *The Map gives, in fact, a complete picture of the final result of en-closure carried out on a large scale for the purposes of Pasture farming by a single larger grazier.*

On No. III. it will be seen that there is a good deal of subdivision. On Nos. IV. and V. the tenants whose strips separated parts of the demesne from each other, have in many cases dropped out, so that the process of aggregation is facilitated: on No. I. the concentration of the demesne into a single large block is complete; though it is still unenclosed, it offers no obstacle to enclosure: on No. VI.consolidation has been followed by enclosure, conversion to pasture and depopulation. Between the state of things on map No. III. and that on map No. VI. there is the greatest possible difference. Yet there is no reason to doubt that Whadborough had once been an open field village with tenants who were mainly engaged in tillage. Map Nos. IV., V., and I. are, as it were, the intervening chapters which join the preface to the conclusion. Occasionally one can see the process of consolidation, which was the necessary preliminary of enclosure, actually taking place. At Harriesham,[414] in Kent, the parson held 3 acres of glebe land in two pieces, one of them lying in the middle of a field belonging to another tenant, who ploughed up its boundaries and added it to his own land. Accordingly, to prevent uncertainty in the future, the owner of the field and the parson executed a deed by which the latter surrendered his claim to the detached pieces of land, and in return got three acres laid out in a single plot. In view of the large blocks which are often held by the farmer of the demesne, one cannot doubt that such consolidation by way of exchange must have been a common arrangement.

It remains to ask how far the type of economy pursued by the large farmer differed from that of the smaller tenants, and in particular whether there are signs of his specialising upon the grazing of sheep. The most complete picture of the agricultural changes of the early sixteenth century, not on the demesne farms alone, but on the holdings of all classes of tenants as well, is given in the well-known returns[415] made by the Commissioners who were appointed by Wolsey in 1517 to investigate enclosures, and these are supplemented by the figures published

---

[414] Maps in All Souls' Muniment Room: "The description of the parsonage of Harriesham in the countie of Kent, with the glebe lands thereunto belonging." Note on back of map: "Memorandum that whereas there are and always have been 4 parcelles of land in Mr. Steed his fielde called Harriesham field belonging unto the parsonage of Harriesham, conteyninge by estimation three acres, whereof the one did lye along by the landes of Sir Edward Wootton, called the Cowe doune, the other ... abutteth on the said Cowe doune toward the east, the other boundes thereof not being certainly known by reason that they were plowed up by one Robert Brinkley, tenant of the whole field, and were laid out by Robert Brinkley as in the Platte doth appeare under the Redd colour; It is now covenanted by the said Mr. Steede and Mr. George Hovenden, incumbent there, by deed bearing date the 20th of July in the 17th year of the Queen's Majestie's reign, that nowe all that the said three acres shall from henceforth be possessed by the parson and his successors for ever in manner and form as it is nowe laid out in the platte in the yellow colour after the maner of a square" [here follow the boundaries].

[415] Leadam, *Domesday of Enclosures*. For a discussion as to whether they suggest that enclosing took place for arable or pasture, see *Trans. Royal Hist. Soc.*, New Series, vol. xiv.

by Miss Davenport[416] as to the relative proportions or arable and pasture land on certain Staffordshire estates. The interpretation of both of these sets of statistics is ambiguous. Mr. Leadam uses them to show that much enclosing took place for arable, and that therefore the statutes and writers of the period exaggerated the movement towards pasture farming. Professor Gay thinks his conclusions untenable, and that a proper interpretation of the Commissioners' returns corroborates the view of contemporary writers that pasture was substituted for tillage on a large scale. Two points emerge pretty clearly from the controversy. The first is that there was a good deal of redistribution of land with the object of better tillage, of the kind which has been described above, and that probably the fact that the word "enclosure" was used to describe this, as well as the conversion of arable to pasture, was responsible for some confusion. The second is that the predominant tendency was towards sheep-farming. To suppose that contemporaries were mistaken as to the general nature of the movement is to accuse them of an imbecility which is really incredible. Governments do not go out of their way to offend powerful classes out of mere lightheartedness, nor do large bodies of men revolt because they have mistaken a ploughed field for a sheep pasture. Even if we accept Mr. Leadam's statistical analysis of the report of the Commission of 1517, his figures still reveal a great deal of conversion to pasture; and it is clear that many cases on which his totals rest are open to more than one interpretation.

If the general correctness of the view of the sixteenth century observers that there was a wide movement towards sheep-farming is accepted, it ought to be represented more fully on the demesne farms than elsewhere, because changes could be applied to them with much less friction than to the lands in which the interests of other tenants were involved. With a view to showing to what extent this is the case two sets of figures are given below; the first is a table taken from Dr. Savine's[417] work on *The English Monasteries on the Eve of the Reformation*, and relates to the demesne lands of forty-one monasteries which were surveyed for the Crown on the occasion of their surrender; some were apparently in the hands of the monastery and some apparently were leased. The second gives the approximate use to which land was put by the farmers of the demesnes on forty-nine manors in the sixteenth and early seventeenth centuries. They are subdivided in three groups, (*a*) manors in Norfolk and Suffolk, (*b*) manors in Wiltshire and Dorsetshire (one), and (*c*) manors in other southern and eastern counties, but including one in Staffordshire and one in Lancashire. For purposes of comparison the table given in Part I. Chapter III., illustrating the use made of the customary holdings, is repeated here: —

---

[416] *Quarterly Journal of Economics*, vol. xi.
[417] *Oxford Studies in Social and Legal History*, vol. i. pp. 171–173.

**TABLE X**

I

| Total Demesne Land of Forty-one Monasteries. | Arable. | Pasture. | Meadow. |
|---|---|---|---|
| Acres. | Acres. | Acres. | Acres. |
| 16780 | 6235¾ | 8691½ | 1852¾ |
|  | (37.1%) | (51.7%) | (11.0%) |

II

| Total Acreage of Sixty-five Farms on Fifty Manors. (Fractions of Acres omitted.) | Arable. | Pasture. | Meadow. | Closes. | Indeterminate. |
|---|---|---|---|---|---|
| Acres. | Acres. | Acres. | Acres. | Acres. | Acres. |
| 16866 | 8302 | 6172 | 1528 | 624 | 240 |
|  | (49.2%) | (36.5%) | (9%) | (3.6%) | (1.3%) |

Composed of (*a*) Thirty-two Farms on<br>Twenty-three Manors in Wilts and One Manor in Dorset

| Total Acreage of Thirty-two Farms. | Arable. | Pasture. | Meadow. | Closes. | Indeterminate. |
|---|---|---|---|---|---|
| Acres. | Acres. | Acres. | Acres. | Acres. | Acres. |
| 8812 | 4390 | 2928 | 754 | 500 | 240 |
|  | (49.8%) | (33.2%) | (8.3%) | (5.6%) | (2.7%) |

(*b*) Sixteen Farms on Thirteen Manors in<br>Norfolk and Suffolk

| Total Acreage of Sixteen Farms. | Arable. | Pasture. | Meadow. | Closes. | Indeterminate. |
|---|---|---|---|---|---|
| Acres. | Acres. | Acres. | Acres. | Acres. | Acres. |
| 4361 | 2393 | 1707 | 261 | ... | ... |
|  | (52%) | (39%) | (5.9%) |  |  |

(*c*) Seventeen Farms on Thirteen Other Manors<br>Mainly in South and Midlands

| Total Acreage of Seventeen Farms. | Arable. | Pasture. | Meadow. | Closes. | Indeterminate. |
|---|---|---|---|---|---|
| Acres. | Acres. | Acres. | Acres. | Acres. | Acres. |

| 3691 | 1519 | 1536 | 512 | 124 | ... |
|---|---|---|---|---|---|
|  | (41.1%) | (41.1%) | (13.8%) | (3.3%) |  |

III

| Total Acreage of Customary Holdings on Sixteen Manors. | Arable. | Pasture. | Meadow. | Closes. | Indeterminate. |
|---|---|---|---|---|---|
| Acres. | Acres. | Acres. | Acres. | Acres. | Acres. |
| 7786 | 6841 | 555 | 390 | ... | ... |
|  | (87.7%) | (7.1%) | (5.1%) |  |  |

The figures in this table do not pretend to complete accuracy, but their classification of the distribution of land between different uses is not far wrong. Of the customary tenants' land about 87 per cent. is arable, and 12 per cent. meadow and pasture. Of the farmers' land about 49 per cent. is arable, 36 per cent. pasture, 9 per cent. meadow. The proportion of pasture to arable is somewhat higher in the southern and midland counties than it is in East Anglia; but the cases examined are too few to allow of any conclusion being drawn from this fact. Without pushing the figures in either table further than they will go, one may suggest that they seem to imply, in the first place, that the large farmer was by no means always a grazier, and that the writers of the period who spoke as though all large-scale farming meant the conversion of arable to pasture were guilty of some exaggeration. In a good many cases the methods of cultivation pursued by the farmer of the demesne differed from those of the customary tenants only in the fact that his holding was larger; as a matter of fact the customary tenants on some manors deserve the name of grazier better than the farmer of the demesne upon others.

But they suggest, in the second place, that these cases were exceptional, and that, on the whole, arable farming played a much more important part on the holdings of the customary tenants than it did on those of the farmers. The former subsisted mainly on the tillage of the land in the open fields. The latter, though they had often much arable, sometimes had none, or next to none at all, and relied to a far greater extent on the opportunities for stock-breeding offered by pasture and meadow land. These figures, however, include some derived from manors where tillage was virtually the only sort of farming carried on, and they do not give any idea of the arrangements prevailing on an estate where pasture-farming had been pushed far. Taking from the fifty manors dealt with above, the twelve which are most typical of the new régime, one gets a very different picture—

**TABLE XI**

| Land Held. | Arable. | Meadow. | Pasture. | Closes. | (Wood, &c.) |
|---|---|---|---|---|---|
| Acres. | Acres. | Acres. | Acres. | Acres. | Acres. |
| 4474 | 922 | 403 | 3065 | 71 | 13 |
|  | (20.6%) | (8.9%) | (68.3%) | (1.5%) |  |

Here arable forms only 23 per cent. of the whole area, while pasture and meadow together form over 77 per cent. This swing of the pendulum from arable husbandry to pasture-farming will not surprise us, if we remember that at the time of the Domesday Survey, and, indeed, throughout the Middle Ages, the area of land under the plough had been, when considered in relation to the population, extraordinarily large. The economic justification of ploughing land which no modern farmer would touch had lain in the fact that the impossibility of moving food supplies had made it necessary for each village to be virtually self-supporting, and had thus prevented the specialisation of districts in different types of agriculture. When the development of trade under the Tudors had combined with the keen demand for wool to introduce a geographical division of labour, the change was naturally all the more violent, because there was, so to speak, so much lee-way to be made up, because so much land was in tillage which had no special suitability for the production of grain. Even so, between 1815 and 1846, the rich water meadows of Oxfordshire were being ploughed up for corn. Even so, after 1879, the collapse of corn-growing was all the more disastrous, because it had been so long delayed.

One would expect the growth of large farms side by side with the customary holdings, especially when the methods of agriculture employed were so different, to result in a powerful reaction of the new interests upon the old, and perhaps in a collision between them, even when no deliberate attempt was made to alter the position of the tenants. And this is what we are told in fact occurred. The customary tenants' holdings and the demesne both formed part of one area, subject to certain rights and privileges defined by the custom of the manor. Both, for example, would lie open to the village cattle after harvest; both were subject to the customary rotation of crops, and necessarily so when the demesne was not separate but mixed with the customary holdings in the open field; both had rights of common on the pasture or waste of the manor. Moreover, the whole organisation of the economic side of manorial life was based on the assumption that tillage was the most important element in it. For example, the apportionment of rights over the waste, the "stint" of animals to be grazed, assumed that no one partner would require to graze more than a certain number, and broke down if he gave himself up to cattle-breeding or sheep-farming, and multiplied his beasts by five or ten. It would be natural, therefore, to look for a straining and shifting of those rights as a probable consequence of the existence side by side of two such different agricultural stages, and of such different types of property. Formerly the respective interests of the lord and the customary tenants had been harmonised by the fact that the labour of the latter supplied the chief means of cultivating the demesne, and that the demesne could hardly be a profitable concern if the number of tenants or their standard of living declined very largely, any more than a gold-mine can pay without gold-miners. But when the demesne was largely used for pasture this consideration of course did not apply, and in any case by the sixteenth century, although the services of the tenants were still part of the means by which the farmers found labour, they were probably an unimportant one. As is shown by the smallness of the holdings on many manors, which were quite insufficient by themselves to support a family, and by the evidence of contemporaries, the farmer had a growing, though still small, labour market into which to dip, and the rough agreement which had existed between the interests of the manorial estate and those of the tenants was therefore no longer existent. Thus a collision of interests, a weakening of communal restrictions before the enterprise of the capitalist farmer, the strengthening of some kinds of property and the weakening of others, and the growth of new sorts of social relations in the villages, were consequences to be expected from the increasing predominance of the large farm, and especially of the large pasture farm.

To sum up the arguments of the chapter. At the beginning of the sixteenth century forces both political—the restriction of the territorial sovereignty of the landlords—and economic—the growth in the demand for wool—were working to produce a change in the methods of agriculture; and at any rate by the middle of the century another powerful motive was added by the fall in the value of money. The result was that there was a movement in the direction of converting arable land to pasture, and of enclosure, which affected all classes of landholders, but which was carried furthest by the large farmers who leased the demesne lands of manors, who could afford to make experiments, and who were under a strong incentive to turn the land to its most profitable use.

# CHAPTER II
# THE REACTION OF THE AGRARIAN CHANGES ON THE PEASANTRY

## *(a) The Removing of Landmarks*

The history of the agrarian problem in the sixteenth and seventeenth centuries—indeed its history ever since—is largely the story of the small cultivator's struggle to protect his interests against the changes caused by the growth of the great estate. In that struggle there is much that is detailed, tiresome, and obscure. The student hears very little about general principles, very much of technicalities about the nature of common appendant and common appurtenant, of stinted and unstinted pastures, of gressums and fines, of copyholds for years, for lives, or of inheritance, of land which is old enclosure that ought to stand, or new enclosure that ought to fall. But at the centre of this maze of dry and infinitely diverse details there is a real regrouping of social forces going on, and a rearrangement, at once rapid and profound, of economic and political ideas. We must no more picture the changes of our period as mere matters of the technique of agriculture, than we must think of the industrial revolution of two centuries later in terms of spinning-jennies and steam-power. On the contrary, these very details are the channel along which rural life is beginning to slip from one form of economic organisation to another, the seed-plot in which new conceptions of social expediency are being brought to maturity. In numberless English villages between 1500 and 1600 large issues are being decided which will profoundly modify the course of social development. Is the communal administration of meadow and wastes to survive (as it has survived in France and Belgium) or is it to disappear? Is England to be a country of large cultivators working with many hired labourers, or of small cultivators working with few? Is leasehold or copyhold to be the predominant form of land tenure? When the final transition to modern agriculture takes place, will England face the change with a population the bulk of which has been rooted in the soil since the Middle Ages, or will the middle classes in rural society have been already so far undermined that opinion turns spontaneously to the great landlord as the sole representative of agricultural progress? Of course the answer to these questions was not given by 1600 or even by 1700; we must not forget Arthur Young and the far more extensive enclosures of the eighteenth century. But in our period development certainly took a distinct bias away from one set of arrangements and in the direction of another. The best standpoint from which to examine its course is found by watching the reaction upon the tenants of the agricultural changes which we have tried to summarise in the preceding sections.

The economic effect of the policy pursued by the large farmer depended upon what proportion of the land he controlled, and in particular upon the part of the manor upon which enclosure was made. He might enclose only the land actually belonging to the demesne farm when he took it over; or he might enclose parts of the waste or meadow over which other tenants had rights of pasture; or he might enclose the holdings in the open arable fields belonging to other tenants, for this purpose evicting, or inducing the lord to evict, them. When only the demesne lands were enclosed the other interests were sometimes little disturbed, unless indeed the demesne had already been parcelled out among some of the smaller tenants, a contingency to be considered later. But, even when that was not the case, the conversion of the demesne to pasture and its enclosure had two consequences which were not unimportant. On the one hand, the wage-earning population of cottagers and younger sons, who had found employment as hired labourers when the demesne was used for tillage, were thrown out of work, and with the limited demand for labour offered by a sixteenth century village, were obliged, one would suppose, to join the armies of tramps who figure so largely in the pages of the writers of the period. As the bailiffs accounts of some manors show, the demesne farm had sometimes employed a quite considerable staff of workmen of different kinds, and though no clear instance of a reduction of the number of employees, consequent on the transition to pasture farming, has come to light, one can occasionally compare the demand for labour under the old régime and under the new in a way which does something to substantiate the lamentations of contemporaries.[418] It is this which gives point to their complaints as to the decay of "hospitality." Hospitality in the sixteenth century does not merely mean a general attitude of open-handed friendliness. When the Government intervenes to enjoin hospitality, we are not to think that, even in that age of grandmotherly legislation, it is going out of its way to insist that every man shall provide his neighbour with a glass of beer and a bed for the night. Hospitality has a quite precise meaning and a quite definite social importance. It is, in the most literal sense, housekeeping, and the household does not merely imply what we mean by "the family," a group of persons connected by blood but pursuing often quite separate occupations, and, except in the small number of cases where property owned by the head of the family supplies a financial basis for unity, possessing quite separate economic interests. It is, on the contrary, a miniature co-operative society, housed under one roof, dependent upon one industry, and including not only man and wife and children, but servants and labourers, ploughmen and threshers, cowherds and milkmaids, who live together, work together, and play together, just as one can see them doing in parts of Norway and Switzerland at the present day. When the economic foundations of this small organism are swept away by a change in the method of farming, the effect is not merely to ruin a family, it is to break up a business. It is analogous not to the unemployment of an individual householder, but to the bankruptcy of a firm.

On the other hand, even when they lost nothing else, the rest of the land-

[418] The Shepe Book of Tittleshall Manor (Holkham MSS., Tittleshall Books, No. 19), shows flocks of 500 to 1000 sheep being managed by a single shepherd, 1543–1549.

holding population was deprived of some of the rights of grazing which they had exercised on the enclosed arable after harvest. If the demesne formed a large proportion of the whole area of the village, or if there was little other pasture, their loss, as the frequent complaints of interference with "shack"[419] prove, might be a very considerable one; for it meant that there might be no means of feeding some proportion of the village beasts. Moreover, the mere presence of a large capitalist who controlled a great part of the land, and converted it to pasture or retained it as arable according to the price of wool and wheat, prejudiced them in various indirect ways. The farmer of the demesne seems at an early date to have had a bad name for hard dealings. He was often a stranger, and therefore indifferent to the influence of local customs and personal relationships. Where the manoral officials had offered direct employment, he was a middleman with a high rent to pay, and, like most middlemen, a channel for pressure without responsibility. As the largest shareholder in the small agricultural community, he could disturb its arrangements by altering his course of cultivation, and, since he was the representative of the lord, he could not easily be checked. Sometimes, indeed, a clause was inserted in his lease expressly providing that he should not disturb the neighbouring peasants.[420] But there are many cases in which there is no mention of formal

---

[419] *e.g.* Holkham MSS., Fulmordeston, Bdle. 6: "To the Right Honourable Sir Edward Cooke, Knight, Attorney General unto the King's Ma^tie. Humblie sheweth unto your lordship yo^r poore and dayley orators ... yo^r worshippes tenants of the Manor of Fulmordeston cum Croxton in the Duchie of Lancaster, and the moste parte of the tenants of the same manor that whereas your said orators in the Hillary Terme last commenced suite in the Duchie Courte against Thomas Odbert and Roger Salisbury, gent., who have enclosed their grounds contrary to the custom of the manor, wherby your wor. loseth your shack due out of the grounds, common lane or way for passengers is stopped up, and your worshipps' poore orators lose their accustomed shack in those grounds, and the said Roger Salisbury taketh also the whole benefit of theire common from them, keepinge there his sheepe in grazinge, and debarring them of their libertie there which for comon right belongeth unto them." For the rest of this document see Appendix I., and compare the following defence to a charge of breaking open an enclosure: "The owners of the said tenements, from time whereof there is no memory to the contrary, have had a common of pasture for themselves and their tenants in one close commonly called 'the new leasue,' in the lordship of Weston in the manner following; that is to say, when the field where the said 'leasue' doth lie, called Radnor field, lieth fallow, then through the whole year; and when the said field is sown with corn, then from the reaping and carrying away of the corn until the same be sown again ... and the said Thomas Dodd further said that he did break open the said close ... being fenced in such time as he ought to have common in the same, to the end that his cattle might take their pasture therein" (*William Salt Collection*, New Series, vol. ix., Chancery Proceedings, Bdle. 8, No. 9).

[420] For complaints of tenants against the exactions, of farmers as early as 1413, see *Victoria County History*, Essex, vol. ii. p. 318. For a stipulation in the farmer's covenant, see the following: "Item a covenant conteyned in this lease that the said Thomas shall permit and suffer the customary Tenants peaceably to have and enjoy their estates, rights, grants, interests, and premises, without any lette, interruption, or contradiction of the said Thomas" (Roxburghe Club, *Pembroke Surveys*, Knyghton); and *Northumberland County History*, vol. v. p. 208, Buston: "The tenants of this town at the beginning of summer have their oxen allway grazed in Shilbottel wood, or else they were not able to maintain their tenements. It is therefore requisite that his lordship or his heire should have respect unto the want of

enclosing, and in which, nevertheless, it is complained that the farmer persistently molests and harries the customary tenants. It was the essence of the open field system of agriculture—at once its strength and its weakness—that its maintenance reposed upon a common custom and tradition, not upon documentary records capable of precise construction. Its boundaries were often rather a question of the degree of conviction with which ancient inhabitants could be induced to affirm them, than visible to the mere eye of sense, and their indefiniteness made the way of the transgressor extremely easy. Even the lord of the manor sometimes found the large farmer too much for his vigilance. "John Langford and his ancesters," the College of All Souls petitioned in Chancery in 1637, "have for many yeares by vertue of several demises farmed and rented of your oratours their said messuage and lands, and used and occupied the same with their own lands, and during the time of such occupation have pulled up, destroyed and removed, the metes, mere londs, and boundaries of your oratours their said lands, and confounded the same so that the same cannot be set forth.... Mr. Langford's lands and grounds lying next adjoining unto the said oratours their grounds, ... the said John Langford hath extended his said cottages, orchards, gardens, and curtilages thereunto belonging, to your oratours their said grounds, and hath made hedges, ditches, fences and mounds wherein and whereby he hath enclosed your oratours their said grounds unto his own cottages and land, ... and intendeth so ... to keep from your orators all the said land so encroached and enclosed."[421] When a farmer would thus calmly expropriate the lord of the manor, it is not surprising to find constant small disputes between him and the other tenants, on the ground of his entering upon their holdings, or "surcharging the fieldes by waye of intercommon and destroying the corn of greane by drifte of cattle over the common of fieldes and suche other."[422] Often, no doubt, the sporadic encroachments which provoked quarrels with the other tenants appeared to the great grazier a natural exercise of his obvious rights. Who should say where one man's land began and another's ended? But it can hardly be doubted that such irregularities were sometimes a deliberate attempt to worry the weaker members of the village community into throwing up their lands, by making profitable cultivation impossible. "If any man do sow any ground," ran the direction given by a lord to the shepherd who looked after the demesne farm on a Suffolk manor, "and the stifts of the field are broken, and may not duly be taken and fed as heretofore they have been used, then the said Tillot to feed off the said corn and drive his sheep on that part of the ploughed land, and to forbid any particular man to sow his ground or any part thereof whereby the sheep-

---

pasture, that in any lease made by his lordship or his heire to any person of the pasture, the said Shilbottel wood, there might be a proviso in the said lease that the said tenants should have their oxen ground there, as they have been accustomed." Instances of the harrying of the peasants by the large farmers are to be found, *ibid.*, vol. i. p. 350 (Tughall), and p. 274 (Newham).

[421] All Souls' Archives, vol. i. p. 203, No. 356.

[422] *Topographer and Genealogist*, vol. i., Survey of Mudford and Hinton. In this case the aggressor was not the farmer of the demesne, but a freeholder owning a third of the manor. To escape his depredations the tenants proposed "to enclose their common fieldes and to assign to Master Lyte and his tenants his third parte in every field by itself, and to extinguish his right of common in the rest."

walks may be hindered."[423] Such an order points to the difficulty of adjusting the different methods of cultivation pursued by the smaller tenants and on the demesne. Though the complaints of the former were often indefinite enough, it is probable that the very difficulty of defining what a large capitalist might or might not do was in itself a substantial grievance. The truth is that it was not easy for the great pasture farm, with its flocks of sheep, to subsist side by side with the smaller arable holdings of the other tenants, without a good deal of friction arising, even in those cases in which no deliberate attempt was made to evict the latter or to deprive them of their rights of common. The traditional organisation of agriculture was based on the assumption that much the same methods of utilising the land would be followed by all the tenants. When that assumption broke down with the growth of large-scale sheep-farming, there was naturally a collision of interests between the great men who made innovations and the small men who adhered to the customary rule.

### *(b) The Struggle for the Commons*

But sporadic encroachments are not the worst which the small man has to fear. He may wake to find the path along which he drives his beasts to pasture blocked by a hedge. When he goes to renew his lease or buy the reversion of his copy, he may be told that his holding is to be merged in a pasture farm. The great estate is not always built up by the mere consolidation of pieces of land which are already united in ownership, though spatially they may be separate. If it were there would be few statutes and few riots; for the law looks with a favourable eye on such attempts at improved cultivation, and the peasants have long been doing on a small scale what the capitalist farmer does on a large. The great estate is formed in another and less innocent way, by throwing together holdings whose possession is separate, though spatially they may be contiguous. It is the result of addition, not simply of organisation; of addition in which the cyphers are the holdings of numerous small tenants. In such a process the opposition between the interests of the peasantry and those of the manorial authorities is brought to a head. If one man is to run a hedge round a pasture, the pasture must first be stripped of the rights of common which enmesh it. If sheep are to be fed on the sites of ruined cottages, their occupants must first be evicted. It is over the absorption of commons and the eviction of tenants that agrarian warfare—the expression is not too modern or too strong—is waged in the sixteenth century. Let us look at both these movements more closely.

The obscurity to one age of the everyday economic arrangements of another is excellently illustrated by the difficulty of appreciating the part which common rights played in English husbandry before the nineteenth century. It is not so long since it became a memory. There are villages where the old men still remember—how could they forget it?—the year when the commons finally "went in." Yet there is hardly a feature in the plain man's view of the nature of a common which corresponds to the reality as it was used by our ancestors, and as it is used to-day by communities whose land system has followed a different course of de-

---

[423] *Victoria County History*, Suffolk, "Social and Economic History."

velopment from our own. He thinks of a common as land which, like a municipal park, "belongs to the public," land which any one may use and any one abuse. In the innocence of his heart he will even move his local authority to put in a claim for its possession, and is very much surprised when its solicitors tell him that he is fighting for the rights of two or three mouldy tenements. Again, he thinks of a common as a place of fresh air and recreation, not of business; as land for which, at the moment, no serious economic use can be found; unprofitable scraps, whose ineligibility has secured them a precarious immunity from park-loving squires and speculative builders. In connection with agriculture he thinks of it not at all—is not waste land the opposite of land which is under cultivation? In one respect he is right. Our existing commons are remnants—remnants which have survived the deluge of eighteenth century Private Acts, mainly because they consist of land too poor to pay counsel's fees. In all other respects he is wrong. In the earlier period the word common implied common exclusiveness quite as much as common enjoyment. The value of a common to the commoners consisted precisely in the guarantee given them by custom that no one might use it except holders of tenements which time out of mind had a right thereto, and that no man might use it to a greater extent than the custom of the manor allowed. And the modern man is especially wrong in regarding commons as though they fell below the margin of economic employment. Commons and common rights, so far from being merely a luxury or a convenience, were really an integral and indispensable part of the system of agriculture, a linch pin, the removal of which brought the whole structure of village society tumbling down.

No one who reads the petitions and the legal proceedings of our period can doubt that this was what the small cultivator felt. No one who consults the surveyors can doubt that he was right. Yet, at first sight, the importance attached to commons is certainly surprising. Is not the outcry disproportionate to the grievance? To riot and rebel when you lose grazing rights—is not this, it may be asked, rather like shooting your landlord because he will not let you keep poultry? The answer is perhaps a twofold one. The peasants' economy in the sixteenth century was one in which, in many parts of England, the pastoral side of agriculture played a very important rôle, and for which, therefore, abundance of pasture land was very essential. As any one who has lived in a Swiss châlet knows, a family which has sufficient cattle and goats on a good mountain can, during half the year, be almost self-sufficing. It has milk, butter, cheese, eggs, and meat. The only thing it really misses is bread, and that it has the means of purchasing, even if it does not, like the sensible people of Lancashire and Yorkshire, and probably of most parts of England before the industrial revolution, bake its own supplies at home or in a common public oven. Our sixteenth century peasants do not keep goats, but they keep a great many horses and cows, on some manors an average of 6 or 8 per holding; they keep a great many sheep, sometimes 150 or 200 each; they meet depressions in the corn trade by falling back on other sides of agriculture, and sending to market miscellaneous produce which, in a time of rising prices, sells well. But to do this successfully they must have plenty of grazing land. A Swiss commune measures its wealth very largely by the quality of its pasture, and will take pains to buy a good one, even though it be a long distance from the village.[424] Can we doubt that the same was true of many parts of England, and that Hales' husbandmen who "could never be able to make up my lordes rent weare it not for a little brede of neate, shepe, swine, gese, and hens,"[425] was typical, not, it is true, of the more substantial men, but of many of the less well-to-do?

But there was another and more fundamental reason for the importance attached to rights of common, and for the disastrous re-action upon the tenantry involved in their curtailment. It was that the possession of pasture was not only a source of subsidiary income but also quite indispensable to the maintenance of the arable holding, which was everywhere the backbone of the tenants' livelihood. Ask a modern small holder, and he will tell you that what he wants is a certain proportion of grass-land to arable, in order that he may feed his horses without having to resort to the hire of extra land, to the purchase of foodstuffs, or to turning them out to pick up a living where they can by the side of the road.[426] In the normal village community this was secured by the apportionment of rights of pasture to each arable holding, the tenants grazing their cattle on the common in the summer, and only feeding them on their separate closes when the approach of winter made shelter a necessity.[427] It is, therefore, a mistake to think of the engrossing of commons by large farmers as affecting the peasant only in so far as he was a shepherd or a grazier. On the contrary, it struck a blow at an indispensable adjunct of his arable holding, an adjunct without which the ploughland itself was unprofitable; for to work the ploughland one must have the wherewithal to feed the plough beasts. It is this close interdependence of common rights with tillage which explains both the manner of their organisation and the distress caused by encroachments upon them. Rights of common of the most general type go with the tenement, not with the tenant, because what is considered is the maintenance of a fully equipped arable holding in the open fields, and for this end it is not necessary to allow common rights to the population of younger sons, servants, or others who do not hold one of these primary units of tillage. The commoners are often "stinted," restricted[428] that is in the number of beasts which they may put upon the pasture, because rights of grazing have to be distributed among all the arable holdings, such holdings being unworkable without them. Rights of common are often apportioned among the tenants "according to the magnitude of their holdings,"

---

[424] For an amusing example see Conway, *The Alps from End to End*, pp. 190–192.

[425] *The Commonweal of this Realm of England*, p. 57.

[426] Ten acres of "turf" to forty acres of arable was the estimate of his requirements made to me by an Oxfordshire small holder.

[427] *Topographer and Genealogist*, vol. i.: "The tenants of Landress have common in a certayne ground called King's Moore for all kinde of cattle, and every one of them may keep in the said moore as much of all kind of cattle in somer as their severall or ingrounde will beare in the wynter, whyche is a great relief to the poore tenants, for as they confesse they keep all their cattle there in the somer, and reserve their ingroundes untouched for the winter."

[428] *e.g. Southampton Court Leet Records* (Hearnshaw), pp. 4–5, 1550: "Item we present that no burgers or comyners at one time comyn above the number of two beasts upon payne of every such defaulte 2s.; provided that iff any of them have two kyne or wenlings, he shall have no horse, and yf he have but one cow he may have one horse."

for, of course, a large holding will need more plough beasts, and therefore more pasture, than a small one. Their boundaries are accurately recorded from this tree to that stone and such and such a hill, because otherwise an invasion of foreigners with their cattle from a neighbouring village may eat them up like locusts. To divide them up among the tenants may do no harm provided the division is an equitable one, for each man will still have his equipment of pasture, though in the form of a limited area instead of in the form of a limited quota of beasts. To appropriate common pastures without compensation may ruin a whole village; it is to seize a piece of free capital without which cows and horses cannot be fed, and thus it is virtually to confiscate the beasts, which are the peasant's tools. When that is done he must either re-assert his rights, or throw up his arable holding, or hire pasture for a money rent; sometimes—a bitter thought—he must hire grass-land from the very man who has robbed him.[429]

One must not, of course, unduly simplify the picture. Different villages are very differently endowed with grazing land. On some there is a common waste, and a common pasture in addition of superior quality, so that the waste can be left to animals which will thrive on rough land. On others there is not even a common waste, and the tenants have to do the best they can on the stubble which lies open after harvest. Nor do they all manage the apportionment of grazing rights in the same way. As we have seen, there has been a movement towards the formation of separate closes; and even when all the pasture is administered in common, it may either be that each villager looks after his own animals, or that the township, intent on seeing that the common is not overstocked, appoints a common shepherd and a common cowherd, who drives them all afield together "under the opening eyelids of the morn." Under all such diversities, however, which can often be paralleled from the practice of continental communes to-day, there is the fundamental fact of the necessity of rights of pasture to successful tillage. Fitzherbert's remark that "an husband cannot well thrive by his corne without he have other cattle, nor by his cattle without corne,"[430] is reiterated in different forms by other surveyors. When they tell us that a common adjoining a town is a "great relief to the poor tenants," and recommend that a special clause be inserted in a farmer's lease binding him not to appropriate the pasture without which the tenants "were not able to maintain their tenements," they are speaking of matters which they understand far better than we possibly can, and must be believed.

The monopolising of commons by manorial authorities who wished to form a large sheep-run can be traced through several stages, of which actual enclosure is only one, and the climax rather than the beginning. It usually begins with the overstocking of the common pasture by the owner of great flocks and herds, and

---

[429] *Topographer and Genealogist*, vol. i.—Rolleston (Stafford): "The said manor is ... well inhabited with divers honest men, whose trade of lyvinge is onlie by husbandry ... and have no large pastures or severall closes ... but have been alwaie accustomed to have their cattle and sometyme their ploughe beasts pastured in the Queen's Majestie's Park of Rolleston, for xxd., the stage ... without which aide and help they were neither able to maintain hospitallitie nor tyllage; and nowe of late yeares the fermor of the herbage hath advanced the stage to 6s. 8d., and yet the Quene's Majesties rent nothing increased."

[430] Fitzherbert, *Book of Husbandry*.

the consequent edging out of the small man, though, of course, when the area is a large one, and when, as in Wiltshire, there are great downs which are suitable for sheep, it may be a long time before the latter feels the pinch severely. But the mere overriding by a capitalist of the customary allotment of pasture rights is usually only the first step. As long as matters are left in this transition stage there is endless friction and disturbance, because each party tries to oust the other, the great man swamping the pasture with his beasts, and the peasants defiantly insisting that the recognised stint shall be observed—a guerilla warfare in which the farmer's servants are matched against the township's cowherd and the common pound. Enclosing follows as a way of regularising the new arrangements, by substituting a tangible and prickly boundary for an ideal limit. Sometimes enclosure is demanded by the peasants and resented by the well-to-do, who think that in the general squabble they will come off best. More often it is carried out with a high hand by the farmer and the lord, who, once they take seriously to cattle-breeding or sheep-farming, have naturally no desire to have a limit set to their investment in stock. Occasionally compensation[431] is given to the dispossessed commoners in the shape of an abatement in their rents, or of a fresh pasture in another quarter. In most of our documents, however, there is little trace of any deliberate re-adjustment of rights. We are simply told that "he holds the whole of the hilly pasture," or that he has "a heath enclosed with a hedge," or that grounds have been "enclosed contrary to the custom of the manor." We can trace the effect in the small number of beasts which other tenants keep, but we are left to conjecture how this state of things was reached. Our impression is that in most cases the enclosing of commons was carried out in the simplest and most arbitrary way, by the lord or the farmer erecting a hedge round such part of the common pasture as he cared to appropriate, and leaving the tenants to make good their demand that it should be removed, if they could.

Could they make it good? The question of the degree to which different classes of tenants could obtain legal redress for disturbance will be discussed later. But we cannot leave this part of our subject without considering shortly the standpoints towards disputes arising out of the loss of rights of common, which were adopted by the peasantry and by legal opinion. One may point out, in the first place, that their standpoints were by no means the same. The contrast which we have already ventured to draw between the considerable elements of practical communism in the working arrangements of the village community and the strict and (so we believe) correct interpretation of the law of the King's Courts, which treats its members simply as holders of individual rights which they on occasion exercise jointly, comes out very strikingly in the different attitudes adopted towards rights of pasture. If we must be careful not to see communism where there are really only

[431] *Northumberland County History*, vol. v., Birling: "Allowed part of 25s. 4d. for focage of Orchard Medow and Mylneside Bank, because they are now enclosed within the lord's new Park, and this allowance shall be made yearly until the tenants of Byrling have and peacefully enjoy another parcel of pasture to the same value 11s. 8d." (Bailiff's Accounts, 1474). R.O. *Misc. Books Land Rev.*, vol. ccxx., f. 236: "Divers parcels of land and pasture of the manor of Farfield, now common of 140 acres, now occupied by the tenants there as commons and given them in exchange in satisfaction of their old common imparked in the new Park, £6, 13s. 8d."

individual rights, we must also be careful not to see only individual rights where there is in fact a considerable amount of communism. However much it may be necessary to emphasise the "rough and rude individualism"[432] latent in these arrangements, we must admit that for the peasants themselves, who make and depend upon them, they contain features which are not easily explained without the use of words which the lawyers are reluctant to allow us—words implying some degree of practical communism. We must remember that the custom of the manor is itself a kind of law, and that though the lawyers who sit in the King's Courts may cast their rules into a feudal mould, which attenuates rights of common to mere concessions made by the lord to individual tenants, yet the law of the village, the custom of the manor, to which the first appeal is made, does treat them as containing a distinctly communal element. In practice the whole body of customary tenants are found managing their commons on a co-operative plan. They regulate their use and re-adjust the regulations, sometimes at almost every meeting of the court. As a community, they hire additional pasture and administer town lands. As a community, they make arrangements for enclosure and even sell part of their common—the common in which only individuals have proprietary rights—to persons who undertake to invest capital in improving it.[433] When all regulations

---

[432] Pollock and Maitland, *History of English Law*, vol. i. p. 606. For the questions concerning common rights see *ibid.*, pp. 594–624, and Maitland, *Domesday Book and Beyond*, pp. 340–356; Vinogradoff, *Villainage in England*, Essay II. chap, ii., and *The Growth of the Manor*, Book II. chap. iv. I have followed Vinogradoff's rather than Maitland's view.

[433] For buying and selling of pasture see below, and for enclosure pp. 168–170. The following seems a clear case of more or less corporate action. Holkham MSS., Burnham, Bdle. 5, No. 94: "Copy of an indenture between [here follows a list of names] of the same town and county, yeomen, as well on the behalf of themselves as of the rest of the comoners and freeholders of the said town of the one part, and Robert Bacon of [illegible] in the County of Norfolk, and Thomas Coke of Grays Inn in the County of Middlesex of the other part, that whereas heretofore Sir Philip [illegible] being lord and owner of the marshes hereafter mentioned ... did by his indenture of bargain and sale bearing date ... 1588, grant bargain and sell unto [list of names as above] all those marsh grounds lying and being in Burnham, to have and to hold the said premises to the parties last before mentioned and their heires to the use of them and their heires for ever, to the intent and purpose notwithstanding that the said parties last before mentioned there, being inhabitants in certain ancient messuages in the said Towne, and all other inhabitants of the said Towne there and afterwards for the tyme being in any of the ancient messuages and cottages in the said towne, for so long time as they shall be there inhabitinge and noe longer, according to the quantity of their tenures within the said Towne might depasture and feede the land as by the said deeds referring thereunto being had may more fully appeare; [it recites that the land] may by wallinge and embankinge the same be improved to more than a [illegible] value, and made fitt for arrable, meadowe, and pasture grounde, whereby tillage may be increased and his Majestie's subjects receive more employment thereby, and danger of drawing [drowning?] of their stock for their feedinge prevented [recites that Robert Bacon and Thomas Coke have undertaken to drain the land in return for receiving three parts of it and that the persons above mentioned] being the major parte of the parties interested in the said salte Marshes, and being enabled by the lawes and Statutes of this realm to contract and bargaine with any person or persons for the draining thereof" [now convey 3 parts of the marshes to the above-mentioned Robert Bacon and Thomas Coke], June 8, 1637. The motive of this agreement was to get the low-lying meadows on the sea-coast drained. Drainage schemes were

fail and the enemy attempts to evade their vigilance by a strategic appearance of benevolence, a town sometimes returns to the charge with words glowing with what can only be called the pride of common property, though the title to that property may be of a very shadowy kind. "Whereas of late days," proclaimed the Court Leet of Southampton in 1579, "there hathe ben a peice of our common and heathe ditched and hedged and enclosed in and planted with willows under the name of a shadow for our cattle, which have hitherto many yeares past prospered verie well as the common was before;—wherefore (therefore) we desire that it may be pulled down again and levelled as before, for we doubt that in short time yt will be taken from our common to some particular man's use, which were lamentable and pitiable and not sufferable. For as our ancestors of their great care and travail have provided that and like other many benefits for their successors, so we thinke it our dutie in conscience to keepe, uphold and maintaine the same as we found yt for our posteritie to come, without diminishing any part or parcel from yt, but rather to augment more to yt yf may be." We need not ask in what sense the Southampton men had inherited the salt marsh from their ancestors, or whether a lawyer would not have made short work of their claim to leave it to posterity. It is enough to realise that they feel it to belong to their town in a quite effective and intimate manner, that they stint it, turn off intruders, guard it for their descendants, defend it, if need be, with bows and arrows and pikes, and the other agricultural implements of that forceful age. We know that people commit many crimes in the name of posterity. But they do not usually think of bequeathing to their grandchildren rights which have never had any existence for themselves. We shall hardly understand all that was meant for a village by the loss of its common pastures unless we allow for that feeling of practical proprietorship, unless we confess that a society of landholders becomes on occasions something very like a landholding society.

But, in the second place, such communal aspirations are a matter of feeling and custom, not of national law. It is hardly necessary to point out that these words do not put an aspect of the case which could be pleaded in court in a dispute as to common of pasture. At the touch of the law, as has often been pointed out, the communal element, of which Southampton makes so much, seems to crumble away. If, to the eye of the peasants, a manor was a more or less self-conscious community with considerable powers of controlling the administration of its pastures, it was, to the eye of the common lawyer, a collection of individuals bound together by their relation to the manorial authorities, but in other respects able to enforce rights of common only in so far as those rights could be shown to be enjoyed by one of the four[434] titles which the law recognised. It is quite true that in practice much in the air about this time, and any one who has seen the country near Holkham and Burnham will know how badly protection from the sea was needed. Two points are worth noticing: (i.) the tenants have no objection to surrendering part of their common if they get a *quid pro quo*; (ii.) they act as a single body. They buy land and they sell land and they can leave it to their heirs. Certain persons in the township act on their behalf, much as directors might act for a body of shareholders. Is it possible to speak of such arrangements simply in terms of individual rights? Are we not driven to think of the township as almost a landholding corporation?

[434] Common appendant, common appurtenant, common in gross, and common par

the use of common pastures extended to persons who could not plead one of those titles, and that the economic working of the village often cannot be brought inside the four corners of a legal formula. But when a right of pasture is challenged by the lord of the manor, the tenant must show that his right falls within them or lose his case. Of those four titles residence in a manor was not one. The occupier who is the unit of English Local Government to-day had, as such, no standing, because he was not, *qua* occupier, a holder of one of the arable shares with which, primarily, rights of pasture went. Again, a great number of cottagers and day labourers, who were not holders of arable, but who in practice used the commons for pigs, geese, poultry, and cows, were likely to be legally in the same unprotected condition; so that it is obvious that, when enclosing took place, there might be a considerable number of persons, perhaps an actual majority of the villagers, who could not even raise the question whether they could obtain redress or not, and that much distress could be caused without any infringement of the law. Of those who could bring their enjoyment of rights of pasture under one of the categories which the law recognised, the freeholders were, of course, in the strongest position. They could plead rights of common appendant to their tenements; probably they could often plead common appurtenant, and common in gross, common by a special personal grant, as well, and they could enforce their rights both by self-help, in the way of throwing down recent enclosures, and by the ordinary remedies of the Assize of Novel Disseisin or an action of trespass.

Moreover, the Statute of Merton, which expressly allowed a lord to enclose commonable land on condition that he left sufficient for the free tenants, did not mean that a lord could arbitrarily cut down rights of common to what he was pleased to think sufficient. If it had, there would have been little enclosing of commons in the sixteenth century, for by that time there would have been little common left to enclose. The question "what is sufficient?" had to be answered by a jury, a jury representing expert knowledge as to local customs and the agrarian usages of the township. The jury could only answer it by taking account of the size of the tenements and of the land available for commoning. In fact, it found itself at once considering the custom of the manor, which stinted rights of pasture according to the economic needs and resources of different villages. Of the position of the customary tenants it is, for reasons which will be given below, less easy to speak.

---

cause de vicinage. This classification is not found in Bracton, and appears to date from the late Middle Ages, see Vinogradoff, *Villainage in England*, Essay II., chap, ii., and the following case: *Coke's Reports*, Part IV., p. 60. Hill, 4 Jac. I. in Communi Banco: "Robert Smith brought an action of Trespass against Stephen Gatewood, gent., quare clausum fregit ... cum quibusdam averiis.... Defendant pleaded a certain custom, 'quod inhabitantes infra eandem villam de Stixwood prædictam infra aliquod antiquum messuagium ibidem ratione commorantiæ et residentiæ suæ in eadem habuerunt et usi fuerunt et consueverunt habere com. Pastur ... pro omnibus et omnimodis bobus et equis et aliis grossis animalibus.' Unanimously resolved that the custom is against law. 1. That there are but four manners of common, common appendant, appurtenant, in gross, and by reason of vicinage, and this common *ratione commorantiæ* is none of them. 2. What estate shall he have, who is inhabitant, in the common, when it appears he hath no estate or interest in the house (but a mere habitation and dwelling) in respect of which he ought to have his common? For none can have interest in a common in respect of a house in which he hath no interest."

Regarded from the standpoint of the economic organisation of the manor, their rights of pasture should have got protection as much as those of the freeholders, for as holders of ancient tenements they required pasture to enable them to carry on their tillage; and since they were, in most parts of the country, by far the most numerous class, the aggregate of their commonable area was much larger than was that of the free tenants. According to the canon of interpretation supplied by Coke,[435] the Statute of Merton would appear, at any rate in the latter part of the sixteenth century, to have been construed as protecting them; and Fitzherbert,[436] though he introduces an additional complication by trying—trying, it seems, quite arbitrarily—to prove that rights of pasture over the waste and rights of pasture on land which was not technically part of the waste, ought to be treated differently, places all tenants on an equal footing in respect of their claim to be left "sufficient common."

The treatment by the law of common rights, in the case both of freeholders and of the customary tenants, seems to fit roughly into this scheme, though the actual facts are somewhat more complex than it would suggest. The cases show that the freeholders had a legal remedy if enclosure deprived them of rights of pasture, and that this remedy was used. A freeholder could say "these be the pastures ... which should be my common ... after the tenure of my freehold"[437] if he proved the fact he got protection, and on manors where the freeholders were numerous and the lord wanted to make very large enclosures, he had to buy them out. It is true also that the freeholders[438] joined with the farmer on some manors in enclosing commonable land, to the detriment of the customary tenants, who apparently sometimes had to acquiesce in it. They show again that a customary tenant could obtain protection for his rights of common pasture both, at any rate in the sixteenth century, from the Common Law Courts, and also, at an earlier date, from the Court of Chancery, provided that he could show that such rights were attached to his holding by the custom of the manor, a very important qualification, to which

[435] Coke, Complete Copyholder, Sect. 53: "When an Act of Parliament altereth the service, tenure, or interest of the land, or other thing in prejudice of the lord or of the Customs of the Manor, or in prejudice of the tenant, then the generall words of such an Act of Parliament extend not to the copyhold; but when an Act is generally made for the good of the commonwealth, and no prejudice may accrue by reason of the alteration of any interest, service, tenure, or Custom, of the Manor, there usually copyhold lands are within the generall purview of such Acts."

[436] Fitzherbert, *Book of Surveying*: "And as for that manner of common, me seemeth the Lord may improve himself of their waste grounds, leaving their own tenants sufficient common, having no regard to the tenants of the other lordship. But as far as all errable lands, meadows, leises, and pastures, the lordes may improve themselves by course of the common law, for the statute speaketh nothing but of waste grounds."

[437] *e.g. Coventry Leet Book*, vol. ii. p. 510.

[438] *Genealoger and Archæologist*, vol. i., Manor of West Coker (Somerset): "The demesnes remayneth in one entier ferm, and is dymysed to one Sir John Seymour, knight, who being confederate with the freeholders of the manor, maketh such inclosers for his owne lucre, and suffreth the freeholders to do the same, nevertheless surcharge the common with their cattle, that in process of tyme yt wilbe the destruccion of the custumarye tenants."

we must return.[439] On the other hand, it is certainly true that both freeholders and customary tenants suffered in our period from a curtailment of common rights, in spite of the qualified protection enjoyed by the latter and the complete protection enjoyed by the former. We cannot, in fact, be content with a mere summary of the legal position, for the law is not always strong enough or elastic enough to cope with shifting economic forces. Or, rather, its arm is short, and it can only grapple with those conflicts which are sufficiently violent to force their way to Westminster.

Some light may be thrown on the kind of trouble of which our period was full by two accounts which have come down to us of disputes concerning rights of common pasture. At Coventry[440] there were in the fifteenth century prolonged quarrels between the City and the Prior and Convent of the Cathedral Church of St. Mary. In 1485 the Prior was accused by the city authorities of wrongfully overcharging the common with sheep and cattle, to the damage of the city. He replied by admitting the legal rights of the other commoners, but by claiming that whereas they could only pasture a limited number of beasts, "by the lawe of this lande the lord of the waste soyle may surcharge and pasture there what nombre hym lykes," and that therefore in overstocking the common he was only exercising his rights. To this the city answered by a rather hesitating appeal to custom, according to which the commoners never had been stinted to a fixed number of beasts, and by pointing out that, if the Prior was allowed to put as many beasts on the common as he pleased, he was virtually confiscating the property of the other commoners. This case brings out very clearly one weakness in the position even of the free tenants. It was that, while they were protected by law against attempts actually to deprive them of rights of common, the protection might be held to be contingent on the lord or his farmer proceeding so far as not to leave them sufficient, and was not available if the encroachments only went so far as to diminish their common pasture. There was a minimum which they could not lose: but above this minimum their rights of pasture were elastic and compressible, and when, as in this case, the pasture was so large as to make any numerical limit to the number of beasts which they might graze unnecessary, the commoners might be deprived of some part of their customary pasture without any infringement of the law.[441]

Another aspect of the problem is illustrated by a story of a similar struggle at Wootton Basset,[442] a small borough in Wiltshire. Early in the seventeenth century

[439] For a discussion of the legal position of the copyholders see below, pp. 287–310.

[440] *Coventry Leet Book*, vol. ii. pp. 445–446 and *passim*.

[441] If the common was so large that it had been unnecessary to "stint" it, why did the city object to the lord putting additional beasts on? I take the situation to be that the Prior—probably tempted by the profitableness of sheep-farming in the latter part of the fifteenth century—diminished the pasture which the city could use, by putting on many more beasts than ever before, which, in the absence of a recognised "stint," he was able to do without violating any custom, as he would have done if there had been a customary limit, as on many manors.

[442] *Topographer and Genealogist*, vol. iii. These are the people whom Heaven protected in the way described on p. 148 note. Observe what this little community endured. (i.) Sir Francis Englefield, senior, seizes 1900 out of 2000 acres of their common. (ii.) Sir Francis Englefield, junior, seizes "the charter of our town ... and the deed of the said common." (iii.)

the mayor and freemen of Wootton Basset petition Parliament to "enact something for us, that we may enjoy our right again." What they want is a restoration of certain rights of common which a powerful neighbour has taken from them. Their story — they seem to rehearse it with tears in their eyes — is a perfect Odyssey of misfortunes. According to them, the manor of Wootton Basset had passed in 1555 into the hands of Sir Francis Englefield, who enclosed a park containing 2000 acres, in which the free tenants had hitherto had rights of pasture, and had them without stint, owing to its great size. This wicked man showed them, however, a sort of contemptuous compassion. He left them 100 acres, with which they had to be content, and the rights over which they carefully apportioned, "to the Mayor for the time being two cowes feeding, and to the constable one cowe feeding, and to every inhabitant of the said Borough, each and every of them, one cowe feeding and no more, as well the poore as the riche." These rights of common were in practice vested in all the tenements in the town (not only, it would appear, the free tenements), and property was bought and sold subject to them. The occasion of the petition was that the grand nephew of the original grantee, having apparently got, by some means which the petitioners could not explain, the title deed of the common into his hands, set out to ruin those whom his ancestor had only robbed. He began lawsuits against the free tenants, excluded them from the 100 acres of common which remained to them, and put his own cattle on it. The suits, according to our story, were purposely deferred, and dragged on so long that one of the free tenants was actually made bankrupt by legal charges and the rest were impoverished, the common being used meantime by the plaintiff, Sir Francis Englefield.

These examples of struggles over rights of common pasture are instructive in several ways. In the first place, they suggest that the freeholders were regarded as having a better title than the rest of the community, and that they led the movement to resist encroachments for that reason. It is the free tenants who petition Parliament for redress, and the free tenants who are sued. If they lose their case it is not worth while, it seems, for the customary tenants to take any action. In the second place, they show that the classes who have the best legal title to right of pasture are not at all commensurate with the classes who will lose if they are taken away. Whatever the legal rights of the other tenants may be they have as much practical benefit out of the common, and as great an interest in protecting it against encroachments, as the freeholders have. When the shearing away of part of it makes it necessary to limit the number of beasts to be kept there, the limitation is applied to free and customary tenements alike without distinction, and both classes of tenements are bought and sold on the understanding that they carry with

He tries to seize the remaining 100 acres, and ruins them by lawsuits "for the space of seven or eight years at the least, and never suffers any one to come to triall in all that space ... that the said Free tenants were not able to wage law any longer, for one John Rous ... was thereby enforced to sell all his land (to the value of £500) with following the suits in law, and many were thereby impoverished." (iv.) He turns them out of their shops in the market-place, and introduces instead "a stranger that liveth not in the town." (v.) He appoints his own nominee as mayor, in defiance of the custom which requires him to appoint one of two men submitted to him by the jury. (vi.) He prevents his victims from signing this petition by threats of eviction. ("They are fearful that they shall be put forth of their bargaines, and then they shall not tell how to live, otherwise they would have set to their hands.")

them a right of common pasture. In the third place, the case of Wootton Basset is one of many examples of the way in which poverty, ignorance of the law, and the practical difficulties of getting justice against a powerful landlord, prevent humble litigants from enforcing their legal rights. Finally, it reinforces what has been said above as to the economic importance of rights of pasture. The arrangements which are made at Wootton Basset when the first assault upon the commons takes place show clearly that grazing land is thought of as a quite indispensable adjunct to every man's holding, and its loss is so disastrous to the community that they are ready to be slowly bled to death by lawyer's fees, rather than be beggared at a blow by submitting tamely without a contest.

### *(c) The Engrossing of Holdings and Displacement of Tenants*

We have dwelt at some length on the loss of rights of common, because the misleading modern associations of the word seem sometimes to prevent a proper appreciation of the very important place which they occupied in the agricultural economy of our period. It must be confessed, however, that, in dealing with them first, we have reversed the order in which grievances due to enclosure were set out by the writers of the time. Though there are many bitter complaints against the enclosure of commons, it was, notwithstanding this, less the loss of rights of pasture than the consolidation of small tenancies into great farms, which aroused public excitement, at any rate, in the southern and midland counties. In the Statutes the words enclosure and depopulation are again and again combined as though they were almost synonymous; and if a contemporary had been asked to explain the special evils most characteristic of enclosing, he would certainly have given the first place to the "engrossing of farms" and "depopulation," the throwing together of peasant holdings and the eviction of their tenants. We must now examine this side of the movement. Did the displacement of tenants through the concentration of properties take place on the large scale suggested by the passionate outbursts of contemporary writers, or were their complaints as to empty villages and ruined churches mere rhetorical exaggeration? Again, what was the legal position of the classes of people who suffered? Were they entirely without the protection of the law, or did they fail to obtain legal protection principally in consequence of ignorance and intimidation?

It is easy to understand the strong motives for throwing together peasant holdings, if we keep our eyes on the picture of agricultural arrangements given in the maps. It will be seen that the different blocks of demesne land are often separated from each other by two or three strips belonging to the smaller tenantry, and that if such strips were removed they could be fitted together into a wide and unbroken expanse of territory. The manorial authorities have often, it is clear, been for a long time consolidating the demesne by exchange and purchase, so as to avoid the wastefulness of having land scattered in a hundred separate pieces, and the only obstacle to its complete unification consists of strips and patches which are held by tenants who are for one reason or another unwilling to sell, small spits and islands which stand out of the surrounding sea. Clearly there is an enormous temptation to make the tide flow over them as well, to complete the circuit by merging them in the demesne. Look, for example, at maps Nos. III., IV., and V. Here it is evident that there has been a good deal of consolidation. Both the tenants and the lord of the manor have been forming their strips into compact blocks. To unity of ownership has been added something like spatial unity. Still the process is by no means complete. There are awkward little pieces of land which interrupt the smooth surface of the great estate, pieces which one will have to walk round, where, if the demesne is used as arable, the demesne plough must stop, where, if it is used as pasture, a fence must be erected to shut out the demesne sheep. Or walk down a typical field and mark how the land is held. Here are the strips which one would pass, if one travelled from end to end of two parallel furlongs at West Lexham[443] in Norfolk in the year 1575. They are copied in order from the map—

| Furlong A. | ac. | ro. | po. | Furlong B. | ac. | ro. | po. |
|---|---|---|---|---|---|---|---|
| 1. Will Yelverton, Freeholder. | | | | 1. Rob. Clemente, Freeholder. | | | |
| 2. Demesne | 2 | 1 | 31 | 2. Demesne | 0 | 2 | 4 |
| 3. Demesne | 0 | 1 | 7½ | 3. Demesne | 1 | 0 | 3 |
| 4. Will Yelverton, Freeholder. | | | | 4. Demesne | 1 | 0 | 39 |
| 5. Demesne | 0 | 2 | 7 | 5. Demesne | 0 | 1 | 24 |
| 6. Demesne | 0 | 3 | 0 | 6. Demesne | 1 | 3 | 0 |
| 7. Demesne | 0 | 1 | 11 | 7. Demesne | 0 | 1 | 11 |
| 8. Demesne | 1 | 2 | 10 | 8. Demesne | 1 | 2 | 10 |
| 9. Demesne | 3 | 2 | 28 | 9. Will Lee, Freeholder. | | | |
| 10. Glebe | | | | 10. Will Gell, Copieholder. | | | |
| 11. Demesne | 1 | 2 | 12 | 11. Demesne | 1 | 1 | 39 |
| 12. Demesne | 3 | 0 | 0 | 12. Demesne | 2 | 3 | 39½ |
| 13. Glebe | | | | 13. Demesne | 2 | 1 | 25 |

These furlongs, though the predominance of demesne land in them makes them not quite typical, illustrate sufficiently the awkward way in which the great farmer's stretch of land is interrupted by the little property of a freeholder or copyholder. The strips of Will Yelverton, Robert Clement, Will Lee, and Will Gell must have been a constant eyesore to the manorial authorities. Buy them out or evict them, and then the two furlongs will consist of nothing but demesne land and glebe. They will be two fields of quite a modern pattern and quite ready for enclosure. Leave these tenants where they are, and they are a permanent obstacle to unified management, all the more annoying because they are so petty. They may even insist on the farmer observing the same course of cultivation as themselves, and on turning their beasts to common on his land after harvest! Is it not inevitable

---

[443] Holkham MSS., Map of West Lexham.

that, as soon as the lord is pushed by economic forces into making his estate yield the maximum money return irrespective of a numerous tenantry or of the ancient methods of tillage, he should try in any way he can to get rid of what to him are troublesome excrescences, that he should begin questioning titles, screwing up rents, turning copyhold to leasehold?

If our hypothesis is correct we ought to be able to find manors where the strips formerly held by tenants have been merged in the demesne, so as to form a continuous expanse, in the hands of the lord or his farmer, out of what was formerly a collection of fragments of separate holdings. To see it verified, let us turn to another manor in the same county, that of Walsingham,[444] which was surveyed in the reign of Henry VIII. Here is a statement of the land which is "in the hands of the lord" in the west field—

IN THE WEST FELDE

1.  In manus domine [sic]  ½ acre of land of the tenement Marre.
2.  In manus domine [sic]  1½ roods of the tenement Furell.
3.  In manus domine [sic]  ½ acre land of the tenement Stanx.
4.  In manus domine [sic]  1 acre, 1 rood land of the tenement Gryne.
5.  In manus domine [sic]  3 roods land of the tenement Scot.
6.  In manus domine [sic]  3½ roods land of the tenement Townsend.
7.  In manus domine [sic]  ½ acre land of the tenement Byelaugh.
8.  In manus domine [sic]  ½ acre land of the tenement Wheteloffe.
9.  In manus domine [sic]  ½ acre land of the tenement Scutt.
10.  In manus domine [sic]  ½ acre land of the tenement Coyefor.
11.  In manus domine [sic]  1 acre with the gravel pit.
12.  In manus domine [sic]  3 roods land of the tenement Nedwyn.
13.  In manus domine [sic]  1 acre land late of J. Cockerell.
14.  In manus domine [sic]  3 roods land of the tenement Gilbert.
15.  In manus domine [sic]  1 acre and 1 rood of the tenement Spotell.
16.  In manus domine [sic]  3 roods land of the tenement Spotell.
17.  In manus domine [sic]  3 roods land of the tenement Husbond.
18.  In manus domine [sic]  1 acre of the tenement Rodengh.
19.  In manus domine [sic]  ½ acre land of the tenement Pymans.
20.  In manus domine [sic]  3 roods of the tenement Scutt.
21.  In manus domine [sic]  1 acre of decay of the tenement Spotell

Here one has a field divided into twenty-one strips. Of these strips eighteen had at one time been in the occupation of separate individuals. The picture is just what we are accustomed to in mediæval surveys. It is illustrated sufficiently for our purpose by the map of part of Salford, on page 163. But some time before this survey of Walsingham was made a great change had taken place. The separate

---

[444] R.O. *Aug. Off. Misc. Bks.*, vol. cccxcix., f. 201 ff.

fragments had been taken out of the hands of the tenants and combined in the hands of the lord; the field is ready for conversion to pasture and for enclosure. How extremely profitable it might be to substitute a single large farm for a number of small holdings is proved by Manorial Rentals. Taking five manors in Wiltshire in the year 1568, one finds that the rents paid by the farmer of the demesne work out at 1s. 6d., 7¾d., 1s. 5¾d., 1s. 1¾d., 1s. 5½d. per acre; those paid by the customary tenants at 7½d., 5d., 1s. 0¾d., 5¾d., 5¾d. per acre.[445]

The difference is, in itself, enough to explain a decided movement towards an increase in the size of the unit of agriculture. But of course a powerful incentive to such procedure was supplied by the growth of pasture farming. In the days when the cultivation of the demesne depended on the labour of the tenants there was obviously bound to be a certain proportion between the land belonging to the former and the land held by the latter, a proportion which might be expressed by saying "no tenants, no demesne cultivation; no demesne cultivation, no income for the lord." But when tillage was replaced by pasture farming this economic rule of three ceased to work. On the one hand, the limit of size imposed on the demesne farm by considerations of management was removed or at any rate enormously extended, for many thousand sheep could be fed by two or three shepherds. On the other hand, the economic motive for preventing a decline in the number of small landholders was weakened, because there was little use for their labour on a pasture farm; while there was a great deal of use for their land, if only it could be cleared of existing rights and added to it. We have, in fact, an ordinary case of the depreciation of particular[446] kinds of human labour in comparison with capital, of the kind to which the modern world has become accustomed in the case of machinery—become accustomed and become callous.

We shall perhaps best give precision to our ideas of the sort of policy which landlords were inclined to adopt, by taking a single concrete instance, though of course conditions varied locally very much from place to place. It comes from Hartley[447] in Northumberland, where Robert Delavale was lord of the manor in

---

[445] The manors are South Newton, Winterbourne Basset, Knyghton, Donnington, and Estoverton and Phipheld (Roxburghe Club, *Surveys of Pembroke Manors*).

[446] This, of course, is not inconsistent with a general appreciation, *i.e.* a general rise in wages and fall in the rate of interest.

[447] *Northumberland County History*, vol. ix. p. 124. For a similar case of evictions by Delavale, showing how they were carried out, *ibid.*, pp. 201–202: "There was in Seaton Delavale township 12 tenements, whereon there dwelt 12 able men sufficiently furnished with horse and furniture to serve his Majestie ... who paid 46s. 8d. rent yearlie a piece or thereabouts. All the said tenants and their successors saving 5 the said Robert Delavale eyther thrust out of their fermholds or weried them by taking excessive fines, increasing of their rents unto £3 a piece, and withdrawing part of their best land and meadow from their tenements ... by taking their good land from them and compelling them to winne moorishe and heathe ground, and after their hedging heth ground to their great charge, and paying a great fine, and bestowing great reparation on building their tenements, he quite thrust them off in one yeare, refusing either to repay the fine or to repay the charge bestowed in diking or building.... The said seven fermholds displaced had to every one of them 60 acres of arable land, viz. 20 in every field at the least, as the tenants affirme, which amounteth to 480 acres of land yearlie or thereabouts, converted for the most part from tillage to pasture,

the reign of Elizabeth. The narrator is his cousin, Joshua Delavale—

"Since which time" (*i.e.* 16 Eliz.), he says, "the said Robert Delavale purchased all the freeholder's lands and tenements, displaced the said tenants, defaced their tenements, converted their tillage to pasture, being 720 acres of arable ground or thereabouts, and made one demaine, whereon there is but three plows now kept by hinds and servants, besides the 720 acres. So that where there was then in Hartley 15 serviceable men furnished with sufficient horse and furniture, there is now not any, nor hath been these 20 years last past or thereabouts."

Here we get a complete example of the various steps which are taken to build up a great pasture farm. The freeholders are bought out; the other tenants are (it is to be inferred) evicted summarily; their houses are pulled down; their land is thrown into the demesne; the whole area is let down to pasture and managed by hired labourers, while the land-holding population is turned adrift. It is worth noticing that the word "enclosing" is not used. All the drastic changes that are usually ascribed to enclosure can on occasion take place without it. Indeed, the more drastic they are the less need is there to complete them by the erection of fences, for the smaller the population left to commit encroachments.

If such a process were general or even common, we should certainly have the materials of a social revolution. But was it? The much discussed question of the effect of the agrarian changes on the numbers of the rural population is one which it is not possible to answer with any approach to accuracy, owing to the difficulty of obtaining a sufficient number of continuous series of surveys and rentals. Those relating to single years tell mainly results, when what we want to see is a process. Nevertheless even single surveys are not altogether without value. They show the distribution of land between different classes at a given moment, and sometimes contain indications of the changes by which the existing distribution was reached. In particular they show us the relative areas of the demesne farm and of the land in the hands of all other classes of tenants. And this has a certain interest. For since the demesne farm on a manor where conditions approximated most closely to those of the Middle Ages and had been least affected by more recent changes, rarely contained more than half the whole manorial territory and generally not so much, there is a *prima facie* case for surmising concentration of holdings and evictions when one finds two-thirds, three-quarters, or even ninety per cent. of it in the hands of one large farmer. It is, however, a very tedious task calculating the acreage held by a number of different tenants, and this may perhaps excuse the small number of instances which are given below. They are as follows:—

and united to the demaine of the lordship of Seaton Delavale."

Table XII

| Manor. | (I.)<br>Whole Area Ascertainable.[448] | (II.)<br>Area held by Farmers of Demesnes. | Percentage of (II.) to (I.). |
|---|---|---|---|
| Donnyngton | 1523½ | 418 | 27.8 |
| Salford | 856 | 295 | 34.4 |
| Estoverton and Phipheld | 1160 | 484¾ | 41.0 |
| Weedon Weston | 715 | 301 | 42.0 |
| South Newton | 1365 | 632 | 46.3 |
| Washerne | 1249 | 707<br>(in hands of lord) | 56.6 |
| Knyghton | 452 | 268 | 59.2 |
| Bishopeston | 1280 | 805 | 62.9 |
| Gamlingay Merton | 283½ | 199¾ | 70.3 |
| Winterborne Basset | 708½ | 532 | 75.1 |
| Billingford | 666 | 507 | 76.1 |
| Gamlingay Avenells[449] | 531¾ | 420¼ | 79.0 |
| Domerham[450] | 960½ | 824½ | 85.8 |
| Ewerne | 473 | 428 | 90.5 |
| Burdonsball | 190 | 190 | 100.0 |
| Whadborough | 469 | 469 | 100.0 |

It will be seen that on eight of these sixteen manors more than two-thirds of the whole area, and on seven more than three-quarters, is in the hands of one individual, the farmer of the demesnes. These figures are at any rate not inconsistent with a considerable consolidation of tenancies and displacement of tenants, though we cannot say that they prove it.

Occasionally the surveys take us behind this presumptive evidence and enable us to trace the building up of large farms out of small holdings. For example, at Ormesby,[451] in 1516, the lord of the manor held 219 acres "late in farm" of six tenants. At Domerham,[452] some time before 1568, enclosure of land in the open fields and conversion of arable to pasture had been carried out by the largest of

---

[448] In several cases the freeholders' lands are not stated in the survey, and are therefore not included in this table.

[449] A few acres described as "held without title" are omitted.

[450] I am not sure that there are not other lands in Domerham not included in the survey or in the demesne. If this is so, the proportion of the latter to the rest of the manorial land would of course be reduced.

[451] R.O. Rentals and Surveys, Gen. Ser., Portf. 22, No. 18.

[452] Roxburghe Club, *Surveys of Pembroke Manors.*

the three farmers. The process had been accompanied by depopulation; for in 1568 his farm included pieces of land which had formerly belonged to four smaller tenants, and the two large farms which he held had formerly been in separate hands. It is probable that at Winterbourne Basset[453] somewhat the same movement had taken place. In 1436 two carucates of land were held by an unspecified number of tenants; in 1568 three customary tenants are still found there, but three-quarters of the manor is in the hands of a single farmer who has recently enclosed a field of 40 acres. Elsewhere one can fill in the picture in somewhat greater detail. At Tughall,[454] in Northumberland, the surveyor tells us in 1567, the demesne lands had been let to a farmer, who acted as the lord's bailiff and collected the rents and services of the other tenants. He used his position to partition the manor so as to get rid of the intermingled holdings, and at the same time so harassed the smaller tenants that they were reduced from twenty-three to eight. At Cowpen[455] a similar concentration of land was going on at the end of the sixteenth century; first five tenancies were thrown into one, and then the whole manor passed into the hands of one large farmer. At Newham,[456] near Alnwick, we are told that a hundred and forty men, women, and children were evicted simultaneously. At Seaton[457] Delavale, the Robert Delavale who had depopulated Hartly, turned adrift seven families out of twelve. The map of a Leicestershire manor which is reproduced opposite page 223 is more eloquent than many lamentations. In "the place where the town of Whadboroughe once stood" there was by 1620 not a single tenant left. The whole of it formed one great expanse of pasture.

But these isolated instances are obviously worthless as a basis for generalisation. The most that can be said of them is that they prove that the writers who spoke of whole towns being depopulated were not romancing. Nor are the statistics offered by contemporaries of any practical help towards determining the social effects of enclosure. Those who state, like Moore[458] (writing in the seventeenth century), that they have seen "in some townes fourteen, sixteen, and twenty tenants discharged of plowing," or, like the Dean of Durham,[459] that "500 ploughs have decayed in a few years" and "of 8000 acres lately in tillage now not 8 score are tilled," may have seen what they say. But these figures are suspiciously round, and the cases are obviously extreme ones, not samples. The one[460] writer who makes an estimate for the whole country, putting the number of persons of all ages

---

[453] *Ibid.*, and Hoare, *History of Wiltshire*, Hundred of Ambresbury.

[454] *Northumberland County History*, vol. i. p. 350.

[455] *Ibid.*, vol. ix., Cowpen.

[456] *Ibid.*, vol. i. p. 275.

[457] *Ibid.*, vol. ix. pp. 201–202.

[458] Moore, *The Crying Sin of England*, &c.

[459] Cal. S. P. D. Eliz., 1595–1597 (p. 347), quoted Gay, *Quarterly Journal of Economics*, vol. xvii.

[460] "Certayne Causes gathered together wherein is shewed the decaye of England only by the great multitude of shepe" (E. E. T. S. date 1550–1553). "It is to understande ... that there is in England townes and villages to the number of fifty thousand and upward, and for every town and village ... there is one plough decayed since the fyrst year of the reign of King Henry VII.... The whiche 50,000 ploughs every plough was able to maintain 6 persons, and nowe they have nothing, but goeth about in England from dore to dore."

displaced between 1485 and 1550 at 300,000, is rash enough to explain how his estimate was reached, and his explanation shows that it was not even a plausible guess.

The returns collected for the Government seem at first to take us on to surer ground. Investigations were made by Royal Commissioners[461] in the years 1517–1519, 1548, 1566, 1607, 1632, 1635, and 1636. The returns collected for twenty-three counties by the Commission of 1517, for four counties by those of 1548–1566, and for six counties by that of 1607 have been printed. According to them, it would appear that between 1485 and 1517 about one-half per cent. of the total area of the counties investigated was enclosed, and 6931 persons displaced, the corresponding figures for the period 1578–1607 being 69,758 acres and 2232 evictions. Both in the earlier, and in the later, period, the county which was affected most severely was Northamptonshire, where 2.21 per cent. of the county was returned as enclosed in the years 1485–1517, and in the years 1578–1607 4.30 per cent., the numbers displaced being respectively 1405 and 1444. If we like, we may adopt the conjectural estimates of Professor Gay, and, assuming that the pace of the movement was the same during the years for which we have not information as during those for which we have, may say with him that from 1455 to 1607 the agrarian changes affected about 2.76 of the whole area of twenty-four counties, and displaced something between 30,000 and 50,000 persons.

The statistics which have been worked up by Mr. Leadam and Professor Gay from the inquiries of the Government are extremely valuable as showing the geographical distribution of the enclosing movement. It is most powerful in the Midland counties, which were in the sixteenth century the chief granary of the country, and its influence is least in the South-West and South-East. In Somersetshire, Devonshire, and Cornwall, Suffolk, Essex and Kent the small enclosures[462] described

---

[461] For a discussion of the value of these reports see Leadam, *Domesday of Enclosures*, and *Trans. Royal Hist. Soc.*, New Series, vol. vi.; Gay, *Trans. Royal Hist. Soc.*, New Series, vol. xiv. and vol. xviii.; Gay, *Quarterly Journal of Economics*, vol. xvii. (1902–1903). A useful summary of the evidence, with a map illustrating the probable geographical distribution of the movement, is given by Johnson, *The Disappearance of the Small Landowner*, pp. 42–54 and Map I.

[462] It is a question how far there had ever been an open field system in some of these counties, *e.g.* Cornwall and Kent. There certainly were some open field villages of the ordinary pattern in Kent (see Slater, *The English Peasantry and the Enclosure of Common Fields*, p. 230). But Kent from an early date develops on its own lines, and does not go through the same stages of manorialism and commutation as other counties. Much of it seems to start at the point which they reach only in the sixteenth century. Cornwall again, though in the sixteenth century there were commons where the villagers pastured their cattle together (see accounts of Landress and Porpehan, *Topographer and Genealogist*, vol. i.), was largely a county of scattered homesteads and very early enclosure (for the "nucleated village" and "scattered homesteads," see Maitland, *Domesday Book and Beyond*, pp. 15–16), pointing to a different system of settlement from that of the counties where the open field system obtained. For enclosures in Devon and Somerset see Cunningham, *Growth of English Industry and Commerce*, Modern Times, Part II., App. B: "A consideration of the cause in question before the lords touchinge depopulation," and Carlyle's *Cromwell*, Letter XXIV. "Lest we should engage our body of horse too far into that enclosed country."

in Part I. had probably often been carried out by the peasants themselves at an early date, with the result that those districts were, compared with the open field villages of the Midlands, little disturbed. Those parts of the country, in fact, where the peasantry have been most progressive, are relatively unaffected by the changes of our period. They have been inoculated and they are almost immune. On the other hand, one is inclined to say that the figures are not of much value for other purposes. In the nature of things they cannot be reliable, and, if they were reliable, they would not really answer the most important questions which are asked about the social results of the changes to which they refer. Let us remember the methods by which they were collected. They are taken from returns which are in the form of answers delivered to commissioners by juries of peasants, juries which we know from the most active of the commissioners to have been occasionally packed by the local proprietors, and often intimidated,[463] and to have been examined by the commissioners under the eyes of their landlords. It is hardly necessary to point out that no evidence of even approximate accuracy would be derived from an inquiry conducted in such a fashion at the present day. Is it probable that it was obtained any more satisfactorily in the sixteenth century?

Nor, if accurate, could these statistics really be used as a means of disproving the accounts given by contemporary writers of the dislocation produced by enclosure. That those accounts were highly coloured, no one familiar with the methods which the age brought to the discussion of economic questions will doubt. Professor Gay does well to warn us against credulity. It is certainly a salutary discipline to turn from the burning words of Latimer or Crowley to these official calculations, and then, by a glance at the chapters of Dr. Slater and Professor Gonner on the enclosures of the eighteenth century, to realise that even in those parts of England where the cry against depopulation had arisen most bitterly two centuries before, there were still thousands of acres to be enclosed by some hundreds of Enclosure Acts. But if we must discount the protests of authors to whom all large economic changes seem to smell of the pit, we must not forget either that their views are formed by the conditions of their age, and that it is just in the conditions productive of this state of mind that even a moderate change is likely to work with the most disastrous effects. We who reckon in millions and count a year lost which does not see some new outburst of economic energy, must be very careful how we apply our statistics to measure the movements of an age where economic life differs not only in quantity but in quality, where most men have never seen more than a hundred separate individuals in the course of their whole lives, where most households live by tilling their great-grandfathers' fields with their great-grandfathers' plough. We must not be too clever—our ancestors would have said too wicked—for our subject. We must not accept an estimate of the amount of depopulation as an explanation of its effects; for the two things are not in *pari materia*. Certainly we must not argue that, because the returns collected by Royal Commissions show that in the counties affected most severely less than one-twentieth of the total area was enclosed, therefore the complaints of observers

---

[463] For intimidation see the case of Wootton Basset, quoted above, pp. 251–253, and below, pp. 302–304. Also Gay, *Trans. Royal Hist. Soc.*, New Series, vol. xviii.; and Hales' defence (appendix to Miss Lamond's introduction to *The Commonweal of this Realm of England*).

must be taken as a hysterical exaggeration of slow and unimportant changes. For one thing, summary tables are no measure of the distress caused by eviction, till we know how the tables are made up. The drifting away of one tenant from each of fifty manors, and the eviction of fifty tenants from one manor, yield precisely the same statistical results when the total displacement from a given county is being calculated. But the former would be scarcely noticeable; the latter might ruin a village. For another thing, the total area of a county is a mere spatial expression, which is important to no one except geographers. What mattered to the peasantry, and what matters to us, is not the proportion which the land enclosed bore to the whole area of the county, but the proportion which it bore to the whole area available for cultivation. This, which is of course not ascertainable, is clearly a very different thing.[464] It is no consolation to a family which has been evicted from a prosperous farm to be told that it can settle on a moor or a marsh, on Blackstone Edge or Deeping Fen. To argue that enclosing was of little consequence, because so small a proportion of the total land area was enclosed, is almost precisely similar to arguing that overcrowding is of little consequence, because the area of Great Britain divided by the population gives a quotient of about one and a half acres to every human being in the country. The evidence of a general trend of opinion during a century and a half—opinion by no means confined to the peasants, or to the peasants' champions like Hales, or to idealists like Sir Thomas More, or to the preachers of social righteousness like Latimer and Crowley, but shared by Wolsey and Thomas Cromwell in the earlier part of the century, Robert Cecil and Francis Bacon[465] at the end of it—to the effect that the agrarian changes caused extensive depopulation, is really a firmer basis for judging their effects than are statistics which, however carefully worked up, are necessarily unreliable, and which, when reliable, are not quite the statistics required. When that opinion is backed by documentary proof that from one village thirty persons, from another fifty, from another the whole population, were displaced, though of course we cannot say that such displacement was general, we can say that it was not unknown, and that if contemporaries were guilty of exaggeration (as they probably were), their exaggeration took the form not of inventing extreme cases, but of suggesting that such extreme cases were the rule. On the whole, therefore, our conclusions as to the quantitative measurement of depopulation caused in the sixteenth century must still, in spite of the researches of Mr. Leadam and Professor Gay, be a negative one. In the first place, we cannot say, even approximately, what proportion of the total landholding population was displaced. In the second place, such figures as we do possess are not of a kind to outweigh the direct evidence of contemporary observers that the movement was so extensive as in parts of England to cause serious suffering and disturbance.

### (d) The Agrarian Changes and the Poor Law

[464] Professor Pollard has good remarks on this point (*Political History of England, 1547–1603*, p. 29).

[465] Wolsey was responsible for the Commission of 1517. For a letter of Cromwell to Henry VIII. on the subject of enclosure, and for the views of Cecil and Bacon, see below, pp. 273–274, 279, 343, 387.

The obscurity in which the statistics of depopulation are involved does not prevent us from seeing that it played an important part in providing an incentive to the organisation of relief on a national and secular basis, which was the most enduring achievement of the social legislation of sixteenth century statesmen. An influential theory of Poor Law History regards the admission finally made in 1601 that the destitute person has, not only a moral, but a legal, right to maintenance, as a last fatal legacy handed to the modern state by the expiring social order of the Middle Ages, a relic of villeinage which was given a statutory basis at the very moment when a little more patience would have shown that a national system of poor relief was not only unnecessary, but positively harmful, in the new mobile society which the expansion of commerce and industry was bringing into existence. "Serfdom," says an eminent exponent of this view, "is itself a system of Poor Law. The Poor Law is not therefore a new device invented in the time of Elizabeth to meet a new disease. The very conception of a society based on status involves the conception of a Poor Law far more searching and rigid than the celebrated 43 Eng. cap. 2.... The collective provision is appropriate to the then expiring condition of status.... A wide diffusion of private property, not collective property, is the obvious and natural method by which the unable-bodied periods of life are to be met. With the disappearance of Feudalism we might have expected that there would have disappeared the custom which made the poor a charge upon the manor or parish of which they had formerly been serfs. This, however, did not happen, and a history of this survival of mediæval custom is the history of the English Poor Law.... To sum the matter up:—In following the development of Poor Law legislation, we watch society struggling to free itself from the fetters of a primitive communism of poverty and subjection, a state of things possessing many 'plausible advantages.' Legislation for the management of the Poor often impeded, and only occasionally expedited, this beneficent process.... It proceeded from ignorance of the true nature of progress, and from a denial or neglect of the power of absorption possessed by a free society."[466] It is obvious that in this passage Mr. Mackay uses his interpretation of Poor Law origins to make a very trenchant criticism upon the whole principle involved in the public maintenance of the destitute. That principle was not introduced because new conditions made its adoption indispensable. It survived from an older order of things into a world in which the only serious causes of destitution are personal and not economic, and in which therefore it is quite inappropriate. To tolerate it is to drag for ever a clanking chain, one end of which is fastened round the bleeding ankles of modern society, and the other anchored in the hideous provisions of the Statute of Labourers. Nor should we be wrong if we said that a similar theory, though less lucidly expressed, has had a considerable influence upon Poor Law practice. For the idea of a Poor Law as an anachronism which is quite out of place in a developed economic society is implied more than once in the celebrated report drafted by Senior and Chadwick in 1834, and has passed from that brilliant piece of special pleading into the minds of three generations of administrators. "A person," they state, "who attributes pauperism to the inability to procure employment, will doubt the efficiency of the cause which we propose to remove it," whereas "whenever inquiries have been made as to the

---

[466] Mackay, *History of the English Poor Law*, 1834–1898, pp. 10–11, 16–17.

previous condition of the able-bodied individuals who live in such numbers on the town parishes, it has been found that the pauperism of the greater number has originated in indolence, improvidence, and vice, and might have been avoided by ordinary care and industry. The majority of the Statutes connected with the administration of public relief have created new evils, and aggravated those which they were intended to prevent."[467]

A discussion of Poor Law theory and history falls outside the limits of this essay. But in forming an estimate of the effects of the agrarian changes which have been described above, it is perhaps not out of place to consider the minor question of the connection between them and the system of Poor Relief which took its final shape in the reign of Elizabeth. Since the distress which the relief institutions of an age exist to meet stands to its general economic conditions in the relation of reverse to obverse, of effect to cause, of disease to environment, much light is thrown on the economic difficulties most characteristic of any period by ascertaining the type of distress with which relieving authorities are most generally confronted. Equally important, any student of Poor Law History, who is not the partisan of a theory, finds himself constantly driven to look for an explanation of Poor Law developments in regions which, at first sight, appear to lie far outside his immediate subject, but where, in reality, is grown the grim harvest which it is the duty of Poor Law authorities, often acting in complete ignorance of its origin, to reap. Much wild theorising and some tragic practical blunders might have been avoided, had it been more generally realised that, of all branches of administration, the treatment of persons in distress is that which can least bear to be left to the exclusive attention of Poor Law specialists, because it, most of all matters, depends for its success on being carefully adapted to the changing economic conditions, the organisation or disorganisation of industry, the stability or instability of trade, the diffusion or concentration of property, by which the nature and extent of the distress requiring treatment are determined.

When one turns to the age in which the Poor Law took shape, the first thing to strike one is that the need for it arises, according to the views expressed by most writers of the period, from that very development in commercial relationships, that very increase in economic mobility, which Mr. Mackay seems to imply should have made it unnecessary. The special feature of sixteenth century pauperism is written large over all the documents of the period—in Statutes, in Privy Council proceedings, in the records of Quarter Sessions. The new and terrible problem is the increase in vagrancy. The sixteenth century lives in terror of the tramp. He is denounced by moralists, analysed into species by the curious or scientific, scourged and buffeted by all men. The destitution of the aged and impotent, of fatherless children and widows, is familiar enough. It has been with the world from time immemorial. It has been for centuries the object of voluntary charitable effort; and when the dissolution of the monasteries dries up one great channel of provision, the Government intervenes with special arrangements[468] to take their place a

[467] *Poor Law Commission Report of 1834*, pp. 264–277, 281.

[468] 27 Hen. VIII., c. 25. Under this Act city and county authorities are to relieve impotent beggars "by way of voluntary and charitable alms." They are also for the first time given power to apprentice vagrant children.

whole generation before it can be brought to admit that there is any problem of the unemployed, other than the problem of the sturdy rogue. The distinction between the able-bodied unemployed and the impotent is one which is visible to the eye of sense. The distinction between the man who is unemployed because he cannot get work and the man who is unemployed because he does not want work, requires a modicum of knowledge and reflection which even at the present day is not always forthcoming. The former distinction, therefore, is not supplemented by the latter until the beginning of the last quarter of the century.[469] In one respect, that of the Law of Settlement, the English Poor Law does show traces of a mediæval origin. In all other respects, so far from being a survival from the Middle Ages, it comes into existence just at the time when mediæval economic conditions are disappearing. It is not accepted at once as a matter of course that the destitute shall be publicly relieved, still less that the able-bodied destitute deserve anything but punishment. Governments make desperate efforts for about one hundred years to evade their new obligations. They whip and brand and bore ears; they offer the vagrant as a slave to the man who seizes him; they appeal to charity; they introduce the parish clergy to put pressure on the uncharitable; they direct the bishops to reason with those who stop their ears against the parish clergy. When merely repressive measures and voluntary effort are finally discredited, they levy a compulsory charge rather as a fine for contumacy than as a rate, and slide reluctantly into obligatory assessments[470] only when all else has failed. And if we ask why the obligation of maintaining the destitute should have received national recognition first in the sixteenth century, we can only answer by pointing to that trend away from the stationary conditions of agriculture to the fluctuating conditions of trade, and in particular to that displacement of the rural population, which we have already seen was one result of enclosure. The national Poor Law is not a mediæval anachronism. It is the outcome of conditions which seem to the men of the sixteenth century new and appalling. Of these conditions the most important are the agrarian changes.

Let us try for a moment to put ourselves in the position of a family which has been evicted from its holding to make room for sheep. When the last stick of furniture has been tumbled out by the bailiff, where, poor houseless wretches, are they to turn? They cannot get work in their old home, even if they can get lodgings, for the attraction of sheep-farming is that the wage bill is so low. Will they emigrate from England like the Scotch crofters? There are people who in the seventeenth century will advise them to seek a haven with the godly folk who have crossed the Atlantic, who will argue that England is overstocked, that "there is such pressing and oppressing in town and country about farms, trades, traffic, so as a man can hardly anywhere set up a trade but he shall pull down two of his neighbours," and point out that "the country is replenished with new farmers, and the almhouses are filled with old labourers," that "the rent-taker lives on sweet morsels, but the

---

[469] 18 Eliz. c. 3 directed that a stock of wool, flax, hemp, iron, or other stuff should be provided in cities, corporate towns, and market towns. The important words which show the change of opinion are, "To the intente also that ... Roges ... may not have any just excuse in saying they cannot get any service or work."

[470] 14 Eliz. c. 5.

rent-payer eats a dry crust often with watery eyes."[471] But enclosures have been going on for a century before the plantations exist to offer a refuge, and in any case the probability of the country folk hearing of them is very remote. Can a man migrate to seek work in another part of the country? Not easily, for, apart from the enormous practical difficulties, the law puts obstacles in his way, and the law is backed up with enthusiasm by every parish and town in the country. There are three possible attitudes which a State may adopt towards the questions arising from the ebb and flow of population. It may argue, with the optimists of 1834, that the mobility of labour is a good thing, a symptom of alertness and energy, and that it will take place of itself to the extent which is economically desirable, provided that no impediments are placed in the way of those who desire to better themselves by looking for work elsewhere. Or, while believing that it is much to be desired that people should migrate freely from place to place in search of employment, it may nevertheless reflect that the mere absence of restrictions does not in fact stimulate such movement, and therefore take upon itself its encouragement through the publication of information and the registration of unemployed workers. Or, subordinating economic to political considerations, it may hold that the movement of a large number of unemployed persons up and down the country is not an indication of a praiseworthy spirit of enterprise, but a menace to public order which must be sternly repressed. We need hardly say that this last view is the one characteristic of the sixteenth century. The attitude towards the man on tramp in search of employment is exactly the opposite of that which is held at the present day. He is not less, but much more, culpable than he who remains in his own parish and lives on his neighbours. He is assumed not to be seeking work but to be avoiding it, and avoiding it in a restless and disorderly manner. Hear what the worthy Harrison says when the State has already made the provision for the unemployed a charge upon each parish: — "But if they refuse to be supported by this benefit of the law, and will rather endeavour by going to and fro to maintain their idle trades, then are they adjudged to be parcel of the third sort (*i.e.* wilful vagrants), and so, instead of courteous refreshing at home, are often corrected with sharp execution and whip of justice abroad. Many there are which, notwithstanding the rigour of the laws provided on that behalf, yield rather with this liberty (as they call it) to be daily under the fear and terror of the whip, than by abiding where they were born or bred, to be provided for by the devotion of the parishes."[472] The village is still thought of as the unit of employment. It is still regarded as being equipped with the means of finding work for all its inhabitants, as though there had been no movement towards pasture-farming to prick a hole in its economic self-sufficiency. The presumption, therefore, is against the man who leaves the parish where he is known to his neighbours. He must prove that he is going to take up work for which he is already engaged. He must get a licence from his last employer. As far as the able-bodied are concerned the Poor Law is in origin a measure of social police. Relief is thrown in as a makeweight, because by the

---

[471] Robert Cushman, "Reasons and Considerations touching the Lawfulness of Removing out of England into the parts of America" (printed by E. Arber, *The Story of the Pilgrim Fathers*).

[472] Harrison in *Elizabethan England* (Withington), chap. x.

end of the sixteenth century our statesmen have discovered that when economic pressure reaches a certain point they cannot control men without it. The whip has no terrors for the man who must look for work or starve. So every Sunday after church, while Parson's sermon is still fresh in our minds, we board out our poor by rotation "among such householders as will maintain them meat and work and such wages as they shall deserve for the week following."[473] Heaven help us if the next parish does not do the same!

And the Poor Law is a police measure for the necessity of which the agrarian changes are largely responsible. In spite of all the obstacles in the way of migration, in spite of whip and courteous refreshment, men do in fact migrate, and not only men, but women and children. By the latter part of the century, at any rate, statesmen have begun to understand that pauperism and vagrancy stand to the depopulation caused by enclosure in the relation of effect to cause. The revolution in the official attitude to the problem caused by this belated illumination is as great as that which has taken place in the last ten years with regard to unemployment. Once the new standpoint has been seized, though opinion, and the opinion not only of the ruling classes, but of burgesses and villagers, still treats the vagrant with iron severity, it never quite relapses into the comfortable doctrine, the grand discovery of a commercial age, that distress is itself a proof of the demerits of its victim, and that Heaven, like a Utilitarian philosopher, permits the existence of destitution only that it may make "less eligible" the lot of "improvidence and vice." It is saved from this last error not by the lore of economists, but because it regards economic questions through the eyes of a sturdy matter-of-fact morality. It is sufficiently enlightened to recognise that even among vagrants there is a class which is more sinned against than sinning, a class of whom it can be asked "at whose hands shall the blood of these men be required?"[474] It is sufficiently ingenuous to answer by pointing to "some covetous man" who, "espying a further commodity in their commons, holds, and tenures, doth find such means as thereby to wipe many out of their occupyings and turn the same unto his private gains."[475] Occasionally the effect of enclosures is brought home to the encloser in a practical way, by compelling him not only to pay a fine to the Crown, but also to make a contribution towards the relief of the poor whose numbers he has increased.[476]

To see the way in which the relation between the problems of pauperism and of agrarian depopulation is regarded, turn to the debates in the House of Commons. In the year 1597, when both questions are acute (the preceding year had seen a recrudescence of agrarian rioting), a member or minister, probably Robert Cecil, is preparing notes for a speech[477] on the subject in Parliament. What are

[473] *Hist. MSS. Com.*, Marquis of Salisbury, Part VII., pp. 160–161: "Orders agreed to by the Justices of the Peace for Cornwall at General Sessions for Bodmin the 5th and Truro the 8th of April, 39 Eliz."

[474] Harrison, *loc. cit.*

[475] *Ibid.*

[476] Camden Society, 1886. Cases in Courts of Star Chamber and High Commission, Michaelmas, 7 Caroli, Case of Archer. (The allusion in the text is to a precedent cited in this case.)

[477] *Hist. MSS. Com.*, Marquis of Salisbury, Part VII., Nov. 1597. "Notes for the present

the points he emphasises? They are the high price of corn caused by bad harvests and the manipulations of middlemen, the enclosing of land and the conversion of arable to pasture, which naturally intensifies the difficulty of securing adequate food supplies, "the decaying and plucking down of houses, ... and not only the plucking down of some few houses, but the depopulating of whole towns ... and keeping of a shepherd only, whereby many subjects are turned without habitation, and fill the country with rogues and idle persons." When Parliament meets in October, the House is at once busy with different aspects of the same question.[478] Bills are introduced dealing with forestallers, regrators, and engrossers of corn, with vagrancy and pauperism, and with enclosures, and a committee is appointed to consider the latter question. In the debates which follow there is the usual division of opinion between the champions of economic reform and the advocates of more, and more ruthless, "deterrence," between those who wish to legislate as to causes and those who are mainly occupied with symptoms. Bacon, master as ever of the science of his subject, insists with invincible logic that pauperism is one part of the general agrarian problem, and he is supported by Robert Cecil. On the other hand, the experts as to pauperism—we can imagine the county justices fresh from their whippings and relief committees and houses of correction, fresh, too, from enclosure and depopulation—complain that their special subject is being overlooked in a general and dangerous discussion on the economic causes of distress, and that the committee "has spent all their travel about the said enclosures and tillage, and nothing about the said rogues and poor." That this should have been the popular line to take needs no explanation. A Parliament which dares discuss not only how to manipulate the lives of the poor, but the fundamental causes of their misery, is a Parliament which the eye of man had not yet, has not yet, beheld. Compared with other representative assemblies, compared with itself at a later date, the Elizabethan House of Commons, debating in an age when it could be said that government was "nothing but a certein conspiracy of riche men procuringe theire owne commodities under the name and title of the Common Wealth," had the grace to show some stirrings of compunction. If members who had grown fat on the tragedy which they were discussing spoke of their victims as members will speak, ministers at least were independent, and could venture, like Cecil, to tell the House unpalatable truths. Of the two Acts against enclosure, which were the result of this session's deliberations, we shall speak later. What is worth noticing here is the disposition, even in a Parliament composed of country gentlemen, to emphasise the connection between the problems with which anti-enclosure and anti-vagrancy legislation have to deal. It is summed up in the eloquent peroration of a nameless member. "As this bill entered at first with a short prayer, 'God speed the plough,' so I wish it may end with such success as the plough shall speed the poor."[479]

What became of the families displaced from the soil between their final eviction and that subsidence upon the stony breast of the Elizabethan Poor Law,

Parliament."

[478] *D'Ewes' Journal*, pp. 551–555; see also Leonard, *The Early History of English Poor Relief*, pp. 73–75.

[479] *Hist. MSS. Com.*, Marquis of Salisbury, Part VII., pp. 541–543.

which, for some of them, was their ultimate fate? There is no certain information to guide us. The tragedy of the tramp is his isolation. Every man's hand is against him; and his history is inevitably written by his enemies. Yet, beneath denunciations hurled upon him by those who lived warm and slept soft, we can see two movements going on, two waves in a vast and silent ebbing of population from its accustomed seats. In the first place there is a steady immigration into the towns on the part of those "who, being driven out of their habitations, are forced into the great cities, where, being very burdensome, men shut their doors against them, suffering them to die in the streets and highways."[480] The municipal records of the periods teem with complaints of the disorder, the overcrowding, the violation of professional bye-laws, caused by rural immigration. The displaced peasant is the Irishman of the sixteenth century, and, like the Irishman, he makes his very misery a whip with which to scourge, not alas! his oppressors, but men who often are not much less wretched than himself. He turns whole quarters into slums, spreads disease through congested town dwellings, and disorganises the labour market by crowding out the native artisan. Gild members find themselves eaten up by unlawful men who have never served an apprenticeship in the town, and retort with regulations requiring the deposit of a prohibitive sum as an entrance fee from all immigrants who want to set up shop, especially from those wretches who are thought to have a large family of children, at present snugly concealed in their last place of residence, but soon to be surreptitiously introduced, a brood of hungry young cuckoos, if once their parents get a footing in the town.[481] Borough authorities, who see cottages "made down" into tenements in which pestilence spreads with fearful rapidity, seek to stamp out the very possibility of invasion by prohibiting the erection of new cottages or the subdivision of old. To judge by their behaviour, the notorious Statute of 1662, which codified the existing customs as to settlement, must have been one of the most popular pieces of legislation ever passed by Parliament. Town[482] after town in the course of the sixteenth century tries to protect itself by a system of stringent inspection worthy of modern Germany. Sometimes there is a regular expulsion of the aliens. "Forasmuch as it is found by daily experience," declare the authorities of Nottingham,[483] "that by the continual building and erecting of new cottages and poor habitations, and by the transferring of barns and suchlike buildings into cottages, and also by the great confluence of many poor people from forrein parts out of this towne to inhabit here, and lykewise by the usual and frequent taking in of inmates into many poor

---

[480] Lansd. MSS. 83, f. 68, quoted Gonner, *Common Land and Enclosure*, p. 156 n.

[481] *e.g. Nottingham Records*, vol. iv. pp. 170–171, Nov. 4, 1577: "Any burgess that hath not been prentice to pay £10 and no pardon. *Records of Leicester*, vol. iii. p. 351, Oct. 17, 1598: "He is inhibited from dwelling in your corporation unless he finds bonds for £200 that neither his wife nor children shall be burdensome to the town." *Southampton Court Leet Records*, vol. i., Part I.: "One William Dye, undertenant to John Netley, dothe lyve idelly and hathe no trade.... He hathe 4 or 5 children in places from whence he came whom he will bring shortly hither, yf he may be suffered here to remayne, whom we desyer may be examined and removed from hence according to the Statute."

[482] Some instances are given by Leonard, *Early History of English Poor Relief*, pp. 107–109.

[483] *Nottingham Records*, vol. iv. pp. 304–307.

habitations here, the poorer sort of people do much increase ... it is ordered that no burgess or freeman on pain of £5 erect any cottage or convert any building into a cottage in the town without license of the Mayor, that no burgess or freeman, without a license, receive any one from the country as a tenant, that every landlord be bound in the sum of £10 to remove all foreign tenants who have entered in the last three years before May 1st next." What most boroughs do for themselves is finally, after many regulations have been made by the Common Council, done for London by Parliamentary legislation. It is not a chance that the end of Elizabeth's reign sees the first two Housing Acts, one[484] in 1589, enacting that only one family may live in a house, the other[485] applying to London alone, and forbidding the division of houses into tenements, the receiving of lodgers, or the erection of new houses for persons who are assessed in the subsidy book at less than £5 in goods or £3 in lands. The evicted peasants are beginning to take their revenge. They have been taking it ever since.

In the second place there is a general movement from the enclosed to the open field villages. The families displaced by enclosure cannot easily enter into industry, even if they wish to do so, for the avenue to most trades is blocked both by the Corporations and by the statutory system of a seven years' apprenticeship, which maintains professional standards at the expense of an unprivileged residuum. What they do is to follow the orthodox advice given to those who have lost their customary means of livelihood. They proceed to colonise, and to colonise in such numbers that they cannot easily be kept out. They settle as squatters on the waste lands of those manors which have not been enclosed, and which, before the waste is turned into a sheep-run, offer no obstacle to immigration. That the possibility of using the manorial waste to accommodate those who had no settled abode had occurred to statesmen as one expedient for meeting the problem of the infirm and destitute, is shown by the sanction expressly given in the Poor Law of 1597[486] to the expenditure of parish funds on the erection of cottages on the waste as residences for the impotent poor. In fact, however, the mobility of labour was becoming such that it was impossible, even if it had been desirable, to reserve those unutilised territories for the maintenance of the impotent. In spite of bitter protests from the existing inhabitants, refugees from other villages swarm down upon them in such numbers that the Act requiring four acres of land to be attached to each cottage cannot be observed, and the issuing of licences for the erection of cottages on the waste for able-bodied men, who have come with their families from a distance, becomes a regular part of the business of Quarter Sessions.[487]

[484] 31 Eliz. c. 7.
[485] 35 Eliz. c. 6.
[486] 39 Eliz. c. 3.
[487] For petitions on this subject see *Hist. MSS. Com.*, Cd. 784, pp. 81–82 (Wiltshire). The Warwickshire Quarter Sessions were much occupied with this, *e.g.* the following: "Trinity Sessions 1625. Fforasmuch as this Court was this present day informed ... by Sir Edward Marrowe, kt., and Thomas Ashley as the lords of the manor of Woolvey in this county ... that the said lords are content that William Wilcox of Woolvey in this countie shall build and erect a cottage for hys habitation hys wyfe and his small children uppon the waste within the said lordshippe, it is therefore ordered that the same being with consent of the lord as aforesaid that the same cottage shall be and continue," and later "which cottage the

Such a redistribution of the population solves one problem only to create others. Stern economists in the seventeenth century lament that the ease with which permission to build cottages on the waste is obtained encourages the existence of an improvident and idle class, which will neither work for wages nor make good use of the land. "In all or most towns where the fields lie open and are used in common, there is a new brood of upstart intruders as inmates, and the inhabitants of unlawful cottages erected contrary unto law.... Loyterers who will not usually be got to work unless they may have such excessive wages as they themselves desire."[488] The opponents of enclosure answer with some justice that, in effect, the open field villages are saddled with the destitution caused by enclosing landlords, who first ruin their tenants and then, like a modern Dock Company which relies on the Poor Rate to save its wage-bill, leave them to be supported by those places to which they are compelled to migrate.[489] The latter difficulty is indeed a very serious one, which not only is the occasion of numberless petitions[490] from villages who wish to be assisted by, or to avoid assisting, their neighbours, but on occasion converts even the country gentry into opponents of enclosure. "We further conceive," write the Justices of Nottingham to the Council, "that if depopulation may be reformed it will bring a great good to the whole Kingdom; for where homes are pulled down the people are forced to seek new habitations in other towns and countries, whereof those towns where they get a settling are pestered so as they are hardly able to live one by another, and it is likewise the cause of erecting new cottages upon the waste and other places who are not able to relieve themselves ... which causes rogues and vagabonds to increase."[491] In the elaborate book of Poor Law orders published in 1631 the Government recognises the genuineness of this grievance, and, to its direction that richer parishes should contribute funds to the aid of the poor, adds a special rider pointing out that such extra contributions would come with special appropriateness from those places where there had been depopulation.

We may now summarise our view of the social effects of the changes introduced by lords of manors, and by the capitalist farmers who manage their estates. When the demesne land is enclosed and converted to pasture, there is an appreciable diminution in the demand for labour, and consequently an increase in unemployment. When the common rights of tenants are curtailed, they lose not only an important subsidiary source of income, but often, at the same time, the means of cultivating their arable holdings. When their holdings are merged in the great estate of the capitalist farmer, they are turned adrift to seek their living in a world

---

Court doth licence" (*Warwick Quarter Sessions MSS. Records*).

[488] "Considerations Concerning Common Fields and Enclosures," Pseudonismus, 1654.

[489] Moore, *The Crying Sin of England in not Caring for the Poor*: "And now alas, saith the poor cottier, there is no work for me, I must go where I may get my living. And hence it comes to pass that the open fielden towns have above double the number of cottiers they had wont to have, so that they cannot live one by another, and so put the fielden towns to vast expense, in caring for these poor that these enclosures have made."

[490] *e.g. Hist. MSS. Com.*, Cd. 784, p. 95 (Wiltshire), pp. 292 and 298 (Worcester).

[491] See Appendix I., No. VI. Miss Leonard (*Trans. Royal Hist. Soc.*, vol. xix.) prints this document as referring to Norfolk, which appears to be an error.

where most trades and most towns are barred against them, where they are punished if they do not find work, and punished if they look for work without permission, where "if the poor being thrust out of their houses go to dwell with others, straight we catch them with the Statute of Inmates; if they wander abroad, they are in danger of the Statute of the Poor to be whipped."[492] Thus, quite apart both from the eternal source of poverty which consists in the recalcitrance of nature to human effort, and from those causes of individual destitution which in all ages and in all economic conditions lie in wait for the exceptionally unfortunate or the exceptionally improvident, for the sick, the aged, and the orphan, there is an increase in the number of those for whom access to the land, their customary means of livelihood, is unobtainable, and consequently a multiplication of the residuum for whom the haunting insecurity of the propertyless modern labourer is, not the exception, but the normal lot. It is this extension of destitution among able-bodied men, who have the will, but not the means, to find employment, which is the peculiar feature of sixteenth century pauperism, and which leads in 1576 to the most characteristic expedient of the Elizabethan Poor Law—the provision of materials upon which the unemployed can be set to work. The recognition that the relief of the destitute must be enforced as a public obligation was not the consequence of the survival of mediæval ideas into an age where they were out of place, but an attempt on the part of the powerful Tudor state to prevent the social disorder caused by economic changes, which, in spite of its efforts, it had not been strong enough to control.

---

[492] *D'Ewes' Journal.* Speech of Cecil, 1597.

# CHAPTER III

## THE QUESTION OF TENANT RIGHT

### *(a) The Tenants at Will and the Leaseholders*

We have said above that we cannot measure the extent of the depopulation caused by enclosure, even for those years with regard to which figures are supplied us by Royal Commissions. But, after all, it is happily less important to arrive at an exact statistical estimate of the acres enclosed and of the number of tenants displaced, than it is to get a general view of the economic forces at work and of the structure of legal relationships upon which they operated. Given the economic reasons for the consolidation of holdings which were dominant in the sixteenth century, they could hardly have failed to result in evictions on a considerable scale, unless the tenants themselves had sufficient legal security to hold their own. If they had such security, the statistical analysis of displacements given above will fall into line with the general situation and be a valuable comment upon it. If they had not, then the figures, while a useful guide to the imagination, may stand when they confirm, but hardly when they contradict, the picture given by contemporaries. The accounts of the latter, though still not freed from the charge of exaggeration, will be supported by what we know of the general disposition of economic and legal forces. They probably heighten the colour and sharpen the outlines, but their indication of tendencies will be correct.

In discussing the position of the small cultivator in the sixteenth century it was pointed out above that similarity of legal status was compatible with the greatest economic variety, and in considering their ability to resist attempted eviction it is essential to remember the converse truth, that tenants who were economically in a similar position were often from the point of view of tenure very different. Just as writers of the time lump together all classes of well-to-do small landholders under the name of yeomen, though the majority of them were not legally yeomen at all, so they constantly speak of evictions, ruinous fines, and rack-rents, without discriminating between the different classes of tenants whose different legal positions make them liable to suffer in very different degrees. One must remember, again, that in the sixteenth century a man might be called a copyholder because he held a copyhold tenement, but at the same time he might have, and very often had, additional land which he had leased from the demesne or from the waste, and in which his legal interest was quite different; he might be a freeholder and at the same time be the farmer who leased the lord's demesne, or he might be freeholder, copyholder, and leaseholder in one, and even hold at the will of the lord other land which he had been allowed to occupy "by grant of the court," for example part of the manorial waste. Hence not only were the positions of tenants at will, lessees, and copyholders considered as classes, different from each other, but there was also a difference in the legal interest which individuals had in different parts of the lands which they cultivated. Even if the law gave protection to copyholders, a point to be discussed later, they might suffer from the consolidation into large farms of those parts of their lands which they did not hold by copy, and the more they had gained in preceding years by adding to their holdings of customary land by leasing part of the demesne and of the waste, the heavier would be their loss when these additions were taken from them, while those whose holdings consisted entirely of such encroachments would be altogether ruined. Again, on those few manors where tenure at the will of the lord had not crystallised into copyhold, the tenant's position was even weaker than that of the lessee, for there was nothing but a custom unenforced by legal documents to prevent his eviction.

There was thus opportunity for a considerable displacement of population without any need of raising the difficult question of the degree of security enjoyed by copyhold tenure. When a manor was occupied only by tenants at will without copies, or when its demesne lands were leased for short terms to a number of lessees, or when its waste had been gradually taken in either by new settlers or by the customary tenants, land could be resumed by the lord without any conflict save, in the first case, with a custom which two centuries before had been powerful but now was weak, and in the second case with a terminable interest. It is not necessary to adduce instances to prove the liability of the tenant at will or lessee to eviction, because the nature of their interest makes it obvious that they could not claim to have complete legal security. Examples of the first kind are, indeed, not very common, owing to the fact that by our period tenure at will of the lord had in most places hardened into copyhold, and their comparative rarity may suggest that tenants at will who had not become copyholders had been displaced on most manors by the beginning of the century. The case of two Wiltshire manors may serve to illustrate their position. At Knyghton[493] the whole manor was in 1554 leased to a farmer, and with the manor the rents and service of six customary tenants holding at will. At Domerham,[494] in 1568, almost the whole of the land was in the hands of three large farmers, but "it has been granted to Richard Compton, Thomas Pryce, John Pryce, and Robert Kynge, to sow of the above said land every year 120 acres." In the second case the precariousness of the tenants' position is obvious; they are mere squatters, who are there, as it were, on sufferance. In the first case it has been recognised and mitigated, as far as the farmer is concerned, by a clause in his agreement binding him to leave the tenants in peaceable enjoyment as long as they pay their rents. But they have no security as against the lord, and are liable to immediate eviction if it proves more profitable to add their holdings to the large farm. When tenants commence an action against a lord for wrongful disseisin, it is sufficient for him to answer that they are "but his tenantry at wyll."[495]

Much more numerous, however, than the tenants at will, were the small lease-

[493] Roxburghe Club, *Surveys of Pembroke Manors.*
[494] *Ibid.*
[495] Leadam, *English Hist. Rev.,* vol. viii. pp. 684–696.

holders who held part of the waste or of the demesne lands. A glance at the table given on page 25 will show that they form about 12 per cent. of the whole manorial population therein represented. But in parts of the country their numbers are far greater. In 1568 they form 20 per cent. of the landholders on four manors in Somersetshire and one in Devonshire.[496] In two villages in Northamptonshire[497] they form nearly two-thirds. On the great manor of Rochdale there are in 1626 as many as 315 leaseholders to 64 freeholders and 233 copyholders. Leaseholders possessed, of course, legal security during the period of their leases, and these were in some cases for as long as ninety-two years. But they, too, had not an interest in the land of the kind which would enable them to offer any permanent barrier to the policy of consolidating holdings. This fact, indeed, was the motive for the care which surveyors showed in discriminating between those parts of the tenants' holdings which were customary land and those which were made up of pieces taken from the demesne or from the waste, as well as for the desire to convert copyhold tenure into leases for years, which was often shown in the sixteenth century by the manorial officials. For an example illustrating the eviction of numerous small tenants who had leased the demesne we may recur to the case of Ablode[498] which has been mentioned above. The lease of that manor to a farmer made by the monastery of St. Peter's in 1516 expressly provided that he should be allowed to get rid of the lessees, to whom the demesne lands had previously been let, as soon as their leases should have expired. Two other examples show the same class encountering exactly the same difficulty under somewhat different circumstances. The first, which relates to the waste, not to the demesne lands, comes from a survey of the lordship of Bromfield and Gale which was made by the Parliamentary surveyors in 1649.[499] "The inclosures before mentioned," they say, "and all the rest of them within the lordship of Bromfield and Gale, fall to the lord of the soyle, because enclosed without license. For although by their fee farm estate they [*i.e.* the tenants] may challenge freedome of commoning, it is by the covenant of the grant as formerly and antiently was accustomed, so that they must take a new grant of all (except some old inclosures which are included in their fee farms), which is the custom of the lordshippe. *And if they should enclose all their common, yet the lord would have a third part.*" The second illustration is given by a petition which some leasehold tenants of Whitby Strand[500] promoted in the Court of Requests in the year 1553. When the monastery of Whitby was dissolved, its property passed first to the Crown, which disposed of it to the Duke of Northumberland, who in turn sold it to Sir John Yorke. The sufferings of the tenants may be told in their own words: "Which saide Sir John, of his extort power and might and by great and sore threatenings of the said tennants ... hathe gotten from them all the leases ... and unreasonably hathe raised rents ... and in consideration also that the said Sir

[496] *Ibid.*, Paynton, Stooke Trister and Cucklington, Donyett, Chedseye, South Brent and Huish. The leases at South Brent are for ninety-two years.

[497] They are Duston in 1561 (R.O. Rentals and Surreys, Portf. 13, No. 23), and Paulspurie in 1541 (*ibid.*, vol. ccccxix., fol. 3).

[498] See pp. 204 and 210.

[499] MS. Transcript by A.N. Palmer of Survey of Lordship of Bromfield and Gale in Wrexham Free Library.

[500] Selden Society, *Select Cases in the Court of Requests.*

John York is a man of power and might, landes, goodes and possessions; greatly frendid.... Your poor oratours ... are not able to sue against him," and petition the Court for redress. The reality of their grievance is shown sufficiently by the fact that whereas, when the estate was in the hands of the monastery, the total rents of twenty-six tenants amounted to £28, 19s. 8½d., an average of about £1, 2s. 1d. per tenant, by the date of these complaints the rents alone, apart from fines, had been forced up to £64, 9s. 9d., averaging per tenant £2, 6s. 6d.

What is the conclusion to be drawn from these three examples? It is surely the special precariousness in the conditions of the sixteenth century of all those tenants whose livelihood lies mainly in land which has been taken from the demesne or from the waste, which is, in fact, in the words of Fitzherbert,[501] "a new thing that hath not gone by custom," a thing which may "fortune to increase or decrease of rent." A piece of demesne may have been let out on lease at a low rent in the year following the great plague, or have been taken from the waste at an even earlier date. It may have remained in the hands of one family for a century without being resumed by the lord, and without any attempt being made to increase the tenants' payments. It may have been cleared and cleaned, hedged and ditched, by the sweat of generations. But, if the manorial officials have done their duty, that land has been marked as a "new thing," something for which no custom can be pleaded and which no prescription can protect. When the lord wishes to alter the condition of its tenure no vested interest can stand against him. He will throw it into a large farm, or double the rent, and the tenants can say nothing; for they are mere lessees, unprotected by the sanctity of manorial custom, and to have his way he need only wait till their leases expire. That this is no impossible supposition is shown by the records of the manor of Hewlington.[502] In 1562 an inquiry was made into the rights of the tenants there, who seem to have been lessees for the term of forty years with a right of renewal to the heir. On investigation being made by the officers of the Crown, to whom the manor belonged, it was found that there was "a decay of the sum of one hundred and five pounds, six shillings, yearly rent, which in ancient tymes had been answered for the said landes"; which decay "as by the auncient records appeareth, did growe by reason of the great mortalitie and plague which in former tymes had been in the reign of Edward III. and also of the Rebellion of Owen Glendower and trouble that therefrom ensued; ... by reason of which mortalitie and rebellion the country was wasted, the Tenants and their houses destroyed, insomuch that the then lords of the soyle were constrayned by their stewards and officers to graunte the said landes at a lesser rent than formerlie was paid for the same to such as could be gotten to take it." Two hundred years after the great plague, its effect in reducing the rents of a few tenants on the Welsh Border is remembered: a commission calculates the sum due to the last penny, and is then required and authorised "to revise the said decayed rent," a fact which the jurors of the manor duly record in their presentment made another sixty years later. No doubt the Crown has an unusually good memory—*nullum tempus occurrit regi*. But what the Crown can do on this grand scale the surveyors of smaller lords do on a smaller one. As soon as the time has come when it is convenient to

[501] Fitzherbert, *Book of Surveying*, p. 32.
[502] For reference, see p. 130, note 253.

get rid of tenants, nothing but the most unassailable title can stand against the proof that such and such a plot of land was once part of the lord's demesne or of the lord's waste. And this, one may suspect, was a great change, which affected many families who thought themselves as safe as their neighbours. For at least two centuries before enclosing became general enough to cause alarm, the demesne and waste lands on one manor after another had been nibbled away by small encroachments; for lords had been glad to find an alternative to the cultivation of the former through labour services, and the colonising of the latter, though sometimes a source of complaint with commoners whose rights of pasture were curtailed, was welcomed by the manorial authorities as a means of improving lands which would otherwise be useless. Both together had been in fact a sort of reservoir of land upon which any surplus population could draw, and from which the more prosperous of the customary tenants could lease additions to their holdings in the manner described above. In our period the tendency is reversed. A lord is anxious to get rid of the obstruction which the small farmer's lease offers to the consolidation of holdings. He wishes to follow the advice of experts and "reduce his demeans into one entier ferme."[503] Titles are questioned, and the small lessee, whose interest is a terminable one and unprotected by any manorial custom, is the first to suffer.

### (b) The Copyholders[504]

But were the tenants at will and the leaseholders the only classes to be evicted? No allusion has yet been made to the most difficult problem which confronts the student of the sixteenth century agrarian changes—the degree of protection enjoyed by the copyholders. If this problem is the most difficult it is also one of the most important. As far as can be calculated, the copyholders far exceeded in number upon most manors all other classes of tenants together. Copyhold tenure was the rule, and tenure at will and leasehold were generally the exception, though the latter was an important exception. If all copyholders had complete security, and were readily protected in their holdings by the courts, there would be little sense in talking of an agrarian revolution; for the changes, though they might still have caused much individual suffering, could hardly have constituted anything like the serious national danger which they were thought to be by many contemporaries. Again, the copyholders were in a special sense the kernel of a manor, the representatives of an ancient social system, around which the newer relationships of leasehold were, so to speak, comparatively modern accretions. It was with them and their business that the manorial courts were concerned; a copyhold tenement could not exist apart from a manor because surrender and admission in the manorial court was essential to its recognition as copyhold; and the very name of "customary tenants," by which copyholders were often described, suggests the special antiquity and fixity of their position. Even in the sixteenth century there were still manors where there were no tenants at all except copyholders, and the mere shedding of the outer layers of small leaseholders, who had sprung up around them,

---

[503] *Topographer and Genealogist*, vol. i., survey of Mudford and Hinton.

[504] In the following section on copyholders I have been guided largely by Dr. Savine's article in the *Quarterly Journal of Economics*, vol. xix.

would have left the organisation of such manors quite intact. It would have cut back recent developments; it would not have shaken rural society very seriously. One's view of the importance of the agrarian changes of the sixteenth century will depend, therefore, to a great extent, upon the opinion which is formed of the legal position of the copyholders.

The problem centres in the question to what extent a copyholder who was threatened with eviction could obtain protection from the courts. It is not at all easy to extract a definite answer on this point from the writers of the period, whose views as to the degree of security enjoyed by copyhold are often inconsistent with each other, and sometimes seem to be inconsistent with themselves. The layman certainly thought that copyhold tenants could be and were evicted, and this view seems to be supported by Fitzherbert.[505] It is true that he draws a sharp distinction between the customary land, the rent of which cannot be altered, and the new intakes from the waste or the demesne, the rent of which can be forced up at the lord's pleasure. But he expressly states that copyhold tenants cannot get protection from the courts: "These manners of tennants shall not plede nor be impleded of their tenements by the king's writte"; and he implies elsewhere that the lord can increase both rent and fines. Kitchin,[506] on the other hand, thinks that the lord can never increase the amount of the admission fine; while Coke,[507] in a well-known passage, emphasises the copyholder's security as long as he makes no breach in the custom by failing in his services, and points out that he can protect himself either by proceedings in Chancery or by a writ of trespass.

It is not surprising, in view of the variety of opinion as to the copyholders' status which obtained in the sixteenth century, that there should have been much disagreement about it among historians. It seems possible, however, at any rate to narrow the limits of conjecture by ruling certain theories out of account. In the first place one can hardly now accept the view put forward by Mr. Leadam,[508] that, at any rate after 1467, all copyholders had complete legal security, as complete, it would appear, as freehold, though guaranteed by different remedies. He holds that copyholders who occupied customary land, and who were "tenants at will according to the custom of the manor," could get redress either by petition in the Court of the lord with an appeal to Chancery, or by an action of trespass in the Common Pleas, the classes who suffered from eviction being "tenants at will at Common Law," who, though sometimes described as inferior copyholders, were not really copyholders at all, because they did not occupy the lands set apart as customary lands. This view, according to which the lord could clear off his estate all the newer copyhold tenancies on the demesne or waste, but was debarred by the courts from touching the tenancies on the customary land of the manor, receives a certain support from the great pains shown by the manorial authorities in distinguishing between the two. But, while it rightly emphasises the special features of the tenure of customary land, it is difficult to reconcile what we actually know of the position of copyholders with this theory as to the complete security

[505] Fitzherbert, *Book of Surveying*, p. 28.
[506] Kitchin, *Court Leet*.
[507] Coke, *The Complete Copyholder*.
[508] Leadam, *Trans. Royal Hist. Soc.*, New Series, vol. vi.

of copyhold tenure. To the objection that contemporaries who could hardly have been mistaken certainly supposed that copyholders suffered, Mr. Leadam would, no doubt, answer that they were thinking of the "inferior copyholders" who held pieces of the demesne or waste. But this answer has got to meet difficulties which are really overwhelming. On the one hand, the historical confirmation which Mr. Leadam seeks, by trying to trace the distinction postulated back into the remote regions of tenure in villeinage, can no longer be accepted now that the difference between villeinage "regardant" and villeinage "en gros," on which he relies, has been proved to refer not to differences in the tenure by which the serfs held their lands, but simply to different methods of pleading, which have nothing to do with the question of the tenant's security, but merely with the form in which cases were argued in the courts.[509] On the other hand, it cannot be made to fit the facts of the copyholders' position in the sixteenth century. The truth is that copyholders were not safe even on the sacred customary land itself. It is quite certain that a great many copyholds were not copyholds of inheritance, but copyholds for life, which returned into the hands of the lord with the death of every tenant. It is certain also, as will be shown later, that fines for admission to customary holdings were on some manors raised enormously during the sixteenth century. How can one reconcile these facts with the view that the lord could make no alteration in the treatment of the customary land which would jeopardise the copyholders' interest?

Nor is it easy to accept the sharply contrasted theory of Professor Ashley.[510] Where Mr. Leadam sees absolute security of tenure guaranteed by the courts, Professor Ashley sees absolute insecurity mitigated by a once powerful but now decaying custom. In the past, when the lord's land had been dependent on labour services for its cultivation, the last thing he wanted to do was to get rid of the tenants, and therefore custom had made it a rule of practice, though not of law, that first villein, and then copyhold, tenements should pass in the manorial court from father to son. But just when this custom was on the way to become law through the action of the courts in extending protection to copyholders, changed economic conditions made pasture farming much more profitable than tillage, and so supplied landowners with a strong motive for breaking it down. In the struggle which followed custom and public opinion were on the side of the tenants, but the law was on the side of the landlords, and copyholders were evicted without being able to obtain any legal redress, not merely through ignorance or intimidation, but because no legal protection was offered them by the courts. There is perhaps only one serious objection to this ingenious theory. But that is insuperable. It is that in certain circumstances, at any rate, the courts did in fact offer protection to copyholders who were threatened with eviction. In the fifteenth century a considerable number of cases came before the Court of Chancery. In the sixteenth century the same business, which in view of the number of copyholders must have been a lucrative one, came before the Common Law Courts. The case of the year 1482,[511] which is quoted by Professor Ashley to show the hesitation which the judges felt as to whether a copyholder had any legal remedy, is really one of a long series

---

[509] Vinogradoff, *Villainage in England,* pp. 48–56.

[510] Ashley, *Economic History,* Part I., vol. ii. pp. 274–282.

[511] Coke upon Littleton, 60 b.

in which the courts considered the claims of copyholders, and which Coke must have had in mind when he said, "Now copyholders stand upon a sure ground: now they weigh not their lord's displeasure, they shake not at every sudden blast of wind, they eat, drink, sleep securely ... let the lord frown, the copyholder cares not, knowing himself safe, and not within any danger."[512] To overlook that series of cases is really to misread a change of the first importance, a change which almost amounted to a legal revolution. Suppose that at the present day the courts were to begin to protect the "tenant right" of workmen who have given their lives to a trade by ruling that any man dismissed after fifteen years continuous service should either be reinstated or receive compensation? The change would be greater—but would it be much greater?—than the momentous departure that was made by the judges who for the first time decided that a man impleaded for a villein tenement should have an action in Chancery. For centuries such actions could not be brought, and if brought would have been simply sent back to the court of the manor with the endorsement "our lord the king does not interfere in matters of villeinage."[513] Now the tide is reversed. From 1439 onwards a stream of equitable jurisdiction flows out from the Chancery to secure the title of the very class which has hitherto had no legal title at all. Tenure in villeinage becomes copyhold. Clearly the discovery of these cases by Dr. Savine[514] must alter the whole standpoint from which we view the struggle between lords and copyholders in the sixteenth century. If one must reject the view of Mr. Leadam that copyholders on customary land had complete legal security, one must also, it would seem, reject the view of Professor Ashley that the courts never interfered in their favour. Somehow or another one must reconcile a good deal of insecurity with a good deal of protection, the complaints of contemporaries that copyholders suffered from enclosures with the equally indisputable fact that they were fairly often protected by the law.

A way leading some distance through this apparent contradiction may, perhaps, be found by recurring to that dependence upon manorial custom which is the characteristic feature of copyhold. A copyholder is a tenant by copy of Court Roll according to the custom of the manor, and this custom is primarily what regulates his rights and obligations. The custom must be an immemorial one; mere prescription is not custom; to be binding it must have "been used time out of mind." Given such a custom, it is this upon which the nature of the copyholder's tenure depends; and it is noticeable that authorities who differ as to the practical outcome of it, all agree that it is with custom that the first appeal lies. But the custom of a manor is a particular and individual thing peculiar to that manor, and determining the relations between lord and tenant there and not elsewhere. In the words of a surveyor, "Their customs are not so universall as if a man have experyence of the customs and services of any mannor he shall thereby have perfect knowledge of all the rest, or if he be experte of the customes of any one mannor in any one countie that he shall nede no further enstruccions for all the residewe of the

---

[512] Coke, *The Complete Copyholder*.

[513] Note-book of Bracton pl., 1237: "Dominus rex non vult se de eis intromittere" (quoted Vinogradoff, *Villainage in England*, p. 46, note 2).

[514] On this point see *English Hist. Review*, vol. viii. p. 296.

mannors within that countie."[515] There are several different sets of customs, and therefore several different sorts of copyhold. There are, in fact, copyholders and copyholders, and there is no general law of copyhold because its essence is to be local and peculiar. The first question, therefore, which has got to be asked, when considering the question of the legal security of copyholders, relates to the custom of the manor on which they are found; for probably, if the parties go to law, this is the first question which will be asked by the court. If it is shown that in getting rid of a tenant the lord has broken the custom of the manor, there is much likelihood in the sixteenth century that the court will restore it. If this is not shown, there is little probability that the court will go behind the custom in favour of the tenants, or try to harmonise it with general principles of equity, except in so far as it declines to take account of customs which are held to be "unreasonable," a word too vague to be much protection to a tenant or much hindrance to a lord. It is this tremendous importance of local custom which causes it to be so minutely entered in manorial documents, and which results both in the constant appeals which are made to it when cases come before the courts, and in the careful recording of contradictory opinions. Surveyors are at pains to emphasise the difference between land which is customary land and land which is not, because, while on the former the introduction of new conditions will be followed by all sorts of friction and disturbance, on the latter the tenants will have no case in opposing them. It is here that Mr. Leadam's distinction between holders of customary land and holders of land taken from the waste or the demesne becomes of real value. It is a particular exemplification of a general rule, the rule that the appeal is always to custom. The meaning of the distinction is not, as Mr. Leadam seems to suggest, that copyholders on the former always had legal protection and copyholders on the latter always had not. It is that the crucial question is always, "What sort of custom are you under?" and that, while on the customary holdings the custom *may* be unfavourable to the tenant's security, it is much more likely to be unfavourable on the newer tenancies formed on land which, perhaps within the memory of persons living, was indubitably the lord's own, not merely in the general sense in which even the villein's land had been the lord's, but in the practical sense that it was part of his demesne to use as he pleased. In fact quite a common answer when copyholders bring an action is the statement that the land in question is not ancient copyhold but part of the demesne;[516] and when the Protector Somerset applied his popular

---

[515] *Topographer and Genealogist*, vol. i. The surveyor is Humberstone.

[516] *Calendar of Proceedings in Chancery in the Reign of Ed. VI.*, vol. i. p. cxxxvii.: "To the Right Honourable Sir Richard Riche, Kt., Lord Riche and Lord Chancellor of England. In humble wise sheweth and complaineth unto your lordeshippe your daley orator Richard Cullyer of Wymondham ... yeoman, and John Cullyer his son," that whereas they "were admitted tenants (of 20 acres) to hold the same to them and their heirs ... and contynued seased of the said 20 acres as of fee, as tenants at will, by copy of Court Roll" now "Thomas Knyvett, Esq. ... of late claimed 10 acres of the said 20 acres to be the demeanes of the said manor." Knyvett (i.) answers, "The said lond ys and have been tyme out of mynde parcell of the demeanes of the moytie of the said manor of Cromwell." (ii.) Denies that "the premises have been used to be dymytted or be dymittable by copie of Court Roll for term of lyfe or lyves as in fee"; on the contrary "yt may appear that the same have been letten by term of yeres."

agrarian policy to his own estates he had to get Parliament to pass a special Act to give the copyholders on his demesnes peculiar security.[517]

The significance of custom is shown in other ways as well. In the numerous petitions in Chancery addressed by copyholders their demand is constantly for a recital or confirmation of manorial customs, and the same line is taken in the fewer cases which come before the Courts of Common Law. Tenants who claim an estate of inheritance and a fixed fine on admission refuse in a body to show their copies to the surveyors, presumably for fear that, if they do, some excuse may be made to upset the custom.[518] Tenants will perjure themselves as to the nature of the custom of their manor in order to be thought to have estates of inheritance. In the days when copyholders (if they exist at all) are still very few and villeins many, men who are really villeins of St. Peter's of Exeter come forward and swear falsely that they hold in socage, "intending all to say that they hold and ought to hold *de stipite in stipitem*, Anglice stock after stock";[519] but the falsehood is exposed, and they are punished with a fine of 30s. The copyhold tenants on the Northumbrian manor of Amble claim in the sixteenth century that manorial custom requires that the next of kin of the whole blood shall succeed his father, and that the fines shall be limited to two years' rent. But the surveyors repudiate their claim, remarking that "we cannot find that they have any such estate of inheritance."[520] Elsewhere the copyholders are more fortunate, and succeed in inducing the manorial authorities themselves to make formal admission of the custom, or in proving its existence to the satisfaction of the courts. In 1567 the Dean and Chapter of Winchester Cathedral, and the one hundred and fifty-eight copyhold tenants on their manor of Crondal, enter into a solemn covenant and bargain—may we not call it a "collective bargain"?—whereby it is agreed that fixed rents, fixed fines, and copyholds of inheritance, "shall be from henceforth for ever accepted, reputed, deamed, and taken to be vearye trewe, just, certaine, and auncient customs, rights, dewtyes, and useages, between the Lorde and the Customarye tenants ...; and shall from henceforth stand, contynewe, remayne, and be of perfect force and strength to conclude and bynde the said Deane and Chapiter, their successors and assignees of the said mannour and hundred and everye parte thereof for ever."[521] The tenants at Elswick[522] go to law with the lord of the manor on the question of the nature of their estates, and, on the records of a custom requiring the admission of a son on his father's death being produced, the custom is confirmed by the court.

----

[517] In 1548 an Act was passed "for the assurance to the tenants of graunts and leases made for the Duke of Somerset's demesne lands." It begins, "Whereas of truth noe custom or usage can or maye by the lawes of this realm be annexed or knytt to any meases, lands, tenements, or hereditaments letten by copye of Court Roll ... albeyt those words 'secundum consuetudinem manerii,' be rehearsed and expressed in the saide Court Rolle or coppie had or made, except that the same meases, lands, tenements, or other hereditaments, so letten be of olde customarie or coppieholde land, and have byn used by all the tyme whereof memory of man is not to the contrary to be letten or demysed by copie of court roll."

[518] See pp. 122–123.

[519] *Hist. MSS. Com.*, Cd. 3218, p. 74. Inquisition of February 20, 1308.

[520] *Northumberland County History*, vol. v. p. 282.

[521] *Crondal Records* (Baigent), Part I. p. 177.

[522] *Northumberland County History*, vol. viii.

Even the Government of Elizabeth, favourable as it was to the small man, would not intervene without first being informed of the nature of the custom. When a tenant appeals to them for protection, they refer the matter to the local justices, with a request to "certifie their opinions of the poor man's right."[523] No doubt once the Courts begin to interfere with the internal business of a manor they tend to break down some of the peculiarities of local custom, and to set up a general pattern of copyhold tenure by ruling out certain customs as "unreasonable." Copyholders for life may not cut down timber,[524] though perhaps copyholders of inheritance may. Two and a half years' rent is held by the reign of Charles I. to be an unreasonable fine, one and a half years' to be reasonable, and the heir shall not forfeit his copyhold if he tenders such a sum when he demands admission.[525] But the definition of what is meant by "unreasonable" has been going on from that day to this, and is perhaps not yet completed. In our period it was only just beginning. At any rate we shall not be far wrong if we say that, speaking broadly, the crucial question is always whether the custom makes it easy for lords to get rid of tenants or whether it makes it difficult. If an ancient custom gives the lord a free hand, he has little trouble in getting his way. If it restricts him, the courts are likely to enforce the restriction, and though the lord still has, of course, the option of extra-legal action by way of persuasion, cajolery, or intimidation, the tenants are likely to be protected by the law.

The dependence of copyhold upon manorial custom offers an explanation of the fact that the changes of the sixteenth century displaced copyholders, although the courts would intervene when a custom which gave them security was proved

---

[523] *Acts of the Privy Council*, vol. xiii. pp. 91–92, 1581. The justices are to decide "if they thinke it agreeable with equite and justice that the poore man should be put in possession of the said landes."

[524] Croke's *Reports*, vol. iii., Trin. 4 Caroli, Rot. dcciv. case 7. Custom that copyholder for life may cut down trees pronounced "a void and unreasonable custom and not allowable by law. For it is the destruction of the inheritance and against the nature of a copyholder for life. But peradventure there may be such a custom for a copyholder of inheritance."

[525] *Ibid.*, vol. iii., p. 198, case 8, Hill, 5 Car., Rot. 125: "The question was whether a lord of a mannor may assess two years and a half value of copyhold land according to racked rent for a fine upon surrender and admittance, and for non-payment enter for forfeiture. And all the Court conceived that one year and a half of rent improved is high enough; and the defendant assessing two years and a half it is unreasonable, and therefore the plaintiff might well refuse the payment thereof." *Ibid.*, vol. i. p. 779, case 13, takes the rule that unreasonable fines need not be paid back to 1600 ("It was holden *per curiam* that if the lord demands an unreasonable fine of his coppyholder where the fine is uncertain, if he denies it, it is not any forfeiture of his copyhold"), but his judgment does not say how many years' rent is a reasonable fine. The *Calendar of Chancery Proceedings, temp.* Eliz., is full of petitions from tenants asking the court to declare fines excessive. The rule that a fine must not exceed two years' rent does not appear to have been accepted as binding till 1781 (*Grant v. Ashe, Douglas Reports*, 722–723). But it is plain from the cases cited above that by 1600 it was recognised that some fines were unreasonable, and by 1630 that a reasonable fine should not exceed one and a half years' rent. The fact that the Chancery intervened to protect the equitable interests of copyholders earlier than the Common Law Courts leads one to suspect that there must be earlier cases than these of the Courts declaring fines unreasonable. But I have not found them.

to exist. The most important questions with regard to the custom which determined the copyholders' position were two: first, whether he had by it an estate of inheritance, or merely an estate for years, for life, or for lives; second, whether his payments were fixed or unalterable, or whether they could be increased at the will of the lord. If it was not an estate of inheritance his holding returned fairly frequently into the hands of the manorial authorities, who could either renew it on the old terms, or lease it at an increased rent, or amalgamate it with a large farm. In the second case, where payments were variable, lords could force a tenant to throw up his land by placing a prohibitive burden upon it. The only way of ascertaining with accuracy the real position of copyholders in our period would be to show the relative proportions in which these four arrangements are found upon each of many hundred manors. And this we cannot yet do. The figures published by Dr. Savine[526] suggest that manors on which copyholders possessed an estate of inheritance, and those where they did not, were about equal in number, while manors on which the fines were uncertain predominated over those on which they were fixed in a proportion of more than two to one. Since it would seem that the ability of the lord to demand what fine he pleased could be used as a means of excluding a successor even when the copy was not merely for life or lives but from father to son, his investigations suggest that the copyholders' tenure was more often insecure than not.

To the examples which he has collected one may perhaps add certain others, inadequate though they are in point of quantity. Taking twenty-one[527] manors in the years 1568–1573, of which three are in Somersetshire, one in Devonshire, and seventeen in Wiltshire, one finds that on only one out of the whole number was the copyholders' estate one of inheritance. On one manor copies were granted for four lives or less—it is expressly stated that they are not to be granted for more—and on nineteen they are granted for three lives or less. On one manor (that where the copyholders had estates of inheritance) the fine was fixed by custom at a sum which is not stated, but which could not be increased. On the remaining twenty the fine was a variable one, the general formula being that land shall be given "for such fines as buyers can fix by bargaining with the lord or his officers, both in possession and in reversion," which means that they were to be fixed by the higgling of the market. Turning next to two manors on the Welsh[528] Border, which were in

---

[526] *Quarterly Journal of Economics*, vol. xix.

[527] Roxburghe Club, *Surveys of Pembroke Manors*. The twenty-one manors are as follows: Washerne, South Newton, North Ugford, Brudecombe, Foughlestone, Chalke, Albedeston, Chilmerke and Rugge, Staunton, Westoverton, Remesbury, Stockton, Dichampton, Berwick St. John, Wyley, North Newton, Byshopeston (all in Wilts), Donyett, Chedseye, South Brent (all in Somerset), and Paynton in Devonshire. Estates of inheritance are found at Byshopeston, and also fixed fines. At Paynton copies are granted for 4 lives or less. The common formula for fines runs: "Pro talibus finibus ut emptores et captores cum domino et officiariis suis concordare vel barganizare possunt tam de terra in possessione quam in reversione."

[528] MSS. Transcript in Wrexham Free Library by A.N. Palmer, of "The Presentment and Verdict for the Manor of Hewlington," 1620 (in which the proceedings in the reign of Elizabeth are recorded), and "The Surveys of the Town and Liberty of Holt," 1620. At Hewlington it is stated that the Crown Commissioners made an arrangement with the tenants

possession of the Crown, one is told that in the reign of Elizabeth the royal officers granted the tenants leases for years, renewable at the will of the tenant, and fixed the fine at two years' rent, thus giving them what was virtually an estate of inheritance. It is possible, however, that the Crown tenants received more favourable treatment than did those on manors which were in private hands. From Northumberland, again, there is a good deal of evidence which it is difficult to summarise. Coke stated that "the customary tenants upon the borders of Scotland ... are mere tenants at will, and though they keep their customs inviolate, yet the lord might, sans controll, evict them."[529] At the beginning of the seventeenth century an order in Chancery ruled that none of the tenants of Lady Cumberland,[530] who paid a fine on the death of lord and tenant, could have an estate of inheritance; and we have clear evidence that the fines paid by the copyhold tenants of the Earl of Northumberland[531] increased very considerably in the course of the sixteenth century. On the other hand such insecurity was not universal. A common rule on the Northumbrian border seems to have given a copyhold for life, with a tenant right of renewal to the heir, provided that a constant custom of renewal could be proved.[532] On the Crown estates in the reign of Elizabeth fines were fixed on conditions which varied from place to place; sometimes they were at discretion, sometimes one year's rent, sometimes two years' rent; and in 1609 the tenants of twelve Tynemouthshire manors got the Courts to confirm a custom limiting their fine to a definite sum, on six of them to £2 on the admission of a descendant, and £4 on alienation, and on the remaining six to one year's rent in the former case and two years' rent in the latter.[533] On eleven out of thirteen manors in Norfolk[534] and Suffolk the fines are uncertain; on one, Wighton, they are said to have been fixed at 4s. per acre "by the space of 100 years at least"; on one, Aldeburgh, there is a curious distinction between the fines paid for land "in the fields," which are

---

"that if the said tenants would relinquish these said pretended estates, revive the said decayed rents, and pay two yeres Rent of the landes to the late Queen for a fine, that then the said tenants and their heirs and assignes should have leases granted them for fortie years, and so from fortie years to fortie years in perpetuity." It is not expressly stated that the same arrangement was made at Holt, but it is to be inferred from the context that it was.

[529] Coke, *The Complete Copyholder.*

[530] *Northumberland County History*, vol. viii. p. 238.

[531] See below, pp. 305–306.

[532] *Northumberland County History*, vol. viii. pp. 238–239.

[533] *Ibid.* For conditions on the Crown estates under Elizabeth see *S. P. D. Eliz.*, vol. xii. pp. 69–70: "Abstract of the Commission to the lord Chancellor ... for letting the queen's lands and tenements in Northumberland within 20 miles of the border and in the seigniories of Middleham and Richmond, Yorkshire and Barnard Castle, Bishopric of Durham," June 24, 1565.

[534] The manors are West Lexham (Holkham MSS., West Lexham, No. 87, Map), Sparham (*ibid.*, Sparham Bdle., No. 5), East Dereham (R.O. Parliamentary Surveys, Norfolk, No. 1), Wighton (R.O. Special Commissions, Duchy of Lancs., No. 839), Stockton Socon (R.O. Parliamentary Surveys, Norfolk, No. 14), Aldeburgh (R.O. *Misc. Bks. Treas. of Receipts*, vol. clxiii.), Chatesham (R.O. *ibid.*, vol. clxiii.), Dodnash (R.O. *ibid.*, vol. clxiii.), Falkenham (R.O. *ibid.*, vol. clxiii.), Stratford iuxta Higham (R.O. Duchy of Lancaster, Rentals and Surveys, 9/13), St. Edmund (R.O. Parliamentary Surveys, Suffolk, No. 14), Mettingham (*Victoria County History*, Suffolk), Mark Soham (*ibid.*).

at the will of the lord, and the fines paid for cottage tenements, which are fixed at 2s. when the site is built upon and 1s. when the site is not covered. Elsewhere when the fine is fixed the ordinary payment seems to be usually two years' rent on descent, with sometimes a small addition, sometimes a small deduction, when the tenement is alienated during the tenant's life. Estates of inheritance and fixed fines do not necessarily go together. The general situation on the small number of manors for which information has been obtained is set out below.[535] Table I relates to duration of tenancies, Table II to the character of admission fines. In each table, line (*a*) gives Dr. Savine's figures, line (*b*) our own, line (*c*) the total of both together.

**TABLE XIII**

I

DURATION OF TENURE

| Manors. | Copyholds of Inheritance. | Copyholds for Years but with Right of Renewal (*i.e.* virtually Copyholds of Inheritance). | Copyholds for Life or Lives. | Copyholds for Years but without Right of Renewal (*i.e.* virtually Leases for Years) |
|---|---|---|---|---|
| (*a*) 82 | 25 | 17 | 40 | ... |
| (*b*) 60 | 22 | 2 | 33 | 3 |
| (*c*) 142 | 47 | 19 | 73 | 3 |

II

CHARACTER OF FINES

| Manors. | Fines Certain. | Fiines Uncertain. | Partly Certain and Partly Uncertain. |
|---|---|---|---|
| (*a*) 86 | 28 | 58 | ... |
| (*b*) 61 | 25 | 35 | 1 |
| (*c*) 147 | 53 | 93 | 1 |

It will be seen that the degree of security enjoyed by copyholders varies very greatly. When the copyhold is one of inheritance, it is legally complete, unless the tenants incur forfeiture by breaking the custom. An estate for life with right of renewal is virtually as good as a copyhold of inheritance. Estates for life or lives are precarious. Copyholds for years without right of renewal are scarcely distinguishable from leases. On the whole, when these examples are added to those of Dr. Savine, it would appear that copyholds for life or lives were more usual than copyholds of inheritance, while fixed fines were the exception and variable fines the general rule.

---

[535] See Appendix II.

## *(c) The Undermining of Customary Tenures*

The importance of the predominance of copyholds for lives for the question of the degree of security enjoyed by the tenant is shown by the efforts which were made by lords of manors, where copyholders had estates of inheritance, to persuade them to give up their copies and take leases instead. It is evident that in this course they encountered a good deal of opposition. On manors, however, where the copyholds escheated to the lord at intervals of one, two, or three lives, he could substitute leases for a regrant of the copies, or throw the holdings into a large farm, or retain them in his own hands. Though such action might be thought harsh, it could hardly be prevented by the tenants, since the lord could always hold the threat of eviction over their heads. One finds some manors where the striking and exceptional preponderance of small leaseholders suggests unmistakably that such a conversion of copyhold to leasehold has taken place,[536] or where the motive of the alteration is shown by the great rise in rents which has followed it. One finds others where the struggle between copyhold and leasehold is going on and is still undecided. In that struggle the chances are against the copyholders, even though their interest is protected by the law, for the law is less powerful than ignorance and fear. How can our peasants, men "very simple and ignorant of their estates,"[537] enter into the respective merits of copies and leases with the powers of the manor, armed with professional advice and all those indefinite but invincible advantages in bargaining which are given by legal knowledge, social influence, and a long tradition of authority? It is so easy to get caught in some legal trap. In the reign of Charles I., the two hundred Crown tenants of the manor of North Wheatley, who have suffered much in the way of rack-renting from the officers of their impecunious lord, engage a lawyer to negotiate the renewal of their leases of the demesne lands. The grant is made to him, as their attorney; but, to their dismay, they find that he declines to fulfil his bargain. He has "afterward, contrary to the Trust committed to him, increased and raised the rent thereof upon the tenants, to his owne privat benefitt."[538] The tenants of Hewlington succeed, as we have seen, in inducing the Crown to recognise their estates of inheritance by granting that their forty years' leases shall be renewable at the will of the tenants. Then unexpectedly a servant of the Earl of Leicester purchases one of the townships. The tenants, in an agony of apprehension, "perceiving that they were like

---

[536] *E.g.* Ormesby in Norfolk, where in 1516 thirty-one tenants holding "in farm" formed the whole landholding population (R.O. Rentals and Surveys, Gen. Ser., Portf. 22, No. 18). For a great rise in rents following a probable substitution of leases for customary tenures, see the case of Lewisham in Kent. On this manor in the reign of Henry VI. the rent of the tenants (tenure unspecified) was £8, 11s. 7d., 9 ploughshares, and 6s. 2½d. in the abbot's hand (R.O. Rentals and Surveys, Gen. Ser., Roll 361). In 1621 it was £23, 1s. 6½d. (R.O. *Misc. Bks. Treas. of Receipt*, vol. clxxiv., fol. 1–34). In the reign of James I. we have full details. The rent of the free tenants was £17, 12s. 10½d.; that of the tenants at will 9d.; that of tenants "per dimissionem" (*i.e.* lease-holders) £72, 9s. 8½d. (R.O. *Misc. Bks. Aug. Off.*, vol. ccccxiv., f. 33–34). It is unfortunate that we are not told how the bulk of the tenants held at the two earlier dates. But is it unreasonable to say that they were probably customary tenants, and that the introduction of leases was followed by a great rise in rents?

[537] Survey of Town and Liberty of Holt, MS. transcript in Wrexham Free Library.

[538] *S. P. D.*, ch. i. vol. cli., No. 38. (See Appendix I., No. iv.)

to have their said landes and tenements after the expiration of their said leases taken from them, and that they had no remedy by the course of the common law to helpe themselves, preferred their Bill to be relieved in Equitie." Chancery comes to their rescue. It decides that the covenant made by the Crown to the effect that their leases should be renewable at the option of the holder is binding not only on the Crown, but on all to whom it might sell the lands in question. But their troubles are not yet finished. It is one thing to get a judgment, another for the judgment to be carried out. The purchaser is servant to a great man and can afford to be dilatory and recalcitrant. We leave these villagers still petitioning "His Highness and His Honourable Council and Commissioners of Revenue that when it shall seem good unto them the said tenants may be admitted to have their leases accordingly."

It is so easy to be intimidated by the fear of aggravating your misfortunes. When an agent frightens some tenants by telling them the unfavourable decision of the Court of Chancery as to the tenant right of the copyholders on a neighbouring estate, do they answer, as they should, that manorial customs vary, and that they will see what the Courts say about their own? No, they make "Humble suit that your lordship will be pleased to grant them leases for twenty-one years, and they will pay, in lieu of their fine, double rent for every farm."[539] Sometimes they live to repent their bargain. "I have persuaded one John Wilson of Over-Buston," writes a manorial official to the Earl of Northumberland, "to deliver me in his copy, and he is content to take a lease at double rent."[540] A strange chance has left us a letter, in which this very John Wilson, labouring horribly amid the intricacies of grammar, expounds through one long, broken-backed sentence, what balm such "contentment" brings. "To the Right Honourable the Earl of Northumberland, the humble petition of John Wilson, his wife and 8 poor children. Humbly complaining showeth ... your petitioner ... that whereas your said petitioner and his predecessors being ancient tenants to your honour, holding one tenement on ferme in Upper Bustone, by virtue of copyhold tenure out of the memory of man, which copies both of your said poor petitioners' great grandfather, his father's father, and his own father are yet extant to be seen: and now of late your said poor petitioner, being under age, helpless and none to do for him, and forced (God knows) by some of your honour's officers to take a lease and pay double and treble rent, in so much that your said poor petitioner, his wife, and 8 poor children is utterly now beggared and overthrown, unless your worthy good honour will be pleased to take a pitiful communication thereof, or otherwise your saide poore petitioner, his wife and poore children knows no other way but of force to give over your honour's land, by reason of the deare renting thereof, and so be constrained to go a-begging up and down the countrie."[541] Poor, patient, stiff-fingered John Wilson, so certain that he has not been treated fairly, so confident that his lordship cannot have meant him to be wronged, so easily circumvented by his lordship's brisk officials! He and his heavy kind are slow to move; but, once roused, they will not easily be persuaded to go back. It was such as he that, at one time or another in the sixteenth century, set half the English counties ablaze with the grievances of

---

[539] *Northumberland County History*, vol. viii. p. 238.
[540] *Ibid.*, vol. v. p. 211. The rent was raised from 18s. to 36s.
[541] *Northumberland County History*, vol. v. p. 210.

the tillers of the soil.

The significance of the predominance of variable fines is very evident if one turns to examine the economic relations between lords and copyhold tenants as they stood in the middle of the sixteenth century. A manor on which there was a large number of customary tenants must have often seemed from the point of the owner a rather disappointing form of property, because the first fruits of economic progress tended to pass into the hands of the tenants. The rents and services due from their holdings were fixed by custom; meanwhile prices were rising with the fall in the value of silver, and the result, as is pointed out by Maitland, was that the economic rent or unearned increment of their properties was intercepted by the copyholders, instead of being drained, as under leasehold, into the pocket of the lord.

An explanation of what is meant can best be given by recurring to the table of rents printed in Chapter III. of Part I. It will be recollected that on the manors there represented the value of the rents got by the lords from the customary tenants was often almost stationary. When the enormous fall in the purchasing power of money is remembered, it is clear that rentals must sometimes have very greatly depreciated, which of course meant that the tenants retained the surplus due to economic progress, a surplus measured by the difference between the "rents of assize" and the full rack-rent for which the holding could be let if put up to competition, and amounting sometimes to more than three-quarters of the latter. At Wilburton, for example (to quote a fresh instance), according to Maitland,[542] a virgate worth £7 or £8 only pays £1 in rent. From the competitive rents of the open market the lord was debarred by the custom of the manor. How could he tap the surplus? He did so, it may be suggested, either by inducing the tenants to exchange their copies for leases, or by raising the fines, when the fines were not fixed by custom, so as to get in a lump sum what he could not get by yearly instalments. In that case the tenant's surplus was on paper only; he was exactly in the position of an investor in a stock of inflated value, the high nominal interest of which has been capitalised in the price paid for the shares. The probability that when fines were movable, they were forced up in the sixteenth century so as to sweep away any unearned increment accruing to the holders of customary land, is not only suggested by the bitter denunciations launched against the practice by contemporaries. It is also indicated by the manorial documents. May not this be the explanation of what Maitland justly calls "the absurdly high price" of £1261 paid in the reign of James I. by the purchasers of Wilburton, a manor the yearly value of which was at the time only £33? The suggestion is confirmed, as far as a few manors are concerned, by the upward movement of fines revealed by the following table—

**FINES PAID ON THREE MANORS IN NORTHUMBERLAND[543]**

|  | 1567. | 1585. |
|---|---|---|
| Acklington | £57, 3s. 8d. or £3, 3s. 4d. | £87, 10s. 0d. or £4, 17s. 2d. |

---

[542] Maitland, *English Historical Review*, vol, ix., "The History of a Cambridgeshire Manor."

[543] *Northumberland County History*, vol. v.

|              | per tenant. | per tenant. |
|--------------|-------------|-------------|
| High Buston  | £11, 14s. 0d. or £2, 18s. 6d. | £18, 0s. 0d. or £4, 10s. 0d. |
|              | per tenant. | per tenant. |
| Birling      | £43, 7s. 6d. or £4, 6s. 9d. | £72, 0s. 0d. or £7, 4s. 0d. |
|              | per tenant. | per tenant. |

### FINES PER ACRE PAID ON SIX MANORS[544] IN WILTS AND ONE IN SOMERSET

1520–39, average fine per acre for each of 42 tenants . . . 1s.   3d.

1540–39, average fine per acre for each of 28 tenants . . . 2s.   11d.

1550–59, average fine per acre for each of 36 tenants . . . 5s.   6d.

1560–69, average fine per acre for each of 36 tenants . . . 11s.  0d.

The figures show a steady upward movement during the third and fourth decades of the century of a little over 100 per cent., a rather less rapid rise between 1549 and 1559, and another rise of 100 per cent. between 1559 and 1569. They are of course too small to be the basis of a wide generalisation, but perhaps they may be held to offer some documentary confirmation of a grievance which bulks large in the literature of the period. The elasticity of fines at any rate corrects the impression which would be formed of the tenants' position from looking only at the comparatively stationary rents. The same tendency is suggested by the details of individual copies. It was a not uncommon practice for a tenant who was in possession and had an estate for life to buy at a later date the right of his heir to succeed him. When this was done we have an opportunity of comparing the fines paid at different periods, and the complaints of contemporaries about unreasonable and excessive fines become intelligible. This may be illustrated by a few extreme instances taken from the manors of Estoverton and Donnington in Wiltshire, and of South Brent in Somersetshire.

|     | Fine for Copy. | | Fine for Reversion. | |
|-----|------|--------|-------------|--------|
| 1.  | 6/8   | (1537) | £5          | (1563) |
| 2.  | 40/—  | (1537) | £13, 6s. 8d. | (1566) |
| 3.  | 54/4  | (1537) | £23         | (1561) |
| 4.  | 60/—  | (1537) | £30         | (1565) |
| 5.  | 20/—  | (1537) | £10         | (1561) |
| 6.  | 20/—  | (1529) | £40         | (1563) |
| 7.  | 33/4  | (1542) | £20         | (1565) |
| 8.  | 66/8  | (1522) | £20         | (1563) |
| 9.  | 13/4  | (1516) | £13, 6s. 8d. | (1563) |

[544] Roxburghe Club, *Surveys of Pembroke Manors*. The manors are South Newton, Washerne, Donnington, Winterbourne Basset, Estoverton and Phipheld, Byshopeston (all Wilts), and South Brent and Huish (Somerset).

| 10. | 40/— | (1513) | £40 | (1565) |
|---|---|---|---|---|
| 11. | 46/8 | (1531) | £20 | (1563) |
| 12. | 6/8 | (1545) | £20 | (1565) |
| 13. | £5, 6s. 8d. | (1545) | £20 | (1558) |
| 14. | £9 | (1532) | £12 | (1557) |

Though these are extreme cases, a considerable rise is the rule and not the exception. The advantage of the fixed rent is in fact neutralised by the movable fine. Such figures give point to Crowley's outbursts, "They take our houses over our heads; they buye our groundes out of handes, they reyse our rents, they levy great, yea unreasonable fines."[545] It is not surprising that the programme[546] of agrarian reform put forward by the Yorkshire insurgents in 1536, and by the rebels under Ket in 1549, should have contained a demand for copyhold lands "to be charged with an easy fine, as a capon or a reasonable sum of money." It is not surprising that the Court of Chancery[547] should have been bombarded with petitions to declare or enforce customs limiting the demands which a lord might make of an incoming tenant. It is perhaps more surprising that, in those cases where the fine was by custom uncertain, the rule that a reasonable fine was about two years' rent should not have been enforced by judges at an earlier date and more generally than it seems to have been. For in the sixteenth century, though many old economic ideas are going by the board, public opinion still clings to the conception that there is a standard of fairness in economic dealings which exists independently of the impersonal movements of the market, which honest men can discover, if they please, and which it is a matter of conscience for public authorities to enforce. Even a good Protestant who hates the Pope will admit that there is more than a little in the Canon Law prohibition of usury,[548] and under usury, be it noted, the plain man includes rack-rents, as well as interest on capital and exorbitant prices. If to a modern economist the demand for reasonable fines and rents savours of sentimentality and confusion, he must logically condemn not only the peasants and their champions, but the statesmen; not only Ket and Hales and More and Latimer, but almost every member of every Elizabethan Privy Council. After all,

---

[545] E. E. T. S., Crowley, *The Way to Wealth*.

[546] See below, pp. 334–337.

[547] *Calendar of Proceedings in Chancery in the Reign of Edward VI.* Bills to establish a fine certain on admission and alienation, to get protection against exorbitant fines, &c. are common. For popular complaints see E. E. T. S., *A Supplication of the Poore Commons*: "These extortioners have so improved theyr lands that they make of a xls. fyne xl. pounds," &c. For an actual instance see the following case. The tenants of Austenfield claim "that of ancient time all the customary tenants of the said manor of Austenfield were finable at fines certain, until of late years the lords moved by covetousness, by troubling and vexing their copyholders, drove many of them, for the buying of their quietness, to be at fines uncertain" (William Salt Collection, vol. ix. Chancery Proceedings. Bdle. 12, No. 70).

[548] Th. Wilson, *A Discourse upon Usurie*, 1584: "And therefore I would not have men altogether to be enemies to the Canon Lawe, and to condemn everything there written, because the Pope was author of them.... Naie, I will saie plainlie that there be some such lawes made by the Pope as be right godlie, saie others what they list."

all the precedents are on the side of an attempt to enforce a standard which shall be independent of the result which might be reached by higgling between this landlord and that tenant. Prices are fixed, wages are fixed, the rate of interest is fixed, though the money market is becoming more and more elusive, more and more critical of old-fashioned attempts at interference; the fines which freeholders must pay on admission have been fixed for centuries. Now that copyhold has got the protection of the Courts, it is not unnatural that tenants should ask the State to do with regard to the bargain most affecting them what it already does for bargains of nearly every other kind. It is not unnatural that, even when the fine is not settled by custom at a definite sum, they should demand nevertheless that the Courts should sanction that establishment of a "common rule," which is the ideal of the economically weak in all ages.

Yet we shall miss the full significance of the movement which we have examined, if we take their demands without analysis, and do not look at the other side of the picture. There was much to be said on the side of the manorial authorities, harsh as they often were. The criticism which Norden,[549] with a surveyor's experience, makes upon the outcry against the upward movement of fines, by pointing out that the whole scale of prices and payments has been shifted by the depreciation in the value of money, is perfectly justified. For money had depreciated, depreciated enormously; and landlords, who were faced with swiftly rising prices on the one hand and fixed freehold and copyhold rents on the other, were in a cleft stick from which it is not easy to blame them for extricating themselves as best they could. The truth is that if we content ourselves with the supposition of an access of exceptional unscrupulousness on the part of lords of manors which was favoured by contemporaries, we shall misread the situation. The real facts were much more complex, much more serious, much more interesting. A large impersonal cause, the flooding of Europe with American silver, upsets all traditional standards of payment. The first brunt is borne by those whose incomes are fixed, or relatively fixed, the owners of landed property, and the wage-earning classes. But all over the country thousands of new bargains are being struck as leases fall in and copies are renewed. Each fresh contract is the opportunity for a readjustment of relationships, for shifting the burden from the shoulders where it rested. The wage-earners do this to some extent, but not successfully; wages do not keep pace with prices. The landlords do it much more effectively. But there is no mechanical means of measuring what change is necessary in order to place them and their tenants in the same position relatively to each other as they were before. Once customary fines are thrown overboard, there is, unless the Government interferes, <u>no other standard</u> except the full fine which can be got in the open market, and,

[549] Norden, *The Surveyor's Dialogue*, Book I.: "*Surveyor.* The tennant leaveth commonly one either in right of inheritance, or by surrender, to succeed him, and he by custome of the manor is to be accepted tenant, alwaies provided he must agree with the lord, if the custome of the manor hold not the fine certain as in few it doth.... *Farmer.* You much mistake it, for I will show by ancient court rolls that the fine of that which is now £20 was then but 13s. 4d., and yet will you say they are now as they were then? *Surveyor.* Yea, and I thinke I erre little in it. For if you consider the state of things then and now, you shall find the proportion little differing; for so much are the prices of things vendible ... now increased as may well be said to exceed the prices then as much as £20 exceede the 13s. 4d."

when the custom of the manor allows it to be demanded, it is demanded. Thus the readjustment, as it were, overshoots itself, and the economic rent, unearned increment, surplus value—it is difficult to avoid phrases which modern associations have made trite—only part of which represents the rise in the price of land caused by the fall in the value of money, tends, instead of being, as hitherto, shared between landlord and copyholder, to be transferred *en bloc* to the former. It is rarely in modern society that classes are sufficiently definite and self-contained, rarely that economic changes are sufficiently catastrophic, for a great shifting of income from one to the other to be detected. Here we can see it going on before our eyes. We can note the result. But in this matter the twentieth century is not in a position to be critical of the sixteenth.

We may now sum up this part of our subject. The extreme lucrativeness of sheep-farming, and the depreciation in the value of money, offered an incentive to landlords to make the most profitable use which they could of their property by amalgamating small holdings into large leasehold farms, which were used mainly, though not entirely, for pasture. To carry out this new policy they had to get rid of the small tenants. When the tenants held at will, or were lessees for a short term of years, lords could do this without difficulty. When they were copyholders for one life or more, they could do it more slowly; but still they could do it in time. When they were copyholders with an estate of inheritance, lords had only two alternatives—to induce them to accept leases, or to raise the fines for admission. The latter course enabled them to offer the tenants the alternative of surrendering their holdings or paying the full competitive price which could be got for them. And thus it caused an almost revolutionary deterioration in their position. Hitherto the custom of the manor had been a dyke which protected them against the downward pressure of competition, and behind which they built up their prosperity. Now the unearned increment was transferred from tenant to landlord by the simple process of capitalising it in the fine demanded on entry. The interest of the customary tenant, therefore, virtually depreciated to the level of that of a leaseholder. The interest of the manorial lord appreciated to the full and effective ownership of all surpluses arising between the grant of one copy and the grant of the next. Thus the differences in the degree of security enjoyed by copyholders are to be explained by differences in manorial customs. Whom custom helps the law helps; who by custom are without protection, are without protection from the law, except in so far as it gradually builds up a doctrine as to what is reasonable. Long after villeinage has disappeared, copyholders still bear traces of having sprung from a class of whom the law was reluctant to take cognizance, traces of being nurtured in a "villein nest."

# PART III
# THE OUTCOME OF THE AGRARIAN REVOLUTION

"Lords spiritual and temporal, have it in your mind
This world as it waveth, and to your tenants be kind."

> —*The Proclamation of the Commons*, Gairdner,
> *Letters and Papers of Henry VIII.*, xii. I. 163.

"We must needs fight it out, or els be brought to the lyke slavery that the Frenchmen are in…. Better yt were therefore for us to dye like men, than after so great misery in youth to dye more miserably in age."—E. E. T. S., Crowley, *The Way to Wealth*.

*Doctor.* "On my faithe youe trouble youreselves … youe that be justices of everie countrie … in sittinge upon commissions almost wekely."

*Knight.* "Surely it is so, yet the Kinge must be served and the commonwealth. For God and the Kinge hathe not sent us the poore lyving we have, but to doe services therefore amonge our neighbours abroad."—*The Commonweal of this Realm of England*.

"We have good Statutes made for the Commonwealth, as touching commoners and inclosers, many meetings and sessions; but in the end of the matter there cometh nothing forth."—Latimer, *First Sermon preached before King Edward VI.*, March 8, 1549.

# CHAPTER I

## THE AGRARIAN PROBLEM AND THE STATE

### *(a) The Political and Social Importance of the Peasantry*

The changes which have been described in the organisation of agriculture created problems which were less absorbing than those arising out of the religious reformation and the relation of England to continental powers. When we turn over the elaborate economic legislation of the reign of Elizabeth, with its attempts to promote industry, to define class relationships, and to regulate with sublime optimism almost every contract which one man can make with another, we are tempted at first to see statesmen giving sleepless nights to the solution of economic problems, and to think of a modern bureaucratic state using the resources of scientific administration to pursue a deliberate and clearly conceived economic policy. But this is both to exaggerate the importance which economic questions occupied in the minds of the governing aristocracies of the age, and to credit them with a foresight which they did not possess. If they are to be called mercantilists, in England, at any rate, they wear their mercantilism with a difference; as a vague habit of mind, not as a reasoned system of economic doctrines. Their administrative optimism is the optimism of innocence as much as of omnipotence; the fruit of a self-confidence which, in the name of the public interests, will prop a falling trade, or cut down a flourishing one, with a bland naïveté unperturbed by the hesitations which perplex even the most courageous of modern protectionists. Though in several departments of life—in commercial policy, in the regulation of the wage contract, in the relief of distress—the main lines drawn by Elizabethan statesmen will stand for two centuries, much of their legislation is very rough and ready; much of it again is undertaken after generations of dilatory experiments; much of it is devoid of any originality, and is a mere reproduction on a national scale of the practice of individual localities, a reproduction which sometimes does less than justice to the original. If it is popular, it is popular because it tells men to do what most decent men have been doing for a long time already, and when it tells them to do something else it is carried out only with great difficulty. If it is permanent, it is permanent not because Parliamentary draughtsmen possess any great skill or foresight, but because, before the rise of modern industry, all social relationships have a great amount of permanence. Though there was much interesting speculation on economic matters, economic rationalism was as a practical force almost negligible; and since the only instrument through which it could have achieved influence was the monarchy, its lack of influence was perhaps politically fortunate.

Sixteenth century England was too busy getting the State on to its feet to produce a Colbert. Lath and plaster Colberts built their card castles on the Council table of James and Charles, and all was in train for the sage paternal monarchy which was the ideal of Bacon. But a wind blew from strange regions beyond their ken, and they were scattered before they could do much either for good or evil, leaving, as they fled, a cloud of dark suspicion round all those who would be wiser in the art of Government than their neighbours, from which, in the lapse of three centuries, the expert has hardly emerged. In spite of mercantilism, economic questions never became in England the pre-occupation of specialists. In spite of the genuine indignation roused by the sufferings of the weaker classes in society, questions affecting them were questions which statesmen did not handle for their own sake, but only in so far as they forced themselves into the circle of political interests by cutting across the order, or military defence, or financial system, of the country. Apart from these high matters of policy most members of the governing classes were inclined to answer petitions on the subject of economic grievances as Paget did to Somerset: Why can't you let it alone? "What a good year ... is victuals so dear in England and nowhere else? If they and their fathers before them have lived quietly these sixty years, pastures being enclosed, the most part of these rufflers have least cause to complain."[550]

The subordinate place occupied by economic questions during our period makes the attention which was given to the results of pasture-farming all the more remarkable. Though to the statesmanship of the sixteenth century the agrarian problem was one of the second order, it was, at any rate till the accession of Elizabeth, the most serious of its own class, and it was important enough to occupy Governments at intervals for over a century and a half. The first Statute against depopulation was passed in 1489;[551] an abortive Bill was introduced into the House of Commons in 1656;[552] and between the two lies a series of seven Royal Commissions, twelve Statutes, and a considerable number of Proclamations dealing with one aspect or another of the enclosing movement, as well as numerous decisions on particular cases by the Privy Council, the Court of Star Chamber, and the Court of Requests. This reaction of the new agrarian developments upon public policy is interesting in several ways. It illustrates the growth of new classes and forms of social organisation, the methods and defects of sixteenth century administration, and the ideas of the period as to the proper functions of the State in relation to an important set of questions, upon which political opinion was in some ways nearer to our own than it was to that of the age following the Civil War. Nor, perhaps, is it altogether without importance from the point of view of general history. We need not discuss how far the reaction of some recent historians against the familiar judgments which contrast Tudor tyranny with the constitutional revolutions of the seventeenth century as darkness with light, is likely to be permanent. But it is perhaps safe to say that it is in the sphere of social policy that their case is

---

[550] Strype, *Ecclesiastical Memorials*. Sir William Paget to the Lord Protector, July 7, 1549.

[551] 4 Henry VII., c. 19.

[552] Journal of House of Commons, December 19, 1656. See Leonard, *Trans. Royal Hist. Society*, vol. xix.

seen at its strongest. After all, tyranny is often the name which one class gives to the protection of another. To the small copyholder or tenant farmer the merciless encroachments of his immediate landlord were a more dreaded danger than the far-off impersonal autocracy of the Crown to which he appealed for defence. The period in which he suffered most in the sixteenth century was the interval between the death of the despotic Henry VIII. and the accession of the despotic Elizabeth. Though the interference of the Tudor, and—in a feebler fashion—of the Stuart, Governments to protect the peasantry was neither disinterested nor always effective, its complete cessation after 1642, and the long line of Enclosure Acts which follow the revolution of 1688, suggest that, as far as their immediate economic interests were concerned, the smaller landholders had more to lose than to gain from a revolution which took power from the Crown to give it to the squires. The writers[553] who after 1750 turned with a sigh from the decaying villages which they saw around them, to glorify the policy of the absolutist Governments of the sixteenth and seventeenth centuries, were received with the ridicule which awaits all who set themselves against a strong current of interests and ideas. But historically they were right. The revolution, which brought constitutional liberty, brought no power to control the aristocracy who, for a century and a half, alone knew how such liberty could be used—that blind, selfish, indomitable, aristocracy of county families, which made the British Empire and ruined a considerable proportion of the English nation. From the galleries of their great mansions and the walls of their old inns their calm, proud faces, set off with an occasional drunkard, stare down on us with the unshakable assurance of men who are untroubled by regrets or perplexities, men who have deserved well of their order and their descendants, and await with confidence an eternity where preserves will be closer, family settlements stricter, dependents more respectful, cards more reliable, than in this imperfect world they well can be. Let them have their due. They opened a door which later even they could not close. They fostered a tree which even they could not cut down. But neither let us forget that to the poorer classes its fruits were thorns and briars, loss of their little properties, loss of economic independence, the hot fit of the hateful Speenhamland policy, the cold fit of the more hateful workhouse system.[554] Those who would understand the social forces of modern England must realise that long disillusionment. Even in the seventeenth century there are whisperings of it. At the end of the Civil War there were men who were dimly conscious that the freedom for which they had fought involved economic, as well as political and ecclesiastical, changes. "Wee the poor impoverisht commoners," wrote the leaders of a little band of agrarian reformers to the Council of War in 1649, "claim freedom in the common lands by vertue of this conquest over the King, which is gotten by our joynt consent.... If this freedom be not granted, wee that are the poor commoners are in a worse case than we were in the King's day."[555] But from the reign of Henry VII. to the Civil War official opinion was as

[553] *e.g.* Price, *Observations on Reversionary Payments*, 1773. See Levy, *Large and Small Holdings*, p. 41.

[554] The general adoption of the "Test Workhouse" for the able-bodied, which dates from the Poor Law Reform Act of 1884, was the direct result of a one-sided reaction against the disastrous Speenhamland policy.

[555] Camden Society, *Clarke Papers*, vol. ii. p. 217.

generally in favour of protecting the peasantry against the ruinous effects of agrarian innovations, as it was on the side of leaving the landlords free to work their will in the two centuries which succeeded. We must explain this state of mind, for it certainly needs explanation; and this will necessitate our looking at the movements of the peasants and at their place in the State. We must estimate how far it was effective in practice; and to do this we must say a few words about the administrative machinery of the Tudors and of the first two Stuarts.

In almost all ages the first task of Governments is the preservation of order. Though the economic ideas of the sixteenth century were very different from those of the nineteenth, one of the reasons which made it impossible for the statesmen of the period to leave the land question altogether alone was the same as that which induced their successors to deal with Irish land in 1870 and 1881. It was that agrarian discontent created a permanent supply of inflammable material, which a spark might turn into a conflagration. The years between 1500 and 1650 are the last great age of the peasant uprisings which, in all countries of Western Europe except France and Ireland, are incredible to-day as a romance of giants, and hardly a generation in that stormy period elapsed without one. Sometimes nothing more happened than a collision of justices and gentry with angry mobs who were tearing down hedges and restoring common to common again under mysterious figures who flit across the darkening country-side with weapons in their hands and the eternal insurrection of the New Testament on their lips—Jack o' the Style, Pyrce Plowman, and that prophetic Captain Pouch, who "was sent of God to satisfie all degrees whatsoever, and in this present work was directed by the Lord of Heaven."[556] Sometimes the discontent swelled to a small civil war, as it did in Lincolnshire and Yorkshire in 1536, and in the eastern and southern counties in 1549. The Lincolnshire rising and the Pilgrimage of Grace were, it is true, mainly motived by discontent with the attack on the abbeys. But the explanation of their objects given by those insurgents who were cross-examined by the Government makes it difficult to agree with Professor Gay that only an insignificant part was played in these movements by agrarian discontent. The truth is that we ought to distinguish between the objects of different sections. The rebels of 1536 were not a class, but almost the whole society of northern England, which suddenly rolls forward with all its members, spirituality and laity, peasants and peers, in fervent motion together. The weaker side of these great conservative demonstrations was that, though all classes were united against the régime typified by Cromwell, all classes were not moved to the same degree by the same grievances. Even when the old religion was the cause that took the gentry into the field, the humbler rebels were brought out as much by hatred of agrarian as of religious innovations. The men of Lincolnshire marched under a banner embroidered with a ploughshare, and laggards were spurred forward with the cry "What will ye do? Shall we go home and keep sheep?"[557] In Cumberland the four Captains of Penrith—Faith, Poverty, Pity,

---

[556] For Captain Pouch see Gay, *Trans. Royal Hist. Soc.*, New Series, vol. xviii. For the other names Cooper, *Annals of Cambridge*, vol. ii. p. 40.

[557] Gairdner, *Letters and Papers of Henry VIII.*, vol. xii., Part I., 70, 1537. Examination of R. Leedes: "The rebels ... were half inclined to go home. But Ralph Green ... encouraged them to go forward, saying, 'God's blood, sirs, what will ye now do? Shall we go home and

and Charity—marched in solemn procession with drawn swords round Burgh Church, and then, having heard Mass, led their followers, with the blessing of the vicar, on a crusade to put an end to gentlemen and to withhold rents and fines.[558] In the North generally the arrival of Aske's messengers was a signal for the wholesale plucking down of new enclosures; a programme of agrarian reform was included in the demands put forward at Doncaster; and Aske himself told the Government at his examination that the practice of letting out farms over the heads of poor tenants was one of the causes of the rising.[559] A well-informed officer of State like Sir William Paget seems to have thought that even the rebellion which took place in Devonshire and Somersetshire in 1549, the causes of which were mainly ecclesiastical, was partly also agrarian.[560] In that year, indeed, nearly the whole of the southern counties, beginning in May with Hertfordshire, from Norfolk in the east to Hampshire in the south and Worcester in the west, were driven into riot by disappointment with the ineffective Royal Commission appointed in the preceding year. In 1550 there were disturbances in Kent, and the Government anticipated their appearance in Essex. In 1552 the Buckinghamshire peasants rose on account of high rents and high prices. In 1554 Wyatt's[561] adherents demanded that all pasture lands which had forcibly been seized by persons in power should be restored. In 1569 an armed band pulled down enclosures near Chinley[562] in Derbyshire, threatened to kill the encloser, and rescued by force those of their number who were arrested. Twenty-six years later, at a time of unusually high prices, even the peasantry of Oxfordshire,[563] that most imperturbable of English counties, planned "to knock down the gentlemen and rich men who made corn so dear, and who took the commons." In 1607 in the Midlands, where in the preceding decade enclosure and depopulation had created a situation as acute as that of half a century before, there was a riot which resulted in the appointment of a Royal Commission.

This was perhaps the last serious agrarian rising which England has seen. But

keep sheep? Nay, by God's body, yet had I rather be hanged,'" and *ibid.*: "The said Trotter says the meaning of the plough borne in the banner was the encouraging of the husbandman."

[558] *Ibid.*, vol. xii., Part I., 687, 1537. Confession of Barnarde Townleye, Clerk: "The beginners of the insurrection in Cumberland were the 4 captains of Penrith; Faith, Poverty, Pity and Charity, as the Vicar of Burgh proclaimed them at each meeting.... Conjectures that the intent was to destroy the gentlemen, that none should pay ingressums to his landlord, and little or no rent or tithe"; also *ibid.*, Examination of Sir Robert Thompson, Vicar of Burgh: "On the Wednesday and Thursday the 4 captains followed examinand in procession with their swords drawn, and examinand said mass, which they called the Captains' mass."

[559] Gairdner, *L. and P. Henry VIII.*, vol. xii., Part I., 687: "They of Kirkby Stephen plucked down the new intacks of enclosures, and sent to other Parishes to do the like, which was done at Burgh, 28th January." For the Doncaster programme see below, p. 334. Aske said (*L. and P.*, vol. xii., Part I., p. 901) that the new farmers of monastic estates "let and tavern out the farms of the same houses to other farmers for lucre."

[560] These particulars are taken from Strype, *Ecclesiastical Memorials.*

[561] Gay, *Trans. Royal Hist. Soc.*, New Series, vol. xviii., which also gives an account of the Midland riot of 1607.

[562] MSS. in possession of Charles E. Bradshaw Bowles, Esq., of Wirksworth, for a transcript of which I am indebted to Mr. Kolthammer. See below, pp. 327–329.

[563] *Hist. MSS. Com.*, MSS. of Marquis of Salisbury, Part VI., pp. 49–50.

though henceforward the hatred of the new agrarian régime ran for the most part underground, it had been burned too deep into the minds of the people to be lightly forgotten, and more than once its smouldering embers flickered up in occasional riots. In the first flush of the army's victory over King and Parliament, when the shattering of authority seemed for a moment to make all things new, not only the political, but the economic, ideas of two centuries later burst for a moment, as in an early spring, into wonderful and premature life. The programme of the Levellers, who more than any other party could claim to express the aspirations of the unprivileged classes, included a demand not only for annual or biennial Parliaments, manhood suffrage, a redistribution of seats in proportion to population, and the abolition of the Veto of the House of Lords, but also "that you would have laid open all enclosures of fens and other commons, or have them enclosed only or chiefly for the benefit of the poor."[564] Theoretical communism, repudiated by some of the Levellers, found its expression in the agitation of the Diggers, those "true born sons and friends of England" who, under Everard and Winstanley, set themselves, in the spirit of an Owenite Community, to convert the waste land at Weybridge into the New Jerusalem.[565] For to many earnest souls the day of the Lord seems very near, and Israel must make ready against it, not with anguish of spirit only, but with spade labour upon the barren earth. The contrast between the prevalence of organised agrarian revolts in the middle of the sixteenth century, dragging on in small sporadic agitations for nearly one hundred years, with their comparative rarity two hundred years later, when similar causes were at work to produce them, marks the new grouping of social classes and economic forces which was going on apace in our period. The intelligence of toiling England, that for a century now has gone to build up a new civilisation in factory and mine, in trade union and co-operative store, still lay in the larger villages, its immemorial home. Discontent travelled across the enclosing counties as it does to-day in a Welsh mining valley, outcoursing oppression itself, like Elijah running before Ahab into Jezreel. "If three or four good fellows would ride in the night with every man a bell, and cry in every town that they pass, 'To Swaffham! To Swaffham!' by the morning there would be ten thousand assembled at the least; and then one bold fellow to stand forth and say, 'Sirs, now we be here assembled, you know how little favour the gentlemen bear us poor men.... Let us

---

[564] The Humble Petition of thousands well affected persons inhabiting the city of London, Westminster, the Borough of Southwark, Hamlets, and places adjacent. In Bodleian Pamphlets, *The Leveller's Petition*, c. 15, 3 Linc. See also Gooch, *English Democratic Ideas in the Seventeenth Century*, pp. 139–226.

[565] Camden Society, *Clarke Papers*, vol. ii. pp. 215–217. Winstanley's letter to Lord Fairfax and the Council of War begins: "That whereas we have begun to dig upon the Commons for livelihood, and have declared unto your excellency and the whole world our reasons, which are four. First, from the righteous law of creation that gives the earth freely to one as well as another, without respect of persons"; also Gooch, *op. cit.* The Owenite note may be more than a mere chance. Owen himself stated ("New View of Society"): "Any merit due for the discovery calculated to effect more substantial and permanent benefit to mankind than any ever yet contemplated by the human mind belongs exclusively to John Bellers." Bellers published his *College of Industry* in 1696, and may easily have been acquainted with the story of the Diggers' agitation.

... harness ourselves.'"[566] Good fellows and bold were not wanting. "From that time forward no man could keep his servant at plough; but every man that could bear a staff went forward."[567] Before the appearance of almost universal leasehold tenure, standing armies, and omnipotent aristocratic Parliaments, unrest among the rural population might cause the Government a not inexpensive campaign, in which the reluctant militia of yesterday were the enthusiastic rebels of to-day, and there was not therefore much disparity between the discipline and equipment of the forces engaged on either side. Both in the mainly agrarian revolts in Norfolk, and in the mainly religious revolts in Devonshire, the peasants fell, as they hoped they might, like men, and it was the arquebuses of the foreign mercenaries which really decided the struggle. Poor homeless hirelings, what could they know but to clamour for their pay, and shoot better men than themselves?

To understand the nature of a body at rest it is sometimes advisable to look at the same body when it is in motion. The agrarian disturbances of our period possess certain features which are of interest even to those who are concerned primarily not with social politics, but with economic organisation. In the first place, they mark the transition from the feudal revolts of the fifteenth century, based on the union of all classes in a locality against the central government, to those in which one class stands against another through the opposition of economic interests. In the Lincolnshire rebellion and in the Pilgrimage of Grace the old spirit predominated. In the North of England the new agrarian régime had not proceeded far enough to sap entirely the ancient bonds between landlord and tenant, and the plunder of the monastic estates had not yet set a commercial aristocracy in the seat of the old-fashioned Catholic landlords. The commons of Westmoreland, who declare that they will trust no gentlemen with their councils, nevertheless feel sufficient confidence in Lord Darcy to write to him for his advice as to how far they will be justified in insisting on reduced admission fines, and in pulling down "all the intakes yt be noysum for poor men."[568] Had the Catholic gentry generally been willing to sacrifice the rents got from pasture-farming, these movements might have found leaders who would have made them more formidable. As it was, even when hatred of the religious changes or of some particular piece of legislation, like the unpopular Statute of Uses, enrolled the gentry with the peasants, as in Lincolnshire and Yorkshire in 1536, the incompatibility of the allies was obvious, and the presence of the wealthier classes inspired distrust among the rank and file, who saw in them the authors of their economic evils, and who, though genuinely concerned at the painful destruction of the social institutions of the old religion, were fighting mainly for the maintenance of "old customs and tenant right," fair rents and security of tenure. In spite of the temporary union of all classes in 1536, the insurgents tended to break up into two camps corresponding roughly with the division between landlord and tenant. In Lincolnshire, though the commons were influenced by the gentry so far as to demand the repeal of the Act of Uses, "not knowing," as a witness said, "what that Act of Uses meant," they showed their

---

[566] Russell, *Ket's Rebellion in Norfolk*, p. 8.

[567] Gairdner, *L. and P. Henry VIII.*, vol. xii., Part I., 201, Examination of John Halom of Calkehill, yeoman.

[568] *Ibid.*, vol. xi., 1080.

distrust of the upper classes by refusing to allow them to discuss their future policy apart from the general body of insurgents, while the extremists clamoured that "they ought to kill some of the justices; also that if they hanged for this, they would not leave one gentleman alive in Lincolnshire."[569] At Richmond all lords and gentlemen were to swear on the mass-book to maintain the profit of Holy Church, to take nothing of their tenants but the usual rents, to put down Cromwell and not to go to London, on pain of death if they refused.[570] For courts have strange arts of seduction, and though London (thank Heaven) is not England now, it was still less England then. The rough rhymes that ran through the North contain the warning of all popular movements against the treachery of leaders, the sad eternal warning which buoys the sands where so many high endeavours have gone to wreck. "All commons stick ye together, rise with no great man till ye know his intent. Keep your harness in your hands, and ye shall obtain all your purpose in all this North land…. Claim ye old customs and tenant right, to take your farms by a God's penny, all gressums and heightenings to be laid down. Then may we serve our sovereign Lord King Henry VIII., God save his noble Grace.

> We shall serve our lands' lords in every righteous cause
> With horse and harness as custom will demand.
> Lords spiritual and temporal have it in your mind
> This world as it waveth, and to your tenants be kind.
> Adieu, gentle commons, thus make I an end:
> Writer of this letter, pray Jesu be his speed;
> He shall be your captain, when that ye have need."[571]

The temporary solidarity which had drawn all classes into the Pilgrimage of Grace, though it flickered up for the last time in the feudal revolt of the northern earls in 1569, was absent altogether from the widespread agitation of 1549 to 1550. Except in Devonshire and Cornwall, the disturbances of those years were purely agrarian, a movement of tenants against landlords. The Eastern rebels were for leaving "as many gentlemen in Norfolk as there be white bulls";[572] the gentry responded by rallying to the Government; and both in that country and in Devonshire the military forces which put down the peasants were led by the two most notoriously unpopular landlords in England, who had built up their estates out of confiscated abbey lands, the Earl of Warwick and Sir William Herbert. In the reign of Henry VII. the problem before Governments had still been to prevent a great landlord from using his authority over his tenants to make war on his neighbours or on the State. Sixty years later it is to prevent tenants in several different counties from combining against landlords. The landed classes recognise the new spirit. They denounce the peasants as communists and agitators; and when they get a free hand, as in the years from 1549 to 1553, they insist on legislation which will

---

[569] Gairdner, *L. and P. Henry VIII.*, vol. xi., 975.

[570] *Ibid.*, vol. xii., Part I., 163.

[571] Gairdner, *L. and P. Henry VIII.*, vol. xii., Part I., 163. The Proclamation of the Commons; see also *ibid.*, 138, the manifesto which says, "Ye shall have captains just and true, and not be stayed by the gentry in no wise."

[572] Russell, *Ket's Rebellion in Norfolk*, Introduction, p. 8. The advice of John Walker of Griston.

make effective combination impossible.

In the second place, the way in which the agrarian agitations were conducted is interesting as showing both the comparative prosperity and independence of the English peasantry, even at a time when the fortunes of many of them were declining, and the general conceptions of social expediency held by what was regarded as the most representative part of the English nation. It would be a mistake to think of the rebels who joined these revolts as mere unorganised malcontents, with nothing to lose. There is no resemblance at all, either in personnel or methods, between the agrarian disturbances of our period and the riots of starving agricultural labourers who burned ricks under Captain Swing in the early nineteenth century. The peasants who formed the backbone of the movements were often well-to-do men, who were fighting to keep their land with the dreadful tenacity of small proprietors. They had arms and were accustomed to their use. They had sufficient money to raise common funds. They included among their number sanguine and pertinacious litigants who, so far from being disposed to throw up their case at the hint of the landlord's displeasure, were quite capable of making his life one long lawsuit. The readiness of a class to make effective the protection given it by the law in the face of the opposition of powerful individuals, quenched, alas! too often by ignorance, and timidity, and generations of dull oppression, is a very good test of its spirit and of the practical freedom which it enjoys. In the sixteenth century, though we certainly see many gross cases of intimidation, we also see tenants appealing to the law courts and to the Government over the heads of lords of manors. Such appeals are a proof of the helplessness of the victims which has been commented on above. But they are also a proof of the persistence and cohesion of some among them. For while in the absence of oppression they would not have been necessary, in the absence of a determination to resist oppression they could not have been made. To enclose was in parts of the country to stir up a hornet's nest. There was not much obsequiousness about the villagers of Thingden,[573] who from 1494 to 1538 pursued their landlord through almost every Court in the Kingdom. The leaders of the popular agitation were often the more prosperous among the middle-classes. Sanders, the general in the interminable struggle over the common lands of the city of Coventry which began in 1460, was a member of the important craft of Dyers, and had occupied the high civic office of Chamberlain.[574] At Louth[575] the initiative among the commons was taken by a tailor and a weaver. Ket[576] himself was a considerable landed proprietor as well as a tanner.

[573] Selden Society, *Select Cases in the Court of Star Chamber*, and Leadam, *E. H. R.*, vol. viii. pp. 684–696.

[574] *Coventry Leet Book*, edited by M.D. Harris, vol. ii. 510 and *passim*.

[575] Gairdner, *L. and P. Henry VIII.*, vol. xii., Part I., 380, The Examination of the Monk late of Louth Park: "Plummer and one James, a tailor, were the most quick and chiefest rulers of the company.... Melton, whom they named 'Captain Cobbles,' was the most chief and busy man among these commoners.... John Tailor, of Louth, webster, brought out of the house a great brand of fire, and the commons carried the books into the market-place."

[576] *Hist. MSS. Com.*, Cd. 2319, p. 75, Copy of Letters Patent (28 May, 4 Ed. VI.) granting to Thomas Audeley ... all that manor called Gunvyles Manor in Norfolk, parcel of the possessions of the said ... Robert Ket, in consideration "boni, veri, fidelis, et magnanimi servitii in conflictu versus innaturales subditos nostros proditores ac nobis rebelles in Com.

The peasants' agitations took the form both of more or less organised risings and of sporadic rioting, which aimed at ends varying from place to place according to the grievances inspired by the varying conditions of different districts. Everywhere there were the throwing down of enclosures and the driving of sheep.[577] In Yorkshire the enclosures which were pulled down seem to have been mainly intakes from the waste, and in Norfolk and the Midlands enclosures of arable land which had been converted to pasture. In Warwickshire the Earl of Warwick's park was demolished, while in Wiltshire, where Sir William Herbert had acquired the lands of Wilton Abbey, and enclosed a whole village in his new park at Washerne, the peasants rose and tore down the palings.[578] In the North generally the bitterest outcry seems to have arisen over the excessive fines and "gressums" charged for the admission of copyholders. In Cumberland[579] there was a general strike against the payment of rents, and almost everywhere there were complaints of the diminution in the area available for pasturing the beasts of commoners through the enclosing by landlords of manorial wastes.

Though it involves abandoning the order of events, let us illustrate by a single example[580] the shape assumed by agrarian rioting, which has not yet become a rebellion. In the summer of 1569, when Cecil and Elizabeth were waiting anxiously for news from those northern counties which "know no other prince but a Percy," there was much running and riding, much sending for warrants and plentiful delay in their execution, in the wild country between Chinley and Bakewell, whose centre is the Peak, and whose principal gorge now carries the most beautiful piece of railway line in England. The Derbyshire peasantry seem to have been ill to deal with. A few years later some of those in Glossopdale succeeded in setting the Earl of Shrewsbury at defiance, and, when evicted from their farms, induced the Council to intervene to insist on their reinstatement.[581] Just now those of them who lived in the neighbourhood of Chinley were in a ferment over the enclosure of some common land. The story is a curious one, and shows both the kind of conditions under which agrarian discontent developed, and the way in which it was associated in the mind of the Government with fears of political disturbance. The Duchy of Lancaster, to whom the land near Chinley belonged, had let a parcel of herbage called Mayston Field to one Lawrence Wynter, his lease to begin as soon as that of the existing tenant had expired. In that age of land speculation land changed hands rapidly. On the same day as Wynter obtained the lease he sold it

nostro Norf.... quorum ... quidam Bobertus Kett existit capitanus et conductor."

[577] Sheep-driving in the sixteenth century was like cattle-driving in Ireland to-day; see Gairdner, *L. and P. Henry VIII.*, vol. xii., Part I., 201: "When they first went to York, they drove one Coppyndale's sheep because he fled away, and sold them again to his deputy for £10," and the behaviour of the Norfolk rebels in 1549.

[578] Gairdner, *L. and P.*, xi., II., 186, and *Rutland MSS.*, p. 36, quoted by Leadam: "There is a great number of the commons up about Salisbury in Wiltshire, and they have plucked down Sir William Herbert's Park that is about his new house ... they say they will not have their common grounds to be enclosed and taken from them."

[579] Gairdner, *L. and P.*, xii., I., 362: "Your rents and others cannot yet be collected."

[580] I take this story from a transcript kindly supplied me by Mr. Kolthammer of MSS. in the possession of Charles E. Bradshaw Bowles of Wirksworth.

[581] Lodge, *Illustrations*, ii. p. 218.

to a certain Richard Celey. Celey transferred it to Godfrey Bradshaw, and Godfrey Bradshaw got rid of it to his brother Anthony. The trouble began when the land came into the hands of Godfrey Bradshaw. He started to hedge and ditch it, which of course involved the exclusion of the other inhabitants from the rights of pasture which they had hitherto enjoyed. Accordingly the villagers, led by twelve of their number, of whom four belonged to one family, removed the ditch, tore down the enclosure, which consisted of "XLIII hundredth quicksetts willowes and willowe stackes ... and did utterlye destroy and cutt the sayd stacks and quick setts in pieces," proceeding at the same time, with the object of protecting their own grazing land against encroachments, themselves to divide up the land into smaller enclosures to be held by each man in severalty. Godfrey Bradshaw then obtained warrants for the preservation of the peace against the ringleaders, and at the same time induced the lessor, who was Sir Ralph Sadler, the Chancellor of the Duchy, to address a letter to them directing them not to interfere with any houses, hedges, or ditches, which might in future be constructed round the land. They received his communication, but massed in force with arms on Chinley Hill, pulled down what still remained of Bradshaw's hedges, and then proceeded to organise the nucleus of a very pretty agitation. They gave part of the herbage, which was nominally in the occupation of the unfortunate lessee, to one William Beard, on condition that, after the manner of his betters in the good old days before the Tudors, he should "maynteyn them geynst the Queenes Majestie," his support taking the form of an agreement that he "should from tyme to tyme send them Ydill ryotouse p'sons to assyste them in these yll doinges." They then raised a fund, presumably by a levy on the inhabitants, called a meeting in the forest of High Peak, and set off about the tenth of June to Bakewell for a further conference, arranging in the meantime that some one should burn Godfrey Bradshaw's house, and that while his enclosures, if re-erected, should be pulled down, the other inhabitants should make haste to divide up the disputed land into twenty-one separate parcels. When the Bradshaws, having got their warrants, tried with the aid of the village constable to execute them, their opponents ("the land was grabbed from him, and he did what any decent man would do"[582]) threatened them with murder, and, on one of the party being actually arrested, came very near to carrying their threat out. "The said p'tyes ... did ryotouslye assemble themselves together in great companies at the town of Hayfield with unlawfull weapons, that is to saye, with bowes, pytchefforkes, clobbes, staves, swords, and daggers drawen, and ryotouslye dyd then and there assaulte and p'sue the sayd Godfrey and Edward Bradshawe, and in ryotouse manner dyd reskewe and take from them the body of the sayd Richard Shower, being attached; the Queenes Officer, George Yeavely of Bawdon, then being p'sent commanding the peace to be kepte." Having chased the enemy for some distance, they camped on the contested territory, and kept a watchful eye and a firm hand for any sign of the reappearance of the detested hedges. More serious still in the eyes of the Government (and this, one suspects, was their undoing), the leaders of this village revolution went so far as to entangle themselves in high politics. At their examination they are asked, "Whether dyd Reynold Kirke about May day last paste, and dyvers tymes since and before, or any other tyme, confederate,

---

[582] Synge, *The Playboy of the Western World*.

consulte, practise, or otherwise confer and talk with one Mr. Bircles of the countye of Chester ... touching or concerning prophesis by noblemen, or otherwise, and what books of prophesie have you or the said Bircles seen or heard, and what is the effect thereof, and how often have you or he perused, used, or conferred of the same, or about such purposes, and with whom?" We do not know how they answered this question. It may be that the anger of these Derbyshire peasants at their vanishing commons was indeed a fraction to be set among weightier assets by schemers in high places, and that the sinister Mr. Bircles had really talked with them of matters more serious than the pulling down of hedges and the baiting of enclosers, of things forbidden to the vulgar, of the scattering of upstart officials, of the restoration of a Catholic monarchy, of Mary, who in the previous year had made her irrevocable plunge across the Border. It may be merely that all in authority had that autumn an unusually bad attack of nerves. In 1569 the North was full of prophets, both noble and other.

It was not always the case, however, that agrarian discontent ended in casual rioting of this kind. Of mere destructive violence there is, indeed, in all the social disturbances of the period, singularly little. There was a good deal in the routine of rural life, with its common administration of land and dependence on a collectively binding custom, to teach habits of discipline and co-operation. It must be remembered that those who took the initiative in breaking the law were not the peasants who pulled down enclosures, but the landlords who made them in defiance of repeated statutes forbidding them. On the whole the organised character of the action taken is more conspicuous than the individual excesses, and if one is to look for a modern analogy to the mixture of deliberation and violence which it shows, it must be sought in an Irish fair rent campaign rather than in the bread riots of a despairing urban proletariat. When the agitation was confined to individual manors it occasionally took the form of agrarian trade unionism. Tenants collectively decline to serve as jurors in the court of the manor till their demands are granted.[583] They raise a common purse.[584] They refuse to pay more than a certain rent. When more than one manor is implicated different localities display a rough cohesion. Whole communities seem to have joined the movement in 1536 and 1540 with a certain formality. In Lincolnshire and Yorkshire townships were brought out on the ringing of the town bell with the cohesion of a

---

[583] Selden Society, *Select Cases in the Court of Requests* (Leadam). Customary tenants of Bradford *v.* Francis: "The said stuard called ... the ... tenants of the manor to be sworn to enquire as they ought to doo, the which to do ... the said tenants ... obstinately and sturdily then and there refused, and said that unless the said defendent ... wold grante them forthwith and immediatelye that they should have and enjoy the commodity of the said three matters ... that they, nor any of them, wolde be sworn at that Court, but wolde depart."

[584] Leadam, *E. H. R.*, pp. 684–696. The tenants at Thingden, in their proceedings against Mulsho, "calle commen Councelles ... and make a commen purse among them, promising all of them to take parte with other, saying that xx. of them would spend xx. score pounds ayenet the said John Mulsho." The tenants of Abbot's Ripton "procured one common purse to be ordeyned together one common stock to thentent obstinately to defend their perverse and ffrowned appetitez." As to Rents, see *L. and P. Henry VIII.*, xii., I., 154: "In many counties little or no ferms will they pay" (Darcy to Shrewsbury).

well-organised trade union; Beverley[585] sent messages to the Lincolnshire rebels under its common seal; and the part which was played by the village officers in the movements of the peasantry is proved by the Proclamation[586] which the Council issued in 1549, when disorders were at their height, forbidding constables, bailiffs, and head-boroughs to call meetings except for the purposes required by the law. Hales,[587] as he rode through the South and Midlands in 1548, was struck by the patience with which people waited for the Government to take action, and attributed the disturbances of the ensuing year to the despair caused by the victory of the local landlords over the Commission, and to the rejection by Parliament of the Bills which he had introduced. Even Ket's campaign in Norfolk, which ended in a sanguinary battle, during the greater part of it was carried on with an orderliness from which the Government which suppressed it might profitably have taken a lesson. Nothing could have been more unlike the popular idea of a *jacquerie*. The peasants enjoyed the enormous joke of making the gentry look foolish a great deal more than cutting their throats, as during the four weeks in which they were "playing" they might have done without any difficulty.

> "Mr. Pratt, your sheep are very fat,
> And we thank *you* for that;
> We have left you the skins to pay your wife's pins,
> And you must thank *us* for that."[588]

These lines, pinned on the carcasses of an enclosing landlord's flocks and herds, are a fair specimen of their humour. Men may well be merry together, when they have seen hovering over the fields of an English county, though but in a fleeting glimpse, the New Jerusalem where the humble are exalted and the mighty put down; and there is no inconsistency between such mundane gaiety and the long pent up passion which on the lips of a nameless labourer burst into the cry, "As sheepe or lambs are a prey to the wolfe or lion, so are the poor men to the rich men."[589] There was much lecturing (the matter is easily imagined) at the Oak of Reformation, and not on one side only, for the peasants were tolerant compared with their betters, and a future archbishop was allowed to address the insurgents on the evils of their ways; much laying down of hedges and enclosures; much slaughtering of that beast of iniquity, the man-devouring sheep. There was none of the massacring of unarmed men which both Henry VIII. and Elizabeth ordered without compunction when they thought the times required it, very little of the "making the public good a pretext for private revenge," against which the in-

---

[585] Gairdner, *L. and P. Henry VIII.*, xii., I., 392.

[586] Proclamation of July 22, 1549. Strype, *Ecclesiastical Memorials*, who remarks that these village officers, "in the places where these risings were, had been the very ringleaders and procurers by their example and exhortation."

[587] *Commonweal of this Realm of England* (Lamond), Appendix to Introduction, lviii.: "In dyvers places wher we were, and wher the people had just cause of Gryef, and have complayned a great many yeares without remedy, there have they byn very quiet, shewed themselves most humble and obedient subiectes taryenge the Kynges Maiesties Reformation."

[588] *Original Papers of the Norfolk and Norwich Archæological Society*, 1905, p. 2.

[589] *Original Papers of the Norfolk and Norwich Archæological Society*, 1905, p. 22.

surgents were warned by Parker. Though for months after the final tragedy the badges of the justly-hated Warwick "were not so fast set up but that they were as fast pulled down" from the city walls, the rebels even in the heat of their early triumphs claimed only to be executing the Protector's Proclamations, and, while indignantly repudiating the name of traitors, showed a complete readiness to negotiate peaceably with the Government. The whole movement was less a rising against the State than a practical illustration of the peasants' ideals, a mixture of May-day demonstration and successful strike embodied in one gigantic festival of rural good fellowship. Its bloody termination was, as far as can be judged, the result of two errors of judgment, one, a pardonable one, on the part of Ket, the other, unpardonable, on the part of a nameless member of the other party.[590] When all was over, and each man reflected after his kind on the great days of Mousehold Heath, what the camp followers, who attach themselves to every popular movement, remembered was that for about a month they had filled their bellies at other people's expense. "'Twas a merry world when we were yonder, eating of mutton." But there were some who, as they saw Ket swinging on the gallows before the City gates, were seized with the tumult of pity and hoarse indignation which serves Englishmen, who are not good at revolutions, in place of the revolutionary spirit. "O Kette," one countryman was heard to say to another, "God have mercy upon thy soul; and I trust in God that the King's Majesty and his Councell shall be enformed once between this and Midsummer evening, that of their own gentleness thou shalt be taken down and buried, not hanged up for winter store; and set a quietness in the realm, and that the ragged staff shall be taken down of their own gentleness from the gentlemen's gates in this City, and to have no more King's arms but one within the City, under Christ."[591] The Council, in its gentleness, thought otherwise. Ket still creaked in his chains, and in the meantime other gallows were rising for other rebels in Somerset, and Devon, and Cornwall.

What were the aims which at intervals between 1530 and 1560 set half the counties of England in a blaze? Let us look at the peasants' programme more closely. It will help us to see the agrarian problem from the inside. Reduced to its elements their complaint is a very simple one, very ancient and yet very modern. It is that what, in effect, whatever lawyers may say, has been their property, is being taken from them. To be told that social disorders take place because an envious proletariat aims at seizing the property of the rich would seem to them a very strange perversion of the truth. They want only to have what they have always had. They are conservatives, not radicals or levellers, and to them it seems that all the trouble arises because the rich have been stealing the property of the poor. Here is part of a colloquy[592] between Jack of the North beyond the Style, Robin and Harry Clowte, Tom of Trumpington, Peter Potter, Pyrce Plowman, and divers other worthies. As

[590] Ket refused the pardon offered on July 31st on the ground that the insurgents had committed no offence requiring to be pardoned, and fighting followed. On August 23rd a pardon was again offered. While it was being read by a herald, a boy standing by insulted him "with words as unseemly as his gesture was filthy" (Holinshed), and was shot by one of the herald's retinue. Ket tried to pacify the anger of his followers at what they took to be treachery, but without effect.

[591] *Original Papers of the Norfolk and Norwich Archæological Society*, 1905, p. 20.

[592] Printed by Cooper, *Annals of Cambridge*, vol. ii. p. 40.

will be seen from the verses, they are birds of night—

> JACK. Now for that Slaunder's sake,
> Companye by night I take,
> And, with all that I may make,
> Cast hedge and ditch in the lake,
> Fyxed with many a stake
> Though it was never so faste
> Yet asondre it is wraste.
>
> *       *       *       *
>
> HARRY CLOWTE. Gud conscience should them move
> Ther neighbours quietly to love,
> And thus not for to wrynche
> The commons styl for to pinch,
> To take into their hande
> That be other mennes land.
>
> JACK. Thus do I, Jack of the Style,
> Now subscrybe upon a tyle.
> This I do and will do with all my myght,
> For sclaundering me yet do I but right,
> For common to common again I restore
> Wherever it hath been yet common before.
> If agayne they enclose it never so faste
> Agayne asondre it shall be wraste.
> They may be ware by that is paste
> To make it agayne is but waste."

To take into your hand what is other men's land, that is the grievance. To restore common to common again, that is the obvious remedy, a remedy which is not seriously opposed to the agrarian policy of most sixteenth century statesmen. But the more far-seeing of the peasants realise what their followers do not, that these troubles which are going on in so many different parts of England cannot be dealt with by isolated bodies of villagers, however good their cause may be. They require the intervention of the Government. How the Government is to intervene they lay down in two documents which are perhaps the only two popular programmes of agrarian reform ever published in England since 1381. The first, contained in two of the articles[593] drawn up at Doncaster in 1536, is short enough:—

"That the lands in Westmoreland, Cumberland, Kendall, Dent, Sedbergh, Furness, and the abbey lands in Mashamshire, Kyrkbyshire, Notherdale, may be by tenant right, and the lord to have, at every change, 2 years' rent for gressum, according to the grant now made by the lords to the commons there. This to be done by Act of Parliament.

"The Statutes for Enclosures and Intacks to be put in execution, and all enclosures and Intacks since the fourth year of Henry VII. to be pulled down, except mountains, forests, and Parks" (a noticeable exception which shows the composite

[593] Gairdner, *L. and P. of Henry VIII.*, xi. 1246.

character of the movement. In the South of England the peasant did not spare parks).

The articles[594] signed by Ket, Aldryche, and Cod in 1549 are a much more elaborate affair. Here are the most noteworthy of them:—

"We pray your grace that where it is enacted for enclosing, that it be not hurtful to such as have enclosed saffren grounds, for they be greatly chargeable to them, and that from henceforth no man shall enclose any more.[595]

"We certify your grace that whereas the lords of the mannors hath been charged with certe fre rent, the same lords hath sought means to charge the freeholders to pay the same rent, contrary to right.

"We pray your grace that no lord of no manor shall comon uppon the commons.

"We pray that priests from henceforth shall purchase no lande neither free nor bondy, and the lands that they have in possession may be letten to temporal men, as they were in the first year of the reign of King Henry VII.[596]

"We pray that reed ground and meadow ground may be at such price as they were in the first year of King Henry VII.

*     *     *     *     *

"We pray that the payments of castleward rent, and blanch ferm and office lands, which hath been accustomed to be gathered of the tenements, whereas we suppose the lords ought to pay the same to their bailiffs for their rents gathering, and not the tenants.[597]

"We pray that no man under the degree of a knight or esquire keep a dove house, except it hath been of an old ancient custom.

"We pray that all freeholders and copyholders may take the profits of all commons, and there to common, and the lords not to common nor to take profits of the same.

"We pray that no feudatory within your shires shall be a councellor to any man in his office making, whereby the King may be truly served, so that a man being of good conscience may be yearly chosen to the same office by the commons of the same shire.

*     *     *     *     *

---

[594] Russell, *Ket's Rebellion in Norfolk*, p. 48.

[595] Some doubt has been expressed as to the interpretation of these words. They should probably be read in the light of what was said above (Part I. chap. iv.) as to enclosures made by the tenants themselves. The rebels point out that a considerable number of people have spent capital on hedging and ditching their lands for the better cultivation of saffron, and therefore ask that, while other enclosures may be pulled down, a special exception may be made in favour of this particular kind of enclosure.

[596] Contrast the feeling in Protestant Norfolk with that of Cornwall and Devon in 1549, and of the North in 1536.

[597] The grammar is bad, but the sense is clear enough. Lords must stop shifting on to tenants burdens which lords ought to bear.

"We pray that copyhold land that is unreasonably rented may go as it did in the first year of King Henry VII., and that at the death of a tenant or of [at] a sale the same lands to be charged with an easy fine, as a capon or a reasonable [sum] of money for a remembrance.

*      *      *      *      *

"We pray that all bondmen may be made free, for God made all free with his precious bloodshedding.

"We pray that rivers may be free and common to all men for fishing and passage.

*      *      *      *      *

"We pray that the poor mariners or Fishermen may have the whole profits of their fishings, as porpoises, grampuses, whales, or any great fish, so it be not prejudicial to your Grace.

*      *      *      *      *

"We pray that it be not lawful to the lords of any manor to purchase land freely, or [and] to let them out again by copy of court roll to their great advancement and to the undoing of your poor subjects.

*      *      *      *      *

"We pray that no man under the degree of ... shall keep any conies upon any of their freehold or copyhold, unless he pale them in, so that it shall not be to the common nuisance.

*      *      *      *      *

"We pray that your Grace give license and authority by your gracious commission under your Great Seal to such commissioners as your poor commons hath chosen, or to as many of them as your Majesty and your Council shall appoint and think meet, for to redress and reform all such good laws, statutes, proclamations, and all other your proceedings, which hath been hidden by your justices of your peace, shreves, escheators, and other your officers, from your poor commons, since the first year of the reign of your noble grandfather, King Henry VII.

*      *      *      *      *

"We pray that no lord, knight, esquire, nor gentleman, do graze nor feed any bullocks or sheep, if he may spend forty pounds a year by his lands, but only for the provision of his house."

The programme of the peasants is partly political. The Northerners insist that Parliament and the Crown must interfere, and the Norfolk leaders ask for a permanent commission to do the work which the county justices, who are interested in enclosing, have wilfully neglected. But it is mainly economic. The State is to do no more than restore the old usages, and the end of all is to be a sort of idealised manorial customary enforced by a strong central Government throughout the length of the land, free use of common lands, reduced rents of meadow and marsh, reasonable fines for copyholds, free fisheries, and the abolition of the lingering disability of personal villeinage. The most striking thing about these demands is their conservatism. Almost exactly a hundred years later agrarian reform will be demanded as part of a new heaven and a new earth. Agrarian agitation will be carried on in terms of theories as to the social contract, of theories as to the origin of private property. Its leaders will be appealing to Anglo-Saxon history to prove to the indifferent ears of a Government which has saved them "from Charles, our Norman oppressor," that "England cannot be a free commonwealth, unless the poore commoners have a use and benefit of the land."[598] They will appeal also to a more awful sanction than that of history. "At this very day," cries Winstanley,[599] "poor people are forced to work for 4d. a day and corn is dear, and the tithing-priest stops their mouths and tells them that 'inward satisfaction of mind' was meant by the declaration 'the poor shall inherit the earth.' I tell you, the scripture is to be really and materially fulfilled.... You jeer at the name of Leveller. I tell you Jesus Christ is the head leveller." Such communistic doctrines are always the ultimate fruit of the breakdown of practical co-operation and brotherliness among men. To human nature, as to other kinds of nature, a vacuum is abhorrent.

But as yet the soil has not been ploughed by a century of political and religious controversy, and there is little sign of these high arguments in the social disturbances of our period. The earliest levellers[600] get their name because they raze not social inequalities but quickset hedges and park palings. What communism there is in the movement is not that of the saints or the theorists, but the spontaneous doctrineless communism of the open field village, where men set out their fields, and plough, and reap, laugh in the fine and curse in the wet, with natural fellowship. The middle-class terror of the appearance in England of the political theories of the German Peasants' War, though it was forcibly expressed by Sir William

---

[598] Camden Society, *Clarke Papers*, vol. ii. p. 217. Letter addressed by the Diggers, December 8, 1649: "To my lord generall and his Councell of War." The allusion to the usurping Normans occurs also (*ibid.*, p. 215) in another letter in a statement of the reasons of the agitation: "Secondly by vertue of yours and our victory over the king, whereby the enslaved people of England have recovered themselves from under the Norman Conquest; though wee do not yet enjoy the benefit of our victories, nor cannot soe long as the use of the Common land is held from the younger brethren by the Lords of Mannours that yet sit in the Norman chair and uphold that tyranny as if the kingly power were in force still."

[599] Winstanley: "The curse and blessing that is in mankind," quoted Gooch, *English Democratic Ideas in the Seventeenth Century.*

[600] A reference to the Levellers occurs in connection with the Midland Revolt of 1607, Lodge, *Illustrations*, iii. 320: "You cannot but have hearde what courses have been taken in Leicestershire and Warwickshire by the two Lord Lieutenants there, and by the gentlemen ... and lastlie howe Sir Anth. Mildmay and Sir Edward Montacute repaired to Newton ... where one thousand of these fellowes who term themselves levellers were busily digging, but weare furnished with many half-pikes, pyked staves, long bills, and bowes and arrows and stones ... there were slaine some 40 or 50 of them and a verie great number hurt" (January 11, 1607, the Earl of Shrewsbury to Sir John Manners, Sir Francis Leake, and Sir John Harper). The name Diggers seems to have cropped up about the same time, v. *Wit and Wisdom*, edited by Halliwell for New Shakespeare Society, pp. 140–141, for a petition from "the Diggers of Warwickshire to all other diggers," and signed "poore Delvers and Day Labourers for ye good of ye commonwealth till death" (quoted by Gay, *Trans. Royal Hist. Soc.*, New Series, vol. xviii.)

Paget[601] in remonstrating with Somerset's policy in 1549, and though John Hales thought it worth while to repudiate it, is not justified by any recorded utterances or programmes which have come to us. There are, indeed, many verbal similarities between the articles of Ket and those put out by the German peasants at Memmingen in 1525, which suggest that some refugee from Germany had carried them with him to the most Protestant county in England. Both, for example, demand a reduction in rents, the abolition of villeinage, and free fisheries. But the contrasts are much more striking, and are due not only to the fact that the onerous villein services which survived in Germany had become almost nominal in England, but to the difference in the spirit of their conception, which leads one to appeal to the New Testament and the other to the customs of the first years of Henry VII. There is, in fact, the same broad difference between the peasant movements in England and Germany as there is between the English and German Reformation. In Germany the ecclesiastical changes spring from a widespread popular discontent, and are swept forward on a wave of radical enthusiasm, which carries the peasants (German Social Democrats are metaphysicians to this day) into the revolutionary mysticism of Münzer. In England changes in Church government are forced upon the people by the State, and outside the South and East of England are regarded with abhorrence. It is not until the later rise of Puritanism that either religious or economic radicalism becomes a popular force. In the middle of the sixteenth century the English peasants accepted the established system of society with its hierarchy of authorities and division of class functions, and they had a most pathetic confidence in the Crown. What they wanted, in the first place, was fair conditions of land tenure, the restoration of the customary relationships which had protected them against the screw of commercial competition. When they went further, they looked for an exercise of Royal Power to reduce to order the petty tyranny of local magnates, and to carry out the intentions of a Government which they were inclined to think meant them well, "to redress and reform all such good laws, statutes, proclamations, and all other your proceedings which hath been bidden by your justices of your Peace ... from your poor commons." Such movements are a proof of blood and sinew and of a high and gallant spirit. They are the outcome of a society where the normal relations are healthy, where men are attached to the established order, where they possess the security and control over the management of their own lives which is given by property, and, possessing this, possess the reality of freedom even though they stand outside the political state. Happy the nation whose people has not forgotten how to rebel.

The social disturbances caused by enclosure, with its accompaniments of rack-renting and evictions, were one cause which compelled the Governments of our period to give attention to the subject. Though no direct concessions were made to them, their lessons were not altogether wasted, because it is plain that they impressed on the minds of statesmen the idea that to prevent disorder it was necessary for the State to interfere in favour of tenants. Rural discontent, which might have been insignificant in an age of greater political stability, derived a factitious importance from the circumstances of the sixteenth century, when it might be exploited by a rebellious minority, which, for all that most men knew, might

[601] See below, pp. 367–368.

really be a majority of the nation, by Yorkist Plotters under Henry VII., religious enthusiasts under Henry VIII., restorers of a Catholic monarchy, supported by a Spanish invasion or a Franco-Scottish alliance, under Elizabeth. Governments so uncertain of their popularity as these had a strong reason for protecting the class which would be the backbone of a revolt. One way in which they could secure themselves against the discontent of the disaffected nobility was to encourage the yeomanry, who might act as a counterpoise. The way in which self-preservation and a popular agrarian policy went hand in hand is illustrated by Burleigh's cynical advice to Elizabeth to make a practice of supporting tenants in any quarrel which might arise between them and Catholic landlords.[602]

But there were other causes as well working in the same direction. No one who reads the writers by whom the agrarian problem is discussed can fail to notice that the official view of the proper system of agrarian relationships was on the whole favourable to the small man, and was, indeed, not very different from that expressed in the demands of the peasants themselves. Not, of course, that the authorities had any intention of depressing landlords or raising peasants, but that the whole established system of Government was based on a certain organisation of social life, and that the Government tended to maintain that organisation in maintaining itself and carrying on the work of the State. For this attitude, which is in striking contrast with the policy of the statesmen of the eighteenth century when faced with an analogous problem, there were several practical reasons which we shall do well to understand. In judging the motives of economic policy in past ages we are even more apt to be misled by modern analogies than we are in estimating its effects. We see that in our own day most of the legislative protection accorded to those who are economically weak has been produced by a combination of two causes, the political enfranchisement of the wage-earning classes and the spread of humanitarian sentiment. We know that in the sixteenth century the first cause was absent and the second was feeble. The Macchiavellis of that iron age were neither democrats nor philanthropists; and when they avow a policy of protecting the weaker classes in society against economic evils we are inclined to think with Professor Thorold Rogers that they are merely hypocritical. But this analogy is a false light. To be influenced by it is to confuse political power with its symbols, and to forget that the economic importance of a class may be a more effective claim to the interest of Governments than the ballot-box. Under the Tudors there were strong practical reasons for protecting the peasantry which are not felt to the same extent to-day. The modern State has so specialised its organs that its maintenance is quite compatible with the existence of the extremes of poverty, not only among the exceptionally unfortunate, but among those whose position is not more insecure than that of their neighbours. They may be able neither to fight, nor

[602] *Somers' Tracts*, vol. i., pp. 164–168: "For their tenantries, this conceit I have thought upon ... that your Majesty, in every shire, should give instruction to some that are indeed trusty and religious gentlemen, that, whereas your Majesty is given to understand that divers popish landlords do hardly use some of your people and subjects, ... you do constitute and appoint them to deal both with entreaty and authority, that such tenants, paying as others do, be not thrust out of their living, nor otherwise molested. This would greatly bind the commons' hearts unto you, on whom indeed consisteth the power and strength of your realm, and it will make them less, or nothing at all, depend upon their landlords."

to take part in public duties, nor to contribute much to the Exchequer. But if their incompetence is a menace, it is a menace which is not felt till after the lapse of generations, a menace the fulfilment of which no single life is long enough to behold. For the State hires specialists to fight, and specialists to keep order; indeed, the poorer they are, the more cheaply it can obtain their services.[603] Its local government is conducted mainly by specialised officials, and the concentration of wealth makes possible a concentration of taxation. The extension of political power has been accompanied by a subdivision of political functions, which has diminished the importance of the individual citizen, and turned him, as far as the routine of Government is concerned, into a sleeping partner, whose consent is necessary, but whose active co-operation is superfluous.

Now we need not point out that this would be as fair a description of large classes of persons in the sixteenth century as it is now, and that the day labourer and handicraftsman who "are to be ruled and not to rule"[604] were, as a class, far more completely beneath the consideration of statesmen than they are at the present day. But we are concerned with the landholding population, not with the landless wage-earner, and in the slightly differentiated state of our period both economic and political conditions made a decline in the standard of life among a class so important as the peasantry a danger which might cause the most authoritarian of Governments to be confronted with very grave practical difficulties. It might find itself unable to raise an effective military force. The States of Continental Europe had introduced standing armies. But England relied mainly on the shire levies, and the shire levies were recruited from the small farmers. Just as the lord of a manor in the North of England, whose tenants held by border service with horse and harness, was anxious to prevent the decline in their numbers which landlords elsewhere were welcoming, so the Government regarded with quite genuine dismay an agrarian movement which seemed to threaten its military resources by impoverishing the finest fighting material in the country. Shadow, Feeble, and Wart may "fill a pit as well as better"; but to make good infantry it requires not "housed beggars," but "men bred in some free and plentiful manner." One Depopulation Statute after another recites how "the defence of this land against our enemies outward is enfeebled and impaired."[605] In the settlement of the North after the Pilgrimage of Grace the Government took care to instruct its officials to see that the Northumbrian tenants, on whom the defence of the border depended, "should be put in comfort, that no more shall be exacted with gyrsums and like charges, instead of which they shall be ready with horse and harness when required."[606] In 1601 Cecil[607] crushed a proposal to repeal the acts then in force against depopula-

[603] For the manner in which the British army is recruited by starvation, see Mr. Cyril Jackson's Report on Boy Labour to the Royal Commission on the Poor Laws and Relief of Distress, Cd. 4632, pp. 166–168.

[604] Smith, *De Republica Anglorum,* Lib. I., chap. xxiv.

[605] 4 *Henry VII.,* c. 19.

[606] Gairdner, *L. and P. Hen. VIII.,* xii., I. p. 595.

[607] *D'Ewes' Journal,* p. 674: "Mr. Secretary Cecil said, '... I think that whosoever doth not maintain the plough destroys this kingdom.... I am sure when warrants go from the Council for levying of men in the counties, and the certificates be returned unto us again, we find the greatest part of them to be ploughmen.'" See also on this point Appendix I., Nos.

tion by pointing out that the majority of the militia levies were ploughmen. And in the instructions for the choice of persons to be enrolled in the trained bands which were issued by the Government of Charles I., particular care was taken to emphasise that they were not to be selected at haphazard, but were to be drawn from the families of the gentry, freeholders, and substantial farmers.[608]

This cogent reason for intervening to protect the peasantry was supported by another which was not less convincing. The classes who suffered most from enclosure were important from a fiscal, as well as a military, point of view. In the simple economic life of that age the connection between the output of wealth and the individual worker's opportunities for production and standard of subsistence, if not more important than to-day, was certainly more patent to observation. "The hole welth of the body of the realm cometh out of the labours and works of the common peple ... a riche welthy body of a realm maketh a riche welthy king, and a poore feble body of a realm must needs make a poore weak feble king."[609] In our period *"pauvre paysans pauvre royaume, pauvre royaume pauvre roi"* was a statement not of any recondite theory, but of an obvious economic fact, and one can hardly be mistaken in supposing that part of the favour which sixteenth century Governments were inclined to show the small farmer was due to the fact that the methods of taxation in use made him important as a source of revenue. To a State which relies largely for its supplies on a direct declaration of income, it is indifferent whether the total assessable income is made up of a few large or many small ones; indeed if the tax be a progressive one, most will be got from the former. But look at the way in which taxation is raised in the sixteenth century. The chief direct tax is the subsidy. A typical subsidy, for example that of the first year of Elizabeth,[610] is assessed partly on the capital value of property, including farm and trade stock and household furniture, partly on the yearly profits of land. When a village of small and fairly prosperous cultivators is wiped out to make room for a large and sparsely populated estate, will the Government get as large a revenue from direct taxation as before? A modern reader may very well answer "Yes." The motive of converting land to pasture is to increase the profits of agriculture. If they are increased, does not this mean a corresponding increase in the taxable wealth of the country? Now to inquire how far one can assume in any age that the personal interests of landlords will lead to land being put to its most productive use would take us far beyond the scope of this essay, and it is unnecessary for our present purpose. For, as far as our period is concerned, the answer is certainly wrong. Apart from the subtler reactions of the agrarian changes upon social welfare, there

iv., v., vi., and viii.

[608] *Original Papers of the Norfolk and Norwich Archæological Society* (1909), p. 144.

[609] Pauli, *Drei volkswirthshaftliche Denkscriften,* How to Reform the Realm in Setting Men to Work to restore Tillage: "The kynge and his lordes have nede to mynyster right ordre of common wele; or els they must needs destroy their own wealth by the very ordenaince of God, for they are upholden and borne upon the body. Yf they will be riche, they must first see all common people have riches."

[610] 1 Eliz. cap. xxi. Prothero Statutes and Constitutional Documents, 1558–1625. Two subsidies of 1s. 8d. and 1s. were imposed on "every pound, as well in coin, ... as also plate, stock of merchandises, all manner of corn and blades, household stuff, and of all other goods moveable," and two subsidies of 2s. 8d. and 1s. 4d. on the "yearly profits" of land.

is then no such identity between the economic interests of the landlord and the economic interests of the State. Speaking broadly, the former consist in securing the largest net income, the latter in securing the largest gross product. And these two things are by no means necessarily found together. If a pasture farm managed by a shepherd and his dog is substituted by an enclosing proprietor for several score of families living by tillage, the rent roll of the estate can hardly fail to be increased, for the value of wool is so high, and the cost of sheep-farming so low, that the net income from which rent can be paid is large. But subsidies are assessed on property, not only on income; and on personal as well as real property. A rise in rents is quite compatible with a falling off in the gross produce of the land, and the conversion of an estate from arable to pasture, by displacing tenants, means a diminution in the farm stock and household property which has hitherto contributed towards the revenue.

Lest such a view should seem unduly theoretical, let us hasten to add that it is one which is endorsed by the authority of contemporaries. When subsidies are being debated in the House of Commons members complain that, while the wealthy are under-assessed, the small men pay more than their share.[611] Political writers from Fortescue[612] to Bacon[613] emphasise the fact that the ability of the country to bear taxation depends on the maintenance of a high level of prosperity among the yeomanry. The yeoman is a man who "makes a whole line in the subsidy book."[614] "The weight thereof," says a pamphleteer in 1647, "falls heavily ... especially upon the yeomanry."[615] The occasional glimpses which we get of harassed collectors trying in vain to screw taxes out of small farmers, whom a rise in rents or a bad season has plunged in distress, show the truth of their accounts. In the reign of Edward VI. subsidies cannot be collected on the northern border owing to the oppression to which some of the tenants have been subjected.[616] From Norfolk in 1628 comes a still more melancholy tale. "The ffarmors and such as use Husbandrye and tilth," write the Commissioners of the subsidy to the Government, "from whom in times past was accustomed to be drawne the greatest part of ye money leviable by way of subsidye, present unto us their pitiful estates, growen into decay through the base price and noe vent in these later years for their corne ... that some of them doo owe unto their landlordes two yeares rent, many of them one years.... All which considered we much feare that the collectors shall

---

[611] *D'Ewes' Journal*, p. 633. "Sir Walter Raleigh said ... 'Call you this par iugum when a poor man pays as much as a rich, and peradventure his estate is no better than he is set at, or little better; when our estates, that be thirty or forty pounds in the queen's books, are not the hundredth part of our wealth?'"

[612] Fortescue, *On the Governance of England*, chap. xii.: "The reaume off Ffraunce givith never ffrely off thair owne good will any subsidie to thair prince, because the commons thereoff be so pouere.... But owre commons be riche, and therefore thai give to thair kynge as somme tymes quinsimes and dessimes, and ofte tymes other grete subsidies."

[613] Bacon, *History of King Henry VII.* (Pitt Press Series), pp. 70–71: "The more gentlemen, ever the lower book of subsidies."

[614] Fuller, *The Holy and Profane State*.

[615] *The Standard of Equality in Subsidiary Taxes and Payments*, London, 1647.

[616] *S. P. D. Ed. VI.*, Addenda IV., p. 26: "Subsidies and duties must be levied on that border for your service, and they are loosed by oppression of your officers."

not gather in the monye soe speedily as they would or we desire."[617] The truth is that so much of the wealth of the country had been in the hands of the more prosperous among the small cultivators that any decline in their position was likely to place the Governments of our period in financial straits. They regard it with the self-interested apprehension which modern statesmen feel lest capital should be "driven abroad." Hence there was a strong fiscal motive for protecting the rural classes. Rebels who pointed out that "A man can have no more of a cat but the skin; that is the King can have no more of us than we have, which in a manner he has already,"[618] or tenants who urged the Crown to protect them on the ground that "they paie your Majesty subsidies, fifteens, and loans,"[619] were using language which the impecunious Government of the sixteenth and seventeenth centuries could understand much better than appeals to humanitarian sentiment. The military, financial, and political importance of the yeomanry was, in fact, great enough to make them one of the classes with whom the defence and order of the country were identified, and therefore sufficient to make them an object of solicitude to statesmen who were concerned with national interests.

Economic policies are not to be explained in terms of economics alone. When an old and strong society is challenged by a new phenomenon, its response is torn from a living body of assumptions as to the right conduct of human affairs, which feels that more than material interests are menaced, and which braces itself anxiously against the shock. The swift agrarian changes of the sixteenth century differ from the swifter changes of the eighteenth, in that enlightened opinion is, on the whole, against them, and that even the technical experts feel misgivings. If the attitude of statesmen is to be explained by the practical reasons which have already been given, the opposition of men like More, Latimer, Crowley, Starkey, and Hales seemed to themselves a plain matter of morals. In Germany Luther denounced the revolting peasants. In England those who in ecclesiastical matters were poles apart united in a plea for economic conservatism. Leading reformers preach and write against enclosing; and terrified landlords complain that "none ever spake so vilely as these so-called commonwealths."[620] Their understanding of the technique of the agrarian changes is often deficient. Like the Carlyles and Ruskins of a later age, they make Philistia merry with their sad blunders over economic details. But it would be a mistake to regard their views of the social effects of enclosing as abnormal or sentimental. They are the last great literary expression of the appeal to the average conscience which had been made by the old agrarian order, the cry of a spirit which is departing, and which, in its agony, utters words that are a shining light for all periods of change.

Several paths of argument lead to their position. There is the traditional importance of tillage. It is a "foundation industry," an industry from which four-

---

[617] *Original Papers of the Norfolk and Norwich Archæological Society,* 1907, pp. 139–140.

[618] Gairdner, *L. and P. Henry VIII.,* xi. 1244. See the remarks about Cromwell: "Item, the false flatterer says he will make the king the richest prince in Christendom.... I think he goes about to make him the poorest."

[619] See Appendix I., iv.

[620] Letter to Mr. Cecill from Sir Anthony Auchar, quoted by Russell, *Ket's Rebellion, in Norfolk,* p. 202.

fifths of the people directly or indirectly get their living. English Governments have always shown it special favour. Its maintenance is almost part of the common law[621] of the land. And it is right that it should be so. For the partition which separates men from starvation is thin, and if tillage fails how shall the people be fed? The Government insists on a certain minimum area being under the plough for exactly the same reason that the city of Coventry, when it is in the grip of a bad harvest, decides to break up part of its common pastures for wheat. All men are agreed that the price of food ought to be fixed by authority, and one cannot control prices unless one can control supplies. There is the argument from social functions. The State is a community of classes. Between classes there must be inequality, for each has a different function, fighting, or merchandise, or handicraft, or husbandry. Unless there is inequality between classes no class can perform its duties or (strange thought) enjoy its rights. But one class must not encroach upon the livelihood of another. If we will not have villein blood on the Council, neither will we let gentlemen take into their hands the holdings of their tenants. For this means that one limb of the body politic drains nourishment from another limb, and that men drop into a superfluous residuum from which the State gets no profit. And within a class there should be substantial equality. When one man has the livelihoods of two must not another man go without any living at all? There is the argument from economic morality. In every bargain there is the possibility of oppression. The unscrupulous man makes the most of this. He regards only his own profit. He is "a great taker of advantages."[622] This is the sin of the usurer, the bodger, and the tyrannous landlord, and of this bad trinity the last is the worst. To oppress men by rack-renting land is particularly detestable. For though in all contracts there is certainly (if only it can be found!) an objective standard of value, yet a man may with reason be in doubt as to what is fair price to charge for an article the value of which has not been fixed by authority. But he can hardly be in doubt as to what is a fair rent. The fair rent is the usual rent; equity is custom. There is the argument from the very nature of the bond between tenant and landlord. Tenure is no longer as sacred a thing as once it was, and, even if it were, men who are legally the descendants of right-less villeins could not easily appeal to its sanctity. But opinion feels that there is something despicably sordid in using this particular

[621] Miss Leonard (*Trans. Royal Hist. Soc.*, New Series vol. xix.) quotes Coke, *Institutes*, Book III., p. 105 (1644 ed.), and *S. P. D. Chas. I.*, clxxxvii., No. 95: "The decay of tillage and houses of husbandry are the undoubted causes and grounds of depopulation, and a crime against the Common Laws of this Realm, and every continuance thereof is a new crime." But the words "against the Common Laws" are hardly to be interpreted strictly.

[622] *S. P. D. Eliz.*, vol. cclxxxvi., Nos. 19 and 20: "He is a great taker of advantages. He granted a lease to his brother, who dying a year past, he sued his brother's wife to overthrow the lease to the undoing of her and her children." For a strong expression of these views see *Hist. MSS. Com.*, MSS. of Marquis of Salisbury, Part II., 1575, Nov. 20. Lord North to the Bishop of Ely: "My lord, it wilbe no pleasure for you to have hir Majestye and the Councell knowe howe wretchedly yowe live within and without your house, howe extremely covetous, how great a grazier, how marvellous a dayrye man, howe ritche a farmer, how grete an owner. It will not lyke yowe that the world knowe of your decayed houses, ... of the leases you pull violently from many, of the copyeholdes that yowe lawlesslye enter into, of the fre land that yowe wrongfully posese.... Yowe suffer no man to live longer under yowe than yowe lyke him."

relation as a financial engine. Though surveyors' economics are as notorious as lawyers' justice,[623] even one of that detested class can preface his business-like account of western manors with words idealising the conditions which have "knit such a knot of colaterall amytie between the Lords and the tenants that the lord tendered his tenants as his childe, and the tenants again loved the lord as naturally as the childe his father."[624] The bond between landlord and tenant is perhaps, indeed, the only economic relationship which has ever yet stirred the affection of large masses of men. It has done so because it has been in the past so much more than economic. The pitiful cry of that nameless old man to whose care Shakespeare commits the blinded Gloucester, "O my good lord, I have been your tenant, and your father's tenant, these fourscore years," is the voice of an attachment which once was real. In the sixteenth century the tie of tenure is still the symbol of greater things, and the wrench which is given it by the partial commercialising of agriculture seems to portend more ruinous innovations. Most men make the State in the image of their own village, or city, or business. It is perhaps not an unfair description of one side of the social philosophy of our period to say that a manor is still a "little commonwealth,"[625] the kingdom still the greatest of manors. If the lord holds from the King, does not the tenant hold from his lord by as good a right? If the tenant who encroaches on his neighbour's strips is checked by the manorial court, should not the lord who depopulates half a village be checked by the King in his High Court of Parliament? If gentlemen oppress yeomen, how can they "live together as they be joined in one body politic under the King?"[626]

It is true that it is just these ideas which in our period are on their trial, and that if one were to seek the watershed where the mediæval theory of land tenure, as something contingent on the fulfilment of obligations, parts company from modern conceptions of ownership, as conferring an unlimited right to unconditional disposal by the owner, one would find it in the century and a half between 1500 and the final abolition of feudal tenures in 1660. The combination of forces both economic and political making for a change of attitude is unmistakable; on the one hand the severance of the personal relationship of tenure through the development of the great leasehold farm, the breaking up of the customary routine of cultivation through the increasing dependence of agriculture on the market, the general revision of contracts brought about through the fall in the value of money; on the other hand the enormous redistribution of landed property through the confiscation of monastic and gild endowments, the consequent creation of a new aristocracy ready to apply commercial ideas to land tenure, the desire of proprietors to escape from the obnoxious feudal incidents and of the Crown to find some more lucrative substitute for them. But the decay of the older conceptions goes on very slowly. The Government is on the whole on the conservative side; for natu-

[623] Norden, *The Surveyor's Dialogue*, p. 1: "Farmer, I have heard much evill of the profession, and to tell you my conceit plainly I think the same both evill and unprofitable ... and oftentime you are the cause that men lose their land and sometimes they are abridged of such liberties as they have long used in mannors."

[624] *Topographer and Genealogist*, vol. i.

[625] Norden, *op. cit.*: "And is not every mannor a little commonwealth, whereof the tenants are the members, the land the body, and the lord the head?"

[626] Gairdner, *L. and P. Henry VIII.*, xii., I., 98, Instructions to the Duke of Norfolk.

rally it has to work on the material to hand, and the best hope of maintaining order lies in the preservation of fixed customary relationships between the different classes in society. Its instinct is therefore still to treat the control and disposition of land as to a special degree a question of public policy, in regard to which landlords are bound "rather to consider what is agreeable ... to the use of the state and for the good of the commonwealth, than to seeke the utmost profit which a landlord for his particular advantage may take among his tenants."[627]

### *(b) Legislation and Administration*

This was its instinct. But can we say more than this? Can we say that the presumption in favour of protecting the small landholder was translated into any definite policy, and that such a policy was carried out in practice? The answer to these questions is by no means easily given. There is the difficulty of making any generalisation which will cover the century and a half during which, from time to time, the agrarian problem claimed public attention. True, this difficulty is not so serious as might at first sight appear, or as it would be in an age of swiftly changing ideas. The political historian may treat the Tudors as one period and the first two Stuarts as another. But the economist finds much the same views on economic matters obtaining under Charles I. as under Henry VIII., and much the same administrative system to carry them out. There is in our period no marked change in responsible opinion upon the enclosing movement. The Commission which deals with the subject in 1607 shows the same attitude as the Commission of 1517. Enclosers are fined in 1637 as they have been fined in the reign of James I. But the opinion which counts is not always responsible opinion. During the six years which intervene between the death of Henry VIII. and the accession of Philip and Mary the Government is in the hands of the great landlords, — landlords who have built up their fortunes out of the spoils of the monasteries, and whom no authority is strong enough to check. By a curious chance the first head of the Government is a man who is an agrarian reformer by conviction. But, when he falls, his colleagues throw over his policy, and turn savagely to the work of crushing out the very possibility of organised protest among the peasantry. These years, the so-called reign of Edward VI., will be an exception to whatever conclusions may be reached as to the policy of the State under the Tudors and the first two Stuarts. Again, there is the difficulty, the great difficulty, of saying how far the interference of Governments is successful even when they honestly desire it to have effect. The modern assumption, which is sometimes all too sanguine, is that a Law is being carried out unless it is proved that it is not. For the sixteenth century there are those who would say that we must assume that a Law is not being administered unless it is proved that it is, and, though scepticism is sometimes pushed to absurd lengths, one certainly cannot build much on the letter of Acts of Parliament. But how exacting are our tests of effective administration to be? All will agree that in our period the mere enacting of a Statute causes and cures very little, unless special efforts are applied to making it work. But is a peremptory order from the Council to the Justices of the Peace, or to the Council of the North, to redress this or that griev-

[627] *Acts of the Privy Council,* New Series, vol. xxvii. p. 129. Letter from the Council to William Harman, Esq.

ance among tenants, a proof that the grievance will be redressed? Or must we be content with nothing less than a record of cases actually handled? If we decline to believe in the efficacy of any economic legislation about which we have not a full list of decisions, we shall have little left to rely on. The famous Statute of Artificers will look shaky, and so will the legislation with regard to prices and quality. Perhaps a reasonable view would be to look askance at mere Acts of Parliament, but to accept action, or orders to take action, on the part of the executive authorities, as a proof that the law is being applied in practice.

Of the Statutes prohibiting the conversion of arable to pasture we need not, then, say much. The long series of Acts[628] which were passed between 1489 and 1597 show little originality. They were at bottom simply a series of great manorial customaries framed to apply to the whole country, or to all parts of the country which were not expressly excepted from their operation, an attempt to maintain the *status quo* obtaining at any time by laying down for the whole country a common rule of cultivation of much the same kind as had been in the past maintained by local customs. They did not prohibit enclosure as such, but they proceeded on the assumption that a fixed proportion of the land, usually the average of a certain number of years preceding the Act, ought to be under the plough, and that the small cultivator's farm accommodation should be maintained or renewed at the expense of the landlord. They differed only in the methods used to achieve this end. The Statutes before 1550 usually insisted merely on the reconversion of pasture land to tillage,[629] the re-edification of decayed houses of husbandry,[630] and the limitation to 2000 of the sheep to be kept by any one farmer.[631] They relied on most unpromising machinery. Like the ancient Statute of Mortmain, they tried to make the feudal contract the means for enforcing the law, by empowering superior lords to take half the profits of mesne lords and tenants who infringed it. The Statutes after 1550 were somewhat bolder in their experiments. The most important departure was the provision, first introduced into the Statutes of 1552[632] and 1555,[633] for the creation of permanent bodies of Commissioners to do the work which, when most landlords were anxious to enclose, no landlord would undertake. Under the Statute of 1555, subsequently declared "too mild and gentle," but on the face of it a drastic measure, the Commissioners were empowered both to bind over offenders to rebuild decayed houses, to plough up pasture land, and to fix the judicial rents

---

[628] A useful list of these Acts, with a summary of their provisions, is given by Slater, *The English Peasantry and the Enclosure of Common Fields*, Appendix D.

[629] 4 Henry VII., c. 19. All occupiers of twenty acres and more which have been in tillage during three years preceding the Act to maintain tillage.

[630] 6 Henry VIII., c. 5, and 7 Henry VIII., c. 1. In parishes "whereof the more part was or were used and occupied to tillage and husbandry," any person who "shall decay a town, a hamlet, a house of husbandry, or convert tillage into pasture," and has not "within one yeere next after such wylfull decaye reedifyed and made ageyn mete and convenyent for people to dwell and inhabyte the same ... and therein to exercyse husbandry and tillage," forfeits one half of his land to the lord of the manor. Land converted to pasture must be tilled "after the maner and usage of the countrey where the seyd land lyeth."

[631] 25 Henry VIII., c. 13.

[632] 5 and 6 Edward VI., c. 5.

[633] 2 and 3 Philip and Mary, c. 2.

which had been demanded by the peasantry and suggested by certain reformers. It was repealed (together with the Statutes of 1536 and 1552) in 1563, the Act[634] of that year confirming the earlier Acts passed in the reign of Henry VIII., and requiring all land which had been under the plough for four successive years since 1529 to be kept in tillage, on pain of a fine of 10s. per acre for all land converted to pasture contrary to the Act. In 1589[635] a Statute was passed for the protection of cottagers, prohibiting the letting of cottages to agricultural labourers with less than four acres of land attached. In 1593[636] it was thought that sufficient land was in tillage to make the maintenance of legislation on the subject unnecessary, and the clause in the Act of 1563, which forbade conversion to pasture, was repealed. But the result seems to have been a recrudescence of the movement for converting arable land to pasture, with the result that in 1597[637] two more Acts were passed, both of which adopted the expedient of setting up a special authority, apart from the ordinary machinery of local government, to enforce the Act, by empowering the Lord Chancellor to nominate bodies of Commissioners. The first enacted that all houses of husbandry decayed within seven years preceding the Act, and half of those decayed within seven years before that, were to be rebuilt and let, the former with not less than 40 acres, and the latter with not less than 20 acres, of land. It also took the significant step of expressly sanctioning the consolidation of intermixed holdings by way of exchange between lord and tenants, or between one tenant and another. The second applied only to twenty-five counties, where, presumably, enclosing had proceeded furthest or was most disastrous in its effects. It enacted that all land converted from tillage to pasture since 1558 should be reconverted within three years, if it had been under the plough for twelve years immediately preceding conversion, and that land which had been in tillage for twelve years preceding the Act should remain in tillage, the penalty for disobedience being a fine of 20s. per acre. These two Acts escaped the general repeal of the laws against depopulation which took place in 1624, and remained on the Statute Book till the Statute Law Revision Act of 1863.

The Statutes are evidence of a state of opinion. To judge how far that opinion wrote itself on the world of affairs we must look elsewhere. Nor are they in themselves very interesting. The genius of sixteenth century statesmanship lay in administration not in legislation. It dwelt not in Parliament but in the Council, and in those administrative courts, the Court of Star Chamber, the Court of Requests, the Council of the North, the Council of Wales, which were the Privy Council's organs. In studying economic questions in the sixteenth and early seventeenth centuries, one is met at every turn by the apparatus of special administrative jurisdictions, which was built up by the Tudors, and which fell to pieces with the final rupture between the Crown and Parliament. On the one hand, they supply the control and stimulus in matters of detailed administration, without which all legislation designed to regulate shifting economic relationships, or running counter to the prejudices of a powerful class, is doomed to be ineffective. Are the Justices of the

---

[634] 5 Elizabeth, c. 2.
[635] 31 Elizabeth, c. 7.
[636] 35 Elizabeth, c. 7.
[637] 39 Elizabeth, c. 1 and c. 2.

Peace lax in carrying out the Statutes for the relief of the poor and punishment of vagrants? The Council will remonstrate. Have they omitted to assess wages and fix prices? The Council will let them know that their neglect has been noted at headquarters and that it must be corrected. Are capitalists in the clothing counties dismissing workmen in times of trade depression? The Council will direct the justices to read them a lesson on the duty of employers to their operatives and to the State, and threaten them with a summons to Whitehall unless they mend their ways. A stream of correspondence pours into London from the Government's agents in the counties—returns as to the supplies of wheat available for consumption, applications for permission to license the export of food-stuffs, statistics as to prices, information as to unemployment, information as to vagrancy based on a "day-count" of vagabonds. The Council digests it, and sends out its mandates to continue this and alter that, to raise wages or reduce prices, to inspect granaries, punish middlemen, whip sturdy rogues, relieve the poor. Bad means of communication, scanty and inaccurate intelligence, incompetent local officials, prevent administration from running smoothly; and as the Civil War approaches incompetence becomes recalcitrance. Nevertheless the engine is a powerful one, and up to a year or two before the meeting of the Long Parliament its throb is felt throughout the country.

Such a system of centralised supervision, which can meet emergencies with promptitude, and can adjust regulations to the varying needs of different years and different localities, is a necessity in any society where economic relationships are made the object of authoritative control. Under the Tudors and first two Stuarts the Council does much that is done to-day by several State departments—the Board of Agriculture and Fisheries, the Board of Education, the Local Government Board, the Home Office, as well as much that is left to Private Bill legislation. But the Council is, of course, much more than an executive organ. It is also a court of law. It does not only make rules, it punishes people for breaking them. Sometimes it exercises jurisdiction itself. More often, at any rate in the cases arising out of the economic questions with which we are chiefly concerned, it issues an order, and leaves the punishment of breaches of it to the Court of Star Chamber and the Court of Requests. Into the controversy as to the constitutional position of these courts we need not enter; we need only point out their extreme importance as buttresses of the Government's control over economic affairs. Both in personnel and procedure they were admirably qualified to be the instruments of a thorough system of State intervention in matters of industry and agriculture. Both of them were committees of the Council, and in both the governmental predominated over the judicial element, the two judges who attended the Court of Star Chamber, and the Masters of Requests who sat in the Court of Requests, being in the position rather of legal advisers or assessors than of judicial authorities. In theory the former court dealt with criminal, the latter with civil cases. But in an age when the majority of the populace were armed, a dispute was extremely likely to terminate in a riot, and in practice there were subjects on which complaints came before either court indifferently. They dispensed with a jury. They took account of equitable considerations which had no place in the common law courts. They were guided by reasons of State, not by the letter of the law, and would punish behaviour as contrary to public policy. For the execution of their rulings they used not only the ordinary officers of the law, the Justices of the Peace, but also special bodies of Commissioners.

Whatever may have been the abuses of this system of administrative jurisdictions, one can easily understand that it was well fitted to deal with the agrarian problem. It is seen at its worst in ecclesiastical matters. It is seen at its best in protecting the poorer classes against economic tyranny; and we shall fail to understand the popularity of the Tudor Governments unless we lay as much emphasis on the good side as on the bad. The Court of Requests in particular is a popular court, a court which punishes the rich, a court which brings, in the words of the aristocratic chronicler, "many an honest man to trouble and vexacion," a court to which the poor "compleyned without number."[638] The notorious difficulty of getting a verdict from a jury of tenants who are liable to eviction means that a landlord can break the law with impunity. Here are courts before which the intimidator can be intimidated; courts which will handle him "on that sort, that what courage soever he hath, his heart will fall to the grounde."[639] The enormous importance of manorial custom in determining the fate of all classes of peasants, except the freeholders, makes it certain that grave injustice will be done to vested interests by any court which confines itself to the strict letter of the law. The Council will direct that "such order be taken in the matter as in justyce and equitie shall appertayn."[640] The mere fact that its ruling is not simply the verdict of a court but the command of the Government, increases the probability that it will receive due attention from those whose duty it is to enforce it. The landlord who has enclosed may be the very man who hears the peasant's complaint. The Council will interfere to insist on the local authorities taking "a more indifferent course."[641]

The activity of the Government in matters of land was not so incessant as it was in the regulation of prices and the administration of the Poor Laws; for its land policy was strongly opposed to the interests of the country gentry who were its officials, and it had to proceed with caution. If we except the first great Commission appointed by Wolsey in 1517, the periods in which it was especially energetic in dealing with the land question were three, the years between 1536 and 1549, the years from 1607 to 1618, the years from 1630 to 1636; and on each of these three occasions there was some temporary cause to explain its peculiar zeal—on the two first the revolts of the peasantry, and on the last the rise in the price of grain, which suggested that an unduly small proportion of the land was under tillage. Nevertheless it handles individual cases with considerable frequency throughout

---

[638] Hall's *Chronicle of Henry VIII.*, p. 585 (Edition 1809), quoted by Leadam, introduction to *Select Cases in the Court of Requests* (Selden Society).

[639] Smith, *De Republica Anglorum*, Lib. III., chap. iv.

[640] *Acts of the Privy Council*, New Series, vol. xiii. pp. 91–92.

[641] *Acts of the Privy Council*, New Series, vol. xxx. pp. 36–37. A letter to the Council in the Marches of Wales, concerning the tenants of Aston in Montgomeryshire: "And if it be true, as they do inform us by their petitions, that examinations in a case concerning one of that Counsell should be taken by a kinsman of his owne and a clerk underneathe him, wee wyshe ... that you would have taken a more indifferent course, especially in a matter of commons, which, concerning many persons, doth easily give occasion of offence and scandal."

the whole period from 1517 to 1640. Usually it acts as a final court of appeal, which intervenes only when other means of redress have broken down, and it is sometimes at pains to explain to offended landlords that it does not intend to debar them from asserting their rights at Common Law, if they can. Its aim is to stop very gross cases of oppression, to prevent the peasants being made the victims of legal chicanery and intimidation, to induce landlords to take a larger view of their responsibilities, to settle disputes by the use of common sense and moral pressure. It steps in when the tenants are poor men who are being ruined by vexatious lawsuits, or when enclosure is thought likely to produce disorder, or to forbid a landlord to take action pending a decision by the courts. It has to hear many cases touching copyholders and many touching commons; for no one is quite certain as to the legal rights of copyholders, and in the matter of commons there is a fearful gulf between law and equity. Occasionally in the reign of Henry VIII., and even in that of Elizabeth, it deals with cases of villeinage. But these, though more numerous than might have been supposed, are nevertheless rare, for the principal economic evils of the period consist not in the revival of old claims, but in the new competitive conditions of agriculture. The treatment of the latter is by no means a simple matter—even the strong Governments of Henry VIII. and Elizabeth will not lightly thrust forceful fingers into the mysterious custom-bound recesses of the manor—and when we have said that on the whole the bias of the Tudor and early Stuart statesmen is against revolutionary changes that damage the peasants, we can say little more without citing individual cases of interference.

Let us look shortly at the more striking among them. The famous Commission upon enclosure appointed by Wolsey in 1517 set a precedent to be followed in several subsequent inquiries, and has left us an invaluable body of information as to the nature and extent of the enclosing movement. It was, however, by no means the first example of the Government intervening in the agrarian problem, and the partial reconversion of pasture to arable, which seems to have resulted from its labours, still left an urgent need for a continuous supervision of the relations between landlord and tenant by some tribunal sufficiently independent to do justice to the weaker party. In 1494 the earliest proceedings in the interminable case[642] of John Mulsho v. the inhabitants of Thingden ended in the Court of Star Chamber (the same court was dealing with the same matter in 1538) with a decree in favour of the tenants. In 1510 the same body was dealing with a quarrel between the Abbot and the copyholders of Peterborough,[643] and in 1516 with a complaint from the inhabitants of Draycote[644] and Stoke Gifford that the lord of the manor had evicted copyholders, stopped up rights of way, and enclosed common land. The policy of Wolsey is sufficiently indicated by the active campaign which he set on foot against depopulation, and requires no further illustration. But it is interesting to observe that his attitude towards the agrarian question was not a mere personal idiosyncrasy, and that it was the same in all essential particulars as that of his successor. Thomas Cromwell must bear the blame for part of the agrarian distress

[642] Selden Society, *Select Cases in the Court of Star Chamber*, edited by Leadam, and Leadam, E. H. R., vol. viii. pp. 684–696.

[643] Leadam, *E. H. R.*, vol. viii. pp. 684–696.

[644] *Ibid.*

which prevailed during the closing years of Henry VIII. and the reign of Edward VI.; for that distress was enhanced by the wild land speculation which followed the secularisation of the monastic estates. In that age, however, such indirect social reactions of their policy were matters quite beneath the consideration of statesmen, and the fact that the Government was responsible for changes which operated most disastrously on the established order of rural society did not prevent administrative interference to impede agrarian innovations from going on to the end of the reign of Henry VIII. Indeed the King, influenced no doubt by the fear that agrarian agitation might add fuel to religious discontent, seems himself to have taken some interest in the matter. In 1534 one finds Cromwell writing to congratulate him on the passage through the House of Commons of a Bill providing that no man shall keep more than 2000 sheep, and that one-eighth of every farmer's land shall always remain in tillage, "The most profitable and most benefycyall thing that ever was done to this the commonwealthe of your realm"[645] and in the following year there is a letter[646] from Cromwell to Rich directing him to apprise the Duke of Suffolk of the King's displeasure at the decay of certain towns which the Duke had promised to repair. The agrarian grievances expressed in the Pilgrimage of Grace were admitted, and in the instructions issued to the officers who were appointed to restore order in the disaffected counties special directions[647] were included to throw open enclosures, and to reduce the excessive fines charged to tenants on admission to their holdings. In the years immediately following the same policy was pursued in other parts of the country. In 1538 the Earl of Derby[648] writes to Cromwell protesting against the pressure put upon him to reinstate seven tenants whom he has turned out. In 1540 a landlord[649] in the Isle of Wight is compelled to restore to their holdings some recently evicted tenants. In 1541 several cases come before the Council. It appoints a Commission to investigate the case of a Northamptonshire[650] landlord who has prevented the tenants of Brigstock from feeding their pigs, calves, and sheep, by cutting up part of a common wood "into several pastures for his own private use and benefit." It meets a complaint from the borderers[651] of the Forest of Dartmoor that the owner of the lands of the monastery of Buckfast is breaking the statute which required the lands of dissolved abbeys to be farmed in the traditional way, by excluding them from the common, with a decision upholding the tenants' case and with the appointment of Commissioners

---

[645] Merriman, *Life and Letters of Thomas Cromwell*, vol. i. p. 273.

[646] *Ibid.*, vol. i. p. 413.

[647] Gairdner, *L. and P. Henry VIII.*, xii., I., 98 and 595.

[648] Gairdner, *L. and P. Henry VIII.*, xiii., I., 334 (see also 66, where an appeal is made January 11, 1536, to Cromwell to protect some tenants in Denbighshire.)

[649] *Proceedings and Ordinances of the Privy Council*, vol. vii. p. 42: "The King's pleasure was signified to John Dawney, Knight, that whereas he had turned certain persons in the Isle of Wight out of their farms, whereof they pretended to have leases, and had demised the same to others that minded not to dwell upon the same, he should take order that the old tenants might enjoy their leases until Michaelmas, come a twelve month, and that in the mean season the King's Highness would see a direction taken in the matter."

[650] *Ibid.*, vol. vii. pp. 225–226. July 30 and August 1, 1541.

[651] *Ibid.*, vol. vii. pp. 123–125. January 25, 1541.

to carry out the award. It sets a certain choleric Sir Nicholas Poyntz,[652] who has dared to procure the imprisonment of a tenant for proceeding against him before the Council, to cool his temper in the Fleet, and when he comes out compels him to grant his victim a new farm in exchange for one which he has surrendered, to reduce his rent from 20s. to 6s., and to pay him forty marks as compensation for his "damages and travailles." In 1543[653] the tenants of Abbots Ripton lay a complaint in the Court of Requests against Sir John St. John on the ground that, in addition to other acts of oppression, he has entered forcibly on their holdings. Sir John replies that they are not copyholders, but merely tenants at will, who are unprotected by any immemorial custom, and after an examination of the manor rolls the court holds that he is right. But the legal insecurity of the tenants does not prevent them from getting protection. The court requires their landlord to grant them leases for years at reasonable rents, and orders that the property which he has distrained shall be restored.

With the Protectorate of Somerset we enter upon a period of more violent agitation and more drastic expedients. There was a large difference between using the jurisdiction of the Council to redress individual cases of hardship and a deliberate attempt to effect a general settlement of the land question upon lines which would do substantial justice to the peasants. The former course involved no perilous assertion of principles, and could be pursued under the guise of a purely conservative policy, merely by referring disputes between landlords and tenants to the Courts of Star Chamber and Requests, which, though in fact administrative and governmental bodies, were none the less protected to some extent against criticism by wearing the appearance of mere legal tribunals. The latter might, perhaps, have been attempted with some faint hope of success, if statesmen had been much more careful than they were to discriminate between the different aspects of the problem with which they were confronted. To us, who look back on the situation from a distance of three and a half centuries, it seems that the one guiding thread, which might have led some way through the welter of confusion, was offered by the sharp distinction drawn by Hales between those enclosures which were made by the exchange and consolidation of strips, with a view to better husbandry, and those which had as their effect the conversion of arable land to pasture, the monopolising of commons, and the eviction of tenants. The arguments in favour of the first type of enclosure were too cogent for any policy which condemned enclosing in general to have the smallest prospect of success. The only possibility of averting the ruin to the peasantry which accompanied depopulation lay in encouraging them generally to follow the example of their brothers in Kent, Essex, Devonshire, and Cornwall, who had for centuries been substituting a more progressive husbandry for the "mingle mangle" of the open fields, without the disastrous consequences entailed by the spread of capitalist agriculture in other parts of the South and Midlands. But such a frank encouragement of certain kinds of enclosure for the sake of repressing others implied an appreciation of the economics of the problem to which comparatively few persons in our period had attained, and was quite beyond the grasp of Governments, which, at their worst, as

[652] *Acts of the Privy Council*, New Series, vol. i. pp. 5 and 9.

[653] Leadam, *E. H. R.*, vol. viii. pp. 684–696.

under Warwick, were quite indifferent to the sufferings of the poorer classes, and, at their best, conceived public interests to be served best by a strict maintenance of customary conditions. Somerset's policy of deliberately restoring ancient relationships with a strong hand could hardly even be begun without those who pursued it taking sides in a bitter economic agitation, and essaying openly to reverse the whole agrarian movement with which, in the course of the past half century, the wealth of the middle and upper classes, at any rate south of the Trent, had become inextricably identified. It involved in fact a return to the policy of Wolsey, and a return to it under conditions which made Wolsey's policy doubly hard to carry out, inasmuch as, on the one hand, the position of Somerset as temporary head of a jealous aristocracy was far weaker than that of the omnipotent Cardinal, and, on the other hand, the lapse of twenty years had seen the growth of a generation to which enclosures were a vested interest.

Yet it would be a mistake to think of the whole agrarian episode between the death of Henry VIII. and the fall of Somerset as the mere freak of a misguided doctrinaire. If we can see difficulties which he did not, if we can smile at the thought of any Government at once so incompetent, and but for Somerset himself, so entirely selfish, carrying out a great conservative revolution in the teeth of the new wealth and power of the country, we must also remember that he was not alone in thinking the spoliation of the weaker rural classes not only, as it certainly was, illegal, but also so patently unjust as to amount to a national crime, and that in that age men overestimated the ability of a Government fiat to modify economic habits almost as much as they underestimated it two and a half centuries later. Somerset can hardly have been ignorant of the tremendous risks involved in his policy. But he may well have thought inaction not only baser than, but almost as dangerous as, action. It was certain that, unless the Government interfered to protect tenants, there would be a series of peasants' revolts. The best answer to the charge of stirring up class hatred, which was made against Somerset, as against all who call attention to its causes, was that agrarian rioting had begun in Hertfordshire[654] before the Commission on Enclosures was sent out, that in those counties where it took its work seriously order was maintained till the end of 1548, and that grave disturbances did not take place until the following year, when it became evident that, both in Parliament and on the Council, the Protector's policy had been beaten by the opposition of the great landowners. Nor is there any reason to doubt the sincerity of Somerset himself (though he, like every one else, had speculated in monastic estates), however much there may be to regret that his policy did not come into stronger hands, or fall upon times which were, from a political point of view, less hopelessly impracticable. An attempt was made to set a good example on the Crown Estates. In 1548, in response to complaints from the tenants at Walton, Weybridge, Esher, and Shepperton, that the making of the royal deer park at Hampton Court was ruining them through the loss of common rights which it entailed, an order[655] was issued dechasing the Park, and throwing open

[654] Appendix to Miss Lamond's edition of *The Commonweal of this Realm of England*, Hale's defence, p. lviii.: "Whas ther not, longe before this Commyssyon was sent forthe, an insurrection in Hertfordshire for the comens at Northall and Cheshunt?"

[655] *Acts of the Privy Council*, New Series, vol. ii. pp. 190–193, May 5, 1548: a complaint

the enclosed lands to the commoners. In the following year Somerset secured the passage through Parliament of a Private Act[656] conferring a good title on those copyholders on his own manors to whom demesne lands had been let, and who, as occupiers of other than customary tenancies, could not claim the protection of manorial custom. It is plain from the comparatively few complaints which came in the sixteenth century from freeholders that, if such a course had been generally pursued, the chief objection to the changes grouped together under the name of enclosure would have been removed, because the harsh disturbance of vested interests which they involved would have been avoided. But that, of course, was quite outside the bounds of political possibility.

The story of Somerset's attempt to deal with the land question is soon told. In 1548 agrarian discontent was at its height. Some time in that year there must have come to the hands of the Government the small tract on the effect of sheep-farming in Oxfordshire, Northamptonshire, Buckinghamshire, and Berkshire, which was printed in 1551 under the name of "Certayne causes of the Present Discontent."[657] In spring and summer Latimer was thundering against the "Step-lords"[658] at Paul's Cross. In autumn Crowley published his "Information and Petition against the Oppressors of the Poor Commons."[659] Above all, the poor commons had earlier in the year shown unmistakable signs of fending for themselves. The result of Somerset's own sympathy with the prevalent discontent was the formation of something like a party, under the name of the "Commonwealth men," with Latimer as its prophet and Hales as its man of action, which had a programme sufficiently definite to put heart into the peasantry and to terrify the great landed proprietors. On June 1st a Royal Commission[660] was appointed to inquire into offences committed against the Acts forbidding conversion of arable to pasture

---

from "many poor men of the Parishes of Walton, Weybridge, East Molson, West Molson, Caverham, Esher, Byfiete, Temsditton ... in the name of the whole parishes before rehearsed, that by reason of the making of the late chase of Hampton Court, forsomyche as their commons, pastures, and meadows be taken in, and that all the said parishes are overlaid with the deer now increasing daily upon them, very many households of the same parishes be let fall down, the families decayed, and the king's liege people much diminished, the country thereabout in manner made desolate."

[656] See p. 294.

[657] Published by the E. E. T. S.

[658] The first sermon preached before King Edward the Sixth, March 8, 1549: "You landlords, you rent-raisers, I may say you step-lords, you unnatural lords, you have for your possession yearly too much. For that herebefore went for twenty or forty pounds by year ... now is let for fifty or an hundred pound by year." See also Latimer, *The Sermon of the Plough*, January 18, 1548.

[659] Strype, *Ecclesiastical Memorials*.

[660] The proclamation appointing the Commission is printed by Strype, *op. cit.*, vol. ii., Book I., chap. ii. The operative part of it runs: "And therefore, He ... hath appointed, according to the said acts and proclamations, a view and inquiry to be made of all such as contrary to the said acts and godly ordinances have made enclosures and pasture of that which was arable ground, or let any house, tenement, or mease decay or fall down, or done anything contrary of the good and wholesome articles contained in the said acts." In my account of the situation under Somerset I have followed the documents printed by Strype, and the appendix to Miss Lamond's introduction to *The Commonweal of this Realm of England*.

and depopulation. The Commission divided itself into several committees to deal with different parts of the country. Only one of them, however, consisting of John Hales and five of his colleagues, got seriously to work. It had a large area to cover—the counties of Oxfordshire, Berkshire, Warwickshire, Leicestershire, Bedfordshire, Buckinghamshire, and Northamptonshire—and one which was the centre of the agitation against enclosure. It seems to have interrupted its labours during autumn and winter, but it was busy in June, July, and August 1548, and again in the summer of 1549, by which time, however, the anger of the landed gentry against its proceedings, and of the peasants against the inactivity of the Commission as a whole, had reached a point which made it hardly possible for it to do more than collect information. Considering the difficulties of its task, and the wide tract of country to be covered, its behaviour appears to have been thorough and business-like. The usual procedure was to empanel a jury of twelve in each place visited, to whom Hales delivered an address explaining the objects and methods of the inquiry, as set out in the instructions issued by the Government to the Commissioners. These stated the Commission to have been formed in particular "for the maintenance and keeping up of houses of husbandry, for avoiding destruction and pulling down of houses for enclosures and converting of arable land into pasture, for limiting what number öf sheep men should have and keep in their possession at one time, against plurality and keeping together of farms, and for maintenance of housekeeping, hospitality, and tillage on the sites ... of such monasteries, priories, and religious houses as were dissolved."[661] Offenders were then presented by the jury, and though, on Hales' advice, a pardon was granted them for their past illegalities, their enclosures seem to have been thrown down, arable which had been turned into pasture to have been ploughed up, and farms which had been united to have been separated.[662]

In the meantime Somerset kept the general policy of agrarian reform alive on the Council. In the autumn of 1548 Hales had returned to London, and, as member for Preston, had prepared three Bills, dealing partly with enclosures and partly with the high prices. The first, requiring re-edification of decayed houses and the maintenance of tillage, and the second, forbidding speculation in food-stuffs, were introduced into the House of Lords. The third, which aimed at encouraging cattle breeding as distinct from sheep grazing, was read first in the House of Commons. Neither Bill came to anything, for Parliament was as angry as the Council with Somerset's policy. But in May 1549 the Protector issued another proclamation against the decay of houses and enclosure; in June he infuriated the upper classes by a proclamation pardoning persons who had taken the law into their own hands by pulling down hedges; and throughout the whole period of his power he used the Court of Requests as an instrument for protecting tenants against landlords.[663]

---

[661] Strype, *Ecclesiastical Memorials.*

[662] For the pardon, see appendix to Miss Lamond's introduction to *The Commonweal,* &c., p. lxi.; for the ploughing up of a park and division of farms, *ibid.,* pp. xli. and lxi.-lxii.; for the Bills introduced by Hales, *ibid.,* xl., xlv.-lii., lxii.-lxv. Strype's account appears to be based on that of Hales.

[663] For these facts, see Strype, *Ecclesiastical Memorials.*

The Secretary[664] to the Council, who was quite ready for a reign of terror provided that the gentry began it, prophesied gloomily that the German peasants' revolt was to be re-enacted in England, and Warwick attacked Hales fiercely for venturing to discharge the duties laid upon him by the Government, of which Warwick was a member.[665] "Sir," wrote a plaintive Norfolk gentleman to Cecil about the time of Ket's rebellion, "Be plain with my Lord's Grace, that under the pretence of simplicity and poverty there may not rest much mischief. So do I fear there doth in these men called Commonwealths and their adherents. To declare unto you the state of the gentlemen (I mean as well the greatest as the lowest) I assure you they are in such doubt that almost they dare touch none of them, but for that some of them have been sent up and come away without punishment, and that Commonwealth called Latimer hath gotten the pardon of others.... I may well gather some of them to be in jealousy of my Lord's friendship, yea and to be plain, think my Lord's grace rather to will the decay of the gentlemen than otherwise."[666] Poor gentlemen! A Government which holds that laws do not exist only to preserve the rich in their possessions! Truly the mountains are removed.

Somerset's Government had too short a life for us to judge how far, in happier political circumstances, he might have succeeded, not in checking agrarian changes, which would in any case have been impossible, but in securing that reasonable consideration should be given to the vested interests of the poorer classes. As Elizabethan statesmen discovered[667] at the end of the century, there was room for a policy which would prevent the wholesale displacement of tenants, and nevertheless offer an encouragement to the formation of the compact holdings out of the scattered strips and common pastures, which the agricultural experts were unanimous in condemning. There are faint indications of an understanding that a fair middle course was possible in a remarkable case which comes from the little Huntingdonshire town of Godmanchester.[668] At Godmanchester there had been the usual changes of the preceding half century. Rents had been raised, cottages pulled down, woods destroyed and turned to pasture, while the meadows, which under the Act of 1547 had been confiscated from the local gild, offered a tempting

---

[664] Strype, *Ecclesiastical Memorials*. Sir William Paget to the Lord Protector, July 7, 1549: "The king's subjects are out of all discipline, out of all obedience, caring neither for Protector nor King. And what is the cause? Your own lenity ... the foot taketh upon him the part of the head, and commons is become king, a king appointing conditions and laws to the governors, saying, 'Grant this and that and we will go home.' ... What then is the matter, troweth your grace?... By my faith, Sir, even that which I said to your grace.... Liberty, Liberty.... In Germany, when the very like tumult to this began first, it might have been appeased with the loss of 20 men, and after with the loss of 100 or 200. But it was thought nothing and might easily be appeased, and also some spiced consciences taking pity of the poor ... thought it a sore matter to lose so many of their country folk, saying they were simple folk.... It cost, ere it was appeased, they say, 1000 or 2000 men."

[665] Appendix to Miss Lamond's introduction to *The Commonweal*, &c., pp. xli. and lii. But of course there was no such thing as collective responsibility for policy in the sixteenth century.

[666] Russel, *Ket's Rebellion in Norfolk*, p. 202.

[667] See p. 355.

[668] *Acts of the Privy Council*, New Series, vol. ii. pp. 294–296.

prey to some enterprising speculator. On complaints coming before the Council in the summer of 1549 a comprehensive scheme of reorganisation was drawn up. All persons with more than one house were to let at the customary rent that which they did not use themselves. All persons who had pulled down houses or converted them to other purposes than the accommodation of tenants were either to rebuild them or to build new ones, and to let them to any one offering the customary rent before Michaelmas 1549. The groves of wood converted to pasture were to be enclosed, so as to prevent the depredations made upon them by straying beasts, and, if necessary, the land was to be sown with acorns. With the gild lands a course was taken which, in the scramble for land which was going on in the middle of the sixteenth century, was unfortunately highly unusual. According to the Council's directions they were to "be divided among the inhabitants thereof in this manner; that is to say to every ploughland five acres, and to every cottager and artificer there dwelling, or which hereafter upon the houses to be now builded shall dwell, one acre, and, if the number do not extend, then for every ploughland four, and so for lack of the rate every ploughland three, and the residue of the said acres falling after that rate to be divided among the cottagers, paying for every of the said acres ¾." This case is the high water mark of administrative interference on behalf of the tenants. The action taken embraces nearly all the expedients of re-edifying decayed cottages, fixing fair rents, preventing common land from passing into the control of a single individual, and making equal allotment among the inhabitants, which had been demanded by the peasants and suggested by their friends. It shows that the enclosing of land hitherto used in common was not resented, provided that the division was made in such a way as to give a fair share to all the parties interested. It may perhaps be taken as a specimen of the kind of policy which lay behind Somerset's expressions of sympathy with the peasantry, and which he would have pursued if his colleagues on the Council had permitted. As it was, he was not strong enough to carry out his programme. While the failure of the Commission resulted in the revolts of 1549, his reluctance to crush their authors, whom he believed to be men goaded into rebellion by intolerable grievances, united the whole weight of the greater property against him as a traitor to his order. In the attack made upon him as by his colleagues, the actions which evoked their special denunciation were those which embodied his agrarian policy, the use of the Court of Requests to protect tenants, the appointment of the Royal Commission to enforce the Acts against enclosures, the pardon granted in June 1549 to the riotous peasants, and the statements attributed to him that "the covetousness of the gentlemen gave cause to the common people to rise," and that "people had good cause to reform the things themselves," because "the lords of Parliament were loathe to incline themselves to reformation of enclosures and other things."[669] To the last a popular hero, the "good Duke" could expect no help from those whom he had befriended, and no mercy from the sordid counter-revolution which he had provoked. His epitaph was given by the sad cries of "Too true," with which the crowd about the scaffold greeted his dying declaration that he had "ever been glad of the furtherance ... of the commonwealth."[670]

---

[669] Strype, *Ecclesiastical Memorials.*

[670] Somerset's execution took place on January 22, 1552, more than two years after

With the fall of Somerset in October 1549 the landowning classes had their revenge, and, under the guidance of Warwick, the policy of the Government swung violently in the opposite direction. The intervention of the Council to protect tenants of course stopped at once; in the two cases which are reported as having come before it in the year 1550 and 1551 the line taken was that the presumption was against the tenants who had broken open enclosures.[671] While, in the absence of John Hales, who appears to have found it convenient to leave the country, the Reports of the Royal Commission were allowed to slumber, the Government, by way of reducing opportunities for undesirable meetings, instructed the Bishop of London to prevent unseasonable preaching in his diocese, and set itself to establish the new agrarian régime by law. The ways in which men seek liberty are infinite in number, but the methods of tyranny are everywhere the same; and the nearest parallel to the behaviour of Somerset's successors is the attitude of the panic-stricken aristocracy of the early nineteenth century towards trade unions. Under an Act of 1550 all meetings of the peasantry were treated as a sort of "illegal conspiracy." Any forty of them who assembled to break down an enclosure might be condemned as traitors. Any twelve who assembled for the same purpose were guilty of felony, as also were those who summoned such a meeting, or who combined to reduce rents or the price of corn. Even the rusty legislation of the thirteenth century was revived by the re-enactment of the Statute of Merton of 1235,[672] which permitted lords to enclose as much as they pleased, provided that "sufficient" remained over for the tenants, with the significant improvement that the latter qualification was swept away by a clause declaring that enclosures might be made "notwithstanding their gainsaying and contradiction." The tyranny of the oligarchy which ruled from 1549 to 1553 has been obscured by the more dramatic events which preceded and succeeded it. But it marks the bottom point in the condition of the sixteenth century peasantry. It indicates how the new agrarian régime will develop when the political forces impeding it are removed. More had asked, What is Government? and had answered that it is "a certein conspiracy of riche men procuringe theire owne commodities under the name and title of a Common Wealth." His immortal definition does less than justice to the cynicism of the generation which succeeded his own. Mary executed Protestants for reasons of religion, as Elizabeth executed Catholics for reasons of State. But Warwick, a hypocrite in religion, was at least guiltless of the hypocrisy of sheltering his land policy "under the name and title of the Common Wealth." It was exactly what it seemed to be, a straightforward attempt to prevent the poor from protesting when their possessions were taken from them by the rich.

The general policy of the Government during the reign of Elizabeth and the he had been deposed from the Protectorate, for supposed complicity in a plot to overthrow the Government. The evidence for the existence of a conspiracy appears to be feeble. See Pollard, *The Political History of England*, 1547–1603, pp. 61–65.

[671] *Acts of the Privy Council*, New Series, vol. iii. pp. 181–182 and 247 and 252. "Mr. Grenewaie was this day before the Counsaill and rebuked sore for his attemptate in causeng Raf Lees hedges to be broaken up; nevertheless considering his long service [as gentleman usher] he was borne withall, and for this tyme without further punishment he was commaunded to make up those hedges again."

[672] 3 and 4 Edward VI. c. 3.

first half of the seventeenth century shows neither the desire of Somerset to undo the agrarian revelation, nor the complete indifference to the interests of the poorer classes of the party which succeeded him. During the reign of Elizabeth there was little agrarian agitation. It is possible that the limits of profitable pasture-farming had been reached. It is possible that the policy of encouraging the export of corn, which had been suggested by Hales, and which was adopted in 1563 and extended in 1571, reacted favourably on arable farming. It is possible, again, that Warwick's measures had had their effect, and that the peasantry had been cowed into silence. Though, on the whole, the Government maintained the traditional attitude, it did not interfere except in circumstances of special hardship, or when there was danger of serious disturbance. Cases of this nature came before it fairly frequently in the reigns of Elizabeth, Charles, and James. One finds it intervening on the ground that the poverty of tenants makes it impossible for them to go to law, or that the offenders concerned are so powerful as to be able to disregard inferior authorities, or that the local authorities themselves have been unfairly biassed, or to prevent disturbances by hearing tenants' grievances, or to compel a great noble, like the Earl of Shrewsbury, to reinstate tenants whom it thinks to have been wrongfully evicted, or to stop action being taken by a landlord pending a decision by the courts in his favour. In 1579 the Council writes to the Lord President of Wales ordering him to take proceedings against two persons who have been enclosing part of the Forest of Fakenham, and have disturbed the copyholders; he is to prevent any further enclosures being made until the whole matter has been considered by the Government.[673] In 1581 it interferes to protect a copyholder who has been kept out of his holding by the Dean and Chapter of Peterborough.[674] In 1586 it directs the Cambridgeshire justices to inquire into the complaint of some tenants who claim that a piece of common pasture has been let over their heads, and to see that both parties to the dispute come before the Justices of Assize.[675] The Justices of Assize in Norfolk are to take action in the matter of a common at Kettlestone which

---

[673] *Acts of the Privy Council*, New Series, vol. xi. pp. 191–192. A letter to the Lord President of Wales that whereas upon complaints exhibited to their lordships by the tenants of the Forest of Fakenham against Sir John Throgmorton, and one Mr. William Bell his stuarde, concerning an inclosure by him made of certen commons ... encroachment upon their copieholds ... it was by them ordered that the suite against the tenants commenced at the Common Lawe in respect of their commons and copieholds should surcease and the matters in controversy abyde triall before their lordships ... and untill the matter should be heard and determined they enjoyned to proceed no further in the inclosure of the said Common ... forasmuch as the tenants do now again complaine that since their lordships' said order Sir John and the said William Bell have inclosed more of the said common ... but hath also caused Bell to proceed against the tenants by *ejectione firmæ* at the Common Lawe, he is therefore required ... to will and command the said Sir John and William Bell to forbear their inclosures of the said Common ... untill the same shall be ... determined by their lordships according to their lordships' form and order."

[674] *Acts of the Privy Council*, New Series, vol. xiii. pp. 91–92. A letter to the Justices of the County of Lincoln: "If they thinke it agreeable with equitie and justice that the poore man should be put in possession of the said Landes, that they give commandment unto the said Lacy to admit him thereunto."

[675] *Ibid.*, vol. xiv. pp. 201–202.

two of the tenants allege to have been overstocked with sheep.[676] Several letters are addressed to the Council of the Marches of Wales ordering them to prevent the eviction of copyholders.[677] A landlord is requested to attend the Council and prove that his tenants' fines are uncertain, and not, as they allege, fixed.[678] The Court of Chancery has dismissed a case arising out of the enclosure of commons at Bath, and the Council orders a retrial.[679] Occasionally it cites offenders into the Court of Star Chamber,[680] and in 1592, just when the Court of Requests was beginning to be attacked by the common lawyers, we find a case as to fold-courses coming before the Court of Requests.[681] More often it appoints special Commissioners to act as arbitrators, or refers petitioners to the Justices of Assize in their county, with a request to take local evidence and inform the Council what they advise. Throughout the reigns of James and Charles we get glimpses of administrative activity which show that the traditional policy was, perhaps fitfully, maintained. In 1603 the Council of the North[682] were instructed to make "from time to time diligent and effectual inquisition of the wrongful taking in of commons and other grounds, and the decay of tillage and of towns or houses of husbandry," and to correct offenders with "some notable punishment." The rebellion in the Midlands in 1607 produced special measures, the chief offenders being summoned before the Council and bound over to rebuild houses which had fallen into decay, while in the following years two Commissions were appointed to compound with enclosers.[683] In Yorkshire the justices are evidently fairly active in 1607 and 1608. A Richmond freeholder who owns two-thirds of the manor is presented "for decaying five husbandries, and also for converting 30 acres of tillage ground to meadow and pasture," and similar presentments are made at Malton, Thirsk,

---

[676] *Ibid.*, vol. xv. pp. 394–395.

[677] See p. 373, n. 1, and *Acts of the Privy Council*, New Series, vol. xvii. p. 76. For a similar letter to the Council of the North, *ibid.*, vol. xxvii. pp. 228–229.

[678] *Ibid.*, vol. xxii. p. 379.

[679] *Ibid.*, vol. xxii. pp. 360 and 370. Letters to the Master of the Rolls ordering retrial of case concerning enclosure of commons at Bath.

[680] *Ibid.*, vol. xvi. pp. 366–367. A letter to the Solicitor: "Whereas divers poor men, tenants of the manor of Chilton, have exhibited very grievous complaints unto their lordships against William Darrell, Esq., of divers and sundry misdemeanors committed by him in breach of her majestie's peace" ... the solicitor is to "cause a byll to be drawn into the Court of Star Chamber against Darrel," and Camden Society 1886, *Cases in the Court of Star Chamber and High Commission*, pp. 44–45.

[681] Holkham MSS., Sparham, Bdle. No. 5, 14th June, 34 Eliz: "In the matter in variance brought before the Queenes Majestie in her Maj[tie's] hon[ble] Court of Requests at the suit of John Byrd against Christopher Saye and other defendants upon the motion of Mr. Edward Coke recorder of the City of London being of Councel with the said defendant.... For that it appeareth that the said Defendant hath had three verdicts and judgments at the Common Law, one of them against the said complainant himself."... The defendant is awarded costs, "and the said complainant shall from henceforth forbear to put any sheepe upon the said ground, and suffer his sheepe to feede there."

[682] Prothero, *Statutes and Constitutional Documents*, 1558–1625, pp. 370–371.

[683] Prothero, *Statutes and Constitutional Documents*, 1558–1625, pp. 470–472, and Gay, *Trans. Royal Hist. Soc.*, New Series, vol. xviii.

and Helmsley.[684] A Justice of Assize writes about the same time from the western counties to the effect that twenty-six houses of husbandry have been rebuilt and the offenders punished.[685] In 1614 the justices of Norfolk inform the Council that in accordance with its directions they have examined the enclosures made in the last two years, and have ordered the hedging and ditching of lands to be stopped till further notice.[686] In the following year one William Combe was negotiating with the corporation of Stratford for their consent to the enclosure and conversion to pasture of his freehold lands lying in the common fields at Welcombe; in 1615 an order made at Warwick Assizes was confirmed by the Chief Justice restraining him from doing so on the ground that it was "against the laws of the realm," and in the following year a peremptory letter was addressed to him by the Council directing his compliance.[687] In 1619 there was a temporary reaction owing to the low price of grain, which led to the appointment of a Commission to grant pardons for breaches of the Acts forbidding enclosure, and in 1624 all the Statutes except the two passed in 1597 were repealed. But this did not stop administrative interference. In 1621 the Justices of Assize for Bedfordshire are directed to check encroachments on a common, and in 1623 a Commission is appointed to remove grievances arising in connection with enclosures at Cheshunt.[688] The rise in corn prices which occurred from 1629 to 1631 produced another burst of activity, which is to be attributed partly to a genuine desire to protect the poorer classes, and partly to the hope that the fines imposed upon enclosers might squeeze a few drops into the Government's ever thirsty Exchequer. In 1630 directions were issued by the Council to the justices of five Midland counties to remove all enclosures made in the last two years on the ground that they led to depopulation and were particularly harmful in time of dearth.[689] In 1632, 1635, and 1636, three Commissions were appointed, and special instructions to enforce the Statutes against enclosure were issued to the Justices of Assize.[690] That the inquiry was not a mere formality is proved by the State Papers of the period. In part of the country, at any rate, land which had been pasture was ploughed[691] up in obedience to the Government's orders, and a list of offenders, including — the Government must have seen his name with grim satisfaction — Lord Saye and Sele, was returned to the Council, some of whom were still being prosecuted in the Court of Star Chamber as late as 1639.

[684] Atkinson, *North Riding Quarter Sessions*, vol. i. pp. 106, 108, 111, 122. The last presentment runs: "Will Marwood of Busby, gentⁿ, for decaying of xxx acres of arable land or thereabouts, and converting of xxx acres of arable land or thereabouts, the same, from tillage into pasture or meadow, and tilled nothing in the same parish in lieu thereof, contrary, etc."

[685] Leonard, *Trans. Royal Hist. Soc.*, vol. xix.

[686] Leonard, *Trans. Royal Hist. Soc.*, vol. xix.

[687] Ingleby, *Shakespeare and the Welcombe Enclosures.*

[688] *S. P. D. J., I.*, vol. cxxiv., December 20, 1621, and *S. P. D.*, Ch. i. cliii., October 2, 1623.

[689] Leonard, *Trans. Royal Hist. Society*, vol. xix.

[690] *Ibid.*

[691] For the ploughing up of pasture, *S. P. D.*, Ch. I. vol. cccciv. 142, and vol. cccclxxv. 72; for Lord Saye and Sele, vol. ccclxii. 60, 1637; order of Council that the Attorney-General should forthwith proceed by information in the Star Chamber against Viscount Saye and Sele for depopulation and conversion of houses and lands.

This is the last occasion on which we can trace the administration of this part of the Tudor State policy. The agitation against enclosures was carried on under the Commonwealth. The diggers under Winstanley came into prominence for a moment, only to be disclaimed by the respectable[692] opponents of enclosure and to be instantly suppressed by the Government, and there was a crop of pamphlets in the years between 1650 and 1660 which dealt with the evils of depopulation in quite the old manner. But the traditional doctrine as to the importance of the peasantry had decayed, and the central machinery for forcing the justices to take action had been destroyed in 1641. The last Bill to regulate enclosures was introduced into the House of Commons in 1656, and was rejected on the second reading.[693]

## *(c) Success and Failure of State Intervention*

It remains to ask how far the policy of trying to check the agrarian changes, which was pursued by Governments for nearly a century and a half, had any effect on economic practice. Statesmen were certainly biassed in favour of protecting the weaker landholding classes. But was their intervention simply the expression of a pious opinion? Was it so entirely futile as—to give a modern parallel—the Small Holdings Act of 1892? Or did it to any extent modify or retard the course of economic events? The view usually taken, that legislation was so ineffective as to be almost negligible, is in accordance with what we know of the character of local administration in the sixteenth century, and is supported by much contemporary evidence. The constant introduction of fresh proposals suggests that the previous laws were disappointing. The failure of existing Acts was the reason given in Somerset's proclamation for the appointment of the Commission of 1548. Hales, who is certainly the most reliable authority on the situation between 1540 and 1550, speaks of them as being notoriously a dead letter.[694] If one looks at the Statutes passed against depopulation in the sixteenth century, with a view to discovering how far they really met the situation, one will be inclined to say that they quite failed to go to the root of the matter. The special evil which they were intended to combat was depopulation caused by evictions. But evictions could be checked only by giving tenants security, which would have meant turning customary into legal titles, and fixing judicial rents for leaseholders and immovable fines for copyholders; in short, the sort of interference which the peasants and their champions demanded, but on which no Government depending on the support of the landed gentry would venture, except upon an extraordinary emergency. In the absence of <u>such an attempt</u> to grapple directly with the fundamental fact that the peasants'

[692] J. Moore, *A Target for Tillage*: "My purpose is not here to plead for ... any other idle drones and wretched atheists.... All these I acknowledge to be the greatest wasters and spoylers of our country, worse by many degrees than any depopulators, oppressors, and decayors of villages.... All these I know abhorre the plough, and are enemies to the State; who yet (I confesse) in their high talke do justify tillage and will be ready no doubt to reforme the decay thereof with spade and pickaxe." (The copy of this pamphlet which I have seen is dated 1611. I have ventured to assume that this is a misprint, and that it should be placed with John Moore's other pamphlets on enclosure, 1653–1656.)

[693] Leonard, *Trans. Royal Hist. Soc.*, vol. xix.

[694] Hale's defence in appendix to Miss Lamond's introduction to *The Commonweal of this Realm of England*.

insecurity made them liable to suffer whenever there was a change in the methods of agriculture, legislation designed merely to prevent those changes was almost certain to be evaded. Even with the best intentions the Statutes could never have been easy to administer. There was the difficulty inherent in the whole Tudor and Stuart policy of authoritative interference with trade and industry, the difficulty of making State action keep pace with economic changes. The Government is often like a man pursuing a tram from one stopping-place to another, and just missing it at each. It insists that land which has hitherto been in tillage shall remain in tillage. But there are a few years of bumper harvests, and the farmers complain that they cannot pay their way.[695] The Government tries to get over the difficulty by allowing them to convert arable to pasture, when a providence unversed in statecraft sends a wet summer, and it scrambles hastily back to the position which it has just abandoned.[696] By excepting from the operation of the Statutes certain districts which are specially suitable for grazing, it encourages a rough local division of labour, one part of a county confining itself to pasture-farming and another to tillage. But then, in pursuit of its traditional and quite reasonable policy of securing that food is cheap, it insists that all farmers are to supply the markets with grain, with the result that those who have specialised in corn-growing are threatened with ruin by the fall in prices which ensues, and that it is even questionable whether they will not convert arable to pasture to evade the obligation imposed upon them.[697] Old enclosures were tolerated and new forbidden. But how distinguish between old and new? Land turned to pasture simply to restore it to a condition in which it would be fit for tillage escaped the condemnation passed on other kinds of "conversion," and one can imagine that nice arguments must have arisen as to a farmer's motives. Again, suppose a man converted to pasture land which should have remained under the plough, and then leased it to some one else, who retained it as pasture, was the lessee guilty of an offence? In a case which came before the Court of Exchequer in 1582, the defendant pleaded that he merely "used" the land as pasture, and had not converted it, while the Crown argued that use was equivalent to conversion, that he was in the position of a man profiting by the continuance of a nuisance, and that a fine of 10s. an acre for each year since the original conversion ought to be imposed.[698] Points like this give

[695] D'Ewes *Journal*, p. 674 (1601). Mr. Johnson said: "In the time of dearth, when we made this Statute, it was not considered that the hand of God was upon us; and now corn is cheap. If too cheap, the husbandman is undone." See also Raleigh's speech in the same debate.

[696] *e.g.* in 1593 the clause in the Act of 1563 forbidding conversion of arable to pasture was repealed. In 1595 and 1596 bad harvests produced loud complaints of high prices, and in 1597 conversion to pasture was again prohibited.

[697] *Original Papers of the Norfolk and Norwich Archæological Society*, 1907, pp. 131 ff.

[698] Moore's *Reports*, p. 117, plea 262, Claypole's case: "Le conseil de Reigne argue que ... l'entent de Estatute fuit que le user sera accompt equivalent en tort al convcon." Judgment was apparently given for the Queen. The decision was quoted as an authority in the debate in Parliament on the Bills introduced in 1597. *Hist. MSS. Com.*, MSS. of Marquis of Salisbury, Part VII., pp. 541–543: "And 26 Eliz. in the Exchequer, in Claypole's case, an information was exhibited upon the Statute of 4 Hen. VII. against a purchaser for converting of tillage into pasture, and adjudged good, though the purchaser were not the converter, but only a continuer of the first conversion. So as this new law tends but for an instruction

colour to Coke's complaint against the whole body of Acts against enclosure that "they were labyrinthes, with such intricate windings or turnings as little or no fruit proceeded from them."

But, of course, the obscurity of the Statutes was the least part of the difficulty with which Governments who wished to protect the peasantry were confronted. Much more serious was the fact that the traditional policy could be carried out only by disregarding the financial interests of the wealthier classes, who could most easily influence Parliament and the Council, and who were locally omnipotent. In the first half of the sixteenth century the high position of many of those who were most deeply implicated in cutting land free from communal restrictions made them almost unassailable. The Royal Commission of 1517 returned among enclosers the names of the Duke of Norfolk, the Earl of Shrewsbury, the Duke of Buckingham, Lord Danbury, Sir William Bolen, Sir R. Sheffield, the Speaker of the House of Commons, Sir J. Witte, the Under-Treasurers of State, and Sir J. Cotton, who was himself one of the Commissioners.[699] The angry unanimity with which Somerset's colleague turned against his land policy was not wonderful, for they were nearly all directly interested in the maintenance of the *status quo*. Warwick, who led the *coup d'état*, had enclosed on a large scale. Sir William Herbert had made extensive enclosures on the lands which he had acquired from the Abbey of Wilton. The St. John family, the Darcy family, the Earl of Westmoreland, had all local troubles with their tenants; and there are some indications that Sir William Paget and the detested and detestable Lord Rich were in the same position.[700]

It is not, however, material to trace the records of individual members of the Council, because their interest in checking the interference of the State with the free disposal of land is evident from the fact that many of them enormously increased their estates through the share which they obtained in the property confiscated from the religious houses and the gilds. A comparison of the lists of Privy Councillors for 1548 and 1552, published by Strype,[701] with Dr. Savine's[702] valuable analysis of the grantees of the monastic estates, show that out of thirty-one persons who got grants of land of £200 a year or more fourteen were members of the Privy Council in one or other of those years, exclusive of the Earl of Warwick and Sir William Herbert. This fact is by itself almost sufficient to explain the impossibility of enforcing the laws forbidding depopulation during the years which followed the death of Henry VIII., and the despair of legal protection which seems to have settled upon the classes affected by the movement. The view sometimes expressed that the religious houses had been easier landlords than the lay owners into whose hands their estates passed, though it can occasionally be corroborated from the complaints made by tenants to the Government, scarcely seems, as yet, to be satisfactorily proved. But the distribution among the wealthier classes of

---

and explanation of the old."

[699] Leadam, *Trans. Royal Hist. Soc.*, New Series, vol. vi.

[700] For Warwick, Herbert, and the St. Johns, see pp. 326, 368, and 362. For Darcy and disturbances in Westmoreland, Gairdner, *L. and P. Henry VIII.*, xii. II., xii. I., 319, xi. 1080. For Paget and Rich, Strype, *Ecclesiastical Memorials*.

[701] Strype, *Ecclesiastical Memorials*.

[702] Fisher, *The Political History of England*, 1485–1547, Appendix II.

land producing a net income of not less than £110,000 gave them an enormous vested interest in preventing and evading legislation to check the most profitable use of the new possessions which were to endow the aristocracy of the future. The supposition of peculiar harshness in the owners to whom the land passed, though probably correct, is really not needed to explain the part which the transference of these vast quantities of land had in augmenting the distress of the rural classes. The worst side of all such great and sudden redistributions of property is that the individual is more or less at the mercy of the market, and can hardly help taking his pound of flesh. A buyer must sell at a profit, or he had much better not have bought. During the decade between 1540 and 1550 there was a furor of land speculation. To the Abbey lands, which came into the market after 1536, were added those of the gilds and chantries in 1547. It is quite clear that some of the grantees of estates did not acquire them with the intention of retaining them, but simply "bought for the rise." The lands of the Abbey of Whitby, for example, pass first to the Crown, and are then sold by it to the Duke of Northumberland, who in turn sells them to Sir John Yorke.[703] A small official in the Royal household buys the Cistercian nunnery at Brewood, and at once puts it up to sale "for suche a price that no man will gladly by hit at hys hand."[704] Trentham is surrendered to the Crown in 1536; in 1540 the Duke of Suffolk obtains a grant of the rents and reversions reserved upon the Crown leases there, and in the same year sells it to one Leveson, who has already acquired lands belonging to Horlton Abbey, and already sold them again to Biddulph.[705] One finds even the champion of the tenants, Somerset himself, getting a grant of land from the Crown on July 1st, leasing part of it for eighty years on July 2nd, and transferring it back to the Crown, subject to the lease, on July 9th.[706] When property changed hands three times in the course of ten days, it could hardly fail to be rack-rented, or the transaction would not pay. What happened to the tenants? Here and there, as at Whitby and Washerne,[707] a bitter outburst against their new masters shows that the result has been what we should expect. But for the rest, a cloud descends and we cannot say. It is only in such occasional glimpses that we catch the solid earth shifting beneath the feet of those who till it. It was such a glimpse which led the last great English peasant, in a time of even more widespread misery, to say that the wretchedness of the landless labourer was the work of the Reformation. Cobbett, and those who follow Cobbett in representing the economic evils of the sixteenth century as the fruit of the religious changes, err in linking as parent and child movements which were rather brother and sister, twin aspects of the individualism which seems inseparable from any swift increase in riches. Their vision of a time when mild ecclesiastics administered their estates as a popular trust lays a spell upon the imagination. In

---

[703] Selden Society, *Select Cases in the Court of Requests* (Leadam).

[704] Hibbert, *The Dissolution of the Monasteries*, pp. 209–210.

[705] *Ibid.*, p. 210.

[706] *Hist. MSS. Com.*, C.D. 3218, pp. 322–323 (MSS. of Earl of Leicester at Holkham Hall).

[707] For Whitby and Washerne, see pp. 285 and 194. In 1545 the tenants of the manor of Egglesdon, formerly the property of the monastery of Sion, proceed against Palmer, the grantee, in the Court of Star Chamber for evicting tenants and other oppressions (Leadam, *E. H. R.*, vol. viii. pp. 684–696).

the religious houses of Lancashire and Yorkshire and Northumberland there may, here and there, even on the eve of the dissolution, have been a reality corresponding to it. But we need hardly go further than Sir Thomas More[708] to learn that for parts, at least, of England it is only a vision; and More does not speak without book. Holy men enclose land, convert arable to pasture, claim villeins, turn copyholds into tenancies at will. If prominent ecclesiastics had really wanted to champion the cause of the peasantry, they had an excellent opportunity when Wolsey sent out the first great Commission into enclosures in 1517. But, in fact, there is no reason to suppose that any protest was made at all comparable to that which came thirty-two years later from Latimer. How could there be? The estates of the larger houses were often scattered over several different counties, and before the dissolution they were quite frequently managed by laymen. In such cases the monks were simply rentiers,[709] who needed to know no more about their tenants than the fellows of an Oxford college know about theirs at the present day.

Nevertheless, though facts will not allow us to accept the view which ascribes the agrarian distress of our period to the Reformation, or even to the particular changes brought about by the secularisation of religious endowments, there was a real connection between them. The Reformation in England is as much a social as a religious revolution. As a social revolution it is the work of the commercial and middle classes. It "made of yeomen and artificers gentlemen, and of gentlemen knights, and so forth upward, and of the poorest sort stark beggars."[710] Their support is given, in the main, on strict business principles. It is purchased by ensuring that every one who counts shall have a solid material interest in supporting the new order. The great Elizabethan families, the Cecils, the Herberts, the Grenvilles, are well paid in advance for their services, and continue to be paid long after their services have ceased. The dissolution of the monasteries does for their plastic consciences what the foundation of the Bank of England did for the politics of the City Interest under William III. Having invested in the Reformation at a time when the Reformation is a gambling stock, they nurse the security with a solicitude which title-deeds have done more to inspire than the New Testament, and are zealous to lay up for themselves treasures in Heaven, as the best insurance for the treasures which they have already accumulated on earth. A man who looks from the win-

---

[708] More, *Utopia*, p. 31 (Pitt Press edition): "Noblemen and gentlemen, yea, and certain abbotts, holy men no doubt ... leave no ground for tillage, they enclose all to pasture." For a case of claiming a bondman, see Selden Society, *Select Cases in the Court of Star Chamber*, Carter *v.* The Abbot of Malmesbury. For conversion of copyholds to tenancies at will, Selden Society, *Select Cases in the Court of Requests*, Kent and other inhabitants of Abbot's Ripton *v.* St. John. The change was alleged to have been made in 1471.

[709] The opposite view is expressed by Gasquet, *Henry the Eighth and the English Monasteries*, chap. xxii. For a criticism of it see Savine, *Oxford Studies in Social and Legal History*, vol. i. pp. 263–267, and pp. 245–260 for facts as to lay administrators. Hibbert, *op. cit.*, pp. 210–211, who writes of Staffordshire, supports Savine rather than Gasquet. The evidence of Aske cannot be quoted as though what was true of the northern houses were true of all. As a matter of fact, lay estates preserved the old conditions in the north long after the dissolution (see pp. 189–191). The hatred of the new landlords is proof that they were specially detestable, rather than that the monasteries had been above all ordinary economic considerations.

[710] Quoted by Gasquet, *op. cit.*, p. 464, from a document written about 1591.

dow of his new mansion on the timber in his new park may well think it worth the sacrifice of many masses. Though the economic effect of endowing our landed gentry is not reducible to figures, it is not rash to say that men who have sprung into wealth by suddenly purchasing new estates will make those estates pay. And this means that ultimately the cost will be borne by their tenants. That the new proprietors will be extraordinarily sensitive to attacks on the rights of property goes without saying. The lectures[711] delivered to the peasants by the *nouveaux riches* of 1549 on the wickedness of agrarian spoliation have an irony which is eternal.

Apart from the special interest which the purchasers of the estates of monastic and gild estates had in keeping a completely free hand over their disposal, the normal organisation of English local government made effective State interference very difficult. As has often been pointed out, its peculiar strength lay in the success with which it made the ordinary relationships between social classes the machinery for executing the mandates of the State, by entrusting administration, not to officials of the Central Government, but to persons who already possessed local authority, and who were confirmed in it, rather than given it, by the Crown. Such a system was favourable to the development of representative government and of political freedom, because it strengthened instead of repressing the local initiative on which the success of representative government ultimately depends. But the very absence of bureaucracy had the disadvantage that it made it almost impossible to enforce the regular administration of the law, whenever it conflicted with the local interests of classes who sat on the county bench. A not unimportant chapter in English history is contained in the complaint of the Norfolk rebels that the legislation of the last fifty years had been "hidden" from them by the Justices of the Peace. The account of the proceedings of the Commission of 1548, which had to drag information out of juries packed with the employees of enclosing landlords, and from witnesses who gave it under threat of eviction—above all, the pained amazement of a great landowner who found that the Commission declined to accept evidence from his servants as unbiassed—is a specimen so typical, that, if it were found in isolation, we could hardly fail to fit it back into its English context.[712] Hales, the one statesman whom the agrarian problem produced, put his finger on the root of the difficulty in the third Bill which he introduced into Parliament in 1548. The substance of its proposals, though sufficiently rigorous to modern notions, was not in itself more drastic than others which actually became

---

[711] *e.g.* Paget's letter to Somerset, July 7, 1549 (Strype, *Ecclesiastical Memorials*). Neville, De furoribus Norfolcensium Ketto Duce, 1575. The words put into the mouths of the landed gentry by Crowley in *The Way to Wealth* (E. E. T. S.) no doubt represent their attitude fairly: "Nowe if I should demand of the gredie cormoraunts what they thinke should be the cause of sedition, they would saie, 'The paisent knaves be too welthy, provender pricketh them. They knowe no obedience, they regard no lawes, they would have no gentlemen, they would have all men like themselves, they would have all things commune. They would not have us master of that which is our owne. They will appoint us what rent we shall take for our grounds.... They will caste down our parkes and lay our pastures open.... They wyll compel the Kyng to graunt theyr requests.... We wyll tech them to know theyr betters, and because they would have all in common we will leave them nothing.'"

[712] Appendix to Introduction to *The Commonweal of this Realm of England* (Lamond), p. lix.

law. Its novelty lay in the machinery by which it was to be enforced. Surveys of pastures were to be made annually by the curate and two men of every parish, and those breaking the law were to be presented for trial. In other words, the initiative in returning offences was to be taken by those chiefly interested in preventing them. According to Hales, it was the last provision for making the administration of the Statute a reality which Parliament found intolerable.[713]

Must we, then, dismiss the efforts of the Tudor and Stuart statesmen to soften the harshness of the agrarian revolution as a mere piece of solemn futility? The simplicity of the solution makes it a tempting one; but it is too simple to be true. In the first place we must notice that our literary evidence is one-sided, because it is fullest for just those years during which an exceptional freedom from restraint was enjoyed by the great landlords. It is inevitable that Latimer and Hales should often be quoted. But one cannot argue from comments on the uselessness of legislation, uttered at a time when the Statutes against enclosing were virtually repealed, to show that the law was equally ineffective under Elizabeth and her two successors. And, in the second place, to hold that the frequent intervention of the Council had no result is really an unjustifiably high-handed proceeding. It runs counter to most of what we know of the administration of the period. A Statute might be a dead letter, but a letter from the Council was meant to be obeyed. By 1552 the Government has discovered the uselessness of relying for the enforcement of the law on the intervention of superior lords, and places its administration in the hands of special Commissioners directly responsible to the Central Government. Such a view runs counter to the opinion of the peasants and of the upper classes. The victims of agrarian oppression recognise that though they have little to hope from the local authorities, who are their landlords and employers, the Government's policy is on the whole favourable to them, and they deluge it with appeals for protection. The justices are naturally no friends to that policy. But in the sixteenth and seventeenth centuries they are by no means the independent autocracy which they became later, and are watched closely by the Privy Council. From Norfolk, Nottinghamshire, Lincolnshire, Derbyshire, Leicestershire, and the west of England, they send returns to the Government of their action,[714] and the Government is quite ready, as we have seen, to revise the action of its delegates when it thinks they have been biassed by personal interests. In Yorkshire the juries of several townships present offenders before the justices. The authorities of Southampton[715] take steps to put the Acts against enclosure into force. The authorities of Norfolk[716] request that

---

[713] *Ibid.*, p. lxv.: "This was it that byt the mare by the thombe."

[714] For Norfolk and the West of England, Leonard, *Trans. Royal Hist. Soc.*, vol. xix. For Nottinghamshire, Lincolnshire and Derbyshire, *S. P. D.*, Ch. I. vol. clxxxv. No. 86, and vol. ccvi. No. 71 (quoted in Appendix I.), and vol. clxxxv. No. 41. For Leicestershire, Privy Council Register, vi. 385, and Gonner, *Common Land and Enclosure*, p. 165. For Yorkshire, see pp. 374–375. Professor Gonner (*op. cit.*, p. 167) estimates that about six hundred persons were fined, the sums obtained from thirteen counties amounting to about £46,800.

[715] Hearnshaw, *Southampton Court Leet Records*, 1550. Presentment of "the names of the Commoners which require redress of the Commons inclosed, as they saye, contrary to the King's Majesty's statutes, and that they may be laid abroad according to the said statutes."

[716] *Original Papers of the Norfolk and Norwich Archæological Society*, 1907, p. 185.

they may enjoy the exemption which has been granted them. When in 1597, a year in which legislation against enclosures is in the air, the Earl of Huntingdon asks the burgesses of Leicester to return his nominee to Parliament, they refuse bluntly to do anything of the kind, on the ground that the candidate in question is "an encloser himself and therefore unlikely to redress that wrong in others."[717] The courts hear a large number of cases dealing with offences committed under the enclosing Statutes.[718] Individuals obtain special permission, either by royal license or by Act of Parliament, to use as pasture land which, like undrained marshes, is obviously unsuitable for ploughing. No one who is reported as having taken part in the Parliamentary discussions of proposed legislation in the closing years of Elizabeth suggests that it must necessarily be a dead letter. The chief fear that seems to have been felt was lest it should prove too effective. In introducing two Bills against enclosure and depopulation in 1597, Bacon apologised to the great landlords for taking action which was likely to prejudice their interests. When the question of continuing the Act against depopulation, which was in force in 1601, was under consideration in the House of Commons, both the members who argued for continuance and those who argued for repeal, assumed that the law was being administered in practice, one speaker urging that it had the result of keeping so much land in tillage as to destroy the farmer's profits by causing excessive supplies of grain to be placed on the market in any but the worst years; another that it pressed hardly on the small farmer, who could not easily find the capital needed to sow as much land as he was legally bound to plough.[719] The ablest and most fully reported speech[720] which has come down to us is that of an anonymous member, who, while approving of the principle of the Bill, attacked it as too loosely drafted to meet the situation. His criticisms are those of a man who understands his subject, and are on just those points of detail which, though important in a measure which is to work, would not be worth considering at all if anything like effective interference were out of the question. After commending the clauses which excepted from the provisions of the Bill land lying temporarily fallow, and which punished the purchasers as well as the original converter of arable which was turned into pasture, he goes on to point out that loopholes have been left in the measure which are likely to stultify its effect. The exemption of Crown lands from its operation will encourage enclosing landlords to exchange properties with the Crown, and then take on lease as tenants the land which they have handed over, since by doing so, they will escape the risk of prosecution. The persistent lobbying of the interests affected — "the ears of our great sheepmasters do hang at the doors of this house" — has resulted in the fine for enclosing being placed as low as 10s. per acre, which is ridiculously disproportionate to the profits to be made by enclosures. The clause excluding from the reconversion prescribed in the Bill lands mown for hay plays into the hands of the enclosers by facilitating the winter feeding of their sheep. The failure to limit the acreage which a man may keep in

[717] Bateson, *Records of the Borough of Leicester*, 1509–1603, pp. 300–301.

[718] Gay, *Quarterly Journal of Economics*, vol. xvii.

[719] For the debates of 1597 and 1601 see *D'Ewes' Journal*, pp. 551 and 674 ff.: a special exemption from the operations of the Act was allowed to a landlord who had got letters patent authorising him to enclose 340 acres "too moist and soft and altogether unfit for tillage."

[720] *Hist. MSS. Com.*, MSS. of Marquis of Salisbury, Part. VII., pp. 541–543.

his own hands will discourage the creation of small holdings. At a later date there is the same belief, both among those who approve, and among those who dislike, enclosure, that enclosing can be checked, at any rate, by the Government. In the keen controversy over enclosures which raged under the commonwealth the opponents of further restriction urged that the mere threat of legislation had resulted in checking agricultural enterprise.[721] Harrington,[722] a specialist, not to say a faddist, on agrarian policy, bases his interpretation of the history of the preceding century on the supposed success of the Tudors in keeping the small cultivator on the soil. Even in the middle of the eighteenth century, when the golden age of the enclosing landlord was just about to dawn, some dim memory of the earlier State policy seems in parts of England to have survived. "Why," asked a foreign traveller,[723] "do your farmers not keep separate closes under turnips to feed sheep in the new approved manner?" "Partly," answer the peasants, "because there is a common rotation of crops which all must follow. But the principal reason of all is that on a common land no one has freedom to enclose his strips without a special permission and Act of Parliament."

What weight is to be attached to this body of opinion that enclosure and conversion to pasture were in practice checked by the opposition of the Government, it is not easy to say. If it is hardly compatible with the view that interference was entirely ineffective, it nevertheless need not imply anything more than a temporary retardation of the movement on those special occasions and in those particular parts of the country that were the object of peculiar attention. The test of comparison with facts by which one would like to try it is difficult to apply. Our knowledge of the real extent of enclosure in the sixteenth century is too scanty to permit of our following with confidence the line of argument which has been ingeniously worked out by Miss Leonard,[724] and which, starting from the indisputable fact that in those Midland counties where enclosure had been felt most acutely in the sixteenth century, there was still much land unenclosed in the seventeenth and eighteenth, suggests that the explanation is to be found in its temporary cessation under the authoritative pressure of the Tudor and Stuart Governments. Nevertheless, without going beyond our evidence, we may venture to

---

[721] Pseudonismus, *A Vindication of the Considerations concerning Common Fields and Enclosures*, 1656: "The Statute of Tillage hath excited some and affrighted others that the land in each field is not and cannot be husbanded as it ought." The "Statute" alluded to is the Bill introduced in this year which did not become law.

[722] Harrington's Works (1700 edition), pp. 388–389.

[723] *Kalm's Account of his Visit to England on his Way to America in 1748*, translated by Joseph Lucas, p. 282. I am indebted for this reference to Dr. Gilbert Slater. The exact words are: "Nor had they any turnip land to feed sheep upon. Therefore they were deprived of the advantage of getting to sell any fat sheep or other cattle. The reason they gave for all this was that their arable was common field, and thus came to lie every other year fallow, when one commoner always had to accommodate his crops to the others; but the principal reason of all was said to be that," and so on as in text. I am not sure that I have interpreted the passage rightly in assuming that it alludes to the *illegality* of enclosure without Act of Parliament. It may merely mean that, without an Act of Parliament, the necessary agreement could not be obtained among all those interested. I follow Dr. Slater's interpretation.

[724] *Trans. Royal Hist. Soc.*, vol. xix.

put forward two propositions. The first is that it is extremely improbable that the anti-enclosing policy which we have traced succeeded in altering permanently or on a large scale the course of economic development. That suggestion is surely incredible in view of the continuance of the complaints against enclosure, and of what we know of the slack and biassed routine of rural administration. To expect the justices to stop enclosing, unless actually compelled to do so, was almost as Utopian as it was to expect them to administer the early Factory Acts two centuries later. The second is that the intervention of the Government certainly mitigated the hardships of the movement to the rural classes. The protection which the Court of Star Chamber and the Court of Requests offered to the equitable interests of tenants, while it could not turn the general course of events, tempered its harshness to individuals. A landlord who was determined to depopulate could hardly in the long run be prevented from succeeding in his object. But he might have to wait till leases or life tenancies had expired, instead of being able to clear his estate at one sweep. He might be compelled, as the St. Johns[725] were in the reign of Henry VIII., as Sir John Yorke in 1553, or Lloyd under Elizabeth, to bind himself to respect the titles of the existing generation of tenants. In the same way the occasional campaigns undertaken for the reconversion of pasture to arable, while they could not turn the tide, almost certainly slackened its course. There is no way of escaping from the positive evidence which we possess that in parts of the country houses which had been pulled down were rebuilt, and that land which had been turned from arable to pasture was turned back again, at the command of the Government, from pasture to arable. We have already described the doings of the justices under James I. Look for a moment at the similar agitation which was started in 1630. The agrarian policy of the Council is seen at its worst under Charles I., because the whole of it is smeared with the trail of finance. Some of the offenders were allowed to compound upon payment of a fine, and one's first inclination is to believe that the Commissions of 1632, 1635, and 1636 were nothing but one of those odious financial engines, like the revival of forest claims and the exaction of fines for knighthood, by which Charles tried to dispense with Parliamentary taxation. That they were this among other things is certain. That they were nothing more than this must be denied, for we have clear evidence from enclosers themselves to the contrary. They do not only, like Lord Brudenell, write to the Council begging that their fines may be reduced from £1000 to £500, and explaining that "the enclosures made within man's memory amount not to the decay of one farm."[726] They are not only haled before the Star Chamber to be rebuked by Laud.[727] They beg to be allowed to pay a fine instead of being imprisoned. They reconvert pas-

[725] For the St. Johns, see pp. 362 and 380. For Sir John Yorke, pp. 285 and 381, and Selden Society, *Court of Requests*, Inhabitants of Whitby *v.* Yorke, 1553: "Be yt remembred that the cause brought before the Queen's Counsaill in her Majestie's Court of Requests.... Ys now ordered by the saide Councill by thagreement of the saide Syr John who hathe promised that the saide parties aforenamed, and every one of them, shall have and quietly eujoye theyr tenements and holdings during the yeres and termes in theyr leases and copies yet enduring, paying theyr Rentes and ffermes accustomed." For Lloyd and the tenants of Hewlington in Denbighshire, see pp. 302–303.

[726] *S. P. D.*, Ch. I., cccxlii., No. 47.

[727] *Ibid.*, cccxiv., No. 29, and Appendix I., No. VIII.

ture to arable. In Northamptonshire[728] a man turns thirty-five acres of arable into pasture. But he ploughs up ninety-five acres of ancient pasture to set off against it. From Nottinghamshire[729] comes a letter explaining that the petitioner has complied with the orders of the Commissioners of Depopulation to throw open all his enclosures, and apologising humbly for keeping hedges round three acres on the ground that they are necessary to mark the boundaries.

On the whole one is inclined to regard the Government's intervention in this matter as resembling in its effects the attempts which were made at the same time to fix prices and wages. It retarded, though it could not check altogether, economic changes. It imposed a brake which somewhat eased the shock of sudden movements. But when the hand of authority was removed, when Commissions were called in and justices ceased to be admonished by the Council, affairs swung back into their original position. A rough attempt to illustrate the occasional retardation of pasture-farming by these spasmodic attacks upon it is given in the diagram opposite.

The figures are taken from a list of Final Concords as to land lying mainly in Staffordshire, but occasionally in other counties as well. The period selected is one in which there were two agitations among the peasants, two important Acts against depopulation, and a Royal Commission. It will be seen that while some of the fluctuations in the percentages of arable and pasture bear no relation to any known activity on the part of the Government, the repeal in 1593 of the Acts for the maintenance of tillage comes as a climax to a well-defined increase in the percentage of pasture, the passage of the two Acts of 1599 is followed by a similar though less marked rise in the percentage of arable, and the riots of 1607, which resulted in the appointment of a Royal Commission, appear to be accompanied by another increase in the area under the plough. Of course the acreage represented is absurdly small, and it is possible that the apparent correlation is a mere coincidence. Still, one is inclined to think that the fluctuations on the chart fit in very well with what we know from other sources of the temporary effect and subsequent ineffectiveness of these transient eruptions of governmental activity. The creation of social habits by continuous pressure, such as is exercised by modern states through their paid inspectorates, is quite foreign to the ideas of the age. The Government, when it is most active, never gets beyond making an example of a few notorious offenders whose sins are sufficiently black to bring in good round sums to the Exchequer, and having vindicated the majesty of the law and pocketed their fines, it leaves the small fry to wonder, and hastily set their house in order against the coming of the Judges of Assize, and then gradually to slide back into the ancient ways when the storm has blown over. After all, the fact that A was punished for enclosing last year is in itself sufficient to make it extremely probable that this year B will escape.

---

[728] *Ibid.*, cccclxxv., No. 72.
[729] *Ibid.*, cccciv., No. 142.

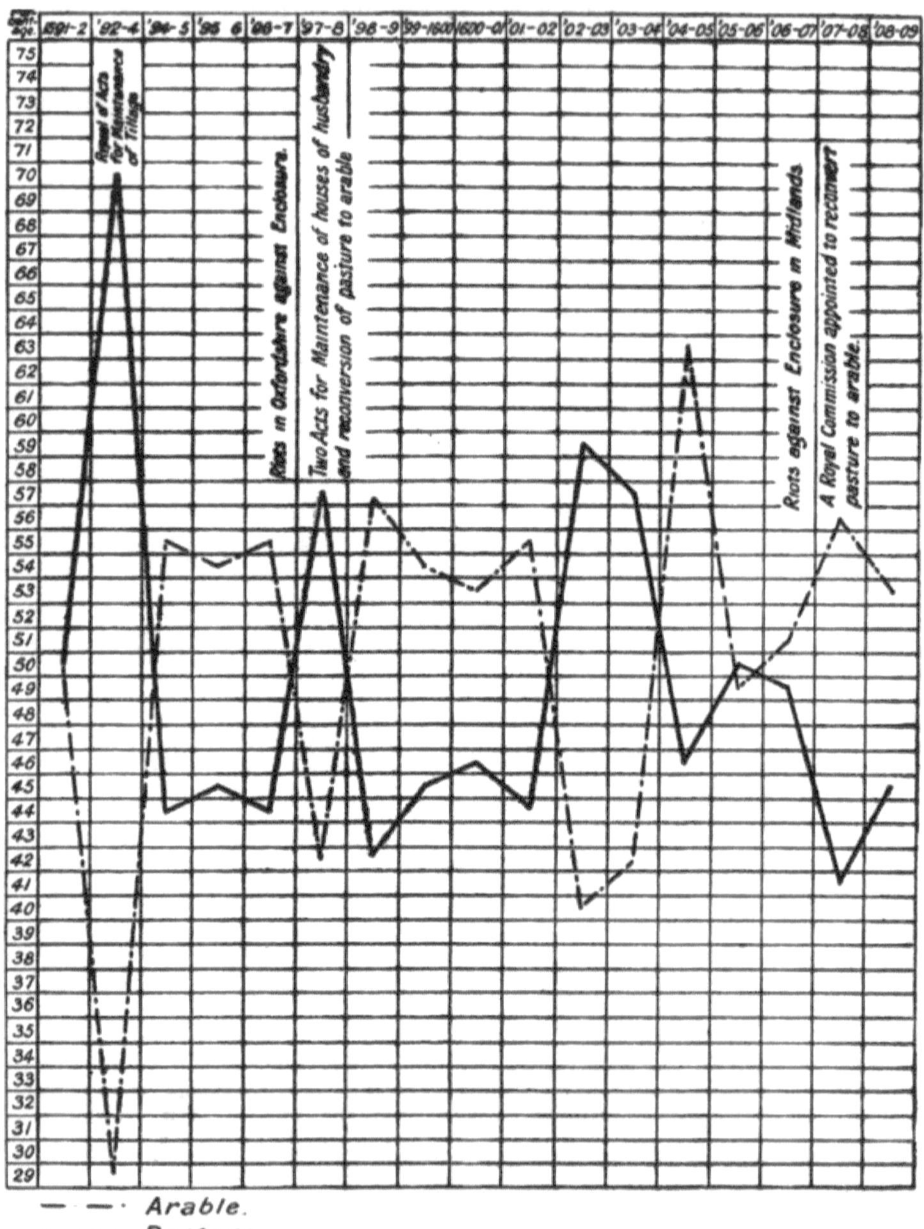



The figures for 1592–3 and 1593–4 have been combined, as the latter are too small to be given separately.

Such "occasional conformity" was, however, too much the rule in all economic matters that were the object of authoritative regulation — and few were not — to be by itself any cause for abandoning it. The real reason for the cessation of interference in the land question which we notice after 1640 is to be found, not in the fact that intervention had invariably proved too ineffective to be worth continuing, but in the change of policy caused by the unchecked domination of Parliament in domestic affairs. The victory of the Parliamentary forces over the Crown meant the triumph of the landed gentry over the only power which was strong enough to enforce the administration of unpopular Statutes in the teeth of their opposition. It prepared the way for the reign of the great landlord who regards himself as charged with a peculiar responsibility for promoting the needs of agriculture, which he alone is presumed to understand—and in fact, to do him justice, does sometimes understand very thoroughly—a weary Titan who pushes forward enclosure from a sheer sense of public duty. On the one hand there is a change in the standpoint from which agrarian policy is regarded. The aim of maintaining a prosperous peasantry becomes subordinate to that of obtaining the maximum output from the soil. This change materially affects the attitude adopted towards enclosure. The Tudor Governments had endeavoured to protect the rights of commoners, because commons were an indispensable adjunct to small-scale subsistence farming. The new view is that commons are waste lands which had much better be improved, and which are most likely to be improved if they pass into the control of men who have capital to spend upon them. Even under the Stuarts this doctrine begins to gather weight, and naturally so, for it both flattered their ambitious conception of the monarchy as a cornucopia whence all economic improvements should flow, and was in line with their general policy of trying to secure cheap food by regulating the supplies of grain. In 1623 Commissioners are busy improving Tiptree Heath, which squatters have occupied without any legal title.[730] In 1637 the King is approached by an influential syndicate which asks for a concession permitting it to reclaim the heaths and barren commons belonging to the Crown, and which displays a glowing prospectus of the advantages which will accrue in the shape of increased supplies of food-stuffs.[731] In 1629 the Commission of Sewers had engaged Vermuyden on his celebrated task of draining the great Level, and, in spite of the fierce opposition of the fenmen, the work was in 1637 adjudged to be completed.[732] All this is quite in the vein of the eighteenth century. It is quite in that vein also for a strong line to be taken against the wastefulness of those who impede good farming, even though the farmer be a grazier, by sowing a few acres here and a few acres there, instead of cultivating a compact holding; in short, by the immemorial system of strip cultivation. The last but one of the Statutes against depopulation[733] was itself the first expressly to authorise that exchanging of holdings for the purposes of more business-like husbandry, which, as we have seen, had been going on informally from an early date. In 1606 we get what may be called the first Enclosure Act of the modern pattern, under which

---

[730] *S. P. D.*, Ch. I., cl., No. 7.

[731] *S. P. D.*, ccclxi., No. 15: "There are many thousand acres of heath and barren commons in England and Wales, not annually worth 6d. an acre, to which your Majesty has right of soil but no benefit thereby, which may be improved to a great value, cause plenty of provision, enrich many thousands, supply the poor."

[732] Cunningham, *Growth of English Industry and Commerce*, Modern Times, Part I., pp. 112–119.

[733] 39 Eliz., c. 2.

certain Herefordshire parishes are allowed to separate and enclose one-third of the land lying in common in each parish.[734] In 1627 a case arising out of a dispute about fold-courses comes before the courts, and sound agricultural doctrine is laid down with a confidence of which Arthur Young himself might have approved. "This Court," say the judges, "was now of opinion that the plowing and sowing of small quantities of land dispersedlye or disorderlye within ye shacks and winter feedinge of ye said ffouldcourses, and the refusal of a few wilfull persons to lett ye owners of ffouldcourses have their quillets of land (Llying intermixt in the places where ye sheep pasture is layd) upon indifferent exchange or other recompense for the same, are things very mischievous and will tend to ye overthrow of very many fould courses."[735] Their opinion is enforced with a judgment decreeing an exchange of lands.

When the whole question comes up again towards the close of the Commonwealth, the old attitude is maintained by the opponents of enclosure, who protest, with all the fervour of Latimer, against the greed of landlords and the pauperising of commoners. But its defenders have overhauled their arguments, and the lines on which the controversy will be fought out for the next century and a half are already obvious. In the eyes of the austere moralists of the Restoration commoners are lewd people, who would be much better employed if at work for wages. All beneath the "nobility and gentry" are "the poor," and the poor themselves (it is well known) are of two kinds, "the industrious poor," who make a living by working for their betters, and "the idle poor," who make a living by working for themselves. Christianity and patriotism require that the latter should enter some "productive employment," and this can best be secured by excluding them from the commons on which their distressingly irregular livelihood depends. Even so Europeans to-day teach habits of industry to the African savage, by taxing him until he can no longer live upon the lands which Europeans desire to exploit. Moreover, the commercial spirit of the later seventeenth century is impatient of antiquated restrictions, and is already groping blindly after some formula which may prove them to be superfluous. Enclosures will increase the output of wool and grain. Each man knows best what his land is best suited to produce, and the general interest will be best served by leaving him a free hand to produce it. "It is an undeniable maxim," writes a pamphleteer, "that every one by the light of nature and reason will do that which makes for his greatest advantage. Whensoever corn bear a considerable rate, viz., wheat four or five shillings, and barley two shillings and sixpence, men may make more profit by ploughing their pasture, and consequently will plough for their own advantage."[736] Hales had said something like this a hundred years before. He had said it to show the need of special measures to divert agricultural enterprise into beneficial channels. Now an identity between the interests of landowners and those of the public is assumed as part of a pre-established harmony, which human intervention may disturb, but which it is neither needed nor competent to secure. Authoritative statecraft fades out in the dawn of reason and the light of nature. With such a wind of doctrine in their sails men are

[734] 4 James I., c. 11.

[735] *Original Papers of the Norfolk and Norwich Archæological Society*, 1907, pp. 70–73.

[736] Lee, *A Vindication of a Regulated Enclosure*, 1656.

steering for uncharted waters.

While opinion on the subject of enclosing was beginning to change even before the Civil War, the final blow at the maintenance of the old policy was struck by the destruction of the Court of Requests and Court of Star Chamber. The abandonment by Governments of all attempts to protect the peasantry against oppression was an indirect consequence of the victory of the Common Law over the prerogative jurisdiction of the Crown. The interference in agrarian matters of the administrative courts of the Tudor monarchy had always been detested by the landed gentry for the very reasons which made it popular with the peasantry. They were the last resort of men who could not get what they considered justice elsewhere. One finds a defendant in whose favour the Common Law Courts have given three decisions being sued again before the Court of Requests.[737] They were the only authority which could prevent a landlord from asserting his claims to a common or to a copyhold by means which the poorer classes found it impossible to resist. Complaints from aggrieved landowners that they are undermining the right of the lord of the manor to exercise jurisdiction over his own copyholders, by trying cases which ought to be heard in manorial courts, that they are interfering with the course of Common Law, that they make it impossible for a lord to "rule his lands" by the countenance which they lend to discontent, are not infrequent[738] in the sixteenth century, and both Wolsey and Somerset were in turn attacked by the upper classes for the favour which they showed to such unconstitutional interference with the rights of property. Such protests are the best proof that the Court of Requests and the Court of Star Chamber had exercised functions which were in some respects beneficial. The strictest constitutionalist will have some sympathy to spare for the address in which Lord Coventry in 1635 charges the Judges of Assize to "beware of the corruptions of sheriffs and their deputies, partiality of jurors, the bearing and siding with men of power and countenance in their country," and to set on foot "strict inquiry after depopulation and enclosures, an oppression of a high nature and commonly done by the greatest persons that keep the juries under their awe, which was the cause there are no more presented and brought in question."[739] Such words paint the ideal of Government by preroga-

---

[737] Holkham MSS., Sparham Bdle., No. 5, see back, p. 374.

[738] Selden Society, *Select Cases in the Court of Requests*, Customarye Tenants of Bradford *v.* Fraunceys: "The seyd defendant seythe that the said bill of complaint ... is mater ... determinable at the comen land and not in this honourable court, whereunto he prayeth to be remitted." Also Gairdner, *L. & P. Henry VIII.*, i., 334, Earl of Derby to Cromwell; and Leadam, *E. H. R.*, vol. viii. pp. 684–696. For attacks on Wolsey's land policy see Herbert, *History of King Henry VIII.*, pp. 297–298 (ed. of 1672): "Also the said Cardinal hath examined divers and many matters in the Chancery, after judgment thereof given at the Common Law, in subversion of your laws, and made some persons restore again to the other party condemned that they had in execution by virtue of the judgment in the Common Law."

[739] Gardiner, *History of England*, 1603–1642, vol. viii., p. 78. Compare the Instructions for the President and Council of the North, 1603 (Prothero, *Statutes and Constitutional Documents*, 1558–1625, pp. 363–378), Article XXVIII.: "Further our pleasure is that the said Lord P. and Council shall from time to time make diligent and effectual inquisition of the wrongful taking in of commons and other grounds and the decay of tillage and of towns or houses of husbandry contrary to the laws, ... and leaving all respect and affection apart

tive, *parcere subjectis et debellare superbos*, which may have floated before the minds of a Bacon or a Strafford, and which had been partially realised under the Government of Elizabeth. When set side by side with the actual practice of the Council under Charles I. they are its final and self-recorded condemnation. For we look for them to be made good in action, and we look, save during a few years, in vain. If much may be forgiven those who boldly do wrong believing it to be right, there is no mercy for "the unlit lamp and the ungirt loin" of a body which, believing a certain system of government to be right, entangles its execution with sloth, and makes a sordid financial instrument out of the very prerogative which itself has declared to be the gift of God for the protection of the poor. The defence which the Council and its courts had offered to the peasantry against economic evils, though real, was too irregular to do more than slightly mitigate the verdict which history has passed upon their employment in the hands of Charles I. Whether the peasants regretted their disappearance we do not know. To those contemporaries whose opinion counted, the occasional onslaughts made by the Council and Star Chamber upon enclosing landlords were an aggravation, not an extenuation, of the indictment brought against them. Though the Grand Remonstrance, in which the Long Parliament sought to unite all classes with a recital of grievance accumulated upon grievance, taunted the Government with its failure to check the conversion of arable land to pasture,[740] the authors of that tremendous indictment had no substitute to suggest for the interference by the Council with "freeholds, estates, suits, and actions," which they denounced; and Laud, who, according to even a friendly critic, "did a little too much countenance the Commission for Depopulation,"[741] lived to be reminded in the day of his ruin of the sharp words with which he had barbed the fine imposed by that body upon an enclosing landlord.[742] The Court of Requests was never formally abolished, but from the closing decade of the sixteenth century it had been gradually stripped of its powers by prohibitions issued by the Common Law Judges, and forbidding plaintiffs to proceed with their cases before it, and after 1642 it quietly disappeared. With the destruction in 1641 of the Court of Star Chamber and the Councils of Wales and of the North, an end was put to the last administrative organs which could bridle the great landed proprietors. Clarendon, himself a relic of an age before the deluge, would seem to have added to his other offences by trying to revive the old policy

---

they shall take such order for redress of enormities used in the same as the poor people be not oppressed and forced to go begging ... and ... if they find any notorious malefactor in this behalf of any great wealth, cause the extremity of the law to be executed against him publicly."

[740] Gardiner, *Constitutional Documents of the Puritan Revolution*, 1625–1660, pp. 212–213, "Conversion of arable into pasture, continuance of pasture, under the name of depopulation, have driven many millions out of the subject's purses, without any considerable profit to his Majesty."

[741] Clarendon's *History of the Rebellion*, I. 204, IV. 63. Clarendon's account of the Grand Remonstrance suggests that the principal grievance was not depopulation, but the fines exacted for it; see the words "with the vexations upon pretence of nuisances in building ... and of depopulation, that men might pay fines to continue the same misdemeanour."

[742] Appendix I., No. VIII.

in a world which would have none of it.[743] But the royalist squirearchy who in 1660 streamed back to their plundered manors, were, when their property was at stake, as sound constitutionalists as Hampden himself, and after 1688 that absorption of the "State" by "Society" which Gneist, a worshipper of the eighteenth century régime, dates with curious perversity from 1832, was, in his sense of the words, complete. Henceforward there was to be no obstacle to enclosure, to evictions, to rack-renting, other than the shadowy protection of the Common Law; and for men who were very poor or easily intimidated, or in enjoyment of rights for which no clear legal title could be shown, the Common Law, with its expense, its packed juries, its strict rules of procedure, had little help. Thus the good side of the Absolute Monarchy was swept away with the bad. Its epitaph was written by Locke:[744] — "The supreme power cannot take from any man any part of his property without his own consent." But it was forgotten as soon as it was written. For to the upper classes in the eighteenth century the possession of landed property by a poor man seemed in itself a surprising impertinence which it was the duty of Parliament to correct, and Parliament responded to the call of its relatives outside the House with the pious zeal of family affection.

---

[743] I make this statement on the authority of Dr. Slater, *Sociological Review*, vol. iv., No. 4, p. 349, but I have been unable to trace his evidence. The only reference I can find bearing on the subject is contained in Article XIII. of the heads of the accusation against Lord Clarendon: "That he hath in an arbitrary way examined and drawn into question divers of his Majesty's subjects concerning their lands, tenements, goods, chattells, and properties, determined thereof at the Council Table, and stopped proceedings at law by the order of the Council Table, and threatened some that pleaded the Statute of 17 Car. I." (The proceedings in the House of Commons touching the impeachment of Edward, late Earl of Clarendon, 1700.)

[744] Locke, *Two Treatises of Government*, Book II., chap. xi.

# CHAPTER II
## GENERAL CONCLUSIONS

Those who have had the patience to follow the detailed changes in rural organisation which have been described above will naturally ask, "What is the upshot of it all? What are the main landmarks which stand out from the bewildering variety of scenery? How does the agrarian England which is sleepily hunting out old guns and older bows on the eve of the Civil War differ from the England which saw the first Tudor 'with general applause and joy, in a kind of military election or recognition, saluted King?'"

At first sight it differs but little. To see our subject in its proper perspective we must emphasise the continuity of economic life between 1485 and 1642 as much as in the preceding pages we have emphasised the novelty of some of its experiments. We must turn from Fitzherbert and Hales to Arthur Young. We must set Latimer's lamentations over the decay of the yeomanry side by side with the figures of Gregory King and the boasts of Chamberlayne and Defoe. We must compare our sporadic enclosures with the two thousand six hundred Enclosure Acts which were passed between 1702 and 1810. The outward appearance of many English villages at the Revolution would be quite unrecognisable to-day, but it can have been but little altered from what it had been at the time of the Peasants' Revolt. It could still be said that three-fifths of the cultivated land of England was unenclosed. And if Piers Plowman had dreamed for four centuries on Malvern Hills he might still have woken to plough his half acre between the balks of a still open field, like that "very wide field," with crooked ways butting upon it and a wicket-gate on its shining horizon, through which Christian sped from Evangelist, crying "Life, Life, Eternal Life."

Ought we, then, to say that the agrarian revolution of the sixteenth century was insignificant, and that it has been magnified into importance only by the rhetorical complaints of unskilful observers? The answer has been given by implication in the preceding pages. The fact that statistical evidence reveals no startling disturbance in area enclosed or population displaced, is no bar to the belief that, both in immediate consequences and in ultimate effects, the heavy blows dealt in that age at the traditional organisation of agriculture were an episode of the first importance in economic and social development. The barometer which registers climatic variations yields no clue to their influence on the human constitution, and the quantitative rule by which we measure economic changes bends in our hands when we use it to appraise their results. The difference between prosperity and distress, or enterprise and routine, or security and its opposite, is scarcely more susceptible of expression in figures than is the difference between civilisation and barbarism itself. In the infinite complexity of human relationships, with their interplay of law with economics, and of economics with politics, and of all with the shifting hopes and fears, baseless anticipations and futile regrets, of countless individuals, a change which to the statistician concerned with quantities seems insignificant, may turn a wheel whose motion sets a world of unseen forces grinding painfully round into a new equilibrium. Not only our estimate of the importance of social alterations, but their actual importance itself, depends upon what we are accustomed to and what we expect. Just as modern manufacturing nations groan over a reduction in exports, which in the reign of Henry VIII. would have passed unnoticed, or are convulsed by a rise in general prices, which, when expressed in percentages, seems ridiculously small, so the stationary rural society of Tudor England may well have been shaken to its core by agrarian changes which, in a world where rural emigration is the rule, would appear almost too minute to be recorded. If contemporaries, to whom the very foundation of a healthy economic life seemed to be shattered, underestimated the capacity of society for readjustment, they were not mistaken in their supposition that the readjustment required would be so vast and painful as to involve the depression of important orders of men, and the recognition of new responsibilities by the State in the agony of transition. If we are busy planting small holders to-day, it is partly because sixteenth century Governments were so often busy with them in vain. The crude barbarities of tramp ward and workhouse were first struck out in an age when most of those who tramped and toiled, who sat in stocks and were whipped from town to town, were not the victims of trade depression or casual employment, but peasants thrown on the labour market by the agrarian revolution.

For, in truth, the change which was coming upon the world in the guise of mere technical improvements was vaster than in their highest hopes or their deepest despondency the men of the Tudor age could have foreseen, and its immediate effects on the technique of agriculture and the standard of rural prosperity were but the tiny beginnings of movements whose origins are overshadowed by their tremendous consequences. It is a shallow view which has no interest to spare for the rivulet because it is not yet a river. Though many tributaries from many sources must converge before economic society assumes a shape that is recognisable as modern, it is none the less true that in the sixteenth century we are among the hills from which great waters descend. By 1642 the channels which will carry some of them have been carved deep and sure. By that time the expansion of the woollen industry has made it certain that England will be a considerable manufacturing nation, and consequently that the ancient stable routine of subsistence farming will gradually give place to agricultural methods which swing this way and that, now towards pasture, now towards arable, according to the fluctuations of the market. It is certain that, sooner or later, the new and more profitable economy of enclosure will triumph. It is certain that the small holder will have a hard struggle to hold his own against the capitalist farmer. It is certain that, owing to the substitution of variable for fixed fines on admission to copyholds, and the conversion of many copyholds into leases for years, a great part of the fruits of economic progress will no longer be retained, as in the fifteenth century, by the mass of the peasants, but will pass, in the shape of increased payments for land, into the pockets of the great landed proprietors. It is almost certain that to any new developments which may be detrimental to them the peasants will be able to offer a much less effective resistance than they have in the past. For the security of many of their class has been undermined; the gulf which separates them from the landed gentry, though still bridged by the existence of many prosperous freeholders, has been widened; and, above all, the destruction of the absolute monarchy has entrenched the great landlords inexpugnably at the heart of government, both central and local, and has made their power as great as their ambitions. Both from below and from above they are unassailable. For a century and a half after the Revolution they have what power a Government can have to make and ruin England as they please.

If we cast our eye over the agrarian changes of our period, with a view to grouping their main elements under a few easily distinguishable categories, we do not find that they present themselves as a simple series of economic sequences. Behind them all there is, it is true, the fundamental economic fact of the decay of subsistence husbandry. The movement away from the strict communal organisation of the open field village was inevitable as soon as markets were sufficiently developed to make agricultural experiments profitable, because experiments could not easily be undertaken without to some extent individualising the methods of cultivation. In particular, the grand innovation of substituting pasture-farming for tillage, whether carried out on a large scale or on a small, was only practicable if individuals were able to break away from the established course of agriculture. But the relaxation of village customs, which allowed a wider scope to individual initiative, did not necessarily involve that formation of large estates out of peasant holdings, which was the special note of the sixteenth century problem, and in fact the gradual nibbling away of customary restrictions went on to some degree among quite small men, long before the enclosure of land by great capitalists became a serious grievance. In the fourteenth century, and even earlier, holdings are becoming partible and unequal, and strips are being interchanged for the purpose of more convenient, because compacter, management. In the sixteenth century there is a good deal of enclosure by the peasants themselves with a view to better arable cultivation or to the more successful keeping of stock. Nor must we forget the example of Kent, Essex, Devonshire, Somersetshire, and Cornwall. Without raising the question whether the predominance of small enclosures in the Western Counties is not partly to be ascribed to peculiarities in their original settlement, we may say without fear of contradiction that the early enclosures of Kent and Essex are the outcome of the spread of commercial forces in those seaboard counties at an earlier date than was possible in the inland districts. Even in the more conservative parts of the country, like the Midlands and Wiltshire, whose geographical position made them the last to respond to the influence of trade its gradual extension was slowly, and in isolated villages, bringing the same departure from the rigid arrangements of mediæval agriculture which in the East of England had developed much more swiftly. How far such enclosure by consent would have proceeded if no other forces had come into play we cannot say. It is not safe, however, to assume that, because in the eighteenth century many villages seemed to observers like Arthur Young to be living in a condition of organised torpor, therefore its effects in facilitating a more economical utilisation of the land are to be dismissed as negligible. Quite apart from the obvious bias given to Young's observations by his questionable doctrine that a high pecuniary return from the soil is the final criterion of successful agriculture, it may well be the case that the decline in the condition of the peasantry, which took place in the sixteenth century, discouraged initiative on the part of small men, and that, since one agent in that decline had been a movement which went by the name of enclosure, its effect was to make them cling all the more closely to the established routine in those parts of the country where they had not been violently shaken out of it.

On such conjectures, however, we need not enter. Even if the movement towards the rearrangement of holdings which has been traced among the peasants themselves was insignificant, and if the larger capitalists were the sole agents through whom a more alert and progressive agrarian régime could be introduced, it is none the less the case that the improvements in the technique of agriculture do not by themselves account for the special social consequences which flowed from the agrarian changes of the sixteenth century. The situation then is not at all similar to that which arose at a later date, when small landholders voluntarily threw up their holdings in order to engage in the more profitable urban industries, and when yeomen like the Peels of their own choice decided that the career of a cotton-spinner was more attractive than that of a farmer. In the period which we have been discussing men do not only leave the land; they are forced off it. Not only economic, but legal, issues are involved, and the latter give a decisive twist to the former. What made the new methods of agriculture not simply an important technical advance in the utilisation of the soil, but the beginning of a social revolution, was the insecurity of the tenure of large numbers of the peasantry, in the absence of which they might gradually have adapted themselves to the altered conditions, without any overwhelming shock to rural life such as was produced by the evictions and by the loss of rights of common. The way in which the economic movement towards enclosure and pasture-farming is crossed, and its consequences heightened, by the law of land tenure, is proved by the comparative immunity of the freeholders from the worst forms of agrarian oppression, by the fact that, even in the middle of the eighteenth century, the purely economic conditions of much of England were by no means unfavourable to small scale farming, and by the anxiety of landlords to induce tenants who had estates of inheritance to surrender them for leases. We cannot therefore agree with those writers who regard the decline in the position of the smaller landed classes, which took place in our period, as an inevitable step in economic progress, similar to the decay of one type of industry before the competition of another. If economic causes made a new system of farming profitable, it is none the less true that legal causes decided by whom the profits should be enjoyed. We have already pointed out that many customary tenants practised sheep-farming upon a considerable scale, and it is not easy to discover any economic reason why the cheap wool required for the development of the cloth-manufacturing industry should not have been supplied by the very peasants in whose cottages it was carded and spun and woven. The decisive factor, which ruled out this method of meeting the new situation created by the spread of pasture-farming, was the fact that the tenure of the vast majority of small cultivation left them free to be squeezed out by exorbitant fines, and to be evicted when the lives for which most of them held their copies came to an end. It was their misfortune that the protection given by the courts since the fifteenth century to copyholders did not extend to more than the enforcement of existing manorial customs. When, in our own day, the same causes which raised the cry of depopulation in sixteenth century England have operated in other countries, their influence has been circumscribed by governmental power, which has stepped ready armed into the field, and has turned customary titles into freeholds and cut back private jurisdictions with a heavy hand. To find a parallel to the sufferings of the English copyholders in the sixteenth century, we must turn to the sweeping invasion of tenant right which at one time made almost every Irishman into a Ket. But the comparison, incomplete in other respects, is most incomplete in this, that even if Tudor Governments, moved by considerations of national strength and order, would have helped the peasants if they could, they could hardly have helped them materially if they would, without a social and administrative revolution which was unthinkable, and which, if carried out, could only have meant political absolutism. Living, as they did, with the marks of villein tenure still upon them, the small cultivators of our period were fettered by the remnants of the legal rightlessness of the Middle Ages, without enjoying the practical security given by mediæval custom, and felt the bitter breath of modern commercialism, undefended by the protection of the all-inclusive modern State which alone can make it tolerable.

For, indeed, it is as a link in the development of modern economic relationships and modern conceptions of economic expediency, that the changes which we have been considering possess their greatest interest. The department of economic life in which, both for good and evil, the modern spirit comes in the sixteenth century most irresistibly to its own, is not agriculture but foreign commerce, company promoting, and the money market, where the relations of man to man are already conceived of as the necessary parts of a vast and complicated mechanism, whose iron levers thrust the individual into actions for the consequences of which he is not responsible, and under whose pressure unknown is driven by unknown to do that which he did not intend. But if the intoxication with dreams of boundless material possibilities, the divorce of economic from moral considerations, the restless experiment and initiative and contempt for restrictions that fetter them, which are the marks of that spirit's operations, are never quite so victorious in agriculture as they are in finance, it is nevertheless in transforming agrarian conditions that its nature and characteristics are most impressively revealed, not because it is felt there first or proceeds there furthest, but because the material which it encounters is so dense, so firmly organised, so intractable, that changes, which in a more mobile environment pass unnoticed, are seen there in high relief against the stable society which they undermine. In truth the agrarian revolution is but a current in the wake of mightier movements. The new world, which is painfully rising in so many English villages, is a tiny mirror of the new world which, on a mightier stage, is ushering modern history in amid storms and convulsions. The spirit which revolts against authority, frames a science that will subdue nature to its service, and thrusts the walls of the universe asunder into space, is the same—

we must not hesitate to say it—as that which on the lips of grasping landlords and stubborn peasants wrangles over the respective merits of "several" and "common," weighs the profits of pasture in an economic scale against the profits of arable, batters down immemorial customs, and, regarding neither the honour of God nor the welfare of this realm of England, brings the livings of many into the hands of one. To the modern economist, who uses an ancient field map to trace the bewildering confusion of an open field village beneath the orderly lines of the dignified estate which lies upon it like a well written manuscript on the crabbed scrawl of a palimpsest, the wastefulness of the old régime, compared with the productiveness of the new, may well seem too obvious to leave room for any discussion of their relative advantages; and indeed the accession of material wealth which followed the first feeble approach towards the methods of modern agriculture is unquestionable. But the difference between such a standpoint and that of our peasants is not one of methods only but of objects, not of means but of ends. We can imagine that to an exposition of the advantages of large scale farming and enclosure, such as many stewards must have made to the juries of many manors, they would have answered something after this fashion:—"True, our system is wasteful, and fruitful of many small disputes. True, a large estate can be managed more economically than a small one. True, pasture-farming yields higher profits than tillage. Nevertheless, master steward, our wasteful husbandry feeds many households where your economical methods would feed few. In our ill-arranged fields and scrubby commons most families hold a share, though it be but a few roods. In our unenclosed village there are few rich, but there are few destitute, save when God sends a bad harvest, and we all starve together. We do not like your improvements which ruin half the honest men affected by them. We do not choose that the ancient customs of our village should be changed!" Such differences lie too deep to be settled by argument, whether they appear in the sixteenth century or in our own day.

# APPENDIX I

## (I)

### [LETTER FROM A BAILIFF, ILLUSTRATING THE RELATIONS BETWEEN FARMER AND LORD, AND DIFFICULTIES WITH FREEHOLDERS]

*Merton MSS., No. 4381*

Good Sir lett me intreat you yf the colledge determyne to make survay this springe of the lands at Kibworth and Barkby to send Mr. Kay or me word a month or 3 weeks before your coming that we may have Beare and other necessaries. And I desire you to gather up all evidences that may be needful for ye Lordshipp, for all testimony will be little enough, the colledge land is soo mingled with Mr. Pochin's frehold and others in our towne. There is an awarde for the keepinge in of the old wol close in our ffields for [from?] Mr. Pochin's occupation, very needefulle for the ynhabitants yf that awarde can be founde at the colledge where yt was loste.

The composition betwixt Mr. Stanford and the towne wold we very gladly see, yt is for tythe willows and partinge grasse, wee thinke that they challenge more than of right they should have. I pray you gather upp what evidence you can for the rents due to the college out of [?], for when some of them are denied I know not where to distraine for them.

I pray you also give order that the evidences may be sought up for the lands lyinge in Barkby Thorpend alias Thurmaston in our parish and parcell of our lordship of the rent per ann. ¾d. as alsoe the evidences of Peppers frehold rent per annum 1d. This rent is denied and not paidd this 20 yeares, and I cannot learne where I should distraine for the same, neither will he pay it unlesse he may knowe for what he payeth the same; he is towards the land [?], and his frehold lyeth in Thurmaston ut supra. And soe with remembrance of my duty desiringe you to pardon my breach of promise for the lease at last Michaelmas, and I hope before this yeare be ended to be as good as my worde, yf it will please you and the company to spare me with your favours untill then, ffor God is my judge I did not breake my promise wilfully nor willingly, but necessity hath noe law. I have lost this sumer 6 horses and was forced to buy in these for my carte. Day [?] groweth scant, therefore I must spare to write, only hoping and desiringe your favour at this tyme I humbly take my leave and rest as I have ever beene your wo[ps] at commandment. Henry Sayer.

Barkby, February 26[th], 1608.

To the w[ll] his very singular<br>ffriend Mr. Brent subwarden at Merton College in Oxon.

## (II)

## [In Illustration of Manorial Customs, cf. pp. 124–131 and 297–301.]

*Manor of Aldeburgh, R.O., Misc. Bks., Treas. of Receipt, Vol. 163, Henry VIII.*

The said Manor has one lete by the year ... and hath also the Court from 3 weeks to 3 weeks called the 3 weeks Court.

Item.—Every tenant payeth for a cottage ground not buylded if it con-
teyn 80 ft. every way

Item.—Every tenant payeth for a cottage ground not buylded if it con-
teyn 80 ft. every way                                                         1d.

Item.—Every tenant payeth for half a cottage which is 40 ft. every way     ½d.

Item.—For every curtilage containing 40 ft. or under                        ½d

Item.—For every fyne of every cotage buylded                               2/-

Item.—For every fyne of every cotage ground unbuilded                       1/-

Item.—Every tenant that taketh any cotage ground to build upon if
he build not within three years he forfeiteth the ground by him
taken.

Item.—Every tenant having a cotage or parcel of a cotage wherein any
tenant dwelleth and keepeth a fire, they owe to pay for the same
a Russhe hen or else 2d. which is for the rushes that they gather
upon the lord's common there.

Item.—If 2 tenants dwell in one house having 2 severall rooms in the
same they to pay yearlie 2 rush hennes or 4d. for them.

Item.—Every freeholder having by copy any arable land or pasture
ground in the field payeth yearly for the same at terms accustomed the rent of old time due at [Michaelmas & Easter] by even
porcions; and for all fines cessed upon the tenaunts for land in the
fields is at the will of the lord, as well at the alienations made as at
the death of any tenant.

Item.—The tenants and copyholders shall do no waste upon the lord's
common ne otherwise upon pain of forfeiture of their tenements.

Item.—All the freeholders shall [pay] double their rent at every death
or alienation made, as relief.

Item.—Certain freeholders and copyholders pay heriot after the death
of any tenant.

Item.—Neither the freeholders nor copyholders shall not surcharge
the lord's comon but to keep after the rate of his tenure. If he otherwise do he shall be amerced.

Item.—No man shall encroche on lord's lands on pain of forfeiture of his tenure.

Item.—Every boat going to the sea on fishing and having 4 men therein payeth yearly to the lord 8d., and 6 men 12d., and so after the rate, for each man 2d., which is by a late composition.

Item.—There is a service paid by certain tenants there called Oryell, which is for the liberty of the common that tenants have in the said lordship.

Item.—The lords of Aldeburgh have the moietie of all wreck of the sea being cast on land or found near the shore within the limits of the same lordship, and the finder thereof hath the other half.

## (III)

### [In Illustration of the Peasants' Grievances]

*Holkham MSS., Fulmordeston MSS., Bdle. 6*

To the Right Honble. Sir Edward Cooke, Knight, Attorney-Generall unto the King's Ma^tie.

Humblie sheweth unto your good lord yo^r poore and dayley orators Thomas Ffawcett, Thomas Humphry, and Nicolas Farnes [?] yo^r worshippes tenants of the Manor of Ffulmordeston cum Croxton in the Duchie of Lancaster and the moste parte of the tenants of the same Manor that whereas yo^r said orators in the Hillary Term laste commenced suite in the Duchie Courte against Thomas Odbert and Roger Salisbury, Gent., who have enclosed their grounds contrary to the custom of the Manor, whereby your wor. loseth your shack due out of those grounds, common lane or way for passengers is stopped up, and your worshippes poore orators lose their accustomed shack in those grounds, and the said Roger Salisbury taketh also the whole benefit of theire comons from them, keepinge there his sheepe in grasinge and debarringe them of their libertie there which for comon right belongeth unto them:—

Which suite and controversie, forasmuch as the same manor is nowe come unto your lordshippe's hands by his most excellent Ma^ties gracious disposinge thereof, youre poore oratours thought it theire duty to impart and lay open unto your wor^pp, and doe most humblie pray and beseech your wor^pp that they may have your lawfull favour herein for the furtherance of their proceedings in this theire suite of lawe, so that the greatness of the said parties adversant unto them, on which they much relie, may not be the more strengthened by your worship's favour, whereby your poore orators may have and enjoy theire former liberties in peace, and be the better able to maintaine themselves in their callings rights and dueties which unto your wor. is belonging and due uppon their Tenures in the saide Mannor.

And according to theire bounden duety your sayde poor orators shall dayly pray to God for your wor. in all encrease of prosperitie and worshippe long to continew.

21 Aug. 1604.

I have considered of this peticion, and seeinge I am lord of the mannor I will do my best endeavour upon hearing of both parties to end the controversie and the defend[ts] need not appeare nor the cause to proceed in the duchy.

EDW. COKE.

## (IV)

### [IN ILLUSTRATION OF THE PEASANTS' GRIEVANCES]

*S. P. Dom. Charles I. Vol. 151, No. 38.*

To the Kings most Excellent Ma[tie].

The humble peticon of yo[r] Ma[te] poore and distressed Tennants of yo[r] Mannor of North Wheatley in the Countie of Nottingham belonging to yo[r] Ma[ties] Duchie of Lancaster.

Most humbly shewing. That yo[r] poore Subiects have tyme out of mynd byn Coppieholders of lands of inheritaunce to them and their heires for ever of the Mannor aforesaid, and paid for every Oxgang of land xvj[s] viij[d] rent, and paid heretofore vpon every Alienacon xij[d] for every Oxgang, but nowe of late, about 4⁰ Jacobi by an order of the Duchie Court they paie ij[s] s vj[d] d vpon euery Alienacon for every acre, w[ch] amounteth nowe to 45[s] an Oxgang.

And whereas some of yo[r] Tennants of the said Mannor have heretofore held and doe nowe hold certayne Oxganges of lands belonging to the said Manor by Coppie from xxj yeres to xxj yeares, and have paid for the same vpon evy Coppy ij[s], and for every Oxgang xvj[s] viij[d] p Ann; they nowe of late by an order in the Duchie Court hold the same by lease vnder the Duchie Seale, and paie vj[li] xiij[s] iiij[d] for a Fyne vpon every lease and xvj[s] viij[d] rent w[th] an increase of vj[s] viij[d] more towards yo[r] Ma[ties] prouision.

And whereas in 11⁰ Edw: 4⁰ yo[r] peticõners did by Copy of Court Roll hold the demeanes of the said Mannor for tearme of yeres att ix[li] vj[s] viij[d] p ann, they afterwards in 6⁰ Eliz: held the same demeanes by lease vnder the seale of the duchie for xxj yeares, att the like rent; and Tenne yeres before their lease was expired, they ymployed one M[r] Markham in trust to gett their lease renewed, whoe procured a newe lease of the demeanes in his owne name for xxj yeres att the old rent, and afterwards contrary to the trust Comitted to him increased and raised the rent thereof vpon the Tenants to his owne privat benefitt to 56[li] p annu.

And whereas the woods belonging to the said Mannor hath within the memory of Man byn the only Comõn belonging to the said Towne, paying yerelie for the herbage and pannage thereof vj[s] viij[d], they nowe alsoe hold the same vnder the Duchie Seale att xvj[li] li xvj[s] ij[d] p annu.

And whereas the Court Rolls and Records of the said Mannor, have alwaies heretofore byn kept vnder severall Locks and Keys, whereof yo{super:r} Ma{super:ts} Stewards have kepte one key and yo{super:r} Ma{super:ties} Tennant (in regard it Concerned their pticuler inheritances) have kept an other keye. But nowe they are att the pleasure of the Stewards and Officers transported from place to place, and the nowe purchasers doe demaund the Custody of them, w{super:ch} may be most preiudiciall to yo{super:r} Ma{super:te} poore Tennants.

Now for asmuch as yo{super:r} Matie: hath byn pleased to sell the said Mannor vnto the Cittie of London, whoe have sold the same vnto M{super:r} John Cartwright and M{super:r} Tho: Brudnell gent: And for that yo{super:r} peticoners and Tennants there (beinge in nomber Two hundred poore men, and there being xj of yo{super:r} Ma{super:te} Tennants there that beare Armes for the defence of yo{super:r} Ma{super:te} Realme, and xij that paie yo{super:r} Ma{super:tie} Subsidies fifteens and Loanes) are all nowe like to be vtterlie vndon, in Case the said M{super:r} Cartwright and M{super:r} Brudnell should (as they saie they will) take awaie from yo{super:r} Tennants the said demeanes and woods after thexpiracon of their leases, and that yo{super:r} poore Tennants should be left to the wills of the purchasers for their Fynes, or that the Records and Court rowles should not be kept as in former tymes in some private place, where the purchasers and Tennants maie both have the custody and viewe of them as occasion shall serve.

Maie it therefore please yo{super:r} Sacred Maj{super:tie} That such order may be taken in the premisses for the reliefe of yo{super:r} poore Tennants of the Mannor aforesaid That they maie not be dispossessed of the demeanes and leases, and that they may knowe the Certayntie of their Fynes for the Coppieholds demeanes and leases and maie have the Court Rolls & Records safely kepte as formerly they have byn. And that yo{super:r} Ma{super:tie} wilbe further pleased to referr the Consideracon hearing, ordering and determynacon of the premisses vnto such Noble men, or other 4 gent: of esteeme in the Country whome yo{super:r} Ma{super:tie} shalbe pleased to appoint, that are neighbours vnto yo{super:r} Tenãnts, and doe best knowe their estate & greevances. That they or any two or three of them may take such order, and soe Cettell the busynes betweene the purchasers & yo{super:r} poore Tennants, as they in their wisdoms and discressions shall judge to be reasonable and fitting, or to Certifie yo{super:r} Ma{super:tie} howe they fynd the same, and in whose defalt it is they cannot determyne thereof. And yo{super:r} poore Tennt̃s as in all humble dutie bound will daielie pray for yo{super:r} Ma{super:tie}.

Whitehall this 10 of Novemb{super:r} 1629.

His Mã is graciously pleased to referre the consideration of this request to the Comĩssion{super:rs} for sale of his lands, that vpon the report vnto his Mã of their opinion and advise his Mã may give further order therein.                    DORCHESTER.

[Endorsed.]    Divers Tenants of his Ma{super:te} mañor of North Wheatley in the Countie
of Nottingham.

(V)

[PAPER ON THE EVILS OF ENCLOSURE, BY AN APPLICANT FOR GOVERNMENT EMPLOYMENT]

*S. P. Dom. Charles I. Vol. 206, No. 70*

Right Ho<sup>le</sup>

Uppon the ix<sup>th</sup> of July and also the 23<sup>d</sup> of Septemb<sup>r</sup> I deliv̄d petitions vnto yo<sup>r</sup> Lo<sup>pp</sup> desireinge to shew y<sup>e</sup> great hurt y<sup>t</sup> ys done to his Ma<sup>tie</sup> & y<sup>e</sup> land by inclosiers w<sup>ch</sup> decay tillage, & depopulate townes in ye best naturall corne countryes, w<sup>ch</sup> affore supplyed the wants of others every way beinge in y<sup>e</sup> middle of y<sup>e</sup> land, for yt their is dearths vppon any vnseasonable seedes tyme or springe, and is a great cause of decayinge of trades and vndoeinge many thousands w<sup>ch</sup> before lived well & now for want of Imployment & dearth of corne, y<sup>er</sup> is multitudes of poor & vagrants complayninge of their miseryes; and are dangerous to y<sup>e</sup> peacable state of y<sup>e</sup> land, by y<sup>er</sup> desire of troubles to revenge them selves. Ye know what lamentable broyles & bloodshedinges were betwixt ye gileadites & ephramites & Israelites & benjamites for ye levits wife & Abia & Jeroboam & Ahay & Peka where was slaine above 700,000 men of warr & many of other sorts, w<sup>ch</sup> was more crewell then by any foraigne enymyes, & wee have incrochinge enemyes y<sup>t</sup> would take y<sup>er</sup> advantage vppon such opertunytyes as y<sup>ei</sup> did when y<sup>e</sup> leaguers in France made warrs against theire Kinge ... for many are of oppinyon that ye Kinges Ma<sup>tie</sup> nor ye lordes doe not truly vnderstand ye secret mischief es w<sup>ch</sup> is done by covetous men by ye cuninge misterie of depopulation nor ye oppressions and causes of dearthes and poverty nor know y<sup>e</sup> readyest waye for remedyes, y<sup>et</sup> beinge as unacquainted in tyllage & husbandrye as in other arts: as appeared by y<sup>e</sup> booke of orders y<sup>e</sup> last yere w<sup>ch</sup> shewed that his Ma<sup>tie</sup> and the lordes had a good desire to remedy the dearth but y<sup>e</sup> corn masters & malsters &c. used such closse dealinges y<sup>t</sup> y<sup>e</sup> dearth was worse as y<sup>e</sup> like in former tymes: soe that no orders will ease dearthes but by causeing more tyllage & y<sup>t</sup> would make plenty & then every man will sell willinglye....

Also many are much deceived by inclosier because there are countries are enclosed & be rich, but these were inclosed when there were but few people & these maintain tyllage husbandry & hospitallyty & sett people on work & have tenements for labourers, these are lyable to musters & all services requirable for ye Kinge & country & taxes & charitable collections but y<sup>e</sup> depopulators in ye champian countryes destroy all meanes of doeinge help or servise for ye Kinge & country what neede soever come.

And although this was the fruitfullest somer that was in many yeares, yet corne holds almost duble price to that which most men expected, because rich men will sell but litle corne before they see the strength of May past & if corne does not prosper then they will keep it expecting a dearth the next yere. Another cause is that all men see how tyllag is yearly decayed in the best champian countryes & people & drunknes increased & no hope of remedy because of y<sup>e</sup> inyquity of y<sup>e</sup> tyme & gentlemen & other have great friends & favour & may doe what they list. And maltsters & ingrossers buy corn as fast as they can, & doe use wayes to have it brought home what lawes or orders to the contrary expectinge a dearth if ye next spring prove not very fruitfull. And if his Ma<sup>ty</sup> & ye lords doe not take some speedy course to cause more tyllage there beinge good ground enough before wete seeds tymes come, then will dearth ensue. And y<sup>n</sup> ye poore hungry people may cry ... where ys corne; And y<sup>n</sup> it will be too late to remedy dearths by any lawes or orders. And now it might be done there beinge aboundance of old resty fatt ground in yᵉ champian countryes which if it were plowed & sowne wᵗ corne, no wett seeds tyme could hurt it soe that they would yield corne to supply all wants beinge in yᵉ midle of yᵉ land my lord if you please to give me leave I will give you yᵉ names of many decayed townes in ye counties of Leicˢ & Northampt, &c., and who decayed them & now the Lord hath swept away yᵉ inclosiers & their posterity out of all & strangers have their houses & pastures. And my desire is yᵗ yoʳ Loᴾ might be acquainted with yᵉ country dissorders & the remydes to reforme yᵉ evills and then ye may better judge of them & acquaint his Maᵗⁱᵉ & yᵉ lords, that by his & their good directions, we shall have plenty and bring much more to his maᵗⁱᵉˢ treasures & the whole land....

Also I doe humbly intreate yoʳ Loᴾˢ favor to let me shew how there may be ymploymᵗ for people & wealth to ye Kinge & ye Kingdome & plenty & cheapnes & have ingrossers frustrated of their game & have lesse wast of corne in ale & beer & less sinninge: & lesse dangers & soe ye lorde keepe you: wᵗʰ my humble sute, to accept of my poore desires for ye deede, with my attendance vpon your Loᴾˢ pleasure.

Your Loᴾˢ to Com̃and<br>RICHARD SANDES.

[Endorsed:—]

Sandes touching Indigence.

## (VI)

## [IN ILLUSTRATION OF ACTION AGAINST ENCLOSURES BY JUSTICES]

*S. P. Dom. Charles I. Vol. 185, No. 86*

Most Honorᵇˡᵉ

Wee have caused a view to bee made according to yoʳ Loᴾˢ Late Lr̃es of all *Inclosures and convʳsions of Arrable Land to meadow and pasture,* wᶜʰ are now in hand or haue beene made wᵗʰⁱn two yeares Last past, And wee haue signifyed yoʳ Loᴾˢ direccõns vnto such ꝑsons as are causers of any such Inclosures & Convtions and have given them notice that they ought not to ꝑcede wᵗʰ hedgeing or dytchinge in of any such grounds but to Let them so rest vntill wee shall have furder orders from yoʳ: honᵒʳˢ: And wee further conceaue that if depopulacõns may bee reformed it will bring a great good to the whole Kingā: for where houses are pulled downe the People are forced to seeke new habitations. In other townes & cuntryes by meanes whereof those Townes where they get a setling are pestred so as they are hardly able to live one by an other, and it is likewise the cause of erecting new Cottages vppon the wasts and other places who are not able to releive themselves nor any such townes able to sustaine or set them on worke wᶜʰ Causes Rogues & vagabonds to encrease. Moreover it doth appeare that in those townes wᶜʰ are depopulated the People being expelled There are few or none Left to serve the King when Souldjours are to bee lodged to appeare at Musters for his Maᵗᵉ seruice wᶜʰ is also a cause that poore Townes where many people are, are put to greater charg in setting forth of souldjours & depopulated Townes are much eased and the Subsidie decayed. All wᶜʰ wee humbly submit to yoʳ Loᴾˢ great wisdome. And will ev rest.

At yo<sup>r</sup> hon<sup>ble</sup> service
humbly to bee comaunded

Fran: Thornhagh     Ro: Sutton vic.

Wee doe herew<sup>th</sup> psent vnto yo<sup>r</sup> Hon<sup>rs</sup>
the names of all such as have made
any Inclosures or convsions w<sup>th</sup> in two
yeares Last past or that were in hand to
make the same.

Matth Palmer

W. Cooper     Gervas Fevery

Tym: Pilsy     Gilbt Millington

Wiłł Coke     Will Moseley

Jo: Woods

[Addressed:]     To the right hon<sup>ble</sup> the Lords of his Mat<sup>s</sup> hon<sup>ble</sup> Privy Counsell humbly present these.

[Endorsed:]     Feb. 1630. From the County of Nottingham touching Inclosures. The inconveniencies of Depopulation.

[No Enclosures]

[This letter is printed by Miss Leonard, *Trans. Royal Hist. Soc.*, New Series, vol. xix. She refers it to Norfolk, which is apparently a mistake.]

# (VII)

## [IN ILLUSTRATION OF ACTION AGAINST ENCLOSURES BY JUSTICES]

*S. P. Dom. Charles I. Vol. 206, No. 71*

Lincoln

An abstract of such depopulators as have bene hetherto dealt withall in Lincolnshyre, & receyued their pardon.

| | |
|---|---|
| The persons in number | 9 |
| The some of their fynes | 300*l* |
| The number of houses by bond to bee erected | 33 |
| The tyme for the ereccon within one yere. | |
| The number of farmes to be contynued that are now standing | 22 |
| The fynes are already payd. | |

Sir Charles Hussey Kn<sup>t.</sup> Fyne, 80ł.

Bond of 200 m̨kes, w<sup>th</sup> Condicon to sett up in Homington 8 farmhouses w<sup>th</sup> Barnes &c. and to lay to evye house 30 acres of land, and to keepe 10 acres thereof yearlye in tyllage.

S<sup>r</sup> Henry Ayscough Knt. Fyne, 20ł.

Bond 200 m̨kcs. To sett vp 8 farmhouses in Blibroughe w<sup>th</sup> 30 acres to evy farme, and 12 thereof to be kept yearlie in tylthe.

S$^r$ Hamond Whichcoote Knt. Fyne, 40ł.

Bond 200 m̨kes. To set up 8 farmhouses &c. in Harpswell, w$^{th}$ 40 acres to eu'y house; and 16 thereof in tyllage.

S$^r$ Edward Carre Kt. Fyne, 30ł.

Bond 100ł. To sett vp 2 Farmhouses in Branswell, and 1 in Aswarby w$^{th}$ 40 acres to eu'y house, 16 in tyllage.

S$^r$ Willm̨aye, Kn$^{t.}$ Fyne, 30ł.

Bond 100ł. To sett up in Graynesby 2 farmhouses w$^{th}$ 2 acres at least to either, 10 in tyllage & to contynue 2 farmes more in Grainsby & 3 in New-bell & Longworth, w$^{th}$ the same quantity, as is now used them, a third ꝑte in tylthe.

S$^r$ Edmund Bussye K$^{t.}$ Fyne, 10ł.

Bond 100ł. To set vp one farmhouse in Thorpe w$^{th}$ 40 acres, 14 thereof in tyllage, And to contynue 14 farmes in Hedor, Oseby, Aseby, & Thorpe, as they now are, w$^{th}$ a third ꝑte in tyllage.

Richard Roseto$^r$ Esq$^{r.}$ Fyne, 10ł.

Bond 50ł. To set vp one farme in Lymber w$^{th}$ 40 acres, 16 in tyllage, and to continewe 1 farme in Limber, and 2 in Sereby, vt sup$^a$

Robert Tirwhilt Esq$^{r.}$ Fyne, 10ł. Bond 50ł.

To set vp one farme in Camtringt$^a$un w$^{th}$ 40 acres. 16 in tyllage.

John Fredway gent. Fyne, 10ł. Bond 40ł.

To set up one farme in Gelson w$^{th}$ 30 acres, 10 thereof in tyllage.

[Endorsed:] Lincoln̨ Depopulato̧r Fyned & pardoned and the reformacons to bee made.

[No date]

# (VIII)

## [Complaints concerning the Procedure of Archbishop Laud in Dealing with Enclosures]

### S. P. Dom. Charles I. Vol. 499, No. 10

That vpon the Commission of enquiry after depopulacoñ The Lord Archbishopp of Cant and other the Commissioners at the solicitacoñ of Tho: Hussey gent. did direct a let̨ nature of a Com̨ission to certain persons w$^{th}$ in the County of Wilts to certifie what number of Acres in South Marston in the ꝑish of Highworth were converted from arable to pasture and what number of ploughes were laid downe &c.

Wherevpon the Archdeacon with two others did retourne Certificate, to the Lord Archbishopp &c.

Upon this Certificate, M^r Anth: Hungerford, M^r Southby with 15 others were convented before his Grace and the other Commissioners at the Councell Board, where being charged with Conversion.

M^r Anth: Hungerford & M^r Southby with some others did averre that they had made noe conversion, other then they had when they came to be owners thereof.

His Grace said that they were to looke noe further then to the owners, And Certificate was retourned that soe many Acres were converted and soe many ploughes let downe.

They alladged that this Certificate was false & made without their privity, and therefore M^r Hungerford in the behalfe of the rest did desire that they might not be iudged upon that Certificate. But that they might haue the like favour as M^r Hussey had, to have Cerf the same nature directed to other Commissioners, or a Commission if it might be granted to examine vpon oath whereby the trueth might better appeare.

His Grace replyed to M^r Hungerford since you desire it & are soe earnest for it you shall not have it.

They did offer to make prove that since the conversion there were more habitacoṇs of men of ability & fewer poore. And that whereas the King had before 4 or 5 souldiers of the Trayned Band he had nowe 9 there. That the Impropriacoṇ was much better to be lett.

His Grace said to the rest of the Lords, wee must deale with these genț as with those of Tedbury to take 150ł fine, and to lay open the inclosures.

Which they refusing to doe they were there threatned with an informacoṇ to be brought ag^t them in the Starrchamḃ And accordingly were within a shorte tyme after by the said M^r Hussey served with sub penas at M^r Attorney his suite in the Starr chamber: And this as M^r Hussey told M^r Hungf^d was done by my Lo: Archbp his command.

[Endorsed:] Depopulation—M^r Hungerford & M^r Southby

# APPENDIX II

**TABLE I. (PP. 19 AND 20)**

This table is based on documents relating to the following manors:—

1. Northumberland.

Acklington (1567, *Northumberland County History*, vol. v. pp. 367–8); Buston (1567, *ibid.*, vol. v. p. 209); Thirston (1567, *ibid.*, vol. vii. pp. 305–6); Birling (1567, *ibid.*, vol. v. pp. 200–1); Amble (1608, *ibid.*, vol. v. p. 281); Hexham (1608, *ibid.*, vol. iii. pp. 86–104).

2. Lancashire.

Warton (Hen. VIII., R.O. Rentals and Surveys, Gen. Ser., Portf. 19, No. 7, ff. 79–87); Whyttington (Hen. VIII., R.O. Rentals and Surveys, Gen. Ser., Portf. 19, No. 7, ff. 47–9); Ashton (Hen. VIII., R.O. Rentals and Surveys, Portf. 19, No. 7, ff. 69–72); Overton (4 Eliz. R.O. Duchy of Lanc., Special Commission, No. 67); Widnes (10 Eliz. R.O. Duchy of Lanc., Special Commission, No. 181); Cartmel (Hen. VIII. (?) R.O. Rentals and Surveys, Gen. Ser., Portf. 22, No. 75); Rochdale (1626, from information kindly supplied by Lieut.-Colonel Fishwick of Rochdale, from a Survey in the Chetham Library, Manchester), Lands of Cockersand Abbey (1501, *Chetham Miscellanies*, vol. iii.).

3. Staffordshire.

Barton (Ph. and M.(?) R.O. Rentals and Surveys, Gen. Ser., Portf. 14, No. 70); Burton Bondend (1597, R.O. Land Rev. Misc. Bks., vol. 185, ff. 70–74); Drayton Basset (1579, R.O. Land Rev. Misc. Bks., vol. 185, ff. 54–68); Wotton in Elishall (1 Ed. VI., R.O. Rentals and Surveys, Gen. Ser., Portf. 14, No. 83); Agarsley (1611, R.O. Rentals and Surveys, Duchy of Lancs., Bdle. 8, No. 29).

4. Leicestershire.

Ulverscroft Priory (31 Hen. VIII., R.O. Land Rev. Misc. Bks., vol. 182, f. 35); Broughton Astley (Eliz. R.O. Rentals and Surveys, Gen. Ser., Bdle. 10, No. 4); Barkby (Hen. VIII., R.O. Rentals and Surveys, Roll 382); Stapleford (10 Eliz., R.O. Rentals and Surveys, Duchy of Lanc., Portf. 6, No. 15); Priory of Launde (31 Hen. VIII, R.O. Land Rev. Misc. Bks. 182, f. 1); College of St. Mary, Leicester (1595, R.O. Rentals, Duchy of Lanc. 6/12); Garradon Abbey (Hen. VIII., R.O. Augm. Off., Misc. Bks. 403, f. 123); Kibworth Beauchamp (1 & 2 Ph. and M., R.O. Land Rev. Misc. Bks. 182, f. 284); Kibworth Harcourt (1636, Merton MSS., Book labelled Kibworth and Barkby, 1636).

5. Northamptonshire.

Duston (3 Eliz., R.O. Rentals and Surveys, Portf. 13, No. 23); Yelvertoft (11 Eliz., R.O. Rentals and Surveys, Portf. 13, No. 52); Warmington and Eaglethorpe (30 Eliz., R.O. Rentals and Surveys, Portf. 13, No. 21); Brigstock (4 James I., R.O. Land Rev. Misc. Bks., vol. 221, f. l); Higham Ferrers (8 James I., R.O. Rentals and Surveys, Portf. 13, No. 34); Paulspurie, *alias* Westpury (32 Hen. VIII., R.O. Rentals and Surveys, vol. 419, f. 3).

6. Norfolk.

Ormesby (7 Hen. VIII., R.O. Rentals and Surveys, Gen. Ser., Portf. 22, No. 18); Barney (29 Hen. VIII., R.O. Rentals and Surveys, Gen. Ser., Portf. 26, No. 57); Great Walsingham (29 Hen. VIII., *ibid.*); Gunthorpe (29 Hen. VIII., *ibid.*); Skerning (Ed. VI., R.O. Rentals and Surveys, Gen. Ser., Portf. 3, No. 23); Metherwolde (1575, R.O. Duchy of Lanc., Rentals and Surveys, Bdle. 7, No. 29a); Brisingham (31 Eliz., R.O. Misc. Bks., Land Rev., vol. 220, f. 220); Aylsham (James I., R.O. Misc. Bks., Augm. Off., vol. 360, f. 1); Scratbye Bardolphes (date uncertain, R.O. Rentals and Surveys, Gen. Ser., Portf. 12, No. 52); Burghe Vaux (1620, R.O. Rentals and Surveys, Gen. Ser., Portf. 12, No. 52); Castons (*c.* 1620(?), R.O. Rentals and Surveys, Gen. Ser., Portf. 12, No. 52 p. 10d); Massingham (Hen. VIII.(?), R.O. Rentals and Surveys, Gen. Ser., Portf. 30, No. 25); Northendall (date uncertain, R.O. Rentals and Surveys, Roll 478, m. 3); Drayton Hall (date uncertain, R.O. Rentals and Surveys, Gen. Ser., Portf. 20, No. 53); East Dereham (1649, R.O. Parliamentary Surveys, Norfolk, No. 10); West Lexham (1595, Holkham MSS., West Lexham MSS., No. 87); Longham Hall and Gunton (1611, Holkham MSS., Tittleshall Bks., No. 62); Longham and Watlington (1611, Holkham MSS., Tittleshall Bks., No. 62); Watlington and Priors (1611, Holkham MSS., Tittleshall Bks., No. 62); Billingford (1565, Holkham MSS., Billingford and Bintry MSS., Bdle. No. 9); Foxley (1568, Holkham MSS., Billingford and Bintry MSS., Bdle. No. 9); Peakhall (1578, Holkham MSS., Tittleshall Bks., No. 12); Wellingham (1611, Holkham MSS., Tittleshall Bks., No. 62); Tittleshall Newhall (Holkham MSS., Tittleshall Bks., No. 62). I have included one manor (R.O. Rentals and Surveys, Gen. Ser., Portf. 3, No. 21), of which I have mislaid the name.

7. Suffolk.

Snape (Hen. VIII., R.O. Misc. Bks., Treas. of Receipt, vol. 163, f. 187); Ashfield (Hen. VIII., R.O. Rentals and Surveys, Gen. Ser., Portf. 14, No. 85); Otley (Hen. VIII., R.O. Misc. Bks., Treas. of Receipt, vol. 163, f. 145); Rodstrete and Brimdishe (Ed. VI., R.O. Misc. Bks., Augm. Off., vol. 414, f. 19–22); Dennington (Ed. VI., R.O. Misc. Bks., vol. 414, f. 22b); Harrolds in Cretingham (Ed. VI., R.O. Aug. Off., vol. 414, f. 25b); Stratford juxta Higham (17 James I., R.O. Duchy of Lanc., Rentals and Surveys, 9/13); Denham (date uncertain, R.O. Rentals and Surveys, Gen. Ser., Portf. 27, No. 32); Dunstall (date uncertain, R.O. Rentals and Surveys, Gen. Ser., Portf. 27, No. 32); Dalham (date uncertain, R.O. Rentals and Surveys, Gen. Ser., Portf. 27, No. 32); Kentford (date uncertain, R.O. Rentals and Surveys, Gen. Ser., Portf.

27, No. 32); Nedham (date uncertain, R.O. Rentals and Surveys, Gen. Ser., Portf. 27, No. 32); Desnage Talmaye, and Cressness[?] in Gaseleye (date uncertain, R.O. Rentals and Surveys, Gen. Ser., Portf. 27, No. 32); Higham (date uncertain, R.O. Rentals and Surveys, Gen. Ser., Portf. 27, No. 32).

8. Wiltshire, Somerset, and Devon.

All are contained in the *Surveys of the Lands of William, Earl of Pembroke*, published by the Roxburgh Club, and edited by Straton, 1565–1573. There are twenty-seven manors in Wiltshire, four in Somersetshire, and one in Devonshire.

9. Hampshire.

Crondal, and Sutton Warblington (*Crondal Records*, Part I., Baigent).

10. Ten other manors in the South of England.

Castle Combe (Wilts, 1454, Scrope, *History of Castle Combe*); Ibstone (Bucks, 1483, Merton MSS., No. 5902); Cuxham (Oxford, 1483, Merton MSS., No. 5902); Malden (Surrey, 1496, Merton MSS., Survey of Malden); Aspley Guise (Bedford, 1542, from information kindly supplied by Mr. G.H. Fowler, of Aspley Guise); Ewerne (Dorset, 1568, *Topographer and Genealogist*, vol i.); Edgeware (Middlesex, 1597, All Souls Estate Maps); Kingsbury (Middlesex, 1597, All Souls Estate Maps); Gamlingay Merton (Cambridge, 1601, Merton Estate Maps); Gamlingay Avenells (Cambridge, 1601, Merton Estate Maps).

*　　　*　　　*　　　*　　　*

The chief criticisms which may be made upon this table are:—

(i) Some of the documents from which the figures are taken are separated from each other by a very long interval of time, so that they do not all represent approximately the same stage of agrarian development. This is a disadvantage. It is possible, for example, that, if the manor of Rochdale could be examined in 1526 instead of in 1626, it would be found that the proportion of copyholders to leaseholders was higher than it is at the later date. This defect, however, is perhaps not so great as to outweigh the value of the general picture of the relative proportion of different classes given by the table. A great majority of the documents from which it is compiled belong to the sixteenth century, and are dated as follows: Those of 10 manors are of an uncertain date, those of 3 fall between 1450 and 1485, of 2 in the reign of Henry VII., of 19 in that of Henry VIII., of 5 in that of Edward VI., of 3 in that of Philip and Mary, of 60 in that of Elizabeth, of 13 in that of James I., of 2 in that of Charles I., of 1 in 1649.

(ii) The lists of tenants given by the surveyors may sometimes not be exhaustive. I am not sure, for example, that all the freeholders on the manor of Crondal, or all the leaseholders at Gamlingay Merton and Gamlingay Avenells, are recorded.

(iii) It is sometimes not clear under what category a tenant should be entered. When there is no clue at all I have entered such tenants as "uncertain." In some cases, however, though there is no entry by the surveyor, there are indications that the tenants are freeholders, customary tenants, or leaseholders, and, when that is so, I have grouped them in the table according to the probabilities of the case. But I do not doubt that I have made some mistakes.

(iv) A special word must be said about Norfolk and Suffolk. In these counties it is quite common to find the same tenant holding both by free and by customary tenure. When this is so, I have entered him both under "freeholders" and under "customary tenants" in the table. This means, of course, that the numbers entered for these two counties in the table exceed the number of individual landholders. As, however, my object was to ascertain the distribution of different classes of tenures, this course, though not satisfactory, seemed the best one to follow. In other counties a similar difficulty hardly ever occurs, a fact which is of some interest as showing the relatively advanced agrarian conditions of Norfolk and Suffolk. In the few cases in which it does occur I have followed the same plan as I have for those two counties.

## TABLE II. (PP. 24 AND 25)

This table is based on documents relating to the undermentioned manors. The sources from which the information is taken are given in the explanation of Table I., and I therefore do not repeat them.

1. Norfolk.

Metherwolde, Northendall, Brisingham, Massingham, Skerning Billingford.

2. Suffolk.

Ashfield, Stratford juxta Higham, Kentford, Dunstall.

3. Staffordshire.

Drayton Basset, Barton, Burton Bondend.

4. Lancashire.

Warton, Overton, Widnes.

5. Northamptonshire.

Paulespurie, Brigstock, Higham Ferrers, Duston.

6. Wiltshire.

South Newton.

7. Leicestershire.

Barkby.

I have thought it worth while to insert this table, but I am not satisfied with it. (i) I am inclined to think that, as stated in the text, fuller information would show that medium-sized holdings of between 20 and 60 acres were more common than it suggests. It is plain that surveyors often could not locate the properties of freeholders, and the larger the property the harder their task. (ii) Even where the holding is set out by the surveyor, one cannot always form an accurate judgment of its size. For example, rights of common, though often expressed in acres, are often expressed in some other way, *e.g.* in the terms of the number of beasts which the tenant may graze; and, again, a man is sometimes said to hold so many acres "cum pertinentiis." What I have done is simply to enter the acreage as given in the surveys. In some cases, therefore, the size of the holding is certainly underestimated.

### TABLE III. (P. 35)

The figures in this table are an analysis of the figures given under the heading of "Customary Tenants" in Table I., and the source from which they are taken will be found by looking at the explanation of that table given above. As I have pointed out in the text, it is probable that not all the "Tenants at Will" should have been entered as "Customary Tenants" in that table. I hope that any error which may have arisen through their inclusion under that heading there may be neutralised by setting them out here. It will be seen that they are not numerous.

### TABLE IV.(PP. 47 AND 48)

This table is based on documents relating to the undermentioned manors. The sources from which the information is taken are given, with a few exceptions (see below), in the explanation of Table I.

1. Wiltshire and Somerset.

South Newton, Byshopeston, Washerne, Knyghton, Donnington, Estoverton and Phipheld, Wynterbourne Basset (all in Wilts), South Brent and Huish (Somerset).

2. Suffolk.

Stratford juxta Higham, Ashfield, Snape, Desnage Talmaye, Chaterham Hall (the last Hen. VIII. R.O. Misc. Bks., Treas. of Receipt, vol. 163, ff. 109–114).

3. Norfolk.

Barney, Great Walsingham, Gunthorpe, Brisingham, Aylsham, Ormesby, Northendall, and one manor, the name of which I have mislaid (see explanation of Table I.).

4. Staffordshire.

Barton, Wotton in Elishall, Agarsley.

5. Lancashire.

Ashton, Whytyngton, Warton, Widnes.

6. Northamptonshire.

Higham Ferrers, Brigstock.

7. Leicestershire.

Launde Priory, Barkby, Kibworth.

8. Northumberland.

High Buston, Acklington, Birling, Thirston, Preston, East Chirton, Middle Chirton, Whitney, Monkseaton, Eardon (the last six all 1539, *Northumberland County History*, vol. viii. p. 230, ff.).

9. Nine manors elsewhere in South of England.

Crondal, Sutton Warblington, Edgeware, Kingsbury, Aspley Guise, Gamlingay Merton, Gamlingay Avenells, Salford, Weedon Weston (two last from surveys on back of All Souls Maps).

In this table are included a few landholders as to whose tenure I am not certain. It has the defect stated in connection with Table I., that in a considerable number of instances the holdings of tenants are not fully expressed in terms of acres, and that therefore it probably somewhat underestimates their area. On the other hand, the holdings of the customary tenants are usually set out by the surveyors much more fully than those of the freeholders.

## Table V (p. 78)

1. Northumberland and Lancashire.

Acklington, Birling, High Buston, Thirston, Whytyngton.

2. Wiltshire and Dorsetshire.

South Newton, Estoverton and Phipheld, Winterbourne Basset, Washerne, Donyngton, Byshopeston, Knyghton, Ewerne (the last in Dorsetshire, *Topographer and Genealogist*, vol. i. There are only three customary tenants on this manor, and only one is represented in the table, as the use made by the others of their land is not ascertainable).

3. Bedfordshire, Northamptonshire, Staffordshire, Leicestershire.

Salford, Weedon Weston, Wotton in Elishall, Kibworth Harcourt.

In connection with this table the following points should be noticed:—

(i) I am not certain that all the tenants represented in it are customary tenants. But with one or two exceptions the holdings of all are not larger than those of the customary tenants on other manors, so that there is no reason to suppose that their agricultural economy differed from that usually followed by the latter.

(ii) More serious, the figures are not completely accurate. I have entered under each denomination, "arable," "meadow," or "pasture," land so entered by the surveyor. In some cases, however, the character of the land is not specified. *E.g.*

it is described simply as a "close," or a tenant is said to hold so many acres of arable "with appurtenances." Further, tenants frequently possess rights of pasture which are not expressed in terms of acres, but are either measured by the number of beasts which they may graze, or are not measured at all (*e.g.* "catalla sine extento"). In the latter case, which does not affect any except the Wiltshire manors, I have not attempted to form any estimate, but have simply taken their holdings as stated by the surveyor. When there is no clue to the character of the land, I have omitted it. When it is plain that the land falls under a special denomination, though this is not specified in the survey, I have placed it under that denomination in my table. *E.g.* at Donyngton nearly every tenant holds "unum clausum noviter extractum de communia," and together they hold in such "closes" 132 acres. I have entered these as "pasture."

### Table VI. (p. 83–85)

1. Ingoldmells, Lincolnshire: Massingberd, Ingoldmells Court Rolls, Preface, p. vii. I quote the words of the editor, "In 1086 the annual value of the manor of Ingoldmells was £10.... In 1295 the rents of the free and bondage tenants were £51, 17s. 1d.... In 1347 the same rents were £61, 9s. 4d., and in 1421 they were £71, 10s. 3d.... But in 1485 £3, 7s. 4d. had to be deducted for lost rents ... from a total of £72, 6s. 8d.... When the manor was sold in 1628 by Charles I., the reserved rent ... was only £73, 17s. 2d.... It is therefore clear that at Ingoldmells the tenants appropriated virtually the whole of the increase in the value of the land."

2. Crondall, Hampshire: Baigent, *Crondal Records*, Part I., pp. 135 and 383.

3. Sutton Warblington, Hampshire: *ibid.*, pp. 141 and 383. At the later date Sutton Warblington appears to have been treated as part of the manor of Crondal, though still itself called a manor.

4. Birling, Northumberland: *Northumberland County History*, vol. v.

5. Acklington, Northumberland: *ibid.*, vol. v.

6. High Buston, Northumberland: *ibid.*, vol. v. (Tenants at will and copyholders only).

7. Amble, Northumberland: *ibid.*, vol. v.

8. Aspley Guise, Bedfordshire. These figures were kindly supplied me by Dr. G.H. Fowler of Aspley Guise as the result of his researches in the Record Office into the history of the manor.

9. South Newton, Wiltshire: Roxburghe Club, *Surveys of Lands of William, first Earl of Pembroke*, edited by Straton. Note (a) The manor of South Newton included the parishes of Childhampton, Stoford, Little Wishford, and North Ugford. I have dealt here only with the Parish of South Newton, (b) The figures relate only to the customary tenants, and do not include the payments of freeholders and *convencionarii*. I have obtained the figure of £8, 3s. 11½d. by adding together the tenants' money payments and the value of their works, which are set down in terms of money. But I am not sure that it is correct. I have omitted the payments of fowls (made at both dates) and the small payments for church shot and maltsilver.

10. Cuxham, Oxfordshire: Merton MSS., Nos. 5902 and 5905.

11. Ibstone, Buckinghamshire: *ibid.*, Nos. 5902 and 5209. (In the earlier rental freeholders as well as customary tenants, and in the later possibly leaseholders as well, are included.)

12. Malden, Surrey: Merton MSS. MSS. both headed "Maldon, Thorncroft, and Farleigh 1841," and giving extracts from early court rolls and rentals.

13. Kibworth, Leicestershire: Merton MSS., Nos. 6375 (Rental), 6362, and 6356 (ministers' accounts). The earliest entry is the payments of the copyholders only: the two later entries are "rents of assize."

14. Standen, Hertfordshire: R.O. Mins. Accts., Gen. Ser., Bdle. 868, No. 17; Bdle. 869, No. 8; Bdle. 869, No. 15; Bdle. 870, No. 4. The earliest entry is "Rents assized £18, 17s. 3d. Lands let at will of lord 60s." The second, third, and fourth give the total income.

15. Feering, Essex: R.O. Mins. Accts., Gen. Ser., Bdle. 841, No. 5; Bdle. 841, No. 23; Mins. Accts., Hen. VIII., No. 951. The first two entries are totals of quarterly rents paid at Christmas, Easter, Birth of St. John the Baptist, and Michaelmas. The last is "assized rent." It is possible, therefore, that the apparent diminution is due to the earlier rentals having included payments not given in the last.

16. Appledrum, Sussex: R.O. Rentals and Surveys, Rolls 643, 644, and Mins. Accts., Gen. Ser., Bdle. 1019, No. 15.

17. Minchinhampton: R.O. Rentals and Surveys, Gen. Ser., Rolls 237 and 241. In the earlier documents the "total rent yearly" is given as £41, 14s. 4d., and the "sum total of works" as £4, 15s.

18. Langley Marish, Berkshire: R.O. Mins. Accts., Gen. Ser., Bdle. 761, No. 4, and Bdle. 762, No. 5; Land Rev. Misc. Bks., vol. 188, f. 196ff. The first entry is the sum total of rents paid quarterly, together with 7s. 4d. of a custom called "vaccage," and 13s. 4d. of common fine at view of frank pledge. (Exactly the same items are entered in the following year.) The second entry is "profits and issues of the manor," and is headed "account of the manor for 83 days," but the similarity of the figure with that of the earlier date makes it hard to believe that the "profits" relate to less than one quarter of the year. The third entry is made up of rents of free and customary tenants, demesne lands held by copy, and customary rents called "Hedage" and "Duply," producing 23s. 3½d.

19. Lewisham, Kent: R.O. Rentals and Surveys, Gen. Ser., Roll 361; Misc. Bks., Treas. of Receipt, vol. 174, f. 1–34; Misc. Bks., Aug. Off., vol. 414, f. 33–4. The first entry is "Rent of the tenants of the manor of Lewisham," the second "Rental of the lordship of Lewisham." The third "Rent of free tenants £17, 12s. 10½d., Rent of tenants *per dimissionem* £72, 9s. 8½d., Rents of tenants at will 9d."

20. Cuddington, Surrey: R.O. Rentals and Surveys, Rolls 669 and 624, Aug. Off., Misc. Bks., vol. 414, f. 3–16. The first entry is "Rents belonging to the manor at the terms of Easter and Michaelmas," i.e. it is for half a year only, and therefore I have ventured to double it. The second and third entries consist of the annual rent of all classes of tenants.

21. Isleworth, Middlesex: R.O. Mins. Accts., Gen. Ser., Bdle. 916, Nos. 11, 21, and 25. The figures at each date refer to the assized rent. At the two earlier dates the assized rent is given for all four quarters of the year. At the last date it is given only for the Michaelmas quarter. In order to make comparison possible, I have given the rents for the Michaelmas quarter throughout. The full entries for the two earlier dates are: 1314–15, £15, 5s. 6d. at Christmas, £17, 1s. 9¾d. at Easter, £15, 5s. 6d. at June 24, £21, 16s. 10d. at Michaelmas, works sold 22s. 1½d; 1386–7, £14, 13s. at Christmas, £16, 19s. 7d. at Easter, £13, 13s. at June 24, £23, 3s. 10½d. at Michaelmas, works sold 106s. 10d.

22. Wootton, Oxfordshire: R.O. Misc. Accts., Bdle. 962, No. 20; Bdle. 963, No. 14; Aug. Off., Misc. Bks., vol. 414, f. 38b. At the two earlier dates the figures given are the assized rents of free and bond tenants and *cotarii*, at the last date they are the rents of free and customary tenants. At that time there was also a rent of 30s. 8½d. from assarts, and a rent of £13, 0s. 11d. from tenants by demission. I have omitted the last two items as there is nothing comparable to them in the earlier entries.

23. Speen, Berkshire: R.O. Mins. Accts., Gen. Ser., Bdle. 750, No. 22; Misc. Bks. Land Revenue, vol. 187, f. 97–101. At the earlier date the figures refer to the assized rents, at the later date to the rents of free tenants, customary tenants, and "firms."

24. Schitlington, Bedfordshire: R.O. Mins. Accts., Gen. Ser., Bdle. 741, Nos. 16, 19, and 27. At the first date the figures refer to the assized rent, and include "Tallage of the vill £10." At the second date they cover the same entries as at the first. At the last date they refer to the rent as it appears in the Rental. At this time there are certain additional entries, viz., "Firm of land £8, 5s. 0¼d., Firm of the manor £4, 15s. 4d., Increase of Rent [of a mill(?)] 13s. 4d., Increase of Rent of 1 messuage, 1 virgate with croft and meadow 13s. 7½d." These I have omitted.

25. Cranfield, Bedfordshire: R.O. Mins. Accts., Gen. Ser., Bdle. 740, Nos. 18, and 25; Mins. Accts., Hen. VIII., No. 4. At the first two dates the figures include rents of free and native tenants and ferm of lands. At the last date the entry is "Rent of the vill, as by the rental, £72, 2s. 1¾d."

26. Holywell, Huntingdonshire: R.O. Mins. Accts., Gen. Ser., Bdle. 877, No. 17, Bdle. 878, No. 1. At the first date the entries include rents assized, and certain miscellaneous items such as "Hewesilver," "Heringsilver," "Brensilver"; at the later date "Rents assized of free and villein tenants £4, 19s. 8d., customary rent lately in works and in new rent £15, 6s. for 17 virgates paying 18s. each, £6, 15s., for 25 cotmen paying 9s. each, 6s. 8d. increment of rent."

The suggestion that it might be of interest to try to discover how far rents were stationary over long periods came to me from reading the article by Maitland on "The History of a Cambridgeshire Manor" in *E. H. R.*, vol. ix., where he points out that copyholders must have enjoyed a considerable unearned increment. The table of rents explained above is unsatisfactory, because of the difficulty of finding a basis for the comparison of payments at different periods. Thus at the earlier dates there are the tenants' works, and (occasionally) tallages to be considered; at the later the rent obtained from leasing the demense. The variety of the sources of manorial revenue makes it impossible to discover a common form to which the payments on all manors can be reduced. The ideal would be to take the villeins' payments and works in (say) the fourteenth century, and to compare them with the payments of the copyhold tenants in the sixteenth century. But since the commonest entry is simply "rents of assize," which included the rents of freeholders as well as of customary tenants, this simple procedure is often impossible.

While the table given on pages 115–117 is certainly not what could be desired, I am inclined to think its inaccuracies do not lie in the direction of exaggerating the fixity of rents, but rather, if anything, in underestimating it, because (i) when a total rent is given for the fifteenth or sixteenth century, without further particulars, it probably often included the rent paid by the farmer of the demesne, which at the earlier period was non-existent, (ii) at the later period the total rent often included payments made for new encroachments in the waste. When this is evidently the case, as at Wootton, and the amount of the new payments is stated, I have omitted them, my object being to compare, when possible, the rents paid by customary tenants at different periods. But often it is not possible to make such an allowance, and therefore I am disposed to think that the figures for the later dates are more likely to be weighted with irrelevant items than are the figures for the earlier dates. This makes the comparatively slow increase in the rents of some manors all the more worthy of notice.

### TABLE VIII (P. 153)

1. Norfolk.

Massingham Priory (two farms, Hen. VIII., R.O. Rentals and Surveys, Gen. Ser., Portf. 24, No. 4, f. 46); Wymondham (Hen. VIII., R.O. Augm. Off., Misc. Bks. 408, f. 25); Marshams (Marham(?), Hen. VIII., Augm. Off., Misc. Bks. 408, f. 19); Thetford (Hen. VIII., Augm. Off., Misc. Bks. 408, f. 22); Bockenham (Hen. VIII., R.O. Augm. Off., Misc. Bks. 408, f. 9–10); Langley (Hen. VIII., R.O. Augm. Off., Misc. Bks. 399, f. 228–9); Walsingham (Hen. VIII., R.O. Augm. Off., Misc. Bks. 399, f. 201); Brisingham (31 Eliz., R.O. Misc. Bks. 220, f. 236); Farfield (31 Eliz., *ibid.*); Wighton (17 Eliz., R.O. Rentals and Surveys, Duchy of Lanc, Bdle. 7, No. 34); Peakhall (1575, Holkham MSS., Tittleshall Bks., No. 12); West Lexham (1575, Holkham MSS., West Lexham MSS., No. 87); Foxley (1568, Holkham MSS., Billingford and Bintry MSS., Bdle. No. 9); Sparham (1590, Holkham MSS., Sparham MSS., Bdle. No. 5); Billingford (between 1564 and 1606, Holkham MSS., Billingford and Bintry MSS., Bdle. No. 9); Fulmordeston (1614, Holkham MSS., Map No. 59).

2. Wiltshire.

South Newton, Estoverton, Wynterbourne Basset, Byshopeston, Donnington, Knyghton, Domerham, Burdonsball, Foughlestone, Brudecomb, Westoverton, Sutton Maundeville, Stockton, Albedeston, Chalke, Bulbridge, Dichampton, Patney, Wyley, Berwick St. John, Remesbury, Staunton, Chilmerke (all 1565–73, Roxburgh Club, *Surveys of Lands of William, First Earl of Pembroke*).

3. Manors in other counties.

Ashton (Lancs., Hen. VIII., R.O. Rentals and Surveys, Gen. Ser., Portf. 19, No. 7, ff. 69–72); Prestwood (Staffs., R.O. Misc. Bks. Land Rev., vol. 185, ff. 155b-7); Gamlingay Merton (Cambridgeshire, 1601, Merton Estate Maps); Gamlingay Avenells (*ibid.*); Salford (Bedfordshire, 1595, All Souls Estate Maps); Weedon Weston (Northants, c. 1595, *ibid.*); Edgeware (Middlesex, 1597, All Souls Estate Maps); Kingsbury (Middlesex, 1597, *ibid.*); Greenham (Bucks, 1595, *ibid.*); Crendon (Bucks, c. 1595, *ibid.*); Harlesden Farm (Middlesex, 1599, *ibid.*); Land in the Parish of Hendon (Middlesex, c. 1599, *ibid.*); Whadborough (Leicestershire, 1620, *ibid.*).

The fact that this table is compiled from documents of different dates makes it impossible to use it as an index of the size of the large leasehold farms at any one period in the sixteenth century. Nor can I hope to have escaped errors of calculation. I hope, however, it may be of some use in illustrating the considerable scale on which some farms were conducted.

### Tables IX, X, and XI (pp. 157, 167–168 and 168)

The farms from which these tables are compiled are included in the list given in explanation of Table VIII. (with one exception, Ewerne in Dorsetshire, *Topographer and Genealogist*, vol. i.), and it is therefore unnecessary to set them out in detail here. The figures as to arable, pasture, and meadow on the demesne of 41 monasteries are taken from Savine, "English Monasteries on the Eve of the Dissolution," *Oxford Studies in Social and Legal History*, vol. i. p. 172.

### Table XIII (p. 219)

This table is compiled from documents relating to the undermentioned manors. When the reference has already been given I do not repeat it here:—23 manors in Wilts, Somerset, and Devon, Roxburghe Club, *Surveys of Lands of William, First Earl of Pembroke*. West Lexham (Norfolk), Sparham (Norfolk), East Dereham (Norfolk), Wighton (Norfolk), Stockton Socon (Norfolk, 1649, R.O. Parly. Surveys, Norf. No. 14); Aldeburgh (Suffolk, Hen. VIII., R.O. Misc. Bks., Treas. of Receipt, vol. 163); St. Edmund (Suffolk, 1650, R.O. Parly. Surveys, Suff. No. 14); Dodnash (Suffolk, Hen. VIII., R.O. Misc. Bks., Treas. of Receipt, vol. 163, f. 79); Chatesham, Suffolk (Hen. VIII., R.O. Misc. Bks., Treas. of Receipt, vol. 163, f. 91); Falkenham (Suffolk, Hen. VIII., R.O. Treas. of Receipt, vol. 163, f. 181); Stratford juxta Higham (Suffolk), Mettingham (Suffolk, *Victoria County History*, chapter on Social and Economic History); Mark Soham (Suffolk, *ibid.*); Bushey (Herts, 7 Eliz., from Court Rolls lent me by the late Miss Toulmin Smith); Ewerne (Dorset, 1567, *Topographer and Genealogist*, vol. i.); Corton (Somerset, *ibid.*); Rolleston (Staffs., *ibid.*); Hewlington (Denbighshire, 4 Eliz., Wrexham Library, Ancient Local Records, vol. ii.); Holt (Denbighshire, *ibid.*); Wotton in Elishall (Staffs.); Burton Bondend (Staffs.); Agarsley (Staffs.); High Furness (Lancs., 28 Eliz., R.O. Duchy of Lancs., Special Commissions, No. 398); Crondal (Hants); Edgeware (Middlesex); Kingsbury (Middlesex); Malden (Surrey, Merton MSS., book labelled Malden, Thorncroft, and Farleigh); Thorncroft (Surrey, *ibid.*); Farleigh (Surrey, *ibid.*); 14 manors in Northumberland (*Northumberland County History*, vol. viii., p. 238); Bradford (Somerset, Selden Society, vol. xii., Leadam, Select Cases in the Court of Requests); Shepton Mallet,

Somerset (Calendar of Proceedings in Chancery, *temp.* Eliz. H.h. i. 27); Newton Tracye (Devon, *ibid.*, H.h. 23, 17); Chudlye (Devon, *ibid.*, L.l. 8, 31); Powlton (Wilts, *ibid.*, M.m. 13); Kibworth Harcourt (Leicestershire, Merton MSS., book containing extracts from Merton Court Rolls); Barkby (Leicestershire, *ibid.*).

*     *     *     *     *

NOTE. — (i) The names of the manors from which Dr. Savine takes his figures are not given. Consequently his information and mine may sometimes overlap, (ii) The MSS. book from which the customs of Farleigh, Thorncroft, and Malden are taken is dated 1841, but it purports to give customs based on ancient court rolls. The same applies to the information as to Kibworth Harcourt and Barkby.

# INDEX

## J

Jack Of The North *241*
Jack Of The Style *242*
John Hales *4, 8, 13, 121, 246, 264, 267*
John Moore *4, 118, 271*
Joshua Delavale *190*
Judges *281, 285, 286*
Juries *21, 27, 28, 194, 276, 277, 285, 287, 293*
Justices *31, 33, 72, 90, 108, 123, 155, 200, 204, 254, 256, 258, 268, 276, 300, 301*
Justices Of Assize *268, 269, 270*

## K

Kalm *279*
Ket's Rebellion *31, 71, 234, 235, 243, 251, 265*
Knight Service *22*

## L

Labour Services *38, 43, 55, 61, 65, 66, 71, 93, 103, 104, 106, 150, 210, 212*
Landholding Peasants *33*
Land Tenure *20, 43, 49, 66, 72, 171, 253, 291*
Leasehold Tenure *66, 101, 154, 155, 234*
Legalisation Of Slavery *33*
Leicester *3, 16, 22, 37, 78, 202, 274, 278, 304*
Letter Of Cromwell *195*
Leyrwite *34, 39*
Liberi Homines And Sochemanni *20*
Lloyd *280*
Locke *287*
Lord Brudenell *280*
Lord Coventry *285*
Lord Danbury *273*
Lord Darcy *234*
Lord North *252*
Lord Rich *97, 273*
Lord Saye And Sele *270*
Lords Of Manors *4, 7, 51, 63, 67, 82, 86, 101, 109, 110, 111, 125, 129, 130, 145, 204, 220, 225, 236*
Lord Thomas Berkeley *130*

## M

Manorial Authorities *23, 33, 34, 35, 49, 53, 56, 58, 60, 63, 66, 69, 86, 87, 93, 94, 102, 105, 111, 114, 115, 117, 131, 145, 150, 154, 175, 178, 181, 186, 187, 210, 211, 215, 217, 225*
Map *51, 120, 126, 160, 161, 163, 164, 165, 187, 193, 218, 313*

Lector House believes that a society develops through a two-fold approach of continuous learning and adaptation, which is derived from the study of classic literary works spread across the historic timeline of literature records. Therefore, we aim at reviving, repairing and redeveloping all those inaccessible or damaged but historically as well as culturally important literature across subjects so that the future generations may have an opportunity to study and learn from past works to embark upon a journey of creating a better future.

This book is a result of an effort made by Lector House towards making a contribution to the preservation and repair of original ancient works which might hold historical significance to the approach of continuous learning across subjects.

HAPPY READING & LEARNING!

LECTOR HOUSE LLP
E-MAIL: lectorpublishing@gmail.com

9 789389 679434